1993 Supplement

CONSTITUTIONAL LAW

1993 Supplement

CONSTITUTIONAL LAW

Second Edition

Geoffrey R. Stone
Harry Kalven, Jr., Professor of Law and Dean
University of Chicago Law School

Louis M. Seidman
Professor of Law
Georgetown University Law Center

Cass R. Sunstein
Karl N. Llewellyn Professor of Jurisprudence
University of Chicago Law School and
Department of Political Science

Mark V. Tushnet
Professor of Law
Georgetown University Law Center

Law School Casebook Series

Little, Brown and Company
Boston New York Toronto London

Library of Congress Catalog Card No. 90-63879

ISBN 0-316-81795-3

ICP

Published simultaneously in Canada
by Little, Brown & Company (Canada) Limited

PRINTED IN THE UNITED STATES OF AMERICA

Contents

Table of Cases

Italics indicate principal and intermediate cases.
All references are to page numbers in the main text.

Table of Authorities

All references are to page numbers in the main text.

McConnell, Accommodation of Religion: An Update and a Response to the Critics, 60 Geo. Wash. L. Rev. 685 (1992), 1541
McConnell, Free Exercise Revisionism and the *Smith* Decision, 57 U. Chi. L. Rev. 1109 (1990), 1531
McConnell, The Origins and Historical Understanding of Free Exercise of Religion, 103 Harv. L. Rev. 1409 (1990), 1510
Michelman, Saving Old Glory: On Constitutional Iconography, 42 Stan. L. Rev. 1337 (1990), 1305
Monaghan, The Protective Power of the Presidency, 93 Colum. L. Rev. 1 (1993), 382
Novick, The Unrevised Holmes and Freedom of Expression, 1991 Sup. Ct. Rev. 303, 305, 1039
Nunn, Rights Held Hostage: Race, Ideology and the Peremptory Challenge, 28 Harv. Civ. R.-Civ. L.L. Rev. 63 (1993), 590
O'Fallon, *Marbury,* 44 Stan. L. Rev. 219 (1992), 30
R. Posner, Sex and Reason (1992), 955
Posner, Democracy and Distrust Revisited, 77 Va. L. Rev. 641 (1991), 575
Post, Racist Speech, Democracy, and the First Amendment, 32 Wm. & Mary L. Rev. 267 (1991), 1176
Powell, The Oldest Question of Constitutional Law, 79 Va. L. Rev. 633, 658 (1993), 224
Raskin, Legal Aliens, Local Citizens: The Historical, Constitutional and Theoretical Meanings of Alien Suffrage, 141 U. Pa. L. Rev. 139 (1993), 727
J. Rawls, Political Liberalism (1993), 768
Redish & Cisar, "If Angels Were to Govern": The Need for Pragmatic Formalism in Separation of Powers Theory, 41 Duke L.J. 449 (1991), 415
Roberts, Punishing Drug Addicts Who Have Babies: Women of Color, Equality, and the Right of Privacy, 104 Harv. L. Rev. 1419 (1991), 967
G. Rosenberg, The Hollow Hope: Can Courts Bring About Social Change? (1991), 532
Rubenfeld, Usings, 102 Yale L.J. 1077 (1993), 1568
Sargentich, The Limits of the Parliamentary Critique of the Separation of Powers, 34 Wm. & Mary L. Rev. 679 (1993), 470
Scalia, The Doctrine of Standing as an Essential Part of Separation of Powers, 17 Suffolk U. L. Rev. 881 (1983), 106
Schauer, Uncoupling Free Speech, 92 Colum. L. Rev. 1321, 1322 (1992), 1090, 1154
Seidman, Brown and Miranda, 80 Calif. L. Rev. 673, 717 (1992), 532

Seidman, Confusion at the Border: Cruzan, "The Right to Die," and the Public/Private Distinction, 1992 Sup. Ct. Rev. 47, 68-70, 985

Shane, The *Rust* that Corrodes: State Action, Free Speech, and Responsibility, 52 Louisiana L. Rev. 1585, 1587 (1992), 1600

Sidak, To Declare War, 41 Duke L.J. 29 (1991), 413

Siegel, Reasoning from the Body: A Historical Perspective on Abortion Regulation and Questions of Equal Protection, 44 Stan. L. Rev. 261 (1992), 932

G. Spann, Race against the Court: The Supreme Court and Minorities in Contemporary America, 2-3 (1993), 757

Stone, Content-Neutral Restrictions, 54 U. Chi. L. Rev. 46 (1987), 1265

Stone, The Equal Access Controversy: The Religion Clauses and the Meaning of "Neutrality," 81 Nw. U.L. Rev. 168, 169-170 (1986), 1353

Stone, Imagining a Free Press, 90 Mich. L. Rev. 1201, 1217-1218 (1992), 1429

Stout, Strict Scrutiny and Social Choice: An Economic Inquiry into Fundamental Rights and Suspect Classifications, 80 Geo. L.J. 1787, 1814-1817 (1992), 579

Strauss, Abortion, Toleration, and Moral Uncertainty, 1993 Sup. Ct. Rev. 1, 27

Strauss, Due Process, Government Inaction, and Private Wrongs, 1989 S. Ct. Rev. 53, 942

Strauss, Persuasion, Autonomy, and Freedom of Expression, 91 Colum. L. Rev. 334 (1991), 1051

Strossen, Regulating Racist Speech on Campus: A Modest Proposal?, 1990 Duke L.J. 484, 1176

C. Sunstein, The Partial Constitution (1993), 765, 802, 1145, 1256, 1263, 1288

Sunstein, Free Speech Now, 59 U. Chi. L. Rev. 255 (1992), 1020, 1319, 1426

Sunstein, Neutrality in Constitutional Law (with Special Reference to Pornography, Abortion, and Surrogacy), 92 Colum. L. Rev. 1 (1992), 932, 942, 1228

Sunstein, What's Standing After Lujan, 91 Mich. L. Rev. 163 (1992), 106

Symposium, Free Speech and Religious, Racial, and Sexual Harassment, 32 Wm. & Mary L. Rev. 207 (1991), 1176

Thomas, *Rouge et Noir* Reread: A Popular Constitutional History of the Angelo Herndon Case, 65 So. Cal. L. Rev. 2599 (1992), 1054

L. Tribe & M. Dorf, On Reading the Constitution (1991), 965

Acknowledgments

Excerpts from the following books and articles appear with the kind permission of the copyright holders:

Aleinikoff, The Case for Race-Consciousness. This article originally appeared at 91 Colum. L. Rev. 1061 (1991). Reprinted by permission.

Alexander, What Makes Wrongful Discrimination Wrong?: Biases, Preferences, Stereotypes, and Proxies, 141 University of Pennsylvania Law Review 149 (1992). Copyright © 1992 by the University of Pennsylvania Law Review.

Amar, The Bill of Rights and the Fourteenth Amendment. Reprinted by permission of The Yale Law Journal Company and Fred B. Rothman & Company for The Yale Law Journal, Vol. 101, pp. 1193-1284.

Baker, Advertising and a Democratic Process, 140 University of Pennsylvania Law Review 2097 (1992). Copyright © 1992 by the University of Pennsylvania Law Review.

Balkin, Tradition, Betrayal, and the Politics of Deconstruction. This article originally appeared in 11 Cardozo L. Rev. 1613 (1990).

Becker, The Politics of Women's Wrongs and the Bill of "Rights": A Bicentennial Perspective, 59 University of Chicago Law Review 453, 456. Reprinted by permission.

Bowman, Street Harassment and the Informal Ghettoization of Women, 106 Harvard Law Review 517, 575 (1993). Copyright © (1993) by the Harvard Law Review Association. Reprinted by permission.

Brown, Separated Powers and Ordered Liberty, 139 University of Pennsylvania Law Review 1513 (1991). Copyright © 1992 by the University of Pennsylvania Law Review.

Calabresi & Rhodes, The Structural Constitution: Unitary Executive, Plural Judiciary, 105 Harvard Law Review 1153 (1992). Copyright © 1992 by the Harvard Law Review Association. Reprinted by permission.

Chang, Discriminatory Impact, Affirmative Action, and Innocent Victims: Judicial Conservatism or Conservative Justices? This article originally appeared at 91 Colum. L. Rev. 790 (1991). Reprinted by permission.

Collins, & Skover, Commerce and Communication. Published originally in 71 Texas Law Review 697, 707, 710, 727, 728, 737, 738, 745 (1993). Copyright 1993 by the Texas Law Review Association. Reprinted by permission.

Delgado, Affirmative Action as a Majoritarian Device: Or, Do You Really Want to be a Role Model? Originally published in 89 Michigan Law Review 1222, 1223, 1224, 1228. Reprinted by permission.

Elhauge, Does Interest Group Theory Justify More Intrusive Judicial Review? Reprinted by permission of the Yale Law Journal Company and Fred B. Rothman & Company from The Yale Law Journal, Vol. 101, pp. 31-110.

Fallon, Making Sense of Overbreadth. Reprinted by permission of the Yale Law Journal Company and Fred B. Rothman & Company from the Yale Law Journal, Vol. 100, pp. 853-908.

Farber, Free Speech Without Romance: Public Choice and the First Amendment, 105 Harvard Law Review 554, 558-561 (1991). Copyright © 1991 by the Harvard Law Review Association. Reprinted by permission.

Farber & Frickey, Is Carolene Products Dead? Reflections on Affirmative Action and the Dynamics of Civil Rights Legislation. © 1991 by California Law Review Inc. Reprinted from California Law Review, Vol. 79, No. 3, pp. 685, 702, 704 by permission.

Flagg, "Was Blind But Now I See": White Race Consciousness and the Requirement of Discriminatory Intent. Originally published in 91 Michigan Law Review 953, 957, 987, 988. Reprinted by permission.

Fried, A New First Amendment Jurisprudence: A Threat to Liberty, 59 University of Chicago Law Review 225, 245-255. Reprinted by permission.

Lawrence, If He Hollers Let Him Go: Regulating Racist Speech on Campus, 1990 Duke Law Journal 431, 439-440. Reprinted by permission of the author.

Michelman, Saving Old Glory: On Constitutional Iconography, 42 Stanford Law Review 1337 (1990). © 1990 by the Board of Trustees of the Leland Stanford Junior University and Fred B. Rothman & Company. Reprinted by permission.

Schauer, Uncoupling Free Speech. This article originally appeared at 92 Colum. L. Rev. 1321 (1992). Reprinted by permission.

Seidman, Brown and Miranda. Portions of this article originally appeared in a different form in California Law Review, Vol. 80, No. 3, pp. 673-717. © 1992 by California Law Review Inc.; permission granted.

Shane, The *Rust* That Corrodes: State Action, Free Speech, and Responsibility. Originally published in 52 La. L. Rev. 1585, 1587 (1992). Copyright 1992, The Louisiana Law Review. All rights reserved.

Stone, Imagining a Free Press. Originally published in 90 Michigan Law Review 1246, 1262, 1263. Reprinted by permission.

Stout, Strict Scrutiny and Social Choice: An Economic Inquiry Into Fundamental Rights and Suspect Classifications, 80 Georgetown Law Journal 1787 (1992). Reprinted with the permission of the publisher, © 1992 The Georgetown Law Journal Association and Georgetown University.

Sunstein, Free Speech Now, 59 University of Chicago Law Review 255, 263-267, 291-292, 301, 304-306 (1992). Reprinted by permission.

Sunstein, Neutrality in Constitutional Law (with Special Reference to Pornography, Abortion, and Surrogacy). This article originally appeared at 92 Colum. L. Rev. 1 (1992). Reprinted by permission.

1993 Supplement

CONSTITUTIONAL LAW

THE CONSTITUTION OF THE UNITED STATES

Page lii. Amendment XIV, Section 4, change the second sentence to read:

But neither the United States nor any State shall assume or pay any debt or obligation incurred in aid of insurrection or rebellion against the United States, or any claim for the loss or emancipation of any slave; but all such debts, obligations and claims shall be held illegal and void.

Page lvi. After Amendment XXVI, add the following:

AMENDMENT XXVII [1992]

No law varying the compensation for the services of the Senators and Representatives shall take effect, until an election of Representatives shall have intervened. [For some questions about this amendment, see Supplement to page 122 below.]

BIOGRAPHICAL NOTES ON SELECTED U.S. SUPREME COURT JUSTICES

Page lxxiii. Before the Van Devanter biography, add the following:

CLARENCE THOMAS (1948-   ): Born into grinding poverty in segregated coastal Georgia, Justice Thomas became the second African American and one of the youngest Justices to join the Court when he was appointed by President Bush in 1991. He was confirmed by the Senate to fill the seat vacated by the retirement of Thurgood Marshall after extraordinary confirmation hearings that opened with a moving account of his personal saga and closed with charges of sexual harassment leveled against him by Anita Hill, who had worked with him at the Department of Education and the Equal Employment Opportunity Commission. A graduate of the Yale Law School, he served as assistant secretary for civil rights at the Department of Education and chair of the Equal Employment Opportunity Commission in the Reagan administration. During his controversial seven-year stewardship of the EEOC, Thomas's fierce opposition to affirmative action antagonized liberals and members of the civil rights community. In 1989, President Bush appointed Thomas to the United States Court of Appeals for the District of Columbia, where he served for fifteen months before his elevation to the Supreme Court. Known as a staunch conservative, Thomas's extrajudicial writings suggest an interest in natural law as a basis for constitutional adjudication.

Chapter One

The Role of the Supreme Court in the Constitutional Scheme

A. INTRODUCTION: SOME NOTES ON THE HISTORY AND THEORY OF THE CONSTITUTION

2. The Federalist Response

Page 20. Before section 2 of the Note, add the following:

For an important recent discussion showing the American progression in the early period from monarchy to republicanism to democracy, see G. Wood, The Radicalism of the American Revolution (1991).

Page 20. At the beginning of the last paragraph, add the following:

See also Ward, The Limits of "Liberal Republicanism": Why Group-Based Remedies and Republican Citizenship Don't Mix, 91 Colum. L. Rev. 581 (1991).

Page 21. Before section 4 of the Note, add the following:

Has the American Constitution had just one, or three, fundamental "constitutional moments?" B. Ackerman, We the People, Vol. 1: Foundations (1991), argues that the founding, the Civil War, and the New Deal resulted in three different constitutional "republics." On Ackerman's account, the Constitution represents a "dualist democracy," that is, a system that distinguishes between the higher politics of constitutional-making and the "normal politics" of day-to-day life. Constitutional politics has many of the features of republican self-governance; normal politics acknowledges the partial truths of pluralism. Ackerman claims that there have been three large periods of constitutional politics, setting forth the nation's basic political aspirations. In his view, much of the work of the Supreme Court can be understood as efforts to synthesize the commitments of these three different republics. Ackerman's arguments are controversial; but as we will see, both the Civil War period and the New Deal did help inaugurate major changes in constitutional law.

Page 30. Before section 2 of the Note, add the following:

The history is illuminatingly discussed in O'Fallon, *Marbury*, 44 Stan. L. Rev. 219 (1992).

D. THE POWER OF REPRISAL: POLITICAL CONTROL OF THE SUPREME COURT

Page 76. Replace the second line of the second paragraph of section 3 with the following:

Justice Samuel Chase was impeached but never convicted. There have been a

Page 84. Before section E, add the following:

C. Sunstein, The Partial Constitution (1993), especially Chapter 5, invokes considerations of this kind in order to argue for a cautious judicial role and in order to emphasize the constitutional duties of legislative and executive officials.

E. "CASE OR CONTROVERSY" REQUIREMENTS AND THE PASSIVE VIRTUES

2. Standing

Page 96. At end of the second full paragraph, add the following:

For a detailed discussion of the relevant history, along with an evaluation of standing limits, see Winter, The Metaphor of Standing and the Problem of Self-Governance, 40 Stan. L. Rev. 1371 (1988).

Page 104. Before section 4 of the Note, add the following:

For the first Supreme Court decision denying standing on zone of interests grounds, see Air Courier Conference v. APWU, 498 U.S. 517 (1991). The case grew out of a decision of the U.S. Postal Service partly to relinquish its monopoly of the mails by allowing private courier services to engage in the practice of "international remailing." With international remailing, such services can bypass the Postal Service and deposit in foreign postal systems letters destined for foreign addresses.

Employees of the Postal Service brought suit. The Court concluded that they were not within the zone of interests of the statutes creating a national postal monopoly. "The particular language of the statutes provides no support" for the view "that Congress intended to protect jobs with the Postal Service." Nor was that claim supported by the history and structure of these statutes. Because the employment interests were statutorily irrelevant, standing was denied.

Consider also International Primate Protection League v. Administrators, 111 S. Ct. 1700 (1991). There the plaintiffs brought suit to challenge the use of certain monkeys in federally funded medical experiments. The suit was filed in state court and removed to federal court; the question raised was whether, assuming that plaintiffs lacked standing to sue, they had standing to contest the removal. The Court said that "standing is gauged by the specific common law, statutory or constitutional claims that a party presents," and quoted the Fletcher article, see pp. 105-106 of text, to the effect that standing "should be seen as a question of substantive law, answerable by reference to the statutory and constitutional provision whose protection is invoked." Here, the Court said, the right to sue in Louisiana court was an injury traceable to the challenged action and likely to be redressed by the remedy they seek.

It is possible that, taken together, these two cases have started to reassert the view that standing is ultimately a question of substantive law: whether relevant statutes and constitutional provisions confer on the plaintiff a right to bring suit.

Page 106. Before "3. Political Questions," add the following:

LUJAN v. DEFENDERS OF WILDLIFE

112 S. Ct. 2130 (1992)

JUSTICE SCALIA delivered the opinion of the Court with respect to Parts I, II, III-A, and IV, and an opinion with respect to Part III-B in which THE CHIEF JUSTICE, JUSTICE WHITE, and JUSTICE THOMAS join.

This case involves a challenge to a rule promulgated by the Secretary of the Interior interpreting §7 of the Endangered Species Act of 1973 (ESA), in such fashion as to render it applicable only to actions within the United States or on the high seas. The preliminary issue, and the only one we reach, is whether the respondents here, plaintiffs below, have standing to seek judicial review of the rule.

I

The ESA seeks to protect species of animals against threats to their continuing existence caused by man. The ESA instructs the Secretary of the Interior to promulgate by regulation a list of those species which are either endangered or threatened under enumerated criteria, and to define the critical habitat of these species. Section 7(a)(2) of the Act then provides, in pertinent part:

> Each Federal agency shall, in consultation with and with the assistance of the Secretary [of the Interior], insure that any action authorized, funded, or carried out by such agency . . . is not likely to jeopardize the continued existence of any endangered species or threatened species or result in the destruction or adverse modification of habitat of such species which is determined by the Secretary, after consultation as appropriate with affected States, to be critical.

In 1978, the Fish and Wildlife Service (FWS) and the National Marine Fisheries Service (NMFS), on behalf of the Secretary of the Interior and the Secretary of Commerce respectively, promulgated a joint regulation stating that the obligations imposed by §7(a)(2) extend to actions taken in foreign nations. The next year, however, the Interior Department began to reexamine its position. A revised joint regulation, reinterpreting §7(a)(2) to require consultation only for actions taken in the United States or on the high seas, was proposed in 1983, and promulgated in 1986.

Shortly thereafter, respondents, organizations dedicated to wildlife conservation and other environmental causes, filed this action against the Secretary of the Interior, seeking a declaratory judgment that the new regulation is in error as to the geographic scope of §7(a)(2), and an injunction requiring the Secretary to promulgate a new regulation restoring the initial interpretation. . . .

II

Over the years, our cases have established that the irreducible constitutional minimum of standing contains three elements: First, the plaintiff must have suffered an "injury in fact" — an invasion of a legally-protected interest which is (a) concrete and particularized, and (b) "actual or imminent, not 'conjectural' or 'hypothetical.'" Second, there must be a causal connection between the injury and the conduct complained of — the injury has to be "fairly . . . traceable to the challenged action of the defendant, and not . . . the result [of] the independent action of some third party not before the court." Third, it must be "likely," as opposed to merely "speculative," that the injury will be "redressed by a favorable decision."

The party invoking federal jurisdiction bears the burden of establishing these elements. Since they are not mere pleading requirements but rather an indispensable part of the plaintiff's case, each element must be supported in the same way as any other matter on which the plaintiff bears the burden of proof, i.e., with the manner and degree of evidence required at the successive stages of the litigation. At the pleading stage, general factual allegations of injury resulting from the defendant's conduct may suffice, for on a motion to dismiss we "presume that general allegations embrace those specific facts that are necessary to support the claim." In response to a summary judgment motion, however, the plaintiff can no longer rest on such "mere allegations," but must "set forth" by affidavit or other evidence "specific facts," Fed. Rule Civ. Proc. 56(e), which for purposes of the summary judgment motion will be taken to be true. And at the final stage, those facts (if controverted) must be "supported adequately by the evidence adduced at trial."

When the suit is one challenging the legality of government action or inaction, the nature and extent of facts that must be averred (at the summary judgment stage) or proved (at the trial stage) in order to establish standing depends considerably upon whether the plaintiff is himself an object of the action (or forgone action) at issue. If he is, there is ordinarily little question that the action or inaction has caused him injury, and that a judgment preventing or requiring the action will redress it. When, however, as in this case, a plaintiff's asserted injury arises from the government's allegedly unlawful regulation (or lack of regulation) of someone else, much more is needed. In that circumstance, causation and redressability ordinarily hinge on the response of the regulated (or regulable) third party to the government action or inaction — and perhaps on the response of others as well. The existence of one or more of the essential elements of standing "depends on the unfettered choices made by independent actors not before the courts and whose exercise of broad and legitimate discretion the courts cannot presume either to control or to predict," ASARCO Inc. v. Kadish, 490 U.S. 605, 615 (1989) (opinion of Kennedy, J.); and it becomes the burden of the plaintiff to adduce facts showing that those choices have been or will be made in such manner as to produce causation and permit redressability of injury. Thus, when the plaintiff is not himself the object of the government action or inaction he challenges, standing is not precluded, but it is ordinarily "substantially more difficult" to establish. . . .

III

A

Respondents' claim to injury is that the lack of consultation with respect to certain funded activities abroad "increases the rate of extinction of endangered and threatened species." Of course, the desire to use or observe an animal species, even for purely aesthetic purposes, is undeniably a cognizable interest for purpose of standing. . . .

[With] respect to this aspect of the case, the Court of Appeals focused on the affidavits of two Defenders' members — Joyce Kelly and Amy Skilbred. Ms. Kelly stated that she traveled to Egypt in 1986 and "observed the traditional habitat of the endangered nile crocodile there and intends to do so again, and hopes to observe the crocodile directly," and that she "will suffer harm in fact as a result of [the] American . . . role . . . in overseeing the rehabilitation of the Aswan High Dam on the Nile . . . and [in] developing . . . Egypt's . . . Master Water Plan." Ms. Skilbred averred that she traveled to Sri Lanka in 1981 and "observed the habitat" of "endangered species such as the Asian elephant and the leopard" at what is now the site of the Mahaweli Project funded by the Agency for International Development (AID), although she "was unable to see any of the endangered species;" "this development project," she continued, "will seriously reduce endangered, threatened, and endemic species habitat including areas that I visited . . . [, which] may severely shorten the future of these species;" that threat, she concluded, harmed her because she "intends to return to Sri Lanka in the future and hopes to be more fortunate in spotting at least the endangered elephant and leopard." When Ms. Skilbred was asked at a subsequent deposition if and when she had any plans to return to Sri Lanka, she reiterated that "I intend to go back to Sri Lanka," but confessed that she had no current plans: "I don't know when. There is a civil war going on right now. I don't know. Not next year, I will say. In the future."

We shall assume for the sake of argument that these affidavits contain facts showing that certain agency-funded projects threaten listed species — though that is questionable. They plainly contain no facts, however, showing how damage to the species will produce "imminent" injury to Mss. Kelly and Skilbred. That the women "had visited" the areas of the projects before the projects commenced proves nothing. [Such] "some day" intentions — without any description of concrete plans, or indeed even any specification of when the some day will be — do not support a finding of the "actual or imminent" injury that our cases require.

Besides relying upon the Kelly and Skilbred affidavits, respondents propose a series of novel standing theories. The first, inelegantly styled "ecosystem nexus," proposes that any person who uses any part of a "contiguous ecosystem" adversely affected by a funded activity has standing even if the activity is located a great distance away. This approach, as the Court of Appeals correctly observed, is inconsistent with our opinion in *National Wildlife Federation*, which held that a plaintiff claiming injury from environmental damage must use the area affected by the challenged activity and not an area roughly "in the vicinity" of it. It makes no difference that the general-purpose section of the ESA states that the Act was intended in part "to provide a means whereby the ecosystems upon which endangered species and threatened species depend may be conserved," 16 U.S.C. §1531(b). To say that the Act protects ecosystems is not to say that the Act creates (if it were possible) rights of action in persons who have not been injured in fact, that is, persons who use portions of an ecosystem not perceptibly affected by the unlawful action in question.

Respondents' other theories are called, alas, the "animal nexus" approach, whereby anyone who has an interest in studying or seeing the endangered animals anywhere on the globe has standing; and the "vocational nexus" approach, under which anyone with a professional interest in such animals can sue. Under these theories, anyone who goes to see Asian elephants in the Bronx Zoo, and anyone who is a keeper of Asian elephants in the Bronx Zoo, has standing to sue because the Director of AID did not consult with the Secretary regarding the AID-funded project in Sri Lanka. This is beyond all reason. Standing is not "an ingenious academic exercise in the conceivable," United States v. Students Challenging Regulatory Agency Procedures (SCRAP), 412 U.S. 669, 688 (1973), but as we have said requires, at the summary judgment stage, a factual showing of perceptible harm. It is clear that the person who observes or works with a particular animal threatened by a federal decision is facing perceptible harm, since the very subject of his interest will no longer exist. It is even plausible — though it goes to the outermost limit of plausibility — to think that a person who observes or works with animals of a particular species in the very area of the world where that species is threatened by a federal decision is facing such harm, since some animals that might have been the subject of his interest will no longer exist, see Japan Whaling Assn. v. American Cetacean Soc., 478 U.S. 221, 231, n.4 (1986). It goes beyond the limit, however, and into pure speculation and fantasy, to say that anyone who observes or works with an endangered species, anywhere in the world, is appreciably harmed by a single project affecting some portion of that species with which he has no more specific connection. . . .

B

The most obvious problem in the present case is redressability. Since the agencies funding the projects were not parties to the case, the District

Court could accord relief only against the Secretary: He could be ordered to revise his regulation to require consultation for foreign projects. But this would not remedy respondents' alleged injury unless the funding agencies were bound by the Secretary's regulation, which is very much an open question. . . .

Respondents assert that this legal uncertainty did not affect redressability (and hence standing) because the District Court itself could resolve the issue of the Secretary's authority as a necessary part of its standing inquiry. Assuming that it is appropriate to resolve an issue of law such as this in connection with a threshold standing inquiry, resolution by the District Court would not have remedied respondents' alleged injury anyway, because it would not have been binding upon the agencies. They were not parties to the suit, and there is no reason they should be obliged to honor an incidental legal determination the suit produced. . . .

A further impediment to redressability is the fact that the agencies generally supply only a fraction of the funding for a foreign project. AID, for example, has provided less than 10% of the funding for the Mahaweli Project. Respondents have produced nothing to indicate that the projects they have named will either be suspended, or do less harm to listed species, if that fraction is eliminated. As in *Simon*, it is entirely conjectural whether the nonagency activity that affects respondents will be altered or affected by the agency activity they seek to achieve. There is no standing.

IV

The Court of Appeals found that respondents had standing for an additional reason: because they had suffered a "procedural injury." The so-called "citizen-suit" provision of the ESA provides, in pertinent part, that "any person may commence a civil suit on his own behalf (A) to enjoin any person, including the United States and any other governmental instrumentality or agency . . . who is alleged to be in violation of any provision of this chapter." The court held that, because §7(a)(2) requires interagency consultation, the citizen-suit provision creates a "procedural right" to consultation in all "persons" — so that anyone can file suit in federal court to challenge the Secretary's (or presumably any other official's) failure to follow the assertedly correct consultative procedure, notwithstanding their inability to allege any discrete injury flowing from that failure. To understand the remarkable nature of this holding one must be clear about what it does not rest upon: This is not a case where plaintiffs are seeking to enforce a procedural requirement the disregard of which could impair a separate concrete interest of theirs (e.g., the procedural requirement for a hearing prior to denial of their license application, or the procedural requirement for an environmental impact statement before a federal facility is constructed next door to them).[7] Nor is it simply a case where concrete injury has been suffered by many persons, as in mass fraud or mass tort situations. Nor, finally, is it the unusual case in which Congress has created a concrete private interest in the outcome of a suit against a private party for the government's benefit, by providing a cash bounty for the victorious plaintiff. Rather, the court held that the injury-in-fact requirement had been satisfied by congressional conferral upon all persons of an abstract, self-contained, noninstrumental "right" to have the Executive observe the procedures required by law. We reject this view.

We have consistently held that a plaintiff raising only a generally available grievance about government — claiming only harm to his and every citizen's interest in proper application of the Constitution and laws, and seeking relief that no more directly and tangibly benefits him than it does the public at large — does not state an Article III case or controversy. . . .

To be sure, our generalized-grievance cases have typically involved Government violation of procedures assertedly ordained by the Constitution rather than the Congress. But there is absolutely no basis for making the Article III inquiry turn on the source of the asserted right. Whether the courts were to act on their own, or at the invitation of Congress, in ignoring the concrete injury requirement described in our cases, they would be discarding a principle fundamental to the separate and distinct constitutional role of the Third Branch — one of the essential elements that identifies those "Cases" and "Controversies" that are the business of the courts rather than of the political branches. "The province of the court," as Chief Justice Marshall said in Marbury v. Madison, 1 Cranch 137, 170 (1803) "is, solely, to decide on the rights of individuals." Vindicating the public interest (including the public interest

7. There is this much truth to the assertion that "procedural rights" are special: The person who has been accorded a procedural right to protect his concrete interests can assert that right without meeting all the normal standards for redressability and immediacy. Thus, under our case law, one living adjacent to the site for proposed construction of a federally licensed dam has standing to challenge the licensing agency's failure to prepare an Environmental Impact Statement, even though he cannot establish with any certainty that the Statement will cause the license to be withheld or altered, and even though the dam will not be completed for many years. (That is why we do not rely, in the present case, upon the Government's argument that, even if the other agencies were obliged to consult with the Secretary, they might not have followed his advice.) What respondents' "procedural rights" argument seeks, however, is quite different from this: standing for persons who have no concrete interests affected — persons who live (and propose to live) at the other end of the country from the dam.

in government observance of the Constitution and laws) is the function of Congress and the Chief Executive. The question presented here is whether the public interest in proper administration of the laws (specifically, in agencies' observance of a particular, statutorily prescribed procedure) can be converted into an individual right by a statute that denominates it as such, and that permits all citizens (or, for that matter, a subclass of citizens who suffer no distinctive concrete harm) to sue. If the concrete injury requirement has the separation-of-powers significance we have always said, the answer must be obvious: To permit Congress to convert the undifferentiated public interest in executive officers' compliance with the law into an "individual right" vindicable in the courts is to permit Congress to transfer from the President to the courts the Chief Executive's most important constitutional duty, to "take Care that the Laws be faithfully executed," Art. II, §3. It would enable the courts, with the permission of Congress, "to assume a position of authority over the governmental acts of another and co-equal department," Frothingham v. Mellon, 262 U.S., at 489, and to become " 'virtually continuing monitors of the wisdom and soundness of Executive action.' " *Allen,* 468 U.S., at 760 (quoting Laird v. Tatum, 408 U.S. 1, 15 (1972)). We have always rejected that vision of our role:

> When Congress passes an Act empowering administrative agencies to carry on governmental activities, the power of those agencies is circumscribed by the authority granted. This permits the courts to participate in law enforcement entrusted to administrative bodies only to the extent necessary to protect justiciable individual rights against administrative action fairly beyond the granted powers. . . . This is very far from assuming that the courts are charged more than administrators or legislators with the protection of the rights of the people. Congress and the Executive supervise the acts of administrative agents. . . . But under Article III, Congress established courts to adjudicate cases and controversies as to claims of infringement of individual rights whether by unlawful action of private persons or by the exertion of unauthorized administrative power.

Stark v. Wickard, 321 U.S. 288, 309-310 (1944). "Individual rights," within the meaning of this passage, do not mean public rights that have been legislatively pronounced to belong to each individual who forms part of the public. See also *Sierra Club,* 405 U.S., at 740-741, n.16.

Nothing in this contradicts the principle that "the . . . injury required by Art. III may exist solely by virtue of 'statutes creating legal rights, the invasion of which creates standing.' " *Warth,* 422 U.S., at 500 (quoting Linda R. S. v. Richard D., 410 U.S. 614, 617, n. 3 (1973)). Both of the cases used by Linda R. S. as an illustration of that principle involved Congress's elevating to the status of legally cognizable injuries concrete, de facto injuries that were previously inadequate in law (namely, injury to an individual's personal interest in living in a racially integrated community, see Trafficante v. Metropolitan Life Ins. Co., 409 U.S. 205, 208-212 (1972), and injury to a company's interest in marketing its product free from competition, see Hardin v. Kentucky Utilities Co., 390 U.S. 1, 6 (1968)). As we said in *Sierra Club*, "[Statutory] broadening [of] the categories of injury that may be alleged in support of standing is a different matter from abandoning the requirement that the party seeking review must himself have suffered an injury." 405 U.S., at 738. Whether or not the principle set forth in Warth can be extended beyond that distinction, it is clear that in suits against the government, at least, the concrete injury requirement must remain.

We hold that respondents lack standing to bring this action and that the Court of Appeals erred in denying the summary judgment motion filed by the United States. The opinion of the Court of Appeals is hereby reversed, and the cause remanded for proceedings consistent with this opinion.

It is so ordered.

JUSTICE KENNEDY, with whom JUSTICE SOUTER joins, concurring in part and concurring in the judgment. . . .

While it may seem trivial to require that Mss. Kelly and Skilbred acquire airline tickets to the project sites or announce a date certain upon which they will return, this is not a case where it is reasonable to assume that the affiants will be using the sites on a regular basis, nor do the affiants claim to have visited the sites since the projects commenced. With respect to the Court's discussion of respondents' "ecosystem nexus," "animal nexus," and "vocational nexus" theories, I agree that on this record respondents' showing is insufficient to establish standing on any of these bases. I am not willing to foreclose the possibility, however, that in different circumstances a nexus theory similar to those proffered here might support a claim to standing. See Japan Whaling Assn. v. American Cetacean Soc., 478 U.S. 221, 231, n. 4 (1986) ("respondents . . . undoubtedly have alleged a sufficient 'injury in fact' in that the whale watching and studying of their members will be adversely affected by continued whale harvesting").

In light of the conclusion that respondents have not demonstrated a concrete injury here sufficient to support standing under our precedents, I would not reach the issue of redressability. . . .

I also join [the] Court's opinion with the following observations. As government programs and policies become more complex and far-reaching, we must be sensitive to the articulation of new rights of action that do not have clear analogs in our common-law tradition. Modern litigation has progressed far from the paradigm of Marbury suing Madison to get his commission, Marbury v. Madison, 1 Cranch 137 (1803), or Ogden seeking an injunction to halt Gibbons' steamboat operations. Gibbons v. Ogden, 9 Wheat. 1 (1824). In my view, Congress has the power to define injuries and articulate chains of causation that will give rise to a case or controversy where none existed before, and I do not read the Court's opinion to suggest a contrary view. See Warth v. Seldin, 422 U.S. 490, 500 (1975); ante, at 22-23. In exercising this power, however, Congress must at the very least identify the injury it seeks to vindicate and relate the injury to the class of persons entitled to bring suit. The citizen-suit provision of the Endangered Species Act does not meet these minimal requirements, because while the statute purports to confer a right on "any person . . . to enjoin . . . the United States and any other governmental instrumentality or agency . . . who is alleged to be in violation of any provision of this chapter," it does not of its own force establish that there is an injury in "any person" by virtue of any "violation." 16 U.S.C. §1540(g)(1)(A).

The Court's holding that there is an outer limit to the power of Congress to confer rights of action is a direct and necessary consequence of the case and controversy limitations found in Article III. I agree that it would exceed those limitations if, at the behest of Congress and in the absence of any showing of concrete injury, we were to entertain citizen-suits to vindicate the public's nonconcrete interest in the proper administration of the laws. . . .

JUSTICE STEVENS, concurring in the judgment. . . .

In my opinion a person who has visited the critical habitat of an endangered species, has a professional interest in preserving the species and its habitat, and intends to revisit them in the future has standing to challenge agency action that threatens their destruction. Congress has found that a wide variety of endangered species of fish, wildlife, and plants are of "aesthetic, ecological, educational, historical, recreational, and scientific value to the Nation and its people." 16 U.S.C. §1531(a)(3). Given that finding, we have no license to demean the importance of the interest that particular individuals may have in observing any species or its habitat, whether those individuals are motivated by aesthetic enjoyment, an interest in professional research, or an economic interest in preservation of the species. Indeed, this Court has often held that injuries to such interests are sufficient to confer standing, and the Court reiterates that holding today.

The Court nevertheless concludes that respondents have not suffered "injury in fact" because they have not shown that the harm to the endangered species will produce "imminent" injury to them. I disagree. An injury to an individual's interest in studying or enjoying a species and its natural habitat occurs when someone (whether it be the government or a private party) takes action that harms that species and habitat. . . .

The plurality also concludes that respondents' injuries are not redressable in this litigation for two reasons. First, respondents have sought only a declaratory judgment that the Secretary of the Interior's regulation interpreting §7(a)(2) to require consultation only for agency actions in the United States or on the high seas is invalid and an injunction requiring him to promulgate a new regulation requiring consultation for agency actions abroad as well. But, the plurality opines, even if respondents succeed and a new regulation is promulgated, there is no guarantee that federal agencies that are not parties to this case will actually consult with the Secretary. Furthermore, the plurality continues, respondents have not demonstrated that federal agencies can influence the behavior of the foreign governments where the affected projects are located. Thus, even if the agencies consult with the Secretary and terminate funding for foreign projects, the foreign governments might nonetheless pursue the projects and jeopardize the endangered species. Neither of these reasons is persuasive.

We must presume that if this Court holds that §7(a)(2) requires consultation, all affected agencies would abide by that interpretation and engage in the requisite consultations. Certainly the Executive Branch cannot be heard to argue that an authoritative construction of the governing statute by this Court may simply be ignored by any agency head. Moreover, if Congress has required consultation between agencies, we must presume that such consultation will have a serious purpose that is likely to produce tangible results. . . .

Although I believe that respondents have standing, I nevertheless concur in the judgment of reversal because I am persuaded that the Government is correct in its submission that §7(a)(2) does not apply to activities in foreign countries. . . .

JUSTICE BLACKMUN, with whom JUSTICE O'CONNOR joins, dissenting. . . .

I think a reasonable finder of fact could conclude from the information in the affidavits and deposition testimony that either Kelly or Skilbred will soon return to the project sites, thereby satisfying the "actual or imminent" injury standard. The Court dismisses Kelly's and Skilbred's general statements that they intended to revisit the project sites as "simply not enough." But those statements did not stand alone. A reasonable finder of fact could conclude, based not only upon their statements of intent to return, but upon their past visits to the project sites, as well as their professional backgrounds, that it was likely that Kelly and Skilbred would make a return trip to the project areas. Contrary to the Court's contention that Kelly's and Skilbred's past visits "proves nothing," the fact of their past visits could demonstrate to a reasonable factfinder that Kelly and Skilbred have the requisite resources and personal interest in the preservation of the species endangered by the Aswan and Mahaweli projects to make good on their intention to return again. . . .

By requiring a "description of concrete plans" or "specification of when the some day [for a return visit] will be," the Court, in my view, demands what is likely an empty formality. No substantial barriers prevent Kelly or Skilbred from simply purchasing plane tickets to return to the Aswan and Mahaweli projects. . . .

The Court also rejects respondents' claim of vocational or professional injury. The Court says that it is "beyond all reason" that a zoo "keeper" of Asian elephants would have standing to contest his government's participation in the eradication of all the Asian elephants in another part of the world. I am unable to see how the distant location of the destruction necessarily (for purposes of ruling at summary judgment) mitigates the harm to the elephant keeper. If there is no more access to a future supply of the animal that sustains a keeper's livelihood, surely there is harm.

I have difficulty imagining this Court applying its rigid principles of geographic formalism anywhere outside the context of environmental claims. As I understand it, environmental plaintiffs are under no special constitutional standing disabilities. . . .

I find myself unable to agree with the plurality's analysis of redressability, based as it is on its invitation of executive lawlessness, ignorance of principles of collateral estoppel, unfounded assumptions about causation, and erroneous conclusions about what the record does not say. In my view, respondents have satisfactorily shown a genuine issue of fact as to whether their injury would likely be redressed by a decision in their favor. . . .

The Court expresses concern that allowing judicial enforcement of "agencies' observance of a particular, statutorily prescribed procedure" would "transfer from the President to the courts the Chief Executive's most important constitutional duty, to 'take Care that the Laws be faithfully executed,' Art. II, sec. 3." In fact, the principal effect of foreclosing judicial enforcement of such procedures is to transfer power into the hands of the Executive at the expense — not of the courts — but of Congress, from which that power originates and emanates. . . .

[There] may be factual circumstances in which a congressionally imposed procedural requirement is so insubstantially connected to the prevention of a substantive harm that it cannot be said to work any conceivable injury to an individual litigant. But, as a general matter, the courts owe substantial deference to Congress' substantive purpose in imposing a certain procedural requirement. In all events, "our separation-of-powers analysis does not turn on the labeling of an activity as 'substantive' as opposed to 'procedural.' " There is no room for a per se rule or presumption excluding injuries labeled "procedural" in nature.

In conclusion, I cannot join the Court on what amounts to a slash-and-burn expedition through the law of environmental standing. In my view, "the very essence of civil liberty certainly consists in the right of every individual to claim the protection of the laws, whenever he receives an injury." Marbury v. Madison, 1 Cranch 137, 163 (1803).

I dissent.

Note: Standing and the Question of Citizens' Suits

1. *Congressional power.* Does *Lujan* mean that Congress is completely without constitutional power to grant standing to citizens? If so, what is the source of this conclusion in Article III or the relevant history? Consider the view that citizen standing was fairly common in England and the colonies at the time of the framing. See Berger, Standing to Sue in Public Actions: Is It a Constitutional Requirement, 78 Yale L.J. 816 (1969); Jaffe, Standing in Public Actions, 74 Harv. L. Rev. 1265, 1274 (1961).

2. *Origins.* The analysis in *Lujan* overlaps a good deal with the analysis in Scalia, The Doctrine of Standing as an Essential Part of Separation of Powers, 17 Suffolk U. L. Rev. 881 (1983). This article therefore deserves considerable attention post-*Lujan.*

3. *Implications.* Consider the following cases in the wake of *Lujan.* (a) Congress tries to grant standing to a citizen to bring suit against a polluter who has violated federal environmental law. (b) Congress tries to grant standing to citizens to enforce the environmental law against both private defendants and government officials — but unlike in *Lujan,* it also says that every victorious plaintiff receives a $200 bounty. (c) The plaintiffs in *Lujan* obtain a plane ticket to go to the relevant nations.

4. For discussion of *Lujan,* see the several articles in 1993 Duke Law Journal 1141; Sunstein, What's Standing After Lujan, 91 Mich. L. Rev. 163 (1992).

Compare with *Lujan* the striking decision in Northeastern Florida Chapter of Associated General Contractors v. Jacksonville, 61 USLW 4626 (1993). Jacksonville enacted an ordinance requiring that 10 percent of the money spent on city contracts be "set aside" for minority business enterprises. A contractors' association, consisting mostly of members who would not qualify as minority enterprises, brought suit, claiming that the set aside violated the equal protection clause. The lower court denied standing on the ground that no member of the association had demonstrated that "but for the program, any AGC member would have bid successfully for any of these contracts." There was therefore no injury in fact.

The Supreme Court responded: "When the government erects a barrier that makes it more difficult for members of one group to obtain a benefit than it is for members of another group, a member of the former group seeking to challenge the barrier need not allege that he would have obtained the benefit but for the barrier in order to establish standing. The 'injury in fact' in an equal protection case of this variety is the denial of equal treatment resulting from the imposition of the barrier, not the ultimate inability to obtain the benefit. And in the context of a challenge to a set-aside program, the 'injury in fact' is the inability to compete on an equal footing in the bidding process, not the loss of a contract. To establish standing, therefore, a party challenging a set-aside program like Jacksonville's need only demonstrate that it is able and ready to bid on contracts and that a discriminatory policy prevents it from doing so on an equal basis."

In an intriguing footnote, the Court added, "It follows from our definition of 'injury in fact' that petitioner has sufficiently alleged both that the city's ordinance is the 'cause' of its injury and that a judicial decree directly to the city to discontinue its program would 'redress' the injury."

Evaluate the following view: There is serious tension between *Lujan* and *Northeastern Florida Chapter of Associated General Contractors.* The injury in *Lujan* could easily have been characterized as an opportunity-type injury, in which case there was indeed injury in fact. And if the injury had been so characterized, there would have been no problem with redressability and causation. Indeed, what the Court did in *Northeastern Florida Chapter* could have been done in many cases denying standing, including Allen v. Wright, Linda R.S. v. Richard D., Simon v. Eastern Kentucky Welfare Rights Organization, and others. The real problem is that the Court has not explained the criteria by which it will decide how to characterize the relevant injury.

3. Political Questions

Page 114. Before "Note: Political Questions," add the following:

The Court rejected a political question claim in United States Department of Commerce v. Montana, 112 S. Ct. 1415 (1992). Congress chose a certain apportionment method for the House of Representatives; several states objected to the choice. Significantly, the Court said that in "invoking the political question doctrine, a court acknowledges the possibility that a constitutional provision may not be judicially enforceable. Such a decision is of course very different from determining that specific congressional action does not violate the Constitution." The Court thus rejected the suggestion that a political question existed when, and only when, there was no constitutional violation. Nonetheless, the Court held that the case was indeed justiciable, because it was no different from *Baker* itself.

NIXON v. UNITED STATES, 113 S. CT. 732 (1993): Nixon, a former district court judge who was convicted of making false statements before a federal grand jury sought judicial review of his subsequent removal from office by impeachment. He claimed that the Senate had failed to "try" him within the meaning of the impeachment clause of Article I. Upon receiving articles of impeachment from the House, the Senate referred the matter to a committee, which reported to the full body. Although the committee presented the Senate with a transcript of the proceedings and Nixon was permitted to make a personal appeal to the Senate, the full body did not receive any of the evidence.

Chief Justice Rehnquist delivered the opinion of the Court:

"[Before] we reach the merits of such a claim, we must decide whether it is 'justiciable,' that is, whether it is a claim that may be resolved by the courts. We conclude that it is not. . . .

A controversy is nonjusticiable — i.e., involves a political question — where there is 'a textually demonstrable constitutional commitment of the issue to a coordinate political department; or a lack of judically discoverable and manageable standards for resolving it' [*Baker*]. But the courts must, in the first instance, interpret the text in question and determine whether and to what extent the issue is textually committed. [The] concept of a textual commitment to a coordinate political department is not completely separate from the concept of a lack of judicially discoverable and manageable standards for resolving it; the lack of judicially manageable standards may strengthen the conclusion that there is a textually demonstrable commitment to a coordinate branch. . . .

"In this case, we must examine Art. I, §3, cl. 6 [which provides 'The Senate shall have the sole Power to try all Impeachments.' This provision] is a grant of authority to the Senate, and the word 'sole' indicates that this authority is reposed in the Senate, and nowhere else. . . .

"Petitioner argues that the word 'try' [requires that] the proceedings must be in the nature of a judicial trial. . . .

"The word 'try,' both in 1787 and later, has considerably broader meanings than those to which petitioner would limit it. [Based] on the variety of definitions, [we] cannot say that the Framers used the word [as] an implied limitation on the method by which the Senate might proceed in trying impeachments. . . .

"The conclusion that the use of the word 'try' [lacks] sufficient precision to afford any judicially manageable standard of review of the Senate's actions is fortified by the existence of the three very specific requirements that the Constitution does impose on the Senate when trying impeachments: the members must be under oath, a two-thirds vote is required to convict, and the Chief Justice presides when the President is tried. These limitations are quite precise, and their nature suggests that the Framers did not intend to impose additional limitations on the form of the Senate proceedings by the use of the word ['try.']

"[The] common sense meaning of the word 'sole' is that the Senate alone shall have authority to determine whether an individual should be acquitted or convicted. . . .

"[Judicial] review would be inconsistent with the Framers' insistence that our system be one of checks and balances. In our constitutional system, impeachment was designed to be the *only* check on the Judicial Branch by the Legislature. [Judicial] involvement in impeachment proceedings, even if only for purposes of judicial review, is counterintuitive because it would eviscerate the 'important constitutional check' placed on the Judiciary by the Framers. Nixon's argument would place final reviewing authority with respect to impeachments in the hands of the same body that the impeachment process is meant to regulate. . . .

"In addition to the textual commitment argument, we are persuaded that the lack of finality and the difficulty of fashioning relief counsel against justiciability. [Opening] the door of judicial review to the procedures used by the Senate in trying impeachments would 'expose the politicial life of the country to months, or perhaps years, of chaos.' This lack of finality would manifest itself most dramatically if the President were impeached. The legitimacy of any successor, and hence his effectiveness, would be impaired severely, not merely while the judicial process was running its course, but during any retrial that a differently constituted Senate might conduct if its first judgment of conviction were invalidated. Equally uncertain is the question of what relief a court may give other than simply setting aside the judgment of conviction. Could it order the reinstatement of a convicted federal judge, or order Congress to create an additional judgeship if the seat had been filled in the interim? . . .

"We agree with Nixon that courts possess power to review either legislative or executive action that transgresses identifiable textual limits. As we have made clear, 'whether the action if [either the Legislative or Executive Branch] exceeds whatever authority has been committed, is itself a delicate exercise in constitutional interpretation, and is a responsibility of this Court as ultimate interpreter of the Constitution.' [*Baker*]. But we conclude, after exercising that delicate responsibility, that the word 'try' in the Impeachment Clause does not provide an identifiable textual limit on the authority which is committed to the Senate."

Justice White, joined by Justice Blackmun, concurred in the judgment:

"Petitioner contends that the method by which the Senate convicted him on two articles of impeachment violates Art. I, §3, cl. 6 of the Constitution, which mandates that the Senate 'try' impeachments. The Court is of the view that the Constitution forbids us even to consider his contention. I find no such prohibition and would therefore reach the merits of the claim. I concur in the judgment because the Senate fulfilled its constitutional obligation to 'try' petitioner. . . .

"[The] discord between the majority's position and the basic principles of checks and balances underlying the Constitution's separation of powers is clear. In essence, the majority suggests that the Framers' conferred upon Congress a potential tool of legislative dominance yet at the same time rendered Congress' exercise of that power one of the very few areas of legislative authority immune from any judicial review. While the majority rejects petitioner's justiciability argument as espousing a view 'inconsistent with the Framers' insistence that our system be one of checks and balances,' it is the Court's finding of nonjusticiability that truly upsets the Framers' careful design. In a truly balanced system, impeachments tried by the Senate would serve as a means of controlling a largely unaccountable judiciary, even as judicial review would ensure that the Senate adhered to a minimal set of procedural standards in conducting impeachment trials."

Justice Souter also concurred in the judgment:

"[The] political question doctrine [derives] in large part from prudential concerns about the respect we owe the political departments. Not all interference is inappropriate or disrespectful, however, and application of the doctrine ultimately turns, as Learned Hand put it, on 'how importunately the occasion demands an answer.'

"This occasion does not demand an answer. [It] seems fair to conclude that the [Impeachment] Clause contemplates that the Senate may determine, within broad boundaries, such subsidiary issues as the procedures for receipt and consideration of evidence necessary to satisfy its duty to 'try' [impeachments].

"One can, nevertheless, envision different and unusual circumstances that might justify a more searching review of impeachment proceedings. If the Senate were to act in a manner seriously threatening the integrity of its results, convicting, say, upon a coin-toss, or upon a summary determination that an officer of the United States was simply 'a bad guy,' judicial interference might well be appropriate. In such circumstances, the Senate's action might be so far beyond the scope of its constitutional authority, and the consequent impact on the Republic so great, as to merit a judicial response despite the prudential concerns that would ordinarily counsel silence. 'The political question doctrine, a tool for maintenance of governmental order, will not be so applied as to promote only disorder.' [*Baker*.]"

A concurring opinion by Justice Stevens has been omitted.

Page 120. Before subsection 3b of the Note, add the following:

The 27th Amendment, requiring that congressional pay raises take effect only after an election has intervened, was ratified by the Michigan legislature on May 7, 1992. The amendment had been among the first proposed by James Madison and sent to the states for ratification by the first Congress. Five states ratified the amendment in 1789-1791 and one in 1873. From 1978 on, ratifications gradually accumulated, and Michigan's was the thirty-eighth ratification.

Is the amendment now part of the Constitution? A federal statute provides that the national Archivist must certify the receipt of a sufficient number of ratifications, after which a constitutional amendment becomes "valid." If the Archivist refused to so certify, on the ground that there was insufficient indication of contemporaneous consensus on the amendment, who would have standing to challenge that refusal? If the Archivist did so certify, who might have standing to challenge that decision and to make the ensuing claim that the amendment was not lawfully included in the Constitution? In any event, is certification necessary under the Constitution?

Suppose no one — member of the public or member of Congress — had standing to raise the question of whether the amendment was part of the Constitution, and the Supreme Court never answers that question. Is it meaningful to say that the amendment is (or is not) part of the Constitution in the same way that the third amendment, or the guaranty clause, is? Suppose Congress adopts the practice of deferring the effective date of pay raises, consistent with the amendment. Does that strengthen or weaken the claim that the amendment is part of the Constitution?

Chapter Two

The Powers of Congress

E. THE PURPORTED DEMISE OF JUDICIALLY ENFORCED FEDERALISM LIMITS ON CONGRESSIONAL POWER

Page 224. Before section 6 of the Note, add the following:

5A. National League of Cities *revived*?: In Gregory v. Ashcroft, 111 S. Ct. 2395 (1991), the Court held that the Age Discrimination in Employment Act did not apply to a state's mandatory retirement provisions applying to appointed state judges. The ADEA bars employers, including state governments, from adopting mandatory retirement policies, but as to state employers, it exempts "appointees on a policymaking level." In interpreting this provision, the Court relied on general propostions about federalism. It noted that the state's retirement provision "is a decision of the most fundamental sort for a sovereign entity," and required that Congress's intention to displace state decisions in this area must be clearly stated.

Justice White, who concurred in the result, objected to the "plain statement" requirement. He asked, "Is the rule limited to federal regulation of the qualifications of state officials? Or does it apply more broadly to the regulation of any 'state governmental functions'? [The] vagueness of the majority's rule undoubtedly will lead States to assert that various federal statutes no longer apply to a wide variety of State activities if Congress has not expressly referred to those activities in the statute. Congress, in turn, will be forced to draft long and detailed lists of which particular state functions it meant to regulate."

NEW YORK v. UNITED STATES
112 S. Ct. 2408 (1992)

JUSTICE O'CONNOR delivered the opinion of the Court.

This case implicates one of our Nation's newest problems of public policy and perhaps our oldest question of constitutional law. The public policy issue involves the disposal of radioactive waste: In this case, we address the constitutionality of three provisions of the Low-Level Radioactive Waste Policy Amendments Act of 1985. The constitutional question is as old as the Constitution: It consists of discerning the proper division of authority between the Federal Government and the States. We conclude that while Congress has substantial power under the Constitution to encourage the States to provide for the disposal of the radioactive waste generated within their borders, the Constitution does not confer upon Congress the ability simply to compel the States to do so. We therefore find that only two of the Act's three provisions at issue are consistent with the Constitution's allocation of power to the Federal Government.

I

We live in a world full of low level radioactive waste. Radioactive material is present in luminous watch dials, smoke alarms, measurement devices, medical fluids, research materials, and the protective gear and construction materials used by workers at nuclear power plants. Low level radioactive waste is generated by the Government, by hospitals, by research institutions, and by various industries. The waste must be isolated from humans for long periods of time, often for hundreds of years. Millions of cubic feet of low level radioactive waste must be disposed of each year.

[In 1971 there were six waste disposal sites, but by 1979 only one remained open, in South Carolina. The state's governor ordered a 50 percent reduction in the waste accepted there. In 1980 Congress adopted a statute declaring that each state was primarily responsible for disposing of low-level radioactive waste produced within its borders, and authorizing states to enter into regional compacts for disposal facilities. By 1985 there were only three disposal sites. In 1985 Congress enacted the amendments at issue in this case. The amendments were based on a proposal from the National Governors' Association and represented a compromise between states with disposal sites and those without them. From 1986 to 1992 states with disposal sites could impose surcharges for waste from elsewhere; after 1992 they could exclude waste from states not participating in their regional compacts.

The 1985 Act had three incentives to induce states to provide for disposal of waste generated within their borders. (1) *Monetary:* Part of the surcharges were transferred to the Secretary of Energy, and that money would be returned to a state that was able to dispose of its own waste by 1993. (2) *Access:* The surcharges for access to existing disposal sites escalate, and after a series of deadlines access to those sites could be denied.

(3) *The take title provision:* If a state was unable to provide for disposal of its own waste by 1996, it was to "take title to the waste" and would "be obligated to take possession of the waste." New York, which generates a relatively large portion of the nation's low-level radioactive waste, identified several possible local disposal sites, but faced political opposition at each location. Instead of proceeding with development of a disposal site, the state challenged the constitutionality of the 1985 Act.]

II

A

In 1788, in the course of explaining to the citizens of New York why the recently drafted Constitution provided for federal courts, Alexander Hamilton observed: "The erection of a new government, whatever care or wisdom may distinguish the work, cannot fail to originate questions of intricacy and nicety; and these may, in a particular manner, be expected to flow from the the establishment of a constitution founded upon the total or partial incorporation of a number of distinct sovereignties." The Federalist No. 82, p.491 (C. Rossiter ed. 1961). Hamilton's prediction has proved quite accurate. While no one disputes the proposition that "the Constitution created a Federal Government of limited powers," Gregory v. Ashcroft, and while the Tenth Amendment makes explicit that "the powers not delegated to the United States by the Constitution, nor prohibited by it to the States, are reserved to the States respectively, or to the people," the task of ascertaining the constitutional line between federal and state power has given rise to many of the Court's most difficult and celebrated cases. At least as far back as Martin v. Hunter's Lessee, 1 Wheat. 304, 324 (1816), the Court has resolved questions "of great importance and delicacy" in determining whether particular sovereign powers have been granted by the Constitution to the Federal Government or have been retained by the States.

These questions can be viewed in either of two ways. In some cases the Court has inquired whether an Act of Congress is authorized by one of the powers delegated to Congress in Article I of the Constitution. See, e.g., Perez v. United States, 402 U.S. 146 (1971); McCulloch v. Maryland, 4 Wheat. 316 (1819). In other cases the Court has sought to determine whether an Act of Congress invades the province of state sovereignty reserved by the Tenth Amendment. See, e.g., Garcia v. San Antonio Metropolitan Transit Authority, 469 U.S. 528 (1985); Lane County v. Oregon, 7 Wall. 71 (1869). In a case like this one, involving the division of authority between federal and state governments, the two inquiries are mirror images of each other. If a power is delegated to Congress in the Constitution, the Tenth Amendment expressly disclaims any reservation of that power to the States; if a power is an attribute of state sovereignty reserved by the Tenth Amendment, it is necessarily a power the Constitution has not conferred on Congress.

It is in this sense that the Tenth Amendment "states but a truism that all is retained which has not been surrendered." United States v. Darby, 312 U.S. 100, 124 (1941). As Justice Story put it, "this amendment is a mere affirmation of what, upon any just reasoning, is a necessary rule of interpreting the constitution. Being an instrument of limited and enumerated powers, it follows irresistibly, that what is not conferred, is withheld, and belongs to the state authorities." 3 J. Story, Commentaries on the Constitution of the United States 752 (1833). This has been the Court's consistent understanding: "The States unquestionably do retain a significant measure of sovereign authority . . . to the extent that the Constitution has not divested them of their original powers and transferred those powers to the Federal Government." Garcia v. San Antonio Metropolitan Transit Authority.

Congress exercises its conferred powers subject to the limitations contained in the Constitution. Thus, for example, under the Commerce Clause Congress may regulate publishers engaged in interstate commerce, but Congress is constrained in the exercise of that power by the First Amendment. The Tenth Amendment likewise restrains the power of Congress, but this limit is not derived from the text of the Tenth Amendment itself, which, as we have discussed, is essentially a tautology. Instead, the Tenth Amendment confirms that the power of the Federal Government is subject to limits that may, in a given instance, reserve power to the States. The Tenth Amendment thus directs us to determine, as in this case, whether an incident of state sovereignty is protected by a limitation on an Article I power.

The benefits of this federal structure have been extensively catalogued elsewhere, see, e.g., Gregory v. Ashcroft, supra; Merritt, The Guarantee Clause and State Autonomy: Federalism for a Third Century, 88 Colum. L. Rev. 1, 3-10 (1988); McConnell, Federalism: Evaluating the Founders' Design, 54 U. Chi. L. Rev. 1484, 1491-1511 (1987), but they need not concern us here. Our task would be the same even if one could prove that federalism secured no advantages to anyone. It consists not of devising our preferred system of government, but of understanding and applying the framework set forth in the Constitution. "The question is not what power the Federal Government ought to have but what powers in fact have been given by the people." United States v. Butler, 297 U.S. 1, 63 (1936).

This framework has been sufficiently flexible over the past two centuries to allow for enormous changes in the nature of government. The Federal Government undertakes activities today that would have been unimaginable to the Framers in two senses; first, because the Framers would not have conceived that any government would conduct such activities; and second, because the Framers would not have believed that the Federal Government, rather than the States, would assume such responsibilities. Yet the powers conferred upon the Federal Government by the Constitution were phrased in language broad enough to allow for the expansion of the Federal Government's role. Among the provisions of the Constitution that have been particularly important in this regard, three concern us here [the Commerce Clause, the General Welfare Clause, and the Supremacy Clause]. . . .

The actual scope of the Federal Government's authority with respect to the States has changed over the years, therefore, but the constitutional structure underlying and limiting that authority has not. In the end, just as a cup may be half empty or half full, it makes no difference whether one views the question at issue in this case as one of ascertaining the limits of the power delegated to the Federal Government under the affirmative provisions of the Constitution or one of discerning the core of sovereignty retained by the States under the Tenth Amendment. Either way, we must determine whether any of the three challenged provisions of the Low-Level Radioactive Waste Policy Amendments Act of 1985 oversteps the boundary between federal and state authority.

B

Petitioners do not contend that Congress lacks the power to regulate the disposal of low level radioactive waste. Space in radioactive waste disposal sites is frequently sold by residents of one State to residents of another. Regulation of the resulting interstate market in waste disposal is therefore well within Congress' authority under the Commerce Clause. Petitioners likewise do not dispute that under the Supremacy Clause Congress could, if it wished, pre-empt state radioactive waste regulation. Petitioners contend only that the Tenth Amendment limits the power of Congress to regulate in the way it has chosen. Rather than addressing the problem of waste disposal by directly regulating the generators and disposers of waste, petitioners argue, Congress has impermissibly directed the States to regulate in this field.

Most of our recent cases interpreting the Tenth Amendment have concerned the authority of Congress to subject state governments to generally applicable laws. This case presents no occasion to apply or revisit the holdings of any of these cases, as this is not a case in which Congress has subjected a State to the same legislation applicable to private parties.

This case instead concerns the circumstances under which Congress may use the States as implements of regulation; that is, whether Congress may direct or otherwise motivate the States to regulate in a particular field or a particular way. Our cases have established a few principles that guide our resolution of the issue.

1

As an initial matter, Congress may not simply "commandeer the legislative processes of the States by directly compelling them to enact and enforce a federal regulatory program." Hodel v. Virginia Surface Mining & Reclamation Assn., Inc., 452 U.S. 264, 288 (1981). In *Hodel*, the Court upheld the Surface Mining Control and Reclamation Act of 1977 precisely because it did not "commandeer" the States into regulating mining. The Court found that "the States are not compelled to enforce the steep-slope standards, to expend any state funds, or to participate in the federal regulatory program in any manner whatsoever. If a State does not wish to submit a proposed permanent program that complies with the Act and implementing regulations, the full regulatory burden will be borne by the Federal Government." . . .

These statements . . . were not innovations. While Congress has substantial powers to govern the Nation directly, including in areas of intimate concern to the States, the Constitution has never been understood to confer upon Congress the ability to require the States to govern according to Congress' instructions. See Coyle v. Oklahoma, 221 U.S. 559, 565 (1911). The Court has been explicit about this distinction. "Both the States and the United States existed before the Constitution. The people, through that instrument, established a more perfect union by substituting a national government, acting, with ample power, directly upon the citizens, instead of the Confederate government, which acted with powers, greatly restricted, only upon the States." Lane County v. Oregon, 7 Wall., at 76. The Court has made the same point with more rhetorical flourish, although perhaps with less precision, on a number of occasions. In Chief Justice Chase's much-quoted words, "the preservation of the States, and the maintenance of their governments, are as much within the design and care of the Constitution as the preservation of the Union and the maintenance of the National government. The Constitution, in all its provisions, looks to an indestructible Union, composed of indestructible States." Texas v. White, 7 Wall. 700, 725 (1869).

Indeed, the question whether the Constitution should permit Congress to employ state governments as regulatory agencies was a topic of lively debate among the Framers. Under the Articles of Confederation, Congress lacked the authority in most respects to govern the people directly. In practice, Congress "could not directly tax or legislate upon individuals; it had no explicit legislative or governmental power to make binding law enforceable as such." Amar, Of Sovereignty and Federalism, 96 Yale L.J. 1425, 1447 (1987).

The inadequacy of this governmental structure was responsible in part for the Constitutional Convention. Alexander Hamilton observed: "The great and radical vice in the construction of the existing Confederation is in the principle of LEGISLATION for STATES or GOVERNMENTS, in their CORPORATE or COLLECTIVE CAPACITIES, and as contradistinguished from the INDIVIDUALS of whom they consist." The Federalist No. 15, p.108 (C. Rossiter ed. 1961). As Hamilton saw it, "we must resolve to incorporate into our plan those ingredients which may be considered as forming the characteristic difference between a league and a government; we must extend the authority of the Union to the persons of the citizens — the only proper objects of government." Id., at 109. The new National Government "must carry its agency to the persons of the citizens. It must stand in need of no intermediate legislations. . . . The government of the Union, like that of each State, must be able to address itself immediately to the hopes and fears of individuals." Id., No. 16, p.116.

The Convention generated a great number of proposals for the structure of the new Government, but two quickly took center stage. Under the Virginia Plan, as first introduced by Edmund Randolph, Congress would exercise legislative authority directly upon individuals, without employing the States as intermediaries. 1 Records of the Federal Convention of 1787, p.21 (M. Farrand ed. 1911). Under the New Jersey Plan, as first introduced by William Paterson, Congress would continue to require the approval of the States before legislating, as it has under the Articles of Confederation. 1 id., 243-244. These two plans underwent various revisions as the Convention progressed, but they remained the two primary options discussed by the delegates. One frequently expressed objection to the New Jersey Plan was that it might require the Federal Government to coerce the States into implementing legislation. As Randolph explained the distinction, "the true question is whether we shall adhere to the federal plan [i.e., the New Jersey Plan], or introduce the national plan. The insufficiency of the former has been fully displayed. . . . There are but two modes, by which the end of a General Government can be attained: the 1st is by coercion as proposed by Mr. P[aterson's] plan[, the 2nd] by real legislation as proposed by the other plan. Coercion [is] impracticable, expensive, cruel to individuals. . . . We must resort therefore to a national Legislation over individuals." 1 id., at 255-256. Madison echoed this view: "The practicability of making laws, with coercive sanctions, for the States as political bodies, had been exploded on all hands." 2 id., at 9.

Under one preliminary draft of what would become the New Jersey Plan, state governments would occupy a position relative to Congress similar to that contemplated by the Act at issue in this case: "The laws of the United States ought, as far as may be consistent with the common interests of the Union, to be carried into execution by the judiciary and executive officers of the respective states, wherein the execution thereof is required." 3 id., at 616. This idea apparently never even progressed so far as to be debated by the delegates, as contemporary accounts of the Convention do not mention any such discussion. The delegates' many descriptions of the Virginia and New Jersey Plans speak only in general terms about whether Congress was to derive its authority from the people or from the States, and whether it was to issue directives to individuals or to States. See 1 id., at 260-280.

In the end, the Convention opted for a Constitution in which Congress would exercise its legislative authority directly over individuals rather than over States; for a variety of reasons, it rejected the New Jersey Plan in favor of the Virgina Plan. 1 id., at 313. This choice was made clear to the subsequent state ratifying conventions. Oliver Ellsworth, a member of the Connecticut delegation in Philadelphia, explained the distinction to his State's convention: "This Constitution does not attempt to coerce sovereign bodies, states, in their political capacity. . . . But this legal coercion singles out the . . . individual." 2 J. Elliot, Debates on the Federal Constitution 197 (2d ed. 1863). Charles Pinckney, another delegate at the Constitutional Convention, emphasized to the South Carolina House of Representatives that in Philadelphia "the necessity of having a government which should at once operate upon the people, and not upon the states, was conceived to be indispensable by every delegation present." 4 id., at 256. Rufus King, one of Massachusetts' delegates, returned home to support ratification by recalling the Commonwealth's unhappy experience under the Articles of Confederation and arguing: "Laws, to be effective, therefore, must not be laid on states, but upon individuals." 2 id., at 56. At New York's convention, Hamilton (another delegate in Philadelphia) exclaimed: "But can we believe that one state will ever suffer itself to be used as an instrument of coercion? The thing is a dream; it is impossible. Then we are brought to this dilemma — either a federal standing army is to enforce the requisitions, or the federal treasury is left without supplies, and the government without support. What, sir, is the cure for this great evil? Nothing, but to enable the national laws to operate on individuals, in the same manner as those of the states do." 2 id., at 233. At North Carolina's convention, Samuel Spencer recognized that "all the laws of the Confederation were binding on the states in their political capacities, . . . but now the thing is entirely different. The laws of Congress will be binding on individuals." 4 id., at 153.

In providing for a stronger central government, therefore, the Framers explicitly chose a Constitution that confers upon Congress the power to regulate individuals, not States. As we have seen, the Court has consistently respected this choice. We have always understood that even where Congress has the authority under the Constitution to pass laws requiring or prohibiting certain acts, it lacks the power directly to compel the States to require or prohibit those acts. The allocation of power contained in the Commerce Clause, for example, authorizes Congress to regulate interstate commerce directly; it does not authorize Congress to regulate state governments' regulation of interstate commerce.

2

This is not to say that Congress lacks the ability to encourage a State to regulate in a particular way, or that Congress may not hold out incentives to the States as a method of influencing a State's policy choices. Our cases have identified a variety of methods, short of outright coercion, by which Congress may urge a State to adopt a legislative program consistent with federal interests. Two of these methods are of particular relevance here.

First, under Congress' spending power, "Congress may attach conditions on the receipt of federal funds." South Dakota v. Dole, 483 U. S., at 206. Such conditions must (among other requirements) bear some relationship to the purpose of the federal spending; otherwise, of course, the spending power could render academic the Constitution's other grants and limits of federal authority. Where the recipient of federal funds is a State, as is not unusual today, the conditions attached to the funds by Congress may influence a State's legislative choices. See Kaden, Politics, Money, and State Sovereignty: The Judicial Role, 79 Colum. L. Rev. 847, 874-881 (1979). . . .

Second, where Congress has the authority to regulate private activity under the Commerce Clause, we have recognized Congress' power to offer States the choice of regulating that activity according to federal standards or having state law pre-empted by federal regulation. This arrangement, which has been termed "a program of cooperative federalism," is replicated in numerous federal statutory schemes. . . .

By either of these two methods, as by any other permissible method of encouraging a State to conform to federal policy choices, the residents of the State retain the ultimate decision as to whether or not the State will comply. If a State's citizens view federal policy as sufficiently contrary to local interests, they may elect to decline a federal grant. If state residents would prefer their government to devote its attention and resources to problems other than those deemed important by Congress, they may choose to have the Federal Government rather than the State bear the expense of a federally mandated regulatory program, and they may continue to supplement that program to the extent state law is not pre-empted. Where Congress encourages state regulation rather than compelling it, state governments remain responsive to the local electorate's preferences; state officials remain accountable to the people.

By contrast, where the Federal Government compels States to regulate, the accountability of both state and federal officials is diminished. If the citizens of New York, for example, do not consider that making provision for the disposal of radioactive waste is in their best interest, they may elect state officials who share their view. That view can always be pre-empted under the Supremacy Clause if it is contrary to the national view, but in such a case it is the Federal Government that makes the decision in full view of the public, and it will be federal officials that suffer the consequences if the decision turns out to be detrimental or unpopular. But where the Federal Government directs the States to regulate, it may be state officials who will bear the brunt of public disapproval, while the federal officials who devised the regulatory program may remain insulated from the electoral ramifications of their decision. Accountability is thus diminished when, due to federal coercion, elected state officials cannot regulate in accordance with the views of the local electorate in matters not pre-empted by federal regulation.

With these principles in mind, we turn to the three challenged provisions of the Low-Level Radioactive Waste Policy Amendments Act of 1985.

III . . .

A

The first set of incentives works in three steps. First, Congress has authorized States with disposal sites to impose a surcharge on radioactive waste received from other States. Second, the Secretary of Energy collects a portion of this surcharge and places the money in an escrow account. Third, States achieving a series of milestones receive portions of this fund.

The first of these steps is an unexceptionable exercise of Congress' power to authorize the States to burden interstate commerce. While the Commerce Clause has long been understood to limit the States' ability to discriminate against interstate commerce, that limit may be lifted, as it has been here, by an expression of the "unambiguous intent" of Congress. Whether or not the States would be permitted to burden the interstate transport of low level radioactive waste in the absence of Congress' approval, the States can clearly do so with Congress' approval, which is what the Act gives them.

The second step, the Secretary's collection of a percentage of the surcharge, is no more than a federal tax on interstate commerce, which petitioners do not claim to be an invalid exercise of either Congress' commerce or taxing power.

The third step is a conditional exercise of Congress' authority under the Spending Clause: Congress has placed conditions — the achievement of the milestones — on the receipt of federal funds. Petitioners do not contend that Congress has exceeded its authority in any of the four respects our cases have identified. See generally South Dakota v. Dole, 483 U.S., at 207-208. The expenditure is for the general welfare, Helvering v. Davis, 301 U.S. 619, 640-641 (1937); the States are required to use the money they receive for the purpose of assuring the safe disposal of radioactive waste. The conditions imposed are unambiguous; the Act informs the States exactly what they must do and by when they must do it in order to obtain a share of the escrow account. The conditions imposed are reasonably related to the purpose of the expenditure; both the conditions and the payments embody Congress' efforts to address the pressing problem of radioactive waste disposal. Finally, petitioners do not claim that the conditions imposed by the Act violate any independent constitutional prohibition. . . .

B

In the second set of incentives, Congress has authorized States and regional compacts with disposal sites gradually to increase the cost of access to the sites, and then to deny access altogether, to radioactive waste generated in States that do not meet federal deadlines. As a simple regulation, this provision would be within the power of Congress to authorize the States to discriminate against interstate commerce. Where federal regulation of private activity is within the scope of the Commerce Clause, we have recognized the ability of Congress to offer states the choice of regulating that activity according to federal standards or having state law pre-empted by federal regulation.

This is the choice presented to nonsited States by the Act's second set of incentives: States may either regulate the disposal of radioactive waste according to federal standards by attaining local or regional self-sufficiency, or their residents who produce radioactive waste will be subject to federal regulation authorizing sited States and regions to deny access to their disposal sites. The affected States are not compelled by Congress to regulate, because any burden caused by a State's refusal to regulate will fall on those who generate waste and find no outlet for its disposal, rather than on the State as a sovereign. A State whose citizens do not wish it to attain the Act's milestones may devote its attention and its resources to issues its citizens deem more worthy; the choice remains at all times with the residents of the State, not with Congress. The State need not expend any funds, or participate in any federal program, if local residents do not view such expenditures or participation as worthwhile. Nor must the State abandon the field if it does not accede to federal direction; the State may continue to regulate the generation and disposal of radioactive waste in any manner its citizens see fit.

The Act's second set of incentives thus represents a conditional exercise of Congress' commerce power, along the lines of those we have held to be within Congress' authority. As a result, the second set of incentives does not intrude on the sovereignty reserved to the States by the Tenth Amendment.

C

The take title provision is of a different character. This third so-called "incentive" offers States, as an alternative to regulating pursuant to Congress' direction, the option of taking title to and possession of the low level radioactive waste generated within their borders and becoming liable for all damages waste generators suffer as a result of the States' failure to do so promptly. In this provision, Congress has crossed the line distinguishing encouragement from coercion. . . .

The take title provision offers state governments a "choice" of either accepting ownership of waste or regulating according to the instructions of Congress. Respondents do not claim that the Constitution would authorize Congress to impose either option as a freestanding requirement. On one hand, the Constitution would not permit Congress simply to transfer radioactive waste from generators to state governments. Such a forced transfer, standing alone, would in principle be no different than a congressionally compelled subsidy from state governments to radioactive waste producers. The same is true of the provision requiring the States to become liable for the generators' damages. Standing alone, this provision would be indistinguishable from an Act of Congress directing the States to assume the liabilities of certain state residents. Either type of federal action would "commandeer" state governments into the service of federal regulatory purposes, and would for this reason be inconsistent with the Constitution's division of authority between federal and state governments. On the other hand, the second alternative held out to state governments — regulating pursuant to Congress' direction — would, standing alone, present a simple command to state governments to implement legislation enacted by Congress. As we have seen, the Constitution does not empower Congress to subject state governments to this type of instruction.

Because an instruction to state governments to take title to waste, standing alone, would be beyond the authority of Congress, and because a direct order to regulate, standing alone, would also be beyond the authority of Congress, it follows that Congress lacks the power to offer the States a choice between the two. Unlike the first two sets of incentives, the take title incentive does not represent the conditional exercise of any congressional power enumerated in the Constitution. In this provision, Congress has not held out the threat of exercising its spending power or its commerce power; it has instead held out the threat, should the States not regulate according to one federal instruction, of simply forcing the States to submit to another federal instruction. A choice between two unconstitutionally coercive regulatory techniques is no choice at all. Either way, "the Act commandeers the legislative processes of the States by directly compelling them to enact and enforce a federal regulatory program," *Hodel*, an outcome that has never been understood to lie within the authority conferred upon Congress by the Constitution.

Respondents emphasize the latitude given to the States to implement Congress' plan. The Act enables the States to regulate pursuant to Congress' instructions in any number of different ways. States may avoid taking title by contracting with sited regional compacts, by building a disposal site alone or as part of a compact, or by permitting private parties to build a disposal site. States that host sites may employ a wide range of designs and disposal methods, subject only to broad federal regulatory limits. This line of reasoning, however, only underscores the critical alternative a State lacks: A State may not decline to administer the federal program. No matter which path the State chooses, it must follow the direction of Congress.

The take title provision appears to be unique. No other federal statute has been cited which offers a state government no option other than that of implementing legislation enacted by Congress. Whether one views the take title provision as lying outside Congress' enumerated powers, or as infringing upon the core of state sovereignty reserved by the Tenth Amendment, the provision is inconsistent with the federal structure of our Government established by the Constitution.

IV . . .

A . . .

First, the United States argues that the Constitution's prohibition of congressional directives to state governments can be overcome where the federal interest is sufficiently important to justify state submission. This argument contains a kernel of truth: In determining whether the Tenth Amendment limits the ability of Congress to subject state governments to generally applicable laws, the Court has in some cases stated that it will evaluate the strength of federal interests in light of the degree to which such laws would prevent the State from functioning as a sovereign; that is, the extent to which such generally applicable laws would impede a state government's responsibility to represent and be accountable to the citizens of the State. . . . [W]hether or not a particularly strong federal interest enables Congress to bring state governments within the orbit of generally applicable federal regulation, no Member of the Court has ever suggested that such a federal interest would enable Congress to command a state government to enact state regulation. No matter how powerful the federal interest involved, the Constitution simply does not give Congress the authority to require the States to regulate. The Constitution instead gives Congress the authority to regulate matters directly and to pre-empt contrary state regulation. Where a federal interest is sufficiently strong to cause Congress to legislate, it must do so directly; it may not conscript state governments as its agents.

Second, the United States argues that the Constitution does, in some circumstances, permit federal directives to state governments. Various cases are cited for this proposition, but none support it. Some of these cases discuss the well established power of Congress to pass laws enforceable in state courts. These cases involve no more than an application of the Supremacy Clause's provision that federal law "shall be the supreme Law of the Land," enforceable in every State. More to the point, all involve congressional regulation of individuals, not congressional requirements that States regulate. Federal statutes enforceable in state courts do, in a sense, direct state judges to enforce them, but this sort of federal "direction" of state judges is mandated by the text of the Supremacy Clause. No comparable constitutional provision authorizes Congress to command state legislatures to legislate. . . .

Third, the United States . . . argues that the Constitution envisions a role for Congress as an arbiter of interstate disputes. The United States observes that federal courts, and this Court in particular, have frequently resolved conflicts among States. Many of these disputes have involved the allocation of shared resources among the States, a category perhaps broad enough to encompass the allocation of scarce disposal space for radioactive waste. The United States suggests that if the Court may resolve such interstate disputes, Congress can surely do the same under the Commerce Clause. The regional compacts support this argument with a series of quotations from The Federalist and other contemporaneous documents, which the compacts contend demonstrate that the Framers established a strong national legislature for the purpose of resolving trade disputes among the States.

While the Framers no doubt endowed Congress with the power to regulate interstate commerce in order to avoid further instances of the interstate trade disputes that were common under the Articles of Confederation, the Framers did not intend that Congress should exercise that power through the mechanism of mandating state regulation. The Constitution established Congress as "a superintending authority over the reciprocal trade" among the States, The Federalist No. 42, p.268 (C. Rossiter ed. 1961), by empowering Congress to regulate that trade directly, not by authorizing Congress to issue trade-related orders to state governments. As Madison and Hamilton explained, "a sovereignty over sovereigns, a government over governments, a legislation for communities, as contradistinguished from individuals, as it is a solecism in theory, so in practice it is subversive of the order and ends of civil polity." Id., No. 20, p.138.

B

The sited State respondents focus their attention on the process by which the Act was formulated. They correctly observe that public officials representing the State of New York lent their support to the Act's enactment. A Deputy Commissioner of the State's Energy Office testified in favor of the Act. Senator Moynihan of New York spoke in support of the Act on the floor of the Senate. Respondents note that the Act embodies a bargain among the sited and unsited States, a compromise to which New York was a willing participant and from which New York has reaped much benefit. Respondents then pose what appears at first to be a troubling question: How can a federal statute be found an unconstitutional infringement of State sovereignty when state officials consented to the statute's enactment?

The answer follows from an understanding of the fundamental purpose served by our Government's federal structure. The Constitution does not protect the sovereignty of States for the benefit of the States or state governments as abstract political entities, or even for the benefit of the public officials governing the States. To the contrary, the Constitution divides authority between federal and state governments for the protection of individuals. State sovereignty is not just an end in itself: "Rather, federalism secures to citizens the liberties that derive from the diffusion of sovereign power." Coleman v. Thompson, 501 U.S. — , — (1991) (Blackmun, J., dissenting). "Just as the separation and independence of the coordinate Branches of the Federal Government serves to prevent the accumulation of excessive power in any one Branch, a healthy balance of power between the States and the Federal Government will reduce the risk of tyranny and abuse from either front." Gregory v. Ashcroft. See The Federalist No. 51, p.323.

Where Congress exceeds its authority relative to the States, therefore, the departure from the constitutional plan cannot be ratified by the "consent" of state officials. An analogy to the separation of powers among the Branches of the Federal Government clarifies this point. The Constitution's division of power among the three Branches is violated where one Branch invades the territory of another, whether or not the encroached-upon Branch approves the encroachment. In Buckley v. Valeo, 424 U.S. 1, 118-137 (1976), for instance, the Court held that the Congress had infringed the President's appointment power, despite the fact that the President himself had manifested his consent to the statute that caused the infringement by signing it into law. See National League of Cities v. Usery, 426 U.S., at 842, n.12. In INS v. Chadha, 462 U.S. 919, 944-959 (1983), we held that the legislative veto violated the constitutional requirement that legislation be presented to the President, despite Presidents' approval of hundreds of statutes containing a legislative veto provision. See id., at 944-945. The constitutional authority of Congress cannot be expanded by the "consent" of the governmental unit whose domain is thereby narrowed, whether that unit is the Executive Branch or the States.

State officials thus cannot consent to the enlargement of the powers of Congress beyond those enumerated in the Constitution. Indeed, the facts of this case raise the possibility that powerful incentives might lead both federal and state officials to view departures from the federal structure to be in their personal interests. Most citizens recognize the need for radioactive waste disposal sites, but few want sites near their homes. As a result, while it would be well within the authority of either federal or state officials to choose where the disposal sites will be, it is likely to be in the political interest of each individual official to avoid being held accountable to the voters for the choice of location. If a federal official is faced with the alternatives of choosing a location or directing the States to do it, the official may well prefer the latter, as a means of shifting responsibility for the eventual decision. If a state official is faced with the same set of alternatives — choosing a location or having Congress direct the choice of a location — the state official may also prefer the latter, as it may permit the avoidance of personal responsibility. The interests of public officials thus may not coincide with the Constitution's intergovernmental allocation of authority. Where state officials purport to submit to the direction of Congress in this manner, federalism is hardly being advanced. . . .

VII

Some truths are so basic that, like the air around us, they are easily overlooked. Much of the Constitution is concerned with setting forth the form of our government, and the courts have traditionally invalidated measures deviating from that form. The result may appear "formalistic" in a given case to partisans of the measure at issue, because such measures are typically the product of the era's perceived necessity. But the Constitution protects us from our own best intentions: It divides power among sovereigns and among branches of government precisely so that we may resist the temptation to concentrate power in one location as an expedient solution to the crisis of the day. The shortage of disposal sites for radioactive waste is a pressing national problem, but a judiciary that licensed extra-constitutional government with each issue of comparable gravity would, in the long run, be far worse.

States are not mere political subdivisions of the United States. State governments are neither regional offices nor administrative agencies of the Federal Government. The positions occupied by state officials appear nowhere on the Federal Government's most detailed organizational chart. The Constitution instead "leaves to the several States a residuary and inviolable sovereignty," The Federalist No. 39, p.245 (C. Rossiter ed. 1961), reserved explicitly to the States by the Tenth Amendment.

Whatever the outer limits of that sovereignty may be, one thing is clear: The Federal Government may not compel the States to enact or administer a federal regulatory program. The Constitution permits both the Federal Government and the States to enact legislation regarding the disposal of low level radioactive waste. The Constitution enables the Federal Government to pre-empt state regulation contrary to federal interests, and it permits the Federal Government to hold out incentives to the States as a means of encouraging them to adopt suggested regulatory schemes. It does not, however, authorize Congress simply to direct the States to provide for the disposal of the radioactive waste generated within their borders. While there may be many constitutional methods of achieving regional self-sufficiency in radioactive waste disposal, the method Congress has chosen is not one of them. The judgment of the Court of Appeals is accordingly affirmed in part and reversed in part.

JUSTICE WHITE, with whom JUSTICE BLACKMUN and JUSTICE STEVENS join . . . dissenting [as to the "take title" holding]. . . .

I

My disagreement with the Court's analysis begins at the basic descriptive level of how the legislation at issue in this case came to be enacted. The Court goes some way toward setting out the bare facts, but its omissions cast the statutory context of the take title provision in the wrong light. To read the Court's version of events, one would think that Congress was the sole proponent of a solution to the Nation's low-level radioactive waste problem. Not so. The Low-Level Radioactive Waste Policy Act of 1980 and its amendatory Act of 1985 resulted from the efforts of state leaders to achieve a state-based set of remedies to the waste problem. They sought not federal pre-emption or intervention, but rather congressional sanction of interstate compromises they had reached. . . .

[The] attempts by States to enter into compacts and to gain congressional approval sparked a new round of political squabbling between elected officials from unsited States, who generally opposed ratification of the compacts that were being formed, and their counterparts from the sited States, who insisted that the promises made in the 1980 Act be honored. In its effort to keep the States at the forefront of the policy amendment process, the National Governors' Association organized more than a dozen meetings to achieve a state consensus.

These discussions were not merely academic. The sited States grew increasingly and justifiably frustrated by the seeming inaction of unsited States in meeting the projected actions called for in the 1980 Act. Thus, as the end of 1985 approached, the sited States viewed the January 1, 1986 deadline established in the 1980 Act as a "drop-dead" date, on which the regional compacts could begin excluding the entry of out-of-region waste. Since by this time the three disposal facilities operating in 1980 were still the only such plants accepting low-level radioactive waste, the unsited States perceived a very serious danger if the three existing facilities actually carried out their threat to restrict access to the waste generated solely within their respective compact regions.

A movement thus arose to achieve a compromise between the sited and the unsited States, in which the sited States agreed to continue accepting waste in exchange for the imposition of stronger measures to guarantee compliance with the unsited States' assurances that they would develop alternate disposal facilities. As Representative Derrick explained, the compromise 1985 legislation "gives nonsited States more time to develop disposal sites, but also establishes a very firm timetable and sanctions for failure to live up [to] the agreement." Representative Markey added that "this compromise became the basis for our amendments to the Low-Level Radioactive Waste Policy Act of 1980. In the process of drafting such amendments, various concessions have been made by all sides in an effort to arrive at a bill which all parties could accept." The bill that in large measure became the 1985 Act "represented the diligent negotiating undertaken by" the National Governors' Association and "embodied" the "fundamentals of their settlement." In sum, the 1985 Act was very much the product of cooperative federalism, in which the States bargained among themselves to achieve compromises for Congress to sanction. . . .

II

To justify its holding that the take title provision contravenes the Constitution, the Court posits that "in this provision, Congress has crossed the line distinguishing encouragement from coercion." . . .

Curiously absent from the Court's analysis is any effort to place the take title provision within the overall context of the legislation. As the discussion in Part I of this opinion suggests, the 1980 and 1985 statutes were enacted against a backdrop of national concern over the availability of additional low-level radioactive waste disposal facilities. Congress could have pre-empted the field by directly regulating the disposal of this waste pursuant to its powers under the Commerce and Spending Clauses, but instead it unanimously assented to the States' request for congressional ratification of agreements to which they had acceded. . . .

A

In my view, New York's actions subsequent to enactment of the 1980 and 1985 Acts fairly indicate its approval of the interstate agreement process embodied in those laws. . . . [The] States — including New York — worked through their Governors to petition Congress for the 1980 and 1985 Acts. As I have attempted to demonstrate, these statutes are best understood as the products of collective state action, rather than as impositions placed on States by the Federal Government. . . .

B

Even were New York not to be estopped from challenging the take title provision's constitutionality, I am convinced that, seen as a term of an agreement entered into between the several States, this measure proves to be less constitutionally odious than the Court opines. First, the practical effect of New York's position is that because it is unwilling to honor its obligations to provide in-state storage facilities for its low-level radioactive waste, other States with such plants must accept New York's waste, whether they wish to or not. Otherwise, the many economically and socially-beneficial producers of such waste in the State would have to cease their operations. The Court's refusal to force New York to accept responsibility for its own problem inevitably means that some other State's sovereignty will be impinged by it being forced, for public health reasons, to accept New York's low-level radioactive waste. I do not understand the principle of federalism to impede the National Government from acting as referee among the States to prohibit one from bullying another.

Moreover, it is utterly reasonable that, in crafting a delicate compromise between the three overburdened States that provided low-level radioactive waste disposal facilities and the rest of the States, Congress would have to ratify some punitive measure as the ultimate sanction for noncompliance. The take title provision, though surely onerous, does not take effect if the generator of the waste does not request such action, or if the State lives up to its bargain of providing a waste disposal facility either within the State or in another State pursuant to a regional compact arrangement or a separate contract. . . .

III

The Court announces that it has no occasion to revisit such decisions as Gregory v. Ashcroft, Garcia v. San Antonio Metropolitan Transit Authority, and National League of Cities v. Usery, 426 U.S. 833 (1976), because "this is not a case in which Congress has subjected a State to the same legislation applicable to private parties." Although this statement sends the welcome signal that the Court does not intend to cut a wide swath through our recent Tenth Amendment precedents, it nevertheless is unpersuasive. . . .

The Court's distinction between a federal statute's regulation of States and private parties for general purposes, as opposed to a regulation solely on the activities of States, is unsupported by our recent Tenth Amendment cases. In no case has the Court rested its holding on such a distinction. Moreover, the Court makes no effort to explain why this purported distinction should affect the analysis of Congress' power under general principles of federalism and the Tenth Amendment. The distinction, facilely thrown out, is not based on any defensible theory. Certainly one would be hard-pressed to read the spirited exchanges between the Court and dissenting Justices in *National League of Cities,* and in Garcia v. San Antonio Metropolitan Transit Authority, as having been based on the distinction now drawn by the Court. An incursion on state sovereignty hardly seems more constitutionally acceptable if the federal statute that "commands" specific action also applies to private parties. The alleged diminution in state authority over its own affairs is not any less because the federal mandate restricts the activities of private parties. . . .

[I] would also submit, in this connection, that the Court's attempt to carve out a doctrinal distinction for statutes that purport solely to regulate State activities is especially unpersuasive after *Garcia.* It is true that in that case we considered whether a federal statute of general applicability — the Fair Labor Standards Act — applied to state transportation entities but our most recent statements have explained the appropriate analysis in a more general manner. Just last Term, for instance, Justice O'Connor wrote for the Court that "we are constrained in our ability to consider the limits that the state-federal balance places on Congress' powers under the Commerce Clause. See Garcia v. San Antonio Metropolitan Transit Authority, 469 U.S. 528 (1985) (declining to review limitations placed on Congress' Commerce Clause powers by our federal system)." Gregory v. Ashcroft. Indeed, her opinion went on to state that "this Court in Garcia has left primarily to the political process the protection of the States against intrusive exercises of Congress' Commerce Clause powers." . . .

[The] more appropriate analysis should flow from *Garcia*. . . . [Where] it addresses this aspect of respondents' argument, the Court tacitly concedes that a failing of the political process cannot be shown in this case because it refuses to rebut the unassailable arguments that the States were well able to look after themselves in the legislative process that culminated in the 1985 Act's passage. Indeed, New York acknowledges that its "congressional delegation participated in the drafting and enactment of both the 1980 and the 1985 Acts." The Court rejects this process-based argument by resorting to generalities and platitudes about the purpose of federalism being to protect individual rights.

Ultimately, I suppose, the entire structure of our federal constitutional government can be traced to an interest in establishing checks and balances to prevent the exercise of tyranny against individuals. But these fears seem extremely far distant to me in a situation such as this. We face a crisis of national proportions in the disposal of low-level radioactive waste, and Congress has acceded to the wishes of the States by permitting local decisionmaking rather than imposing a solution from Washington. New York itself participated and supported passage of this legislation at both the gubernatorial and federal representative levels, and then enacted state laws specifically to comply with the deadlines and timetables agreed upon by the States in the 1985 Act. For me, the Court's civics lecture has a decidedly hollow ring at a time when action, rather than rhetoric, is needed to solve a national problem.[3] . . .

3. With selective quotations from the era in which the Constitution was adopted, the majority attempts to bolster its holding that the take title provision is tantamount to federal "commandeering" of the States. In view of the many Tenth Amendment cases decided over the past two decades in which resort to the kind of historical analysis generated in the majority opinion was not deemed necessary, I do not read the majority's many invocations of history to be anything other than elaborate window-dressing. Certainly nowhere does the majority announce that its rule is compelled by an understanding of what the Framers may have thought about statutes of the type at issue here. Moreover, I would observe that, while its quotations add a certain flavor to the opinion, the majority's historical analysis has a distinctly wooden quality. One would not know from reading the majority's account, for instance, that the nature of federal-state relations changed fundamentally after the Civil War. That conflict produced in its wake a tremendous expansion in the scope of the Federal Government's law-making authority, so much so that the persons who helped to found the Republic would scarcely have recognized the many added roles the National Government assumed for itself. Moreover, the majority fails to mention the New Deal era,

V

The ultimate irony of the decision today is that in its formalistically rigid obeisance to "federalism," the Court gives Congress fewer incentives to defer to the wishes of state officials in achieving local solutions to local problems. This legislation was a classic example of Congress acting as arbiter among the States in their attempts to accept responsibility for managing a problem of grave import. The States urged the National Legislature not to impose from Washington a solution to the country's low-level radioactive waste management problems. Instead, they sought a reasonable level of local and regional autonomy consistent with Art. I, §10, cl. 3, of the Constitution. By invalidating the measure designed to ensure compliance for recalcitrant States, such as New York, the Court upsets the delicate compromise achieved among the States and forces Congress to erect several additional formalistic hurdles to clear before achieving exactly the same objective. Because the Court's justifications for undertaking this step are unpersuasive to me, I respectfully dissent.

JUSTICE STEVENS, concurring in part and dissenting in part.

---

in which the Court recognized the enormous growth in Congress' power under the Commerce Clause. See generally F. Frankfurter & J. Landis, The Business of the Supreme Court 56-59 (1927); H. Hyman, A More Perfect Union: The Impact of the Civil War and Reconstruction on the Constitution (1973); Corwin, The Passing of Dual Federalism, 36 Va. L. Rev. 1 (1950); Wiecek, The Reconstruction of Federal Judicial Power, 1863-1875, 13 Am. J. Legal Hist. 333 (1969); Scheiber, State Law and "Industrial Policy" in American Development, 1790-1987, 75 Calif. L. Rev. 415 (1987); Ackerman, Constitutional Politics/Constitutional Law, 99 Yale L.J. 453 (1989). While I believe we should not be blind to history, neither should we read it so selectively as to restrict the proper scope of Congress' powers under Article I, especially when the history not mentioned by the majority fully supports a more expansive understanding of the legislature's authority than may have existed in the late 18th-century.

Given the scanty textual support for the majority's position, it would be far more sensible to defer to a coordinate branch of government in its decision to devise a solution to a national problem of this kind. Certainly in other contexts, principles of federalism have not insulated States from mandates by the National Government. The Court has upheld congressional statutes that impose clear directives on state officials, including those enacted pursuant to the Extradition Clause, the post-Civil War Amendments, South Carolina v. Katzenbach, 383 U.S. 301, 319-320, 334-335 (1966), as well as congressional statutes that require state courts to hear certain actions, see, e.g., Testa v. Katt, 330 U.S. 386, 392-394 (1947).

Under the Articles of Confederation, the Federal Government had the power to issue commands to the States. See Arts. VIII, IX. Because that indirect exercise of federal power proved ineffective, the Framers of the Constitution empowered the Federal Government to exercise legislative authority directly over individuals within the States, even though that direct authority constituted a greater intrusion on State sovereignty. Nothing in that history suggests that the Federal Government may not also impose its will upon the several States as it did under the Articles. The Constitution enhanced, rather than diminished, the power of the Federal Government.

The notion that Congress does not have the power to issue "a simple command to state governments to implement legislation enacted by Congress," is incorrect and unsound. There is no such limitation in the Constitution. The Tenth Amendment surely does not impose any limit on Congress' exercise of the powers delegated to it by Article I. Nor does the structure of the constitutional order or the values of federalism mandate such a formal rule. To the contrary, the Federal Government directs state governments in many realms. The Government regulates state-operated railroads, state school systems, state prisons, state elections, and a host of other state functions. Similarly, there can be no doubt that, in time of war, Congress could either draft soldiers itself or command the States to supply their quotas of troops. I see no reason why Congress may not also command the States to enforce federal water and air quality standards or federal standards for the disposition of low-level radioactive wastes.

The Constitution gives this Court the power to resolve controversies between the States. Long before Congress enacted pollution-control legislation, this Court crafted a body of "interstate common law," Illinois v. City of Milwaukee, 406 U.S. 91, 106 (1972), to govern disputes between States involving interstate waters. In such contexts, we have not hesitated to direct States to undertake specific actions. For example, we have "imposed on States an affirmative duty to take reasonable steps to conserve and augment the water supply of an interstate stream." Thus, we unquestionably have the power to command an upstate stream that is polluting the waters of a downstream State to adopt appropriate regulations to implement a federal statutory command.

With respect to the problem presented by the case at hand, if litigation should develop between States that have joined a compact, we would surely have the power to grant relief in the form of specific enforcement of the take title provision. Indeed, even if the statute had never been passed, if one State's radioactive waste created a nuisance that harmed its neighbors, it seems clear that we would have had the power to command the offending State to take remedial action. If this Court has such authority, surely Congress has similar authority. . . .

Note: New York v. United States *and the Future of Federalism*

1. Justice White suggested that, under the Court's holding, Congress could still "condition the payment of funds [for example, from the surcharge account] on the State's willingness to take title if it has not already provided a waste disposal facility," or "regulate directly the producers of the waste" by, for example, banning the shipment of waste from New York unless the state either creates a disposal site or takes title to the waste. Do you agree? If Justice White is correct, are his solutions more or less intrusive on state interests than the one the Court held unconstitutional? Consider the Court's discussion of the location of political responsibility for siting decisions.

2. Justice O'Connor's opinion stresses the change in the theory of the national government from the Confederation period to the Constitution. Is a system in which the national government can direct *only* individuals to act more or less centralized than one in which it can (also) direct states to act?

3. Consider H. Jefferson Powell, The Oldest Question of Constitutional Law, 79 Va. L. Rev. 633, 658 (1993):

> [Justice O'Connor's] federalism is one of process, not of substance. [This] turns the primary Anti-Federalist criticism [upside] down. The Anti-Federalist concern was that the Constitution ultimately would reduce the states to the status of municipal corporations not by preempting their processes but by preempting their business. [O'Connor's] federalism accepts as legitimate the effective extension of congressional authority to all areas of major legislative interest; yet this extension is precisely the consequence of adopting the Constitution that the Anti-Federalists predicted and "new federalism" was meant to rebut.
>
> Justice O'Connor's federalism thus endorses exactly the result the Federalists denied that the Constitution would produce — the reduction of the states to autonomous governmental processes concerned with only those affairs left to them by Congress.

Chapter Three

Judicial Efforts to Protect the Expansion of the Market against Assertions of Local Power

B. PROTECTION AGAINST DISCRIMINATION

Page 286. At the end of section 1 of the Note, add the following:

In Chemical Waste Management Inc. v. Hunt, 112 S. Ct. 2009 (1992), the Court relied on *City of Philadelphia* to invalidate a fee imposed on all hazardous waste originated out-of-state and sent to a private disposal facility. "Here, the additional fee applies only to interstate hazardous waste, but at all points from its entrance into Alabama until it is [landfilled], every concern [applies] perforce to local hazardous waste, which pays no additional fee." Chief Justice Rehnquist dissented.

Page 288. As subsection 5c of the Note, add the following:

Collins, Justice Scalia and the Elusive Idea of Discrimination Against Interstate Commerce, 20 New Mex. L. Rev. 555, 555-556 (1990), distinguishes between "laws that discriminate against interstate commerce without regard to the laws of any other state and those that burden commerce only when other states' laws are taken into account." Collins argues that only the former, which he calls "independent discrimination," ought to be unconstitutional, because only they resemble protectionist tariffs closely enough. Does the distinction make sense of the cases here and later in the chapter?

For a recent discussion of discrimination, see Wyoming v. Oklahoma, 112 S. Ct. 789 (1992), holding unconstitutional an Oklahoma statute requiring coal-fired electric utilities in the state to burn a mixture containing at least 10 percent Oklahoma-mined coal. This "preference for coal from domestic sources cannot be characterized as anything other than protectionist."

Page 293. Before section 5 of the Note, add the following:

In Fort Gratiot Sanitary Landfill Inc. v. Michigan Department of Natural Resources, 112 S. Ct. 2019 (1992), the Court invalidated a Michigan statute barring private solid waste disposal facilities from accepting solid waste generated outside the county in which they are located, unless the county made an exception through its comprehensive plan for solid waste disposal. It cited *Dean Milk.* Note that the statute in *Fort Gratiot* effectively barred out-of-state waste from disposal anywhere in the state. Chief Justice Rehnquist, joined by Justice Blackmun, dissented.

Page 315. At the end of the paragraph at the top of the page, add the following:

In connection with inferences from Congress's failure to act, consider the implications of the following sequence of cases. In 1967 the Court held unconstitutional attempts by states to collect use taxes (see casebook page 326) not from purchasers but from out-of-state mail-order sellers who had neither outlets nor sales representatives in the state. National Bellas Hess, Inc. v. Department of Revenue, 386 U.S. 753 (1967). The Court gave two reasons. First, the states violated the due process clause of the fourteenth amendment in attempting to tax entities with insufficient connections with them. Second, requiring the sellers to collect the use taxes imposed an unconstitutional burden on interstate commerce. Note that the due process holding probably (why only probably?) barred Congress from enacting a statute allowing states to require mail-order sellers to collect use taxes.

In Quill Corp. v. North Dakota, 112 S. Ct. 1904 (1992), the Supreme Court revisited this issue. It overruled the due process holding of *National Bellas Hess* but reaffirmed the commerce clause holding. Five Justices joined an opinion by Justice Stevens that justified the result on the ground that it developed a "bright-line rule" to

> demarcat[e] a discrete realm of commercial activity that is free from interstate taxation. [Like] other bright-line tests, the *Bellas Hess* rule appears artificial at the edges. [This] artificiality, however, is more than offset by the benefits of a clear rule. Such a rule firmly establishes the boundaries of legitimate state authority to impose a duty to collect sales and use taxes and reduces litigation concerning those taxes.

Justice Scalia, joined by Justices Kennedy and Thomas, concurred in the result, relying entirely on stare decisis considerations regarding the commerce clause holding. Justice White dissented from the commerce clause holding.

Justice Stevens's opinion concluded by pointing out that the issue was "not only one that Congress may be better qualified to resolve, but also one that Congress has the ultimate power to resolve." It also noted that congressional action might have been "dictated" by the due process holding in *National Bellas Hess,* "but today we have put that problem to rest. Accordingly, Congress is now free to decide whether, when, and to what extent the States may burden interstate mail-order concerns with a duty to collect use taxes."

D. PREEMPTION

Page 356. Before the Note, add the following:

GADE V. NATIONAL SOLID WASTE MANAGEMENT ASSOCIATION

112 S. Ct. 2374 (1992)

JUSTICE O'CONNOR announced the judgment of the Court and delivered an opinion, Parts I, III, and IV of which represent the views of the Court, and Part II of which is joined by THE CHIEF JUSTICE, JUSTICE WHITE, and JUSTICE SCALIA.

In 1988, the Illinois General Assembly enacted the Hazardous Waste Crane and Hoisting Equipment Operators Licensing Act and the Hazardous Waste Laborers Licensing Act. The stated purpose of the acts is both "to promote job safety" and "to protect life, limb and property." In this case, we consider whether these "dual impact" statutes, which protect both workers and the general public, are pre-empted by the federal Occupational Safety and Health Act of 1970 and the standards promulgated thereunder by the Occupational Safety and Health Administration (OSHA).

I

The OSH Act authorizes the Secretary of Labor to promulgate federal occupational safety and health standards [and] the Superfund Amendments and Reauthorization Act of 1986 (SARA) [requires] the Secretary to establish standards for the initial and routine training of workers who handle hazardous wastes.

In response to this congressional directive, OSHA promulgated regulations on "Hazardous Waste Operations and Emergency Response," including detailed regulations on worker training requirements. The OSHA regulations require, among other things, that workers engaged in an activity that may expose them to hazardous wastes receive a minimum of 40 hours of instruction off the site, and a minimum of three days actual field experience under the supervision of a trained supervisor. [On-site] managers and supervisors directly responsible for hazardous waste operations must receive the same initial training as general employees, plus at least eight additional hours of specialized training on various health and safety programs. Employees and supervisors are required to receive eight hours of refresher training annually. . . .

In 1988, while OSHA's interim hazardous waste regulations were in effect, the State of Illinois enacted the licensing acts at issue here. The laws are designated as acts "in relation to environmental protection," and their stated aim is to protect both employees and the general public by licensing hazardous waste equipment operators and laborers working at certain facilities. Both acts require a license applicant to provide a certified record of at least 40 hours of training under an approved program conducted within Illinois, to pass a written examination, and to complete an annual refresher course of at least eight hours of instruction. [Employees] who work without the proper license, and employers who knowingly permit an unlicensed employee to work, are subject to escalating fines for each offense.

[National Solid Waste Management Association sought a declaratory judgment that the licensing acts were pre-empted by the OSHA regulations.]

II

["The] question whether a certain state action is pre-empted by federal law is one of congressional intent. ' "The purpose of Congress is the ultimate touchstone." ' " "To discern Congress' intent we examine the explicit statutory language and the structure and purpose of the statute."

In the OSH Act, Congress endeavored "to assure so far as possible every working man and woman in the Nation safe and healthful working conditions." To that end, Congress authorized the Secretary of Labor to set mandatory occupational safety and health standards applicable to all businesses affecting interstate commerce, and thereby brought the Federal Government into a field that traditionally had been occupied by the States. Federal regulation of the workplace was not intended to be all-encompassing, however. First, Congress expressly saved two areas from federal pre-emption. Section 4(b)(4) of the OSH Act states that the Act does not "supersede or in any manner affect any workmen's compensation law or . . . enlarge or diminish or affect in any other manner the common law or statutory rights, duties, or liabilities of employers and employees under any law with respect to injuries, diseases, or death of employees arising out of, or in the course of, employment." Section 18(a) provides that the Act does not "prevent any State agency or court from asserting jurisdiction under State law over any occupational safety or health issue with respect to which no [federal] standard is in effect."

Congress not only reserved certain areas to state regulation, but it also, in §18(b) of the Act, gave the States the option of pre-empting federal regulation entirely. That section provides:

> Submission of State plan for development and enforcement of State standards to preempt applicable Federal standards.
>
> Any State which, at any time, desires to assume responsibility for development and enforcement therein of occupational safety and health standards relating to any occupational safety or health issue with respect to which a Federal standard has been promulgated [by the Secretary under the OSH Act] shall submit a State plan for the development of such standards and their enforcement.

About half the States have received the Secretary's approval for their own state plans as described in this provision. Illinois is not among them.

[Pre-emption] may be either expressed or implied, and "is compelled whether Congress' command is explicitly stated in the statute's language or implicitly contained in its structure and purpose." Jones v. Rath Packing Co., 430 U.S. 519, 525 (1977). Absent explicit pre-emptive language, we have recognized at least two types of implied pre-emption: field pre-emption, where the scheme of federal regulation is " 'so pervasive as to make reasonable the inference that Congress left no room for the States to supplement it,' " (quoting Rice v. Santa Fe Elevator Corp., 331 U.S. 218, 230 (1947)), and conflict pre-emption, where "compliance with both federal and state regulations is a physical impossibility," Florida Lime & Avocado Growers, Inc. v. Paul, 373 U.S. 132, 142-143 (1963), or where state law "stands as an obstacle to the accomplishment and execution of the full purposes and objectives of Congress." Hines v. Davidowitz, 312 U.S. 52, 67 (1941).

Our ultimate task in any pre-emption case is to determine whether state regulation is consistent with the structure and purpose of the statute as a whole. Looking to "the provisions of the whole law, and to its object and policy," we hold that nonapproved state regulation of occupational safety and health issues for which a federal standard is in effect is impliedly pre-empted as in conflict with the full purposes and objectives of the OSH Act. The design of the statute persuades us that Congress intended to subject employers and employees to only one set of regulations, be it federal or state, and that the only way a State may regulate an OSHA-regulated occupational safety and health issue is pursuant to an approved state plan that displaces the federal standards. The principal indication that Congress intended to pre-empt state law is §18(b)'s statement that a State "shall" submit a plan if it wishes to "assume responsibility" for "development and enforcement . . . of occupational safety and health standards relating to any occupational safety or health issue with respect to which a Federal standard has been promulgated." The unavoidable implication of this provision is that a State may not enforce its own occupational safety and health standards without obtaining the Secretary's approval, and petitioner concedes that §18(b) would require an approved plan if Illinois wanted to "assume responsibility" for the regulation of occupational safety and health within the State. Petitioner contends, however, that an approved plan is necessary only if the State wishes completely to replace the federal regulations, not merely to supplement them. She argues that the correct interpretation of §18(b) is that posited by Judge Easterbrook below: i.e., a State may either "oust" the federal standard by submitting a state plan to the Secretary for approval or "add to" the federal standard without seeking the Secretary's approval.

Petitioner's interpretation of §18(b) might be plausible were we to interpret that provision in isolation, but it simply is not tenable in light of the OSH Act's surrounding provisions. "We must not be guided by a single sentence or member of a sentence, but look to the provisions of the whole law." The OSH Act as a whole evidences Congress' intent to avoid subjecting workers and employers to duplicative regulation; a State may develop an occupational safety and health program tailored to its own needs, but only if it is willing completely to displace the applicable federal regulations.

Cutting against petitioner's interpretation of §18(b) is the language of §18(a), which saves from pre-emption any state law regulating an occupational safety and health issue with respect to which no federal standard is in effect. Although this is a saving clause, not a pre-emption clause, the natural implication of this provision is that state laws regulating the same issue as federal laws are not saved, even if they merely supplement the federal standard. Moreover, if petitioner's reading of §18(b) were correct, and if a State were free to enact nonconflicting safety and health regulations, then §18(a) would be superfluous: there is no possibility of conflict where there is no federal regulation. Because "it is our duty 'to give effect, if possible, to every clause and word of a statute,'" we conclude that §18(a)'s preservation of state authority in the absence of a federal standard presupposes a background pre-emption of all state occupational safety and health standards whenever a federal standard governing the same issue is in effect. . . .

Looking at the provisions of §18 as a whole, we conclude that the OSH Act precludes any state regulation of an occupational safety or health issue with respect to which a federal standard has been established, unless a state plan has been submitted and approved pursuant to §18(b). Our review of the Act persuades us that Congress sought to promote occupational safety and health while at the same time avoiding duplicative, and possibly counterproductive, regulation. It thus established a system of uniform federal occupational health and safety standards, but gave States the option of pre-empting federal regulations by developing their own occupational safety and health programs. [To] allow a State selectively to "supplement" certain federal regulations with ostensibly nonconflicting standards would be inconsistent with this federal scheme of establishing uniform federal standards, on the one hand, and encouraging States to assume full responsibility for development and enforcement of their own OSH programs, on the other.

We cannot accept petitioner's argument that the OSH Act does not pre-empt nonconflicting state laws because those laws, like the Act, are designed to promote worker safety. In determining whether state law "stands as an obstacle" to the full implementation of a federal law, "it is not enough to say that the ultimate goal of both federal and state law" is the same. "A state law also is pre-empted if it interferes with the methods by which the federal statute was designed to reach that goal." The OSH Act does not foreclose a State from enacting its own laws to advance the goal of worker safety, but it does restrict the ways in which it can do so. If a State wishes to regulate an issue of worker safety for which a federal standard is in effect, its only option is to obtain the prior approval of the Secretary of Labor, as described in §18 of the Act.

III

Petitioner next argues that, even if Congress intended to pre-empt all nonapproved state occupational safety and health regulations whenever a federal standard is in effect, the OSH Act's pre-emptive effect should not be extended to state laws that address public safety as well as occupational safety concerns. As we explained in Part II, we understand §18(b) to mean that the OSH Act pre-empts all state "occupational safety and health standards relating to any occupational safety or health issue with respect to which a Federal standard has been promulgated." We now consider whether a dual impact law can be an "occupational safety and health standard" subject to pre-emption under the Act.

The OSH Act defines an "occupational safety and health standard" as "a standard which requires conditions, or the adoption or use of one or more practices, means, methods, operations, or processes, reasonably necessary or appropriate to provide safe or healthful employment and places of employment." Any state law requirement designed to promote health and safety in the workplace falls neatly within the Act's definition of an "occupational safety and health standard." Clearly, under this definition, a state law that expressly declares a legislative purpose of regulating occupational health and safety would, in the absence of an approved state plan, be pre-empted by an OSHA standard regulating the same subject matter. But petitioner asserts that if the state legislature articulates a purpose other than (or in addition to) workplace health and safety, then the OSH Act loses its pre-emptive force. We disagree.

Although "part of the pre-empted field is defined by reference to the purpose of the state law in question, . . . another part of the field is defined by the state law's actual effect." English v. General Electric Co., 496 U.S. 72, 84 (1990) (citing Pacific Gas & Electric Co. v. State Energy Resources Conservation and Development Comm'n, 461 U.S. 190, 212-213 (1983)). In assessing the impact of a state law on the federal scheme, we have refused to rely solely on the legislature's professed purpose and have looked as well to the effects of the law. . . .

Our precedents leave no doubt that a dual impact state regulation cannot avoid OSH Act pre-emption simply because the regulation serves several objectives rather than one. [Whatever] the purpose or purposes of the state law, pre-emption analysis cannot ignore the effect of the challenged state action on the pre-empted field. The key question is thus at what point the state regulation sufficiently interferes with federal regulation that it should be deemed pre-empted under the Act. . . .

[The] Court of Appeals [held] that, in the absence of the approval of the Secretary, the OSH Act pre-empts all state law that "constitutes, in a direct, clear and substantial way, regulation of worker health and safety." We agree that this is the appropriate standard for determining OSH Act pre-emption. On the other hand, state laws of general applicability (such as laws regarding traffic safety or fire safety) that do not conflict with OSHA standards and that regulate the conduct of workers and non-workers alike would generally not be pre-empted. Although some laws of general applicability may have a "direct and substantial" effect on worker safety, they cannot fairly be characterized as "occupational" standards, because they regulate workers simply as members of the general public. In this case, we agree with the court below that a law directed at workplace safety is not saved from pre-emption simply because the State can demonstrate some additional effect outside of the workplace. . . .

IV

We recognize that "the States have a compelling interest in the practice of professions within their boundaries, and that as part of their power to protect the public health, safety, and other valid interests they have broad power to establish standards for licensing practitioners and regulating the practice of professions." But under the Supremacy Clause, from which our pre-emption doctrine is derived, "any state law, however clearly within a State's acknowledged power, which interferes with or is contrary to federal law, must yield." We therefore reject petitioner's argument that the State's interest in licensing various occupations can save from OSH Act pre-emption those provisions that directly and substantially affect workplace safety. . . .

The judgment of the Court of Appeals is hereby Affirmed.

JUSTICE KENNEDY, concurring in part and concurring in the judgment.

Though I concur in the Court's judgment and with the ultimate conclusion that the state law is pre-empted, I would find express pre-emption from the terms of the federal statute. I cannot agree that we should denominate this case as one of implied pre-emption. The contrary view of the plurality is based on an undue expansion of our implied pre-emption jurisprudence which, in my view, is neither wise nor necessary. . . .

Our decisions establish that a high threshold must be met if a state law is to be pre-empted for conflicting with the purposes of a federal Act. Any conflict must be "irreconcilable. . . . The existence of a hypothetical or potential conflict is insufficient to warrant the pre-emption of the state statute." In my view, this type of pre-emption should be limited to state laws which impose prohibitions or obligations which are in direct contradiction to Congress' primary objectives, as conveyed with clarity in the federal legislation.

I do not believe that supplementary state regulation of an occupational safety and health issue can be said to create the sort of actual conflict required by our decisions. The purpose of state supplementary regulation, like the federal standards promulgated by the Occupational Safety and Health Administration (OSHA) is to protect worker safety and health. Any potential tension between a scheme of federal regulation of the workplace and a concurrent, supplementary state scheme would not, in my view, rise to the level of "actual conflict" described in our pre-emption cases. Absent the express provisions of §18, [I] would not say that state supplementary regulation conflicts with the purposes of the OSH Act, or that it "interferes with the methods by which the federal statute was designed to reach [its] goal."

The plurality's broad view of actual conflict pre-emption is contrary to two basic principles of our pre-emption jurisprudence. First, we begin "with the assumption that the historic police powers of the States [are] not to be superseded . . . unless that was the clear and manifest purpose of Congress." Second, " 'the purpose of Congress is the ultimate touchstone' " in all pre-emption cases. A free-wheeling judicial inquiry into whether a state statute is in tension with federal objectives would undercut the principle that it is Congress rather than the courts that pre-empts state law.

Nonetheless, I agree with the Court that "the OSH Act pre-empts all state 'occupational safety and health standards relating to any occupational safety or health issue with respect to which a Federal standard has been promulgated.' " I believe, however, that this result is mandated by the express terms of §18(b) of the OSH Act. It follows from this that the pre-emptive scope of the Act is also limited to the language of the statute. When the existence of pre-emption is evident from the statutory text, our inquiry must begin and end with the statutory framework itself.

A finding of express pre-emption in this case is not contrary to our longstanding rule that we will not infer pre-emption of the States' historic police powers absent a clear statement of intent by Congress. Though most statutes creating express pre-emption contain an explicit statement to that effect, a statement admittedly lacking in §18(b), we have never required any particular magic words in our express pre-emption cases. Our task in all pre-emption cases is to enforce the "clear and manifest purpose of Congress." We have held, in express pre-emption cases, that Congress' intent must be divined from the language, structure, and purposes of the statute as a whole. The language of the OSH statute sets forth a scheme in light of which the provisions of §18 must be interpreted, and from which the express pre-emption that displaces state law follows. . . .

In this regard I disagree with the dissent, and find unconvincing its conclusion that Congress intended to allow concurrent state and federal jurisdiction over occupational safety and health issues. The dissent would give the States, rather than the Federal Government, the power to decide whether as to any particular occupational safety and health issue there will exist a single or dual regulatory scheme. Under this theory the State may choose exclusive federal jurisdiction by not regulating; or exclusive state jurisdiction by submitting a state plan; or dual regulation by adopting supplementary rules, as Illinois did here. That position undermines the authority of OSHA in many respects. For example, §18(c)(2) of the OSH Act allows OSHA to disapprove state plans which "unduly burden interstate commerce." The dissent would eviscerate this important administrative mechanism by allowing the States to sidestep OSHA's authority through the mechanism of supplementary regulation. Furthermore, concurrent state and federal jurisdiction might interfere with the enforcement of the federal regulations without creating a situation where compliance with both schemes is a physical impossibility, which the dissent would require for pre-emption. I would not attribute to Congress the intent to create such a hodge-podge scheme of authority. . . .

The necessary implication of finding express pre-emption in this case is that the pre-emptive scope of the OSH Act is defined by the language of §18(b). Because this provision requires federal approval of state occupational safety and health standards alone, only state laws fitting within that description are pre-empted. For that reason I agree with the Court that state laws of general applicability are not pre-empted. I also agree that "a state law requirement that directly, substantially, and specifically regulates occupational safety and health is an occupational safety and health standard within the meaning of the Act," and therefore falls within the scope of pre-emption. So-called "dual impact" state regulations which meet this standard are pre-empted by the OSH Act, regardless of any additional purpose the law may serve, or effect the law may have, outside the workplace. As a final matter, I agree that the Illinois Acts are not saved because they operate through a licensing mechanism rather than through direct regulation of the workplace. I therefore join all but Part II of the Court's opinion, and concur in the judgment of the Court.

JUSTICE SOUTER, with whom JUSTICE BLACKMUN, JUSTICE STEVENS, and JUSTICE THOMAS join, dissenting.

[In] light of our rule that federal pre-emption of state law is only to be found in a clear congressional purpose to supplant exercises of the States' traditional police powers, the text of the Act fails to support the Court's conclusion.

I

[The] plurality today finds [conflict] pre-emption. [Thus], under the plurality's reading, any regulation on an issue as to which a federal standard has been promulgated has been pre-empted. As one commentator has observed, this kind of purpose-conflict pre-emption, which occurs when state law is held to "undermine a congressional decision in favor of national uniformity of standards," presents "a situation similar in practical effect to that of federal occupation of a field." L. Tribe, American Constitutional Law 486 (2d ed. 1988). Still, whether the pre-emption at issue is described as occupation of each narrow field in which a federal standard has been promulgated, as pre-emption of those regulations that conflict with the federal objective of single regulation, or, as JUSTICE KENNEDY describes it, as express pre-emption, the key is congressional intent, and I find the language of the statute insufficient to demonstrate an intent to pre-empt state law in this way.

II

Analysis begins with the presumption that "Congress did not intend to displace state law." "Where, as here, the field which Congress is said to have pre-empted has been traditionally occupied by the States, 'we start with the assumption that the historic police powers of the States were not to be superseded by the Federal Act unless that was the clear and manifest purpose of Congress.' This assumption provides assurance that the 'federal-state balance,' will not be disturbed unintentionally by Congress or unnecessarily by the courts. But when Congress has 'unmistakably . . . ordained,' that its enactments alone are to regulate a part of commerce, state laws regulating that aspect of commerce must fall." Subject to this principle, the enquiry into the possibly pre-emptive effect of federal legislation is an exercise of statutory construction. If the statute's terms can be read sensibly not to have a pre-emptive effect, the presumption controls and no pre-emption may be inferred.

III

At first blush, respondent's strongest argument might seem to rest on §18(a) of the Act. [Where] there is no federal standard in effect, there is no pre-emption. The plurality reasons that there must be pre-emption, however, when there is a federal standard in effect, else §18(a) would be rendered superfluous because "there is no possibility of conflict where there is no federal regulation."

The plurality errs doubly. First, its premise is incorrect. In the sense in which the plurality uses the term, there is the possibility of "conflict" even absent federal regulation since the mere enactment of a federal law like the Act may amount to an occupation of an entire field, preventing state regulation. Second, the necessary implication of §18(a) is not that every federal regulation pre-empts all state law on the issue in question, but only that some federal regulations may pre-empt some state law. The plurality ignores the possibility that the provision simply rules out field pre-emption and is otherwise entirely compatible with the possibility that pre-emption will occur only when actual conflict between a federal regulation and a state rule renders compliance with both impossible. Indeed, if Congress had meant to say that any state rule should be pre-empted if it deals with an issue as to which there is a federal regulation in effect, the text of subsection (a) would have been a very inept way of trying to make the point. It was not, however, an inept way to make the different point that Congress intended no field pre-emption of the sphere of health and safety subject to regulation, but not necessarily regulated, under the Act. Unlike the case where field pre-emption occurs, the provision tells us, absence of a federal standard leaves a State free to do as it will on the issue. Beyond this, subsection (a) does not necessarily mean anything, and the provision is perfectly consistent with the conclusion that as long as compliance with both a federal standard and a state regulation is not physically impossible, each standard shall be enforceable. If, indeed, the presumption against pre-emption means anything, §18(a) must be read in just this way.

Respondent also relies on §18(b). [Respondent] argues that the necessary implication of this provision is clear: the only way that a state rule on a particular occupational safety and health issue may be enforced once a federal standard on the issue is also in place is by incorporating the state rule in a plan approved by the Secretary.

As both the plurality and JUSTICE KENNEDY acknowledge, however, that is not the necessary implication of §18(b). The subsection simply does not say that unless a plan is approved, state law on an issue is preempted by the promulgation of a federal standard. In fact it tugs the other way, and in actually providing a mechanism for a State to "assume responsibility" for an issue with respect to which a federal standard has been promulgated (that is, to pre-empt federal law), §18(b) is far from pre-emptive of anything adopted by the States. Its heading, enacted as part of the statute and properly considered under our canons of construction for whatever light it may shed, speaks expressly of the "development and enforcement of State standards to preempt applicable Federal standards." The provision does not in any way provide that absent such state pre-emption of federal rules, the State may not even supplement the federal standards with consistent regulations of its own. Once again, nothing in the provision's language speaks one way or the other to the question whether promulgation of a federal standard preempts state regulation, or whether, in the absence of a plan, consistent federal and state regulations may coexist. The provision thus makes perfect sense on the assumption that a dual regulatory scheme is permissible but subject to state pre-emption if the State wishes to shoulder enough of the federal mandate to gain approval of a plan. . . .

IV

In sum, our rule is that the traditional police powers of the State survive unless Congress has made a purpose to pre-empt them clear. The Act does not, in so many words, pre-empt all state regulation of issues on which federal standards have been promulgated, and respondent's contention at oral argument that reading subsections (a), (b), and (h) could leave no other "logical" conclusion but one of pre-emption is wrong. Each provision can be read consistently with the others without any implication of pre-emptive intent. They are in fact just as consistent with a purpose and objective to permit overlapping state and federal regulation as with one to guarantee that employers and employees would be subjected to only one regulatory regime. Restriction to one such regime by precluding supplemental state regulation might or might not be desirable. But in the absence of any clear expression of congressional intent to pre-empt, I can only conclude that, as long as compliance with federally promulgated standards does not render obedience to Illinois' regulations impossible, the enforcement of the state law is not prohibited by the Supremacy Clause. I respectfully dissent.

Note: Preemption after **Gade**

1. Consider whether the distinction between express preemption and implied conflict preemption, which divides the Justices, is adequately explained by them. If congressional intent is the touchstone, what is the justification for implied conflict preemption?

2. Is there a change in the degree of deference to state interests expressed in *Gade* as compared to *PG&E*? If so, is that change justified by the fact that the subject matter of federal regulation differs (if it does)? By changes in how Congress has exercised its power to preempt in recent years?

3. For additional discussions of preemption, see Wisconsin Public Intervenor v. Mortier, 111 S. Ct. 2476 (1991); Cipollone v. Liggett Group, Inc., 112 S. Ct. 2608 (1992) (defining standards for preemption of state law claims for negligent failure to warn and express warranty or misrepresentation in connection with federally required warnings).

Chapter Four

The Distribution of National Powers

B. EXECUTIVE AUTHORITY

1. The General Framework

Page 382. Before section 6 of the Note, add the following:

For a detailed, historical analysis of implied presidential power, see Monaghan, The Protective Power of the Presidency, 93 Colum. L. Rev. 1 (1993). Professor Monaghan concludes that "except perhaps when acting pursuant to some 'specific' constitutional power, the President has no inherent power to invade private rights; the President not only cannot act *contra legem*, he or she must point to some affirmative legislative authorization when so acting." On the other hand, Monaghan argues, the President does possess a narrow inherent power to "protect the personnel, property, and instrumentalities of the United States from harm."

2. Presidential Power and Domestic Affairs

Page 404. After the fourth paragraph, add the following:

On judicial review of removal from office following impeachment, see Nixon v. United States, 113 S. Ct. 732 (1993), considered more fully in Chapter 1, §3 of this Supplement.

3. Presidential Power and Foreign Affairs

Page 413. Before section 5 of the Note, add the following:

c. *The Persian Gulf War.* On August 8, 1990, six days after Iraq invaded Kuwait, President Bush deployed the largest American combat force since the Vietnam War to protect Saudi Arabia from an Iraqi attack. Throughout the fall, soldiers and reservists from around the nation were sent to the Persian Gulf region. In October, both the House and the Senate passed resolutions that supported the defensive operations but stopped short of declaring war. On November 8, notwithstanding the limited congressional authorization, President Bush doubled the existing 230,000 American troops in the Gulf in order to provide the United States with "an adequate *offensive* military operation." On November 29, at the behest of the Bush administration, the United Nations Security Council passed a resolution demanding that Iraq unconditionally withdraw from Kuwait by January 15, 1991, and authorizing member nations to "use necessary means" to free Kuwait and force Iraqi compliance.

Tensions escalated throughout the next month, and on January 8, the President formally requested Congress to pass a joint resolution supporting "the use of all necessary means" to achieve the goals of the United Nations Resolution. Four days later, Congress complied. House Joint Resolution 77, 105 Stat. 3 (1991), approved the use of American military force against Iraq after January 15, provided that the President determined and reported to Congress that all diplomatic efforts had been exhausted. Five days later, on January 17, the United States and its allies unleashed Operation Desert Storm, flying over 1400 air sorties against Iraqi targets. On February 24, the allies launched a land invasion of Kuwait. Three days later, President Bush asserted that Kuwait had been liberated and ordered a cease-fire. Iraq immediately announced that it would comply with all United Nations Security Council resolutions passed during the crisis.

Did the President have the constitutional authority to approve the buildup in Saudi Arabia without congressional approval? Would it have been constitutional for him to have launched Operation Desert Storm in the absence of House Joint Resolution 77? After President Bush's November 8 announcement of an intent to gain an offensive capability, fifty-four members of Congress filed suit to enjoin the President from ordering American forces into war "absent meaningful consultation with and genuine approval by Congress." In Dellums v. Bush, 752 F. Supp. 1141 (D.D.C. 1990), the district court rejected the plaintiffs' motion for a preliminary injunction for lack of ripeness. In the course of so holding, however, the court said that it had "no hesitation in concluding that an offensive entry into Iraq by several hundred thousand United States servicemen [could] be described as a 'war' within the meaning of [the Constitution]" and that "in principle, an injunction may issue at the request of members of Congress to prevent the conduct of war which is about to be carried on without congressional authorization."

Was House Joint Resolution 77 constitutionally adequate to authorize Operation Desert Storm? During debate on the floor, both sponsors and opponents of the Resolution spoke of it as equivalent to a declaration of war. But consider Sidak, To Declare War, 41 Duke L.J. 29, 33, 68 (1991):

> To commence warfare on the scale witnessed against Iraq, the President needed to receive a formal declaration of war. He did not. [Although] politically significant, [the Joint Resolution] was a legal nullity, a merely precatory or hortatory gesture. . . .
>
> [Adherence] to formalism in matters that affect the separation of powers, including the initiation of war, is more likely than constitutional informality and political improvisation to produce predictability and clarity in the specification of the responsibilities of political officials in Congress and the executive branch; to facilitate the effective monitoring of these political officials as they discharge their responsibilities; and to permit the electoral process to function as an effective means to reward fidelity, good judgment, and resourcefulness, and likewise to punish infidelity, folly, and indolence. One of the most important of all constitutional formalities is the declaration of war.

For an opposing point of view, see Koh, The Coase Theorem and the War Power: A Response, 41 Duke L.J. 122, 127 (1991):

> [Members] of Congress were painfully aware not only that they were voting on the functional equivalent of a declaration of war, but also that their votes would be intensely scrutinized. Pre-vote speeches were nationally televised, and the roll-call votes were published in every newspaper. [Given] these indicia of public accountability, it is difficult to see what additional accountability would have been gained had the resolution been styled as a declaration of war.

C. LEGISLATIVE AUTHORITY

2. *Congressional Power and Domestic Affairs*

Page 415. Before the Note, add the following:

For a defense of "pragmatic formalism," see Redish & Cisar, "If Angels were to Govern": The Need for Pragmatic Formalism in Separation of Powers Theory, 41 Duke L.J. 449 (1991). For an alternative approach, see Brown, Separation of Powers and Ordered Liberty, 139 U. Pa. L. Rev. 1513, 1515-1516 (1991):

> Missing from the analysis of both camps is an appropriate external value, [a] norm that is consistent with the reasons for separating powers in the first place. [A] counter-majoritarian approach much better addresses the underlying purposes of separation of powers. Unlike both the formalist and functionalist schools, an "ordered liberty" analysis would have the Court examine governmental acts in light of the degree to which they tend to detract from fairness and accountability in the process of government. If the process is impaired in this way, then the action poses a threat to individual liberty.

Page 418. At the end of the first full paragraph, add the following:

In Touby v. United States, 111 S. Ct. 1752 (1991), a unanimous Court, per Justice O'Connor, rejected a nondelegation doctrine challenge to certain aspects of the Controlled Substances Act. The act authorizes the Attorney General to schedule as a "controlled substance" any drug that he has found to meet certain statutory criteria relating, inter alia, to a "history and current pattern of abuse" and a risk to the public health. If the drug is scheduled, its manufacture, possession, or distribution becomes a criminal offense.

Petitioner conceded that the act provided an "intelligible principle" sufficient to meet ordinary nondelegation doctrine requirements. He contended, however, that something more is required when Congress authorizes another branch to promulgate regulations that contemplate criminal sanctions. The Court declined to rule on this contention because the statute "passes muster even if greater congressional specificity is required in a criminal context."

The Court also rejected petitioner's contention that the statute concentrates too much power in the hands of the Attorney General by allowing him to define the very crimes that he then has the responsibility to prosecute.

> This argument has no basis in our separation-of-powers jurisprudence. The principle of separation of powers focuses on the distribution of powers *among* the three coequal Branches; [it] does not speak to the manner in which authority is parceled out within a single Branch. [Petitioners'] argument that [scheduling] authority should have been vested in one executive officer rather than another does not implicate separation-of-powers concerns; it merely challenges the wisdom of a legitimate policy judgment made by Congress.

Page 425. Replace line 17 with the following:

power to conduct trials following impeachment, the Senate's power over presidential appointments, and the

Page 430. At the bottom of the page, add the following:

For a use of game theory to argue that the Court's *Chadha* decision increased the power of the President at the expense of Congress contrary to the original intent of the framers, see Eskridge & Ferejohn, The Article I, Section 7 Game, 80 Geo. L.J. 523 (1992). See also Eskridge & Ferejohn, Making the Deal Stick: Enforcing the Original Constitutional

Structure of Lawmaking in the Modern Regulatory State, 8 J. Econ. & Org. 165 (1992).

Page 460. Line 8.

The first word should be "Government."

Page 461. Before Section 3, add the following:

f. *"Congress v. the President" versus "Congress v. the courts."* Is there a connection between the debate over Congress's assertion of power to control executive authority and the debate over its assertion power to control the jurisdiction of the federal courts, discussed at pp.78-83 of the main text? Steven Calabresi and Kevin Rhodes spell out an elaborate textual argument for such a connection in The Structural Constitution: Unitary Executive, Plural Judiciary, 105 Harv. L. Rev. 1153 (1992). For example,

> Opponents of a broad congressional jurisdiction-stripping power contend that such a power [undermines] the Framers' decision to make the national courts co-equal with the President and Congress and thus violates the scheme of government implicit in the first three Articles of the Constitution. . . .
>
> Similarly, a broad power to insulate officers exercising executive power from control by the President poses a functional threat to the President's independence. In both instances, Congress diminishes the role of the other two departments: Article III courts have fewer classes of cases to decide, and the President has less supervisory authority to exercise.

Consider the extent to which this parallel (and the textualist-originalist approach that supports it) might be undermined by the unanticipated growth of executive power and the emergence of the administrative state. Consider the extent to which the parallel might be strengthened by the (equally unanticipated?) growth of judicial power that has accompanied the use of nontextualist forms of judicial review.

g. Recall that in Buckley v. Valeo, page 436 of the main text, the Court upheld the Federal Campaign Act insofar as the powers that it delegated to the Federal Election Commission were "essentially of an investigative and informative nature, falling in the same general category as those which Congress might delegate to one of its own committees." Does this holding survive *Chadha*? Would it survive the approach outlined in Justice Stevens's concurring opinion in *Bowsher*? Does *Bowsher* raise nontrivial questions about direct congressional control over the policies adopted by administrative agencies through the passage of ordinary legislation contravening those policies? Consider the following:

METROPOLITAN WASHINGTON AIRPORTS AUTHORITY v. CITIZENS FOR THE ABATEMENT OF AIRCRAFT NOISE, 111 S. Ct. 2298 (1991): Before 1986, National and Dulles Airports, outside of Washington D.C., were operated by the federal government. In that year, Congress enacted the Transfer Act, which authorized the transfer of the airports to the Metropolitan Washington Airport Authority, an entity created by statutes enacted by Virginia and the District of Columbia. However, Congress conditioned the transfer on the creation of a Board of Review with the power to veto major decisions made by the directors of the Authority. The Transfer Act provided that the Board of Review would consist of nine members of Congress, who would serve "in their individual capacities, as representatives of users of the [airports]." Eight of the nine were to be members of various committees with jurisdiction over transportation issues. All nine were to be appointed by the Authority's board of directors from lists provided by the Speaker of the House and the President *pro tempore* of the Senate. Virginia and the District of Columbia thereupon amended their statutes to authorize creation of the Board of Review, and its members were appointed by the directors pursuant to the statutory procedure.

Respondents, representing citizens who resided under the flight paths of aircraft using National Airport, sought a declaration that the power of the board of review to veto actions of the Authority violated separation of powers principles. In a 6 to 3 decision the Court, per Justice Stevens, held that the statute was unconstitutional.

The Court began its analysis by rejecting arguments that separation of powers principles were inapplicable because the Board of Review was created by state statutes: "We [confront] an entity created at the initiative of Congress, the powers of which Congress has delineated, the purpose of which is to protect an acknowledged federal interest, and membership in which is restricted to congressional officials. Such an entity necessarily exercises sufficient federal power as an agent of Congress to mandate separation-of-powers scrutiny."

The Court distinguished South Carolina v. Dole, page 242 of the main text, which had upheld a federal grant of highway funds to a state conditioned on the state's prohibition of the possession of alcoholic beverages by persons under the age of 21: "[*Dole*] did not involve separation-of-powers principles. It concerned only the allocation of power between the Federal Government and the States. Our reasoning that, absent coercion, a Sovereign State has both the incentive and the ability to protect its own rights and powers and therefore may cede such rights and powers [is] inapplicable to the issue presented by this case. [The] question [here] is whether the maintenance of federal control over the airports by means of the Board of Review [is] invalid, not because it invades any state power, but because Congress' continued control violates the separation-of-powers principle, the aim of which is to protect not the States but 'the whole people from improvident laws.' "

Having established that the Board of Review was subject to scrutiny under separation of powers principles, the Court then held that those principles had been violated: "The abuses by the monarch recounted in the Declaration of Independence provided dramatic evidence of the threat to liberty posed by a too powerful executive. But, as James Madison recognized, the representatives of the majority in a democratic society, if unconstrained, may pose a similar threat. [The Court here quoted from The Federalist No. 48, page 360 of the main text]. . . .

"To forestall the danger of encroachment 'beyond the legislative sphere,' the Constitution imposes two basic and related constraints on Congress. It may not 'invest itself or its Members with either executive power or judicial power.' And, when it exercises its legislative power, it must follow the 'single, finely wrought and exhaustively considered procedures' specified in Article I.

"The first constraint is illustrated by the Court's holding in [*Bowsher*]. . . .

"The second constraint is illustrated by our decision in *Chadha*. . . .

"The Court of Appeals found it unnecessary to discuss the second constraint because the court was satisfied that the power exercised by the Board of Review over 'key operational decisions is quintessentially executive.' We need not agree or disagree with this characterization [to] conclude that the Board of Review's power is constitutionally impermissible. If the power is executive, the Constitution does not permit an agent of Congress to exercise it. If the power is legislative, Congress must exercise it in conformity with the bicameralism and presentment requirements of Art I, §7. [See *Chadha*]."

In a footnote at the end of its opinion, the Court noted that it need not address the claim that the Transfer Act violated the Ineligibility Clause of article I, §6, which prohibits members of Congress from holding any "Office under the United States" or the claim that it violated the appointments clause of art. II, §2, cl. 2.

Justice White, joined by Chief Justice Rehnquist and Justice Marshall, dissented. He argued that separation of powers principles were inapplicable because the Authority and the board were creatures of state law: "As an initial matter, the Board may not have existed but for Congress, but it does not follow that Congress created the Board or even that Congress' role is a 'factor' mandating separation-of-powers scrutiny. [The] majority's conclusion ignores the entire series of voluntary and intervening actions, agreements, and enactments on the part of the Federal Executive, Virginia, the District and the Authority, without which the Transfer Act would have been a nullity and the Board of Review would not have existed."

Turning to the merits of respondents' separation of powers claim, Justice White began by challenging the majority's attempt "to clear the path for its decision by stressing the Framers' fear of overweening legislative authority. It cannot be seriously maintained . . . that the basis for fearing legislative encroachment has increased or even persisted rather than substantially diminished. At one point Congress may have reigned as the preeminent Branch, much as the Framers predicted. It does so no longer. This century has witnessed a vast increase in the power that Congress has transferred to the Executive. Given this shift in the constitutional balance, the Framers' fears of legislative tyranny ring hollow when invoked to portray a body like the Board as a serious encroachment on the powers of the Executive."

If the Board really was exercising federal executive power, White maintained, the majority had inexplicably failed to rely on the ineligibility clause, which was directly on point. "If the Board did exercise executive authority that is federal in nature, the Court would have no need to say anything other than that congressional membership on the Board violated [this] express constitutional [limitation]. The majority's failure is either unaccountable or suggests that it harbors a certain discomfort with its own position that the Board in fact exercises significant federal power. Whichever is the case, the Court instead relies on expanding nontextual principles as articulated in [*Bowsher*]. . . .

"As *Bowsher* made clear, a 'critical factor' in determining whether an official is 'subservient to Congress' is the degree to which Congress maintains the power of removal. [Here] Congress exercises no such power. Unlike the statutes struck down in *Bowsher* and *Myers*, the Transfer Act contains no provision authorizing Congress to discharge anyone from the board. . . .

"Nor has Congress improperly influenced the appointment process, which is ordinarily a less important factor in separation-of-powers analysis in any event. . . .

"Twice in recent Terms the Court has considered [appointment] mechanisms [similar to the Transfer Act] without suggesting that they raised any constitutional concern. In *Bowsher*, the Court voiced no qualms concerning Presidential appointment of the Comptroller General from a list of three individuals suggested by the House Speaker and the President *pro tempore*. Likewise, in *Mistretta*, the Court upheld Congress' authority to require the President to appoint three federal judges to the Sentencing Commission after considering a list of six judges recommended by the Judicial Conference of the United States. . . .

"The majority alternatively suggests that the Board wields an unconstitutional legislative veto contrary to *Chadha*. [The] problem with this theory is that if the Board is exercising federal power, its power is not legislative. . . .

"Before their transfer to the Airports Authority, National and Dulles were managed by the Federal Aviation Administration, which in turn succeeded the Civil Aeronautics Agency. There is no question that these two agencies exercised paradigmatic executive power or that the transfer of the airports in no way altered that power, which is now in the hands of the Authority. [*Chadha*] is therefore inapposite."

The Court holds that the transfer act is unconstitutional regardless of whether the Board of Review is exercising executive or legislative authority. Assume first that it is exercising executive authority. What then explains the Court's decision to eschew reliance on the relatively clear requirements of the appointments and ineligibility clauses in favor of the more amorphous, arguably nontextual, *Bowsher* principle? Recall Chief Justice Burger's forceful invocation of textualism in *Chadha*. Does *Metropolitan Washington Airports Authority* suggest an abandonment of this approach in separation of powers cases?

It seems to follow from the Court's failure to reach the appointments and ineligibility clause arguments that the act is unconstitutional simply because congressional control over the Board of Review turned it into an "agent of Congress," and that the particular technique by which the control was exercised was relatively unimportant. Suppose that Congress chose to exercise control over airport decisions by

a. refusing to enact legislation transferring authority over the airports unless the Board of Review established certain substantive policies favored by Congress;

b. refusing to enact legislation transferring authority over the airports unless the President promised to appoint certain named individuals to the Board of Review;

c. enacting legislation requiring the Board of Review to establish certain substantive policies regarding airport use;

d. refusing to enact legislation transferring authority over the airports and enacting all airport rules in the form of federal statutes subject to presidential veto.

Would any of these techniques be unconstitutional? If not, how are they distinguishable from what Congress in fact did? Are alternatives *a* and *c* distinguishable because they involve congressional control over discrete questions, rather than generalized, pervasive congressional control? Is alternative *b* distinguishable because the President could always break his promise? Are alternatives *c* and *d* distinguishable because they preserve presidential involvement in policy decisions through the veto power? Do any of these distinctions have a basis in the constitutional text?

Alternatively, assume that the Board of Review is exercising legislative authority. Is there then any explanation for why it was constitutional for the Federal Aviation Administration to run the airport prior to the transfer?

Page 470. At the end of the first paragraph in the Note, add the following:

Many contemporary critics have argued that American politics is characterized by undesirable "gridlock." Is the Constitution responsible for lethargic government? Would a parliamentary system function more efficiently? For a skeptical view, see Sargentich, The Limits of the Parliamentary Critique of the Separation of Powers, 34 Wm. & Mary L. Rev. 679 (1993).

Chapter Five

Equality and the Constitution

A. RACE AND THE CONSTITUTION

2. *Reconstruction and Retreat*

Page 491. Before the first full paragraph, add the following:

For a reinterpretation of Justice Harlan's dissent claiming that it should be read as a "discourse on the fundamental rights of citizenship, not the equal protection of the laws," see Aleinikoff, Re-reading Justice Harlan's Dissent in *Plessy v. Ferguson:* Freedom, Antiracism, and Citizenship, 1992 U. Ill. L. For. 961.

4. *Southern Desegregation*

Page 511. After the second full paragraph, add the following:

Does this history suggest that *Brown* would have been unnecessary if the Supreme Court had taken action to guarantee the political participation of blacks? Consider Klarman, The Puzzling Resistance to Political Process Theory, 77 Va. L. Rev. 747, 805, 813 (1991):

> [The] vital question is whether the racial climate that made *Brown* a judicial possibility could also have rendered *Brown* unnecessary if black ballots had been guaranteed. Although I do not believe this question can be answered with certainty, the historical record belies the authoritatively negative response that most constitutional law scholars instinctively provide. . . .
>
> [To] the extent that post-*Brown* Supreme Court decisions deserve even partial credit for the demise of southern school segregation, it is crucial to note that those decisions *post*-dated the emergence of a national political coalition committed to eliminating racial segregation and discrimination. [A] great deal of the school desegregation that ultimately flowed from *Brown* appears to have been more directly attributable to the intervention of a racially-enlightened national political process than to the Supreme Court.

6. Desegregation and the Limits of Judicial Power

Page 527. Before section 3 of the Note, add the following:

Consider Board of Education of Oklahoma City Public Schools v. Dowell, 111 S. Ct. 630 (1991). In 1963, a district court found that Oklahoma City had intentionally segregated its schools and was currently operating a "dual school system." In 1972, after finding that previous desegregation efforts had failed, the court ordered adoption of a plan involving extensive bussing of school children.

In 1984, the school board adopted a new plan that relied on neighborhood assignments for students in lower grades. Plaintiffs challenged the plan on the ground that it amounted to a return to segregation, but the district court found that the school system was integrated, that unitariness had been achieved, and that court-ordered desegregation must therefore end. The court of appeals reversed, holding that a desegregation decree must remain in effect until a school district can show "grievous wrong evoked by new and unforseen conditions."

In a 5 to 3 decision, the Court, per Chief Justice Rehnquist, held that the court of appeals had applied the wrong standard.

> [A] finding by the District Court that the Oklahoma City School District was being operated in compliance with the commands of the Equal Protection Clause [and] that it was unlikely that the school board would return to its former ways, would be a finding that the purposes of the desegregation litigation had been fully achieved. No additional showing of "grievous wrong evoked by new and unforeseen conditions" is required of the school board. . . .
>
> A district court need not accept at face value the profession of a school board which has intentionally discriminated that it will cease to do so in the future. But in deciding whether to modify or dissolve a desegregation decree, a school board's compliance with previous court orders is obviously relevant. [The] test espoused by the Court of Appeals would condemn a school district, once governed by a board which intentionally discriminated, to judicial tutelage for the indefinite future. Neither the principles governing entry and dissolution of injunctive decrees, nor the commands of the Equal Protection Clause of the Fourteenth Amendment, require any such Draconian result.

The Court remanded the case to the district court to determine whether the board had made a sufficient showing of constitutional compliance to allow the injunction to be dissolved. It instructed the district court to address itself to whether the board had complied in good faith with the desegregation decree and whether the vestiges of past discrimination had been eliminated to the extent practicable.

The Court noted, however, that even if the school board should be released from the injunction implementing the desegregation plan, plaintiffs could nonetheless challenge the new neighborhood schools on equal protection grounds. "A school district which has been released from an injunction imposing a desegregation plan no longer requires court authorization for the promulgation of policies and rules regulating matters such as assignment of students and the like, but it of course remains subject to the mandate of the Equal Protection Clause of the Fourteenth Amendment."

Justice Marshall, joined by Justices Blackmun and Stevens, dissented:

> [The] standard for dissolution of a school desegregation decree must reflect the central aim of our school desegregation precedents. [*Brown*] rested on the Court's recognition that state sponsored segregation conveys a message of "inferiority as to [the] status [of Afro-American school children] in the community that may affect their hearts and minds in a way unlikely ever to be undone." . . .
>
> [A] desegregation decree cannot be lifted so long as conditions likely to inflict the stigmatic injury condemned in *Brown I* persist and there remain feasible methods of eliminating such conditions. Because the record here shows, and the Court of Appeals found, that feasible steps could be taken to avoid one-race schools, it is clear that the purposes of the decree have not yet been [achieved].

In Freeman v. Pitts, 112 S. Ct. 1430 (1992), the Court, in an opinion by Justice Kennedy, held that "federal courts have the authority to relinquish supervision and control of school districts in incremental stages, before full compliance has been achieved in every area of school operations." Although many schools in the DeKalb County System remained racially imbalanced, the district court found that the Board had "achieved maximum practical desegregation," and that the remaining imbalance resulted from demographic factors not traceable to the initial constitutional violations. The court therefore released the Board from judicial supervision with regard to pupil assignments despite its finding that the board had not attained unitary status with regard to other aspects of the system such as "quality of education." The Supreme Court approved this incremental approach:

> [Upon] a finding that a school system subject to a court-supervised desegregation plan is in compliance in some, but not all areas, the court in appropriate cases may return control to the school system in those areas where compliance has been achieved, limiting further judicial supervision to operations that are not yet in full compliance with the court decree. In particular, the district court may determine that it will not order further remedies in the area of student assignments where racial imbalance is not traceable, in a proximate way, to constitutional violations.

Page 530. At the end of the first paragraph, add the following:

5. *"Freedom of choice."* Do the *Green* and *Swann* standards apply in a context where individuals are not compelled to utilize the facility in question? Consider Bazemore v. Friday, 478 U.S. 385 (1986). Prior to 1965, the North Carolina Agricultural Extension Service operated racially segregated 4-H and Homemaker Clubs. In response to the 1964 Civil Rights Act, the service discontinued its segregated club policy and opened any club to any otherwise eligible person regardless of race. Despite this change of policy, many clubs remained racially segregated, and petitioners brought this action seeking to compel the Extension Service to take affirmative measures designed to integrate the clubs. The district court denied relief after finding that any racial imbalance was the result of a wholly voluntary choice by private individuals, and the Supreme Court affirmed. The Court, in an opinion by Justice White, distinguished *Green* as follows:

> While school children must go to school, there is no compulsion to join 4-H or Homemaker Clubs, and while School Boards customarily have the power to create school attendance areas and otherwise designate the school that particular students may attend, there is no statutory or regulatory authority to deny a young person the right to join any Club he or she wishes to join.

Is this distinction persuasive? Compare Justice Brennan's argument in a dissenting opinion joined by Justices Marshall, Blackmun, and Stevens:

> Prior to the early 1960's, the 4-H Clubs were organized in the public schools, which were at the time, of course, still segregated. Thus, those who wanted to join 4-H were, in effect, "assigned" to join the club in their segregated school. It is the racial segregation resulting from this practice that the State is under a duty to eradicate.
>
> As a result, this case is in fact indistinguishable from *Green*. . . .
>
> Nothing in our earlier cases suggests that the State's obligation to desegregate is confined only to those activities in which members of the public are compelled to participate. On the contrary, it is clear that the State's obligation to desegregate formerly segregated entities extends beyond those programs where participation is compulsory to voluntary public amenities such as parks and recreational facilities.

What implications does *Bazemore* hold for a court's remedial powers concerning state universities formerly segregated by law? Consider the following:

UNITED STATES v. FORDICE, 112 S. CT. 2727 (1992): For years, Mississippi's public university system was segregated by law. Although the state eventually ended its system of formal racial exclusion, various colleges in the system retained their racial identities. By the mid-1980s, more than 99 percent of the state's white students were enrolled at four of the universities, which were overwhelmingly white. Seventy-one percent of the black students attended three other universities, where the racial composition ranged from 92 to 99 percent black.

In this suit, petitioners alleged that the state had violated its constitutional obligations by reenforcing the historic, race-based distinctions among the universities. Relying upon *Bazemore*, the trial court ruled for the defendant. It found that in the higher education context "the affirmative duty to desegregate does not contemplate either restricting choice or the achievement of any degree of racial balance." The Supreme Court, in an opinion by Justice White, reversed:

"We do not agree [that] the adoption and implementation of race-neutral policies alone suffice to demonstrate that the State has completely abandoned its prior dual system. That college attendance is by choice and not by assignment does not mean that race-neutral admissions policy cures the constitutional violation of a dual system. [Even] after a State dismantles its segregative *admissions* policy, there may still be state action that is traceable to the State's prior *de jure* segregation and that continues to foster segregation. [If] policies traceable to the *de jure* system are still in force and have discriminatory effects, those policies too must be reformed to the extent practicable and consistent with sound educational practices.

"[In *Bazemore*], the District Court had found that the policy of segregation had been completely abandoned and that no evidence existed of any lingering [discrimination]; any racial imbalance resulted from the wholly voluntary and unfettered choice of private individuals. In this context, we held inapplicable the *Green* Court's judgment that a voluntary choice program was insufficient to dismantle a *de jure* system in public primary and secondary schools, but only after satisfying ourselves that the State had not fostered segregation by playing a part in the decision of which club an individual chose to join.

"*Bazemore* plainly does not excuse inquiry into whether Mississippi has left in place certain aspects of its prior dual system that perpetuate the racially segregated higher education system. . . .

"[There] are several surviving aspects of Mississippi's prior dual system which are constitutionally suspect, for even though such polices may be race-neutral on their face, they substantially restrict a person's choice of which institution to enter and they contribute to the racial identifiability of the eight public universities. Mississippi must justify these polices or eliminate them.

[The Court focused on four "suspect" aspects of the state's system: differing admission standards for various state universities, program duplication, institutional mission assignments for the various universities, and the continued operation of all eight universities within the system.]

"Because the former *de jure* segregated system of public universities in Mississippi impeded the free choice of prospective students, the State in dismantling that system must take the necessary steps to ensure that this choice now is truly free. [That] an institution is predominantly white or black does not in itself make out a constitutional violation. But surely the State may not leave in place policies rooted in its prior officially-segregated system that serve to maintain the racial identifiability of its universities if those policies can practicably be eliminated without eroding sound educational policies.

"If we understand private petitioners to press us to order the upgrading of [the historically black universities] *solely* so that they may be publicly financed, exclusively black enclaves of private choice, we reject that request. The State provides these facilities for *all* its citizens, and it has not met its burden under *Brown* to take affirmative steps to dismantle its prior *de jure* system when it perpetuates a separate, but "more equal" one. Whether such an increase in funding is necessary to achieve a full dismantlement under the standards we have outlined, however, is a different question, and one that must be addressed on remand."

Justice Thomas filed a concurring opinion: "I write separately to emphasize that [the Court's] standard is far different from the one adopted to govern the grade-school context in [*Green*]. In particular, because it does not compel the elimination of all observed racial imbalance, it portends neither the destruction of historically black colleges nor the severing of those institutions from their distinctive histories and traditions. . . .

"[We] focus on the specific *policies* alleged to produce racial imbalance, rather than on the *imbalance* itself. Thus, a plaintiff cannot obtain relief merely by identifying a persistent racial imbalance, because the district court cannot provide a reassignment remedy designed to eliminate that imbalance directly. Plaintiffs are likely to be able to identify [specific] policies traceable to the *de jure* era that continue to produce a current racial imbalance. As a practical matter, then, the district courts administering our standard will spend their time determining whether such policies have been adequately justified — a far narrower, more manageable task than that imposed under *Green*. . . .

"[We] do not foreclose the possibility that there exists 'sound educational justification' for maintaining historically black colleges *as such*.

Despite the shameful history of state-enforced segregation, these institutions have survived and flourished. . . .

"Obviously, a State cannot maintain such traditions by closing particular institutions, historically white or historically black, to particular racial groups. Nonetheless, it hardly follows that a State cannot operate a diverse assortment of institutions — including historically black institutions — open to all on a race-neutral basis, but with established traditions and programs that might disproportionately appeal to one race or another. [It] would be ironic, to say the least, if the institutions that sustained blacks during segregation were themselves destroyed in an effort to combat its vestiges.

Justice O'Connor also filed a concurring opinion.

Justice Scalia filed an opinion concurring in the judgment in part and dissenting in part: "[The] Court is essentially applying to universities the amorphous standard adopted for primary and secondary schools in [*Green*]. Like that case, today's decision places upon the State the ordinarily unsustainable burden of proving the negative proposition that *it* is not responsible for extant racial disparity in enrollment. *Green* requires school boards to prove that racially identifiable schools are *not* the consequence of past or present discriminatory state action; today's opinion requires state university administrators to prove that racially identifiable schools are *not* the consequence of any practice or practices [held] over from the prior *de jure* regime. This will imperil virtually any practice or program plaintiffs decide to challenge — just as *Green* has — so long as racial imbalance remains. And just as under *Green*, so also under today's decision, the only practicable way of disproving that 'existing racial identifiability is attributable to the State,' *is to eliminate extant segregation, i.e., to assure racial proportionality in the schools.* . . .

"Ironically enough, [today's] decision seems to prevent adoption of a policy of [equal funding for historically black universities]. [Equal] funding, like program duplication, facilitates continued segregation — enabling students to attend schools where their own race predominates without paying a penalty in the quality of education. Nor could such an equal-funding policy be saved on the basis that it serves what the Court calls a 'sound educational justification.' The only conceivable *educational* value it furthers is that of fostering schools in which blacks receive their education in a 'majority' setting; but to acknowledge that as a 'value' would contradict the compulsory-integration philosophy that underlies *Green*. Just as vulnerable, of course, would be all other programs that have the effect of facilitating the continued existence of predominantly black institutions." . . .

"What the Court's test is designed to achieve is the elimination of predominantly black institutions. [In] a perverse way, [the] insistence

[that] such institutions not be permitted to endure perpetuates the very stigma of black inferiority that *Brown I* sought to destroy. . . .

"I [predict that this decision will result in] a number of years of litigation-driven confusion and destabilization in the university systems of all the formerly *de jure* States, that will benefit neither blacks nor [whites]. Nothing good will come of this judicially ordained turmoil, except the public recognition that any Court that would knowingly impose it must hate segregation. We must find some other way of making that point."

For a careful and detailed discussion of *Fordice*, see Davis, The Quest for Equal Education in Mississippi: The Implications of *United States v. Fordice*, 62 U. Miss. L. Rev. 405 (1993).

Page 532. Before Section B, add the following:

For an extended and careful discussion of *Brown*'s impact, see G. Rosenberg, The Hollow Hope: Can Courts Bring About Social Change? (1991). Rosenberg concludes that there is "little evidence that the judicial system [produced] much of the massive change in civil rights that swept the United States in the 1960s. [While] we can never know what would have happened if the Court had not acted as it did [the] existence and strength of pro-civil-rights forces at least suggest that change would have occurred [without judicial intervention], albeit at a pace unknown." Moreover, Rosenberg suggests, civil rights litigation "siphon[ed] off crucial resources and talent [thereby] weakening political efforts."

> A further danger of litigation as a strategy for significant social reform is that symbolic victories may be mistaken for substantive ones, covering a reality that is distasteful. Rather than working to change that reality, reformers relying on a litigation strategy for reform may be misled (or content?) to celebrate the illusion of change.

See also Seidman, Brown and Miranda, 80 Calif. L. Rev. 673, 717 (1992):

> It came to be seen that the *Brown* Court offered the country a kind of deal, and, from the perspective of defenders of the status quo, not a bad one at that. Prior to *Brown* [contradictions] in the ideology of the separate-but-equal doctrine were permanently destabilizing and threatened any equilibrium.
>
> By purporting to resolve those contradictions, *Brown* also served to end their destabilizing potential. The Court resolved the contradictions by definitional fiat: separate facilities were now simply proclaimed to be inherently unequal. But the flip side of this aphorism was that once white society was willing to make facilities legally nonseparate, the demand for equality had been satisfied and blacks no longer had just cause for complaint. The mere existence of *Brown* thus served [to] legitimate current arrangements. True, many blacks remained poor and disempowered. But their status was now no

longer a result of the denial of equality. Instead, it marked a personal failure to take advantage of one's definitionally equal status.

Page 540. Before section 2 of the Note, add the following:

Consider in this regard Gregory v. Ashcroft, 111 S. Ct. 2395 (1991). The Missouri Constitution provides that "[all] judges other than municipal judges shall retire at age of seventy years." The Supreme Court, in an opinion written by Justice O'Connor, sustained this provision against equal protection attack.

> The Missouri mandatory retirement provision, like all legal classifications, is founded on a generalization. It is far from true that all judges suffer significant deterioration in performance at age 70. It is probably not true that most do. It may not be true at all. [But the] people of Missouri rationally could conclude that the threat of deterioration at age 70 is sufficiently great, and the alternatives for removal sufficiently inadequate, that they will require all judges to step aside at age 70.

Justice Blackmun, in an opinion joined by Justice Marshall, dissented on statutory grounds without reaching the constitutional question.

Would it be constitutional for Missouri to establish a mandatory retirement age of 50 for judges? Could Missouri provide that no person over the age of 70 could form a binding contract or drive an automobile?

B. EQUAL PROTECTION METHODOLOGY: RATIONAL BASIS REVIEW

Page 544. At the bottom of the text page, add the following:

CHAPMAN v. UNITED STATES, 111 S. Ct. 1919 (1991): Federal law provides for a mandatory minimum sentence of five years for the offense of distributing more than one gram of a "mixture or substance containing a detectable amount of [LSD]." Petitioners were convicted of selling ten sheets of blotter paper containing LSD. The district court held that they were subject to the mandatory minimum because the drug, together with the blotter paper, weighed more than one gram. Petitioners argued that if the statute were construed to require inclusion of the paper or other carrier medium when calculating the weight of the drug, it would violate the equal protection component of the Fifth Amendment's due process clause. They pointed out that this construction would mean that a major wholesaler caught with thousands of doses of pure LSD would not be subject to the mandatory minimum (because even thousands of doses would weigh less than a gram), while a minor pusher with a much smaller number of doses on blotter paper, or even one dose on a sugar cube, would be.

Chief Justice Rehnquist delivered the Court's opinion: "We find that Congress had a rational basis for its choice of penalties for LSD distribution. The penalty scheme [is] intended to punish severely large-volume drug traffickers at any level. It assigns more severe penalties to the distribution of larger quantities of drugs. By measuring the quantity of the drugs according to the 'street weight' of the drugs in the diluted form in which they are sold, rather than according to the net weight of the active component, the statute [increases] the penalty for persons who possess large quantities of drugs, regardless of their purity. That is a rational sentencing scheme. . . .

"Although LSD is not sold by weight, but by dose, and a carrier medium is not, strictly speaking, used to 'dilute' the drug, that medium is used to facilitate the distribution of the drug. Blotter paper makes LSD easier to transport, store, conceal, and sell. It is a tool of the trade for those who traffic in the drug, and therefore it was rational for Congress to set penalties based on this chosen tool. Congress was also justified in seeking to avoid arguments about the accurate weight of pure drugs which might have been extracted from blotter paper had it chosen to calibrate sentences according to that weight. . . .

"While hypothetical cases can be imagined involving very heavy carriers and very little LSD, those cases are of no import in considering a claim by persons such as petitioners, who used a standard LSD carrier. . . .

"Petitioners argue that those selling different numbers of doses and, therefore, with different degrees of culpability, will be subject to the same minimum sentence because of choosing different carriers. The same objection could be made to a statute that imposed a fixed sentence for distributing any quantity of LSD, in any form, with any carrier. Such a sentencing scheme — not considering individual degrees of culpability — would clearly be constitutional. [That] distributors of varying degrees of culpability might be subject to the same sentence does not mean that the penalty system for LSD distribution is unconstitutional."

Justice Stevens, joined by Justice Marshall, filed a dissenting opinion that did not reach the constitutional issue.

Page 555. At the end of section 1 of the Note, add the following:

Compare *City of Cleburne* with Heller v. Doe, — S. Ct. — (1993), where the Court in a 5-4 decision rejected an equal protection attack against

Kentucky statutes that allowed for involuntary commitment for the mentally retarded on the basis of clear and convincing evidence, while mandating a "beyond a reasonable doubt" standard for involuntary commitment based on mental illness. In an opinion by Justice Kennedy, the Court held that Kentucky might rationally conclude that a higher standard of proof was necessary for mental illness because it was more difficult to diagnose. A higher burden of proof therefore tended "to equalize the risks of an erroneous determination that the subject of a commitment proceeding has the condition in question." A higher standard might also be justified because "[the] prevailing methods of treatment for the mentally retarded, as a general rule, are much less invasive than are those given the mentally ill."

The Court also upheld Kentucky's decision to allow close relatives of the mentally retarded, but not the mentally ill, to participate as parties in the commitment proceedings. The Court reasoned that because mental retardation manifested itself early in the developmental process, Kentucky might reasonably conclude that close relatives had a valuable contribution to make to the proceedings. Mental illness, in contrast, might manifest itself suddenly only after minority. "In addition, adults previously of sound mental health who are diagnosed as mentally ill may have a need for privacy that justifies the State in confining a commitment proceeding to the smallest group compatible with due process."

Justice Souter wrote a dissenting opinion in which he was joined in full by Justices Blackmun, and Stevens. Justice O'Connor would have invalidated the differential standards of proof but upheld the provision permitting relatives of the mentally retarded to participate as parties.

Is the *Heller* Court's willingness to accept generalizations about the mentally retarded consistent with its approach in *City of Cleburne*? Is it relevant that in *Heller*, the Court was measuring the rights of the mentally retarded against those of another relatively disadvantaged group?

Page 556. After section 2 of the Note, add the following:

2A. Fritz *and public choice theory.* D. Farber & P. Frickey, Law and Public Choice: A Critical Introduction 137 (1991), say that the statute involved in *Fritz* "embodied a proposal from a joint labor-management negotiating committee, which had formed at the request of Congress. The members of this committee were not appointed by public officials, and no one on the committee represented the workers who bore the brunt of the bill — nonrailroaders who had earlier worked between ten and twenty-five years in the railroad industry." Should this affect the constitutional analysis? How?

Page 560. Before section 2 of the Note, add the following:

Compare the cases cited in the main text with Burlington Northern Railroad Co. v. Ford, 112 S. Ct. 2184 (1992) (using rational basis review to uphold a state venue rule permitting a plaintiff to sue a corporation incorporated within the state only in the county of its principal place of business, but permitting a similar suit in any county against a corporation incorporated outside the state).

Page 565. Before Part C, add the following:

For the Court's most recent discussions of "actual purpose" review, compare Nordlinger v. Hahn, 112 S. Ct. 2326 (1992) with Federal Communications Commission v. Beach Communications, Inc., — S. Ct. — (1993). In *Nordlinger,* the Court considered a portion of California's constitution, as amended by "Proposition 13," that capped property taxes for current owners at 1 percent of the property's assessed value as of the 1975-1976 year with small annual adjustments for inflation. In contrast, newly purchased property was assessed at its value at the time of purchase. This scheme meant that new owners were required to pay dramatically higher taxes even though their land might be less valuable than land owned by pre-1975 purchasers.

In an opinion by Justice Blackmun, the Court rejected an equal protection challenge to these disparities. Applying rational basis review, the Court held that the scheme rationally furthered the state's interest in preserving the continuity and stability of local neighborhoods and in protecting the reliance interests of existing owners.

In their challenge to the California scheme, plaintiffs relied upon the Court's earlier decision in Allegheny Pittsburgh Coal Co. v. Webster County, 488 U.S. 226 (1989). In *Allegheny Pittsburgh,* the Court held that the equal protection clause invalidated the practice of a county tax assessor who assessed recently purchased property on the basis of its purchase price, while making only minor modifications in the assessments of property that had not been recently sold.

The *Nordlinger* Court distinguished *Allegheny Pittsburgh* because in that case state law provided for assessments of property at its true current value, and there was no indication that the policies underlying California's acquisition value scheme could conceivably have been the purpose for the *Allegheny Pittsburgh* tax assessor's unequal valuations.

> To be sure, the Equal Protection Clause does not demand for purposes of rational-basis review that a legislature or governing decisionmaker actually articulate at any time the purpose or rationale supporting its classification. Nevertheless, this Court's review does require that a purpose may conceivably

or "may reasonably have been the purpose and policy" of the relevant governmental decisionmaker. Allied Stores of Ohio, Inc. v. Bowers, 358 U.S. 522, 528-529 (1959). *Allegheny Pittsburgh* was the rare case where the facts precluded any plausible inference that the reason for the unequal assessment practice was to achieve the benefits of an acquisition-value tax scheme. By contrast, [Proposition 13] was enacted precisely to achieve the benefits of an acquisition-value system.

In a concurring opinion, Justice Thomas argued that *Allegheny Pittsburgh* was indistinguishable and should be overruled.

According to the Court, [the] problem in *Allegheny Pittsburgh* was that the Webster County scheme, though otherwise rational, was irrational because it was contrary to state law. Any rational bases underlying the acquisition-value scheme were "implausible" (or "unreasonable") because they were made so by the Constitution and laws of the [state]. . . .

[But even] if the assessor did violate West Virginia law, [she] would not have violated the Equal Protection Clause. A violation of state law does not by itself constitute a violation of the Federal Constitution.

In a dissenting opinion, Justice Stevens argued that the California scheme was irrational:

[Proposition] 13 sweeps too broadly and operates too indiscriminately to "rationally further" the State's interest in neighborhood perservation. . . .

It is just short of absurd to conclude that the legitimate state interest in protecting a relatively small number of economically vulnerable families is "rationally furthered" by a tax windfall for all 9,787,887 property owners in California. . . .

The second state interest identified by the Court is the "reliance interests" of the earlier purchasers. Here I find the Court's reasoning difficult to follow. [In] this case, those who purchased property before Proposition 13 was enacted received no assurances that assessments would only increase at a limited rate; indeed, to the contrary, many purchased property in the hope that property values (and assessments) would appreciate substantially and quickly.

In Federal Communications v. Beach Communications, Inc., decided the term following *Nordlinger,* the Court exhibited a much more hostile approach to actual purpose review. In the Cable Communications Policy Act of 1984, Congress exempted from otherwise applicable regulation cable facilities that served buildings under common ownership or management so long as they provided services without using public rights-of-way. Respondents, who provided satellite master antenna service to a complex of buildings that were not under common ownership, claimed that there was no rational basis for the distinction and that it therefore violated the equal protection component of the Fifth Amendment's due process clause.

In an opinion by Justice Thomas, the Court emphatically rejected this challenge.

> In areas of social and economic policy, a statutory classification that neither proceeds along suspect lines nor infringes fundamental constitutional rights must be upheld against equal protection challenge if there is any reasonably conceivable state of facts that could provide rational basis for the classification. . . .
>
> [Because] we never require a legislature to articulate its reasons for enacting a statute, it is entirely irrelevant for constitutional purposes whether the conceived reason for the challenged distinction actually motivated the legislature.

In a concurring opinion, Justice Stephens argued that

> this formulation sweeps too broadly, for it is difficult to imagine a legislative classification that could *not* be supported by a "reasonably conceivable state of facts." Judicial review under the "conceivable set of facts" test is tantamount to no review at all.
>
> I continue to believe that when Congress imposes a burden on one group, but leaves unaffected another that is similarly, though not identically situated, "the Constitution requires something more than merely a 'conceivable' or 'plausible' explanation for the unequal treatment" *Fritz* (Stevens, J. concurring in judgment. In my view, when the actual rationale for the legislative classification is unclear, we should inquire whether the classification is rationally related to "a legitimate purpose that we may *reasonably presume* to have motivated an impartial legislature." *Id.* (emphasis added).

Page 575. After the second line, add the following:

Consider Farber & Frickey, Is *Carolene Products* Dead? Reflections on Affirmative Action and the Dynamics of Civil Rights Legislation, 79 Cal. L. Rev. 685, 702, 704 (1991):

> The primary flaw in the Ackerman model is that it neglects the importance of ideology. . . .
>
> What *Carolene Products* calls prejudice may play the role of [motivating] ideology. The power a minority group can muster will be limited to the extent that other voters (and legislators) are ideologically motivated to suppress it. . . .
>
> [It] is untenable to conclude that [the undeniable progress toward black political power] has resulted in parity. Although there is no way to gauge political influence, it is far from clear that blacks have as much political clout as other groups of similar size. For example, in 1980, the elderly made up about the same proportion of the population as blacks. Although no one has studied the issue, it seems clear to us that the elderly have had considerably more success in the legislative arena than have blacks. The virtually sacrosanct status of Social Security strongly attests to the soundness of this conclusion, as does an ever-expanding federal prohibition on age discrimination. Similarly, farm-

ers now make up only three percent of the population, considerably less than blacks, but their "influence on legislation beneficial to their interests has been enormous."

C. EQUAL PROTECTION METHODOLOGY: HEIGHTENED SCRUTINY AND THE PROBLEM OF RACE

1. Race-Specific Classifications That Expressly Disadvantage Racial Minorities

Page 575. Before the first full paragraph, add the following:

Consider Posner, Democracy and Distrust Revisited, 77 Va. L. Rev. 641, 646 (1991):

> [Defects in representation are] found in a number of other cases [that] Ely does not discuss. [A] large and amorphous majority may be at the mercy of the very sort of interest group that Ely conceives it to be the fundamental purpose of the Constitution to protect. There is (a related point) the electorate's pervasive ignorance of, and substantial indifference to, the effects of public policies. There is also the fact that representatives are not perfect agents of the electors. [And] there is the fact that [we] vote for people rather than policies — which means that, at best, we are voting for a package of policies — and it is easy to show that particular policies may end up being adopted that are not the preference of a majority of the voters.
>
> No doubt most of the problems of representation are beyond the practical reach of judicial correction. But if they are left unsolved, it is by no means clear that the judicial initiatives that Ely commends will improve the functioning of representative government, or even that those he opposes will *not* improve it.

Page 579. Before the Note, add the following:

Do economic models of the political process help explain the strict scrutiny of racial classifications? Consider Stout, Strict Scrutiny and Social Choice: An Economic Inquiry into Fundamental Rights and Suspect Classifications, 80 Geo. L. J. 1787, 1814-1817 (1992):

> [Social] choice theory suggests that strict judicial scrutiny of statutes employing suspect classifications may [serve] an important economic function. If statutes employing suspect classifications are inordinately likely to be wealth transferring rather than wealth creating, strict judicial scrutiny that discourages such legislation reduces the deadweight losses associated with competing for and enacting it. . . .

> If legislatures can dole out resources or impose burdens according to race, racial interest groups have tremendous incentive to seek purely redistributive legislation. . . .
>
> A classification based on an immutable trait is both less likely to serve a welfare-increasing function, and more likely to provide opportunities to exploit others without risk to oneself. . . .
>
> Social choice theory thus supports the notion that classifications based on immutable traits such as race or gender deserve stricter scrutiny under the Equal Protection Clause than classifications based on characteristics that are changeable, such as age, health, or wealth.

2. *Non-Race-Specific Classifications That Disadvantage Racial Minorities*

Page 585. Before the last paragraph, add the following:

Compare Alexander, What Makes Wrongful Discrimination Wrong? Biases, Preferences, Stereotypes, and Proxies, 141 U. Pa. L. Rev. 149, 213 (1992):

> If one lacks a preferred trait that one would have possessed were one not the victim of wrongful discrimination, may one demand in addition to compensation from one's victimizers that others overlook the absence of the trait? Surely not. If I was a promising neurosurgeon before my hands were mangled by a drunk driver, I cannot ask others to ignore my lack of dexterity in their choice of neurosurgeons. [Preferences] for scarce traits do not become immoral merely because the scarcity is in part due to the immoralities of others, even when just reparations have not been fully paid.

Page 590. Before the last full paragraph, add the following:

In Powers v. Ohio, 111 S. Ct. 1364 (1991), the Court, in an opinion by Justice Kennedy, held that "a criminal defendant may object to race-based exclusions of jurors effected through peremptory challenges whether or not the defendant and the excluded juror share the same race." Justice Scalia, joined by Chief Justice Rehnquist, dissented. Justice Kennedy also wrote for the Court in Edmonson v. Leesville Concrete Co, 111 S. Ct. 2077 (1991), holding that race-based peremptory challenges by private litigants in civil actions violated the Constitution. Justice O'Connor, joined by Chief Justice Rehnquist and Justice Scalia, dissented.

In Georgia v. McCollum, 112 S. Ct. 2348 (1992), the Court, in an opinion by Justice Blackmun, held that the *Batson* prohibition against race-based peremptory challenges applied to the defense as well as the prosecution. Consider Judge Thomas's attack on *Batson* in his opinion concurring in the judgment:

> [I] am certain that black criminal defendants will rue the day that this court ventured down this road that inexorably will lead to the elimination of peremptory strikes.
>
> In *Strauder* [we] invalidated a state law that prohibited blacks from serving on juries. In the course of the decision, we observed that the racial composition of a jury may affect the outcome of a criminal case. . . .
>
> I do not think that this basic premise of *Strauder* has become obsolete. . . .
>
> In *Batson,* however, this Court began to depart from *Strauder* by holding that, without some actual showing, suppositions about the possibility that jurors may harbor prejudice have no legitimacy. We said, in particular, that a prosecutor could not justify peremptory strikes "by stating merely that he challenged jurors of the defendant's race on the assumption — or his intuitive judgment — that they would be partial to the defendant because of their shared race." [Our] decision in *Strauder,* [however,] rested on precisely such an "assumption" or "intuition." We reasonably surmised, without direct evidence in any particular case, that all-white juries might judge black defendants unfairly.

Does *McCollum* pose a conflict between the defendant's interest in a jury that is free of racial bias on the one hand and the juror's interest in not being rejected for jury service on the basis of racial generalizations on the other? If so, how should the conflict be resolved?

For a commentary on the *Batson* problem, see Nunn, Rights Held Hostage: Race, Ideology and the Peremptory Challenge, 28 Harv. Civ. R.-Civ. L. L. Rev. 63 (1993); Underwood, Ending Race Discrimination in Jury Selection: Whose Right Is It, Anyway?, 92 Colum. L. Rev. 725 (1992).

Page 600. Before "Note: The Problem of Proof" add the following:

Does Washington v. Davis rest on a similar acceptance of white norms as the point of departure for equal protection analysis? Consider Flagg, "Was Blind but Now I See": White Race Consciousness and the Requirement of Discriminatory Intent, 91 Mich. L. Rev. 953, 957, 987-988 (1993):

> The most striking characteristic of whites' consciousness of whiteness is that most of the time we don't have any. I call this the transparency phenomenon: the tendency of whites not to think about whiteness, or about norms, behaviors, experiences, or perspectives that are white-specific. Transparency operates to require black assimilation even when pluralism is the articulated goal; it affords substantial advantages to whites over blacks even when decisionmakers intend to effect substantive racial justice. . . .
>
> [The Washington v. Davis] rule recreates transparency at the level of constitutional doctrine, for it affords a presumption of race neutrality to facially

neutral criteria of decision without regard to the possibility that those criteria in fact reflect white-specific characteristics, attitudes, or experiences. The rule tends to reassure whites that all is well so long as we avoid the conscious use of race-specific bases for decision. . . .

The requirement of discriminatory intent also legitimates unconscious race discrimination by reinforcing a popular white story about progress in race relations. The central theme of this story is that our society has an unfortunate history of race discrimination that is largely behind us.

3. *Classifications that describe racial minorities.* Should a statute be subject to strict scrutiny even if it does not use race per se as a classifying principle if it disadvantages individuals based on characteristics that effectively describe members of a minority race?

Suppose, for example, that it could be shown that, as a statistical matter, blacks default on loans more frequently than whites. Obviously, a law requiring a state lender to charge higher interest rates to blacks than to whites would be subject to strict scrutiny. But suppose further that there is a high degree of residential segregation in the state. It is therefore also possible to show a correlation between default rates and the zip code of the borrower — a correlation that is entirely the product of the fact that blacks live in the neighborhoods with high default rates. How should a court treat a statute requiring higher interest rates for borrowers with certain zip codes? Is such a statute subject only to low-level review because the purpose of its drafters was to avoid defaults rather than to harm blacks? Or is it subject to strict scrutiny because, whatever their purpose, the drafters of the statute are using zip codes as a proxy for race? Would the case be different if there was a high correlation between zip code and race but the correlation between zip code and default rates was unrelated to race? Consider the following:

HERNANDEZ v. NEW YORK, 111 S. Ct. 1859 (1991): Hernandez claimed that the prosecutor at his criminal trial had used peremptory challenges to exclude Latinos from the jury. The prosecutor told the trial judge that the challenges were based on his fear that the challenged bilingual jurors would have difficulty following only the official interpreter for Spanish speaking witnesses rather than their own understanding of the testimony. The trial court rejected the defendant's claim, and the Supreme Court affirmed.

Justice Kennedy delivered an opinion for a plurality of the Court:

"A court addressing this issue must keep in mind the fundamental principle that 'official action will not be held unconstitutional solely because it results in a racially disproportionate impact. . . . Proof of racially discriminatory intent or purpose is required to show a violation of the Equal Protection Clause.' [*Arlington Heights*]. . . .

"A neutral explanation in the context of our analysis here means an explanation based on something other than the race of the juror. . . .

"The prosecutor here offered a race-neutral basis for these peremptory strikes. As explained by the prosecutor, the challenges rested neither on the intention to exclude Latino or bilingual jurors, nor on stereotypical assumptions about Latinos or bilinguals. The prosecutor's articulated basis for these challenges divided potential jurors into two classes: those whose conduct during the *voir dire* would persuade him they might have difficulty in accepting the translator's rendition of Spanish-language testimony and those potential jurors who gave no such reason for doubt. Each category would include both Latinos and non-Latinos. While the prosecutor's criterion might well result in the disproportionate removal of prospective Latino jurors, that disproportionate impact does not turn the prosecutor's actions into a *per se* violation of the Equal Protection Clause. . . .

"If a prosecutor articulates a basis for a peremptory challenge that results in the disproportionate exclusion of members of a certain race, the trial judge may consider that fact as evidence that the prosecutor's stated reason constitutes a pretext for racial discrimination. . . .

"In the context of this trial, the prosecutor's frank admission that his ground for excluding these jurors related to their ability to speak and understand Spanish raised a plausible, though not a necessary, inference that language might be a pretext for what in fact were raced-based peremptory challenges. . . .

"The trial judge in this case chose to believe the prosecutor's race-neutral explanation for striking the two jurors in [question]. [The] trial court's decision on the ultimate question of discriminatory intent represents a finding of fact of the sort accorded great deference on appeal. . . .

"In holding that a race-neutral reason for a peremptory challenge means a reason other than race, we do not resolve the more difficult question of the breadth with which the concept of race should be defined for equal protection purposes. We would face a quite different case if the prosecutor had justified his peremptory challenges with the explanation that he did not want Spanish-speaking jurors. It may well be, for certain ethnic groups and in some communities, that proficiency in a particular language, like skin color, should be treated as a surrogate for race under equal protection analysis. And [a] policy of striking all who speak a given language, without regard to the particular circumstances of the trial or the individual responses of the jurors, may be found by the trial judge to be a pretext for racial discrimination. But that case is not before us."

Justice O'Connor, joined by Justice Scalia, concurred in the judgment:

"[I] believe that the plurality opinion goes farther than it needs to in assessing the constitutionality of the prosecutor's asserted justification for his peremptory strikes. . . .

"In this case, the prosecutor's asserted justification for striking certain Hispanic jurors was his uncertainty about the jurors' ability to accept the official translation of trial testimony. If this truly was the purpose of the strikes, they were not strikes because of race, and therefore did not violate the Equal Protection Clause. [They] may have acted like strikes based on race, but they were *not* based on race. No matter how closely tied or significantly correlated to race the explanation for a peremptory strike may be, the strike does not implicate the Equal Protection Clause unless it is based on race. . . .

"Disproportionate effect may, of course, constitute evidence of intentional discrimination. The trial court may, because of such effect, disbelieve the prosecutor and find that the asserted justification is merely a pretext for intentional race-based discrimination. But if, as in this case, the trial court believes the prosecutor's nonracial justification, and that finding is not clearly erroneous, that is the end of the matter."

Justice Stevens, joined by Justice Marshall, dissented:

"A violation of the Equal Protection Clause requires what our cases characterize as proof of 'discriminatory purpose.' By definition, however, a prima facie case is one that is established by the requisite proof of invidious intent. Unless the prosecutor comes forward with an explanation for his peremptories that is sufficient to rebut that prima facie case, no additional evidence of racial animus is required to establish an equal protection violation. In my opinion, the Court therefore errs when it concludes that a defendant's *Batson* challenge fails whenever the prosecutor advances a nonpretextual justification that is not facially discriminatory."

Justice Blackmun also dissented.

Page 605. Before Section 3, add the following:

Most of the Court's vote dilution jurisprudence has concerned claims that minority voting strength is diminished by spreading minority voters thinly so as to deny them majority status in any particular district. In Voinovich v. Quilter, 113 S. Ct. 1149 (1993), the Court considered the opposite claim. Respondents brought a fifteenth amendment challenge to a state reapportionment scheme that grouped African-American voters together in five districts, thereby creating "safe" African-American seats in these districts. Respondents argued that the plan unconstitutionally diluted African-American voting strength by reducing African-American influence in other districts where they would have been a significant minority if they had not been concentrated in the "safe" districts. The District court upheld the claim, finding that the state's reapportionment board had acted "intentionally and for the purpose of political advantage."

The Supreme Court, in a unanimous opinion by Justice O'Connor, reversed. The Court began its constitutional analysis by noting that it had never decided "whether the Fifteenth Amendment applies to vote-dilution claims." Assuming arguendo that the fifteenth amendment was applicable, the Court held that the District Court's decision must nonetheless be reversed because its finding of intentional discrimination was clearly erroneous. The Court noted that the Board relied on information provided by various African-American groups and that the Ohio NAACP had endorsed large parts of the plan.

Why might African-American organizations endorse a plan that grouped most African-Americans into a few districts in which they formed a majority rather than spreading them over a greater number of districts? Might they have reasons for endorsing such a plan even if it had the effect of reducing the overall political influence of African-Americans? Which sort of plan raises the most serious constitutional problems: one that spreads a minority population evenly across districts, thereby denying them majority status anywhere, or one that groups them into a few districts, thereby leaving all the others without substantial minority populations?

For the Court's latest treatment of race-based districting designed to enhance the political power of a minority group, see Shaw v. Reno, 113 S. Ct. — (1993), excerpted in Chapter 6, §1 of this Supplement.

3. Race-Specific Classifications That Are Facially Neutral

Page 615. At the end of section 1 of the Note, add the following:

In Powers v. Ohio, 111 S. Ct. 1364 (1991), the Court, in a 7 to 2 decision written by Justice Kennedy, held that a white criminal defendant could assert the claim of a black potential juror subject to a race-based peremptory challenge. Consider the views of Justice Scalia expressed in a dissenting opinion joined by Chief Justice Rehnquist:

> [When a] group, like all others, has been made subject to peremptory challenge on the basis of its group characteristic, its members have been treated not differently but the same. In fact, it would constitute discrimination to exempt them from the peremptory-strike exposure to which all others are subject. . . .

> Unlike the categorical exclusion of a group from jury service, which implies that all its members are incompetent or untrustworthy, a peremptory strike on the basis of group membership implies nothing more than the undeniable reality [that] all groups tend to have particular sympathies and hostilities. [Since] that reality is acknowledged as to all groups, and forms the basis for peremptory strikes as to all of them, there is no implied criticism or dishonor to a strike.

Compare Justice Kennedy's response in his opinion for the Court:

> We reject [the] view that race-based peremptory challenges survive equal protection scrutiny because members of all races are subject to like treatment, which is to say that white jurors are subject to the same risk of peremptory challenges based on race as are all other jurors. The suggestion that racial classifications may survive when visited upon all persons is no more authoritative today than the case which advanced the theorem, Plessy v. Ferguson. This idea has no place in our modern equal protection jurisprudence. It is axiomatic that racial classifications do not become legitimate on the assumption that all persons suffer them in equal degree. Loving v. Virginia.

Page 636. Before subsection 1f of the Note, add the following:

Compare Delgado, Affirmative Action as a Majoritarian Device: Or, Do You Really Want to Be a Role Model?, 89 Mich. L. Rev. 1222, 1223-1224 (1991):

> Affirmative action [generally] frames the question of minority representation in an interesting way: Should we as a society admit, hire, appoint, or promote some designated number of people of color in order to promote certain policy goals, such as social stability, an expanded labor force, and an integrated society? [Minorities] are hired or promoted not because we have been unfairly treated, denied jobs, deprived of our lands, or beaten and brought here in chains. [The] system thus bases inclusion of people of color on principles of social utility, not reparations or *rights*. When those in power decide the goal has been accomplished, or is incapable of being reached, what logically happens? Naturally, the program stops. At best, then, affirmative action serves as a homeostatic device, assuring that only a small number of women and people of color are hired or promoted. Not too many, for that would be terrifying, nor too few, for that would be destabilizing. Just the right small number, generally those of us who need it least, are moved ahead.

Page 636. Before section 2 of the Note, add the following:

Compare Professor Van Alstyne's views with those expressed in Aleinikoff, A Case for Race-Consciousness, 91 Colum. L. Rev. 1061, 1087-1088, 1109-1110 (1991):

> [Recognizing] race validates the lives and experiences of those who have been burdened because of their race. White racism has made "blackness" a relevant category in our society. Yet colorblindness seeks to deny the continued social significance of the category, to tell blacks that they are no different from whites, even though blacks as blacks are persistently made to feel that difference. . . .
>
> Race-consciousness [should] play a double role in ending black invisibility. It demands that people of color attain visible and important positions in society that challenge traditional views of where they "belong"; and it demands that whites recognize the holders of such positions as people of color. Such use of race [will] help remove the effects of past discrimination. Yet it is not "remedial" in the sense used by the Court; it is not a response to discrete discriminatory acts. Rather, it attempts to attack the underlying structure of thought that supports inequality and that allows society to define discrimination in a way guaranteed to ensure no material change in the lives of black people.

See also Gotanda, A Critique of "Our Constitution is Color-Blind," 44 Stan. L. Rev. 1, 18-19 (1991):

> In everyday American life, [color-blind] nonrecognition is self-contradictory because it is impossible not think about a subject without having first thought about it at least a little. Nonrecognition differs from nonperception. Compare color-blind nonrecognition with medical color-blindness. A medically color-blind person is someone who cannot see what others can. [To] be racially color-blind, on the other hand, is to ignore what one has already noticed. [This] is not just a semantic distinction. The characteristics of race that are noticed (before being ignored) are situated within an already existing understanding of race. That is, race carries with it a complex social meaning. . . .
>
> This pre-existing race consciousness makes it impossible for an individual to be truly nonconscious of race. To argue that one did not *really* consider the race of an African-American is to concede that there was an identification of Blackness. Suppressing the recognition of a racial classification in order to act as if a person were not of some cognizable racial class is inherently racially premised.

Page 638. Before section 3 of the Note, add the following:

For an argument that racist attitudes remain pervasive in our culture and that affirmative action is necessary to counteract current, rather than merely historical racism, see Aleinikoff, The Constitution in Context: The Continuing Significance of Racism, 63 U. Col. L. Rev. 325 (1992).

Page 645. Before subsection 2b of the Note, add the following:

Consider the following critique of the "role model" argument in Delgado, Affirmative Action as a Majoritarian Device: Or, Do You Really Want to Be a Role Model?, 89 Mich. L. Rev. 1222, 1228 (1991):

The job of role model requires that you *lie* — that you tell not little, but big, whopping lies, and that is bad for your soul. Suppose I am sent to an inner city school to talk to kids and serve as role model of the month. I am *expected* to tell the kids that if they study hard and stay out of trouble, they can become a law professor like me. That, however, is a very big lie: a whopper.

4. *Race-Specific Classifications That Benefit Racial Minorities*

Page 675. At the end of section 5 of the Note, add the following:

Consider Chang, Discriminatory Impact, Affirmative Action, and Innocent Victims: Judicial Conservatism or Conservative Justices?, 91 Colum. L. Rev. 790, 790-793 (1991):

Imagine a white person. He is of moderate means, attended suburban schools, and has worked hard to become a police officer. Today he is unemployed, however, because the government, his employer, has adopted an affirmative action program. Suffering from a governmental choice to cure the lingering effects of historic injustices, he is an "innocent victim" of the racial discrimination pervasive in America's past. He believes this is unfair. He hopes it is unconstitutional.

Now imagine a black person. He is poor, attended inner city schools, and has worked hard because he wants to become a police officer. He will not achieve this goal, however, because he cannot pass the government's qualifying test. Suffering from a governmental choice not to address the lingering effects of historic injustices, he, also, is an "innocent victim" of racial discrimination in America's past. He believes this is unfair. He hopes it is unconstitutional.

In [*Wygant*], the Supreme Court determined that the harmful effects suffered by whites from government policies designed to serve the *permissible purpose* of redressing the continuing effects of past racial discrimination are constitutionally significant inequalities that can be justified only by "compelling" state interests. In Washington v. Davis, however, the Court determined that the harmful effects disproportionately suffered by blacks from government policies designed to serve a *permissible purpose*, but which reinforced the effects of past racial discrimination, have no such constitutional significance, but are matters of equity fully within legislative discretion. . . .

[A] principled judicial conservative should enforce the same values when scrutinizing claims of unconstitutional racial discrimination by either facially neutral laws or affirmative action programs: in both contexts, the challenged regulation should be invalidated only upon a finding that it was adopted for purposes that are constitutionally prohibited — specifically, purposes reflecting racial prejudice.

D. EQUAL PROTECTION METHODOLOGY: HEIGHTENED SCRUTINY AND THE PROBLEM OF GENDER

3. *Archaic and Overbroad Generalizations versus Real Differences*

Page 700. Before section 3 of the Note, add the following:

Does society's failure to protect adolescents from the negative consequences of unwanted pregnancies itself constitute an equal protection violation? Consider Colker, An Equal Protection Analysis of United States Reproductive Health Policy: Gender, Race, Age, and Class, 1991 Duke L.J. 324:

> Because of the extensive record of society coercing pregnant adolescents to undergo childbirth, despite the dramatic negative consequences of such childbirth on the lives of pregnant adolescents as well as her future offspring, this group is deserving of treatment as a "suspect class." Moreover, their political powerlessness, as evidenced by their legal inability to vote and their low voting turnout when they can vote, contributes to their entitlement.

Page 707. Before Section 4, add the following:

Consider MacKinnon, Reflections on Sex Equality under Law, 100 Yale L.J. 1281, 1298-1301 (1991):

> The inequality of women to men deserves a theory of its own. The status of women resembles other bases for inequality, but, like every inequality, is also particular and unique. . . .
>
> Existing legal templates utterly fail to capture the particular way in which the legal system organizes its participation in the subordination of women. [Facial] sex classifications may be relatively peripheral to women's inequality, including by law. . . .
>
> Law actively engages in sex inequality by apparently prohibiting abuses it largely permits, like rape, and by hiding the deprivations it imposes beneath ostensibly gender-neutral terms, like abortion. [Most] of the sexual assaults women experience do not fit the legal model of the ideal violation. Most rapes are by familiars not strangers, by members of one's own ethnic group not others, at home not on the street. [The] law of rape is designed so that rape is what somebody else does and what almost never happens: so that what is done all the time, presumably including by those who design and interpret and enforce the laws, can be done.
>
> Similarly, when convenient to do away with the consequences of sexual intercourse (meaning children), women get abortion rights. Women can have abortions so men can have sex. When not convenient, and for those men who seek to control women through controlling their children instead of through controlling their ability to have them, and for those women (such as women of color) for whom more drastic means are deemed convenient,

women are deprived of procreative choice through sterilization abuse the law either actively promotes or fails to recognize or redress, forced obstetrical interventions the law permits, fetal rights the law defines against women's rights, and criminalized and underfunded and bureaucratically burdened abortions the law deems adequate. In this light, the theme of the laws of sexual assault and reproduction is male control of, access to, and use of women.

4. *Benign Gender Classifications and Discrimination against Men*

Page 716. Before section 2 of the Note, add the following:

Professor Klarman has argued that the Burger Court shifted equal protection analysis from a focus on egalitarian results to emphasis on cleansing the legislative process from improper considerations. See Klarman, An Interpretive History of Modern Equal Protection, 90 Mich. L. Rev. 213, 284 (1991). Does this altered focus explain the Court's decisions concerning statutes that discriminate against men? Consider id., at 308:

> A legislative inputs focus justifies these decisions without requiring one to subscribe to special judicial solicitude for males. All of the laws [invalidated by the Court] were grounded in conventional gender stereotypes — respectively, that nursing is a female profession, that women are financially dependent upon their husbands, and that young females are less aggressive and more responsible than their male counterparts. These statutes, then, as the products of legislative decisionmaking contaminated by stereotypical thinking, were constitutionally objectionable on a legislative inputs understanding of equal protection. . . .
>
> [The] thought processes of the enacting legislature were dispositive. [Whether] women were ostensibly benefited, harmed, or some of each was of no moment.

5. *The Equal Rights Amendment*

Page 718. Before Section E, add the following:

Is male domination built into the structure of the Constitution? Consider Becker, The Politics of Women's Wrongs and the Bill of "Rights": A Bicentennial Perspective, 59 U. Chi. L. Rev. 453, 456 (1992):

> The Bill of Rights incorporates a private-public split with only negative rights under a limited government. As a result, women's activities and concerns — from economic rights to religion — seem beyond the proper scope of government. That women are poorer than, and subordinate to, men appears "natural" and pre-political. . . .
>
> Any [written set of cryptic, abstract, and negative rights enforced by judges] will better protect the powerful against government action harmful to their interests than the less powerful, who need protection against the powerful as

> well as against the government. [The] less powerful need many concrete, positive rights. These rights require detailed implementation schemes and the expenditure of funds. Judges are not likely to order either when enforcing abstract clauses.

E. EQUAL PROTECTION METHODOLOGY: OTHER CANDIDATES FOR HEIGHTENED SCRUTINY

1. *Alienage*

Page 719. In the third full paragraph, correct the title of the Lopez article to read:

Undocumented Mexican Migration: In Search of a Just Immigration Law and Policy.

Page 727. At the end of the second line on the page, add the following:

For an intriguing history of alien voting and an argument that "state enfranchisement of noncitizens is neither forbidden by the Constitution, as is commonly assumed, nor compelled by it," see Raskin, Legal Aliens, Local Citizens: The Historical, Constitutional and Theoretical Meanings of Alien Suffrage, 141 U. Pa. L. Rev. 1391 (1993).

Page 754, line 23. After the citation to Vance v. Bradley, add the following:

Gregory v. Ashcroft, 111 S. Ct. 2395 (1991) (utilizing rational basis review to uphold state constitutional provision requiring judges to retire at age 70).

Page 757. At the end of the Note, add the following:

Consider G. Spann, Race against the Court: The Supreme Court and Minorities in Contemporary America 2-3 (1993):

> There is a fundamental flaw in any model of judicial review that posits the Court as a check on majoritarian excesses. The viability of such a model depends upon a qualitative distinction between the way in which the Court ascertains the contours of minority rights and the way in which minority interests are assimilated into the political process. However, the constraints within which the Supreme Court is required to operate make it vulnerable to the same political considerations that govern majoritarian responses to minority interests. [Indeed], far from serving the countermajoritarian function envisioned by the traditional model of judicial review, the Supreme Court is

better understood as serving the veiled majoritarian function of promoting popular preferences at the expense of minority interests. So viewed, the gesture of judicial review becomes simply a less-immediate form of majoritarianism. The only significant difference that exists between political and judicial dispositions of minority interests is that judicial majoritarianism functions with undetected effectiveness precisely because it transpires behind the veil of judicial review.

Chapter Six

Implied Fundamental Rights

A. INTRODUCTION

Page 762. At the end of the first paragraph of section 4 of the Note, add the following:

For additional historical evidence on the original understanding of the relevance of original intent, see Baade, "Original Intent" in Historical Perspective: Some Critical Glosses, 69 Tex. L. Rev. 1001 (1991).

Page 765. Before section 6 of the Note, add the following:

C. Sunstein, The Partial Constitution (1993) argues that the constitutional commitment to "deliberative democracy" should be the source of interpretative principles; this approach has a clear connection to Ely's.

Page 768. At the end of section 6 of the Note, add the following:

Kaplin, The Process of Constitutional Interpretation: A Synthesis of the Present and a Guide to the Future, 42 Rutgers L. Rev. 983 (1990). See also the important discussion of the role of the Court as an exemplar of public reason in J. Rawls, Political Liberalism (1993).

B. THE PRIVILEGES OR IMMUNITIES CLAUSE

Page 777. Before section 4 of the Note, add the following:

e. Amar, The Bill of Rights and the Fourteenth Amendment, 101 Yale L.J. 1193 (1992), argues for "refined incorporation":

> *[A]ll* of the privileges and immunities of citizens recognized in the Bill of Rights became applicable against states by dint of the Fourteenth Amendment. But not all of the provisions of the original Bill of Rights were indeed rights of citizens. Some instead were at least in part rights of states, and as

such, awkward to incorporate fully *against* states. . . . Brennan posed the wrong question: Is a given provision of the original Bill of Rights really a *fundamental* right? The right question is whether the provision really guarantees a privilege or immunity of individual citizens rather than a right of states or the public at large.

D. SUBSTANTIVE DUE PROCESS: THE PROTECTION OF ECONOMIC INTERESTS AND THE PROBLEM OF "REDISTRIBUTION"

Page 802. Before the Note, add the following:

See C. Sunstein, The Partial Constitution (1993) for a general elaboration of this view and for many applications.

Page 807. Before "Note: The End of An Era," add the following:

For a general discussion of the action/inaction issue, and related issues, see C. Sunstein, The Partial Constitution (1993).

Page 813. Before section 4 of the Note, add the following:

But see Elhauge, Does Interest Group Theory Justify More Intrusive Judicial Review?, 101 Yale L.J. 31 (1991). Elhauge offers a number of arguments in favor of a negative answer to the conclusion posed in his title. He argues:

> What interest group theory does identify are the factors that make certain groups more willing than others to expend resources on petitioning for governmental action. However, identifying those factors cannot alone demonstrate which groups' petitioning efforts are *normatively* disproportionate. Such a normative conclusion is only possible if we have some baseline for determining what level of petitioning activity is normatively proportional to each group's interest. Interest group theory does not itself provide such a normative baseline. Rather, implicit normative baselines are adopted, usually without any discussion, when analysis draws normative implications from the degree of political influence predicted by interest group theory.

Elhauge also claims that "interest group theory does not establish . . . that the litigation process is, overall, less defective than the political process" and that "more intrusive judicial review would have several adverse effects on the transaction costs of legal change."

E. FUNDAMENTAL INTERESTS AND THE EQUAL PROTECTION CLAUSE

1. Voting

Page 855. Before section C, add the following:

SHAW v. RENO
113 S. Ct. — (1993)

JUSTICE O'CONNOR delivered the opinion of the Court.

This case involves two of the most complex and sensitive issues this Court has faced in recent years: the meaning of the constitutional "right" to vote, and the propriety of race-based state legislation designed to benefit members of historically disadvantaged racial minority groups. As a result of the 1990 census, North Carolina became entitled to a twelfth seat in the United States House of Representatives. The General Assembly enacted a reapportionment plan that included one majority-black congressional district. . . . Appellants allege that the revised plan, which contains district boundary lines of dramatically irregular shape, constitutes an unconstitutional racial gerrymander. The question before us is whether appellants have stated a cognizable claim.

I

The voting age population of North Carolina is approximately 78% white, 20% black, and 1% Native American; the remaining 1% is predominantly Asian. The black population is relatively dispersed; blacks constitute a majority of the general population in only 5 of the State's 100 counties. Geographically, the State divides into three regions: the eastern Coastal Plain, the central Piedmont Plateau, and the western mountains. The largest concentrations of black citizens live in the Coastal Plain, primarily in the northern part. The General Assembly's first redistricting plan contained one majority-black district centered in that area of the State.

Forty of North Carolina's one hundred counties are covered by section 5 of the Voting Rights Act of 1965, which prohibits a jurisdiction subject to its provisions from implementing changes in a "standard, practice, or procedure with respect to voting" without federal authorization. The jurisdiction must obtain either a judgment from the United States District Court for the District of Columbia declaring that the proposed change "does not have the purpose and will not have the effect of denying or abridging the right to vote on account of race or color" or administrative preclearance from the Attorney General.

[The] first of the two majority-black districts contained in the revised plan, District 1, is somewhat hook shaped. Centered in the northeast portion of the State, it moves southward until it tapers to a narrow band; then, with finger-like extensions, it reaches far into the southern-most part of the State near the South Carolina border. District 1 has been compared to a "Rorschach ink-blot test," Shaw v. Barr, 808 F. Supp. 461, 476 (EDNC 1992) (Voorhees, C. J., concurring in part and dissenting in part), and a "bug splattered on a windshield," Wall Street Journal, Feb. 4, 1992, p. A14.

The second majority-black district, District 12, is even more unusually shaped. It is approximately 160 miles long and, for much of its length, no wider than the I-85 corridor. It winds in snake-like fashion through tobacco country, financial centers, and manufacturing areas "until it gobbles in enough enclaves of black neighborhoods." . . .

II

A

"The right to vote freely for the candidate of one's choice is of the essence of a democratic society. . . ." For much of our Nation's history, that right sadly has been denied to many because of race. . . . Ostensibly race-neutral devices such as literacy tests with "grandfather" clauses and "good character" provisos were devised to deprive black voters of the franchise. Another of the weapons in the States' arsenal was the racial gerrymander — "the deliberate and arbitrary distortion of district boundaries . . . for [racial] purposes." . . . In some States, registration of eligible black voters ran 50% behind that of whites. Congress enacted the Voting Rights Act of 1965 as a dramatic and severe response to the situation.

But it soon became apparent that guaranteeing equal access to the polls would not suffice to root out other racially discriminatory voting practices. Drawing on the "one person, one vote" principle, this Court recognized that "the right to vote can be affected by a dilution of voting power as well as by an absolute prohibition on casting a ballot." . . . Congress, too, responded to the problem of vote dilution. In 1982, it amended the Voting Rights Act to prohibit legislation that results in the dilution of a minority group's voting strength, regardless of the legislature's intent.

An understanding of the nature of appellants' claim is critical to our resolution of the case. In their complaint, appellants did not claim that the General Assembly's reapportionment plan unconstitutionally "diluted" white voting strength. They did not even claim to be white. Rather, appellants' complaint alleged that the deliberate segregation of voters into separate districts on the basis of race violated their constitutional right to participate in a "color-blind" electoral process.

Despite their invocation of the ideal of a "color-blind" Constitution, see Plessy v. Ferguson, 163 U.S. 537, 559 (1896) (Harlan, J., dissenting), appellants appear to concede that race-conscious redistricting is not always unconstitutional. That concession is wise: This Court never has held that race-conscious state decisionmaking is impermissible in all circumstances. What appellants object to is redistricting legislation that is so extremely irregular on its face that it rationally can be viewed only as an effort to segregate the races for purposes of voting, without regard for traditional districting principles and without sufficiently compelling justification. For the reasons that follow, we conclude that appellants have stated a claim upon which relief can be granted under the Equal Protection Clause. . . .

III

A

Classifications of citizens solely on the basis of race "are by their very nature odious to a free people whose institutions are founded upon the doctrine of equality." Hirabayashi v. United States, 320 U.S. 81, 100 (1943). They threaten to stigmatize individuals by reason of their membership in a racial group and to incite racial hostility. Accordingly, we have held that the Fourteenth Amendment requires state legislation that expressly distinguishes among citizens because of their race to be narrowly tailored to further a compelling governmental interest.

These principles apply not only to legislation that contains explicit racial distinctions, but also to those "rare" statutes that, although race-neutral, are, on their face, "unexplainable on grounds other than race."

Appellants contend that redistricting legislation that is so bizarre on its face that it is "unexplainable on grounds other than race," demands the same close scrutiny that we give other state laws that classify citizens by race. Our voting rights precedents support that conclusion. . . .

The difficulty of proof, of course, does not mean that a racial gerrymander, once established, should receive less scrutiny under the Equal Protection Clause than other state legislation classifying citizens by race. Moreover, it seems clear to us that proof sometimes will not be difficult at all. In some exceptional cases, a reapportionment plan may be so highly irregular that, on its face, it rationally cannot be understood as anything other than an effort to "segregate . . . voters" on the basis of race. Gomillion, in which a tortured municipal boundary line was drawn to exclude black voters, was such a case. So, too, would be a case in which a State concentrated a dispersed minority population in a single district by disregarding traditional districting principles such as compactness, contiguity, and respect for political subdivisions. We emphasize that these criteria are important not because they are constitutionally required — they are not — but because they are objective factors that may serve to defeat a claim that a district has been gerrymandered on racial lines.

Put differently, we believe that reapportionment is one area in which appearances do matter. A reapportionment plan that includes in one district individuals who belong to the same race, but who are otherwise widely separated by geographical and political boundaries, and who may have little in common with one another but the color of their skin, bears an uncomfortable resemblance to political apartheid. It reinforces the perception that members of the same racial group — regardless of their age, education, economic status, or the community in which they live — think alike, share the same political interests, and will prefer the same candidates at the polls. We have rejected such perceptions elsewhere as impermissible racial stereotypes. By perpetuating such notions, a racial gerrymander may exacerbate the very patterns of racial bloc voting that majority-minority districting is sometimes said to counteract.

The message that such districting sends to elected representatives is equally pernicious. When a district obviously is created solely to effectuate the perceived common interests of one racial group, elected officials are more likely to believe that their primary obligation is to represent only the members of that group, rather than their constituency as a whole. This is altogether antithetical to our system of representative democracy. . . .

For these reasons, we conclude that a plaintiff challenging a reapportionment statute under the Equal Protection Clause may state a claim by alleging that the legislation, though race-neutral on its face, rationally cannot be understood as anything other than an effort to separate voters into different districts on the basis of race, and that the separation lacks sufficient justification. It is unnecessary for us to decide whether or how a reapportionment plan that, on its face, can be explained in nonracial terms successfully could be challenged. Thus, we express no view as to whether "the intentional creation of majority-minority districts, without more" always gives rise to an equal protection claim. We hold only that, on the facts of this case, plaintiffs have stated a claim sufficient to defeat the state appellees' motion to dismiss.

C

The dissenters consider the circumstances of this case "functionally indistinguishable" from multimember districting and at-large voting systems, which are loosely described as "other varieties of gerrymandering." We have considered the constitutionality of these practices in other Fourteenth Amendment cases and have required plaintiffs to demonstrate that the challenged practice has the purpose and effect of diluting a racial group's voting strength. At-large and multimember schemes, however, do not classify voters on the basis of race. Classifying citizens by race, as we have said, threatens special harms that are not present in our vote-dilution cases. It therefore warrants different analysis. . . .

Finally, nothing in the Court's highly fractured decision in UJO — on which the District Court almost exclusively relied, and which the dissenters evidently believe controls, forecloses the claim we recognize today. UJO concerned New York's revision of a reapportionment plan to include additional majority-minority districts in response to the Attorney General's denial of administrative preclearance under section 5. In that regard, it closely resembles the present case. But the cases are critically different in another way. The plaintiffs in UJO — members of a Hasidic community split between two districts under New York's revised redistricting plan — did not allege that the plan, on its face, was so highly irregular that it rationally could be understood only as an effort to segregate voters by race. Indeed, the facts of the case would not have supported such a claim. . . . UJO's framework simply does not apply where, as here, a reapportionment plan is alleged to be so irrational on its face that it immediately offends principles of racial equality.

IV

JUSTICE SOUTER contends that exacting scrutiny of racial gerrymanders under the Fourteenth Amendment is inappropriate because reapportionment "nearly always requires some consideration of race for legitimate reasons." JUSTICE SOUTER'S reasoning is flawed. . . .

That racial bloc voting or minority political cohesion may be found to exist in some cases, of course, is no reason to treat all racial gerrymanders differently from other kinds of racial classification. Justice Souter apparently views racial gerrymandering of the type presented here as a special category of "benign" racial discrimination that should be subject to relaxed judicial review. As we have said, however, the very reason that the Equal Protection Clause demands strict scrutiny of all racial classifications is because without it, a court cannot determine whether or not the discrimination truly is "benign." Thus, if appellants' allegations of a racial gerrymander are not contradicted on remand, the District Court must determine whether the General Assembly's reapportionment plan satisfies strict scrutiny. We therefore consider what that level of scrutiny requires in the reapportionment context.

The state appellees suggest that a covered jurisdiction may have a compelling interest in creating majority-minority districts in order to comply with the Voting Rights Act. The States certainly have a very strong interest in complying with federal antidiscrimination laws that are constitutionally valid as interpreted and as applied. But in the context of a Fourteenth Amendment challenge, courts must bear in mind the difference between what the law permits, and what it requires.

For example, on remand North Carolina might claim that it adopted the revised plan in order to comply with the "nonretrogression" principle. Under that principle, a proposed voting change cannot be precleared if it will lead to "a retrogression in the position of racial minorities with respect to their effective exercise of the electoral franchise." Beer v. United States, 425 U.S. 130, 141 (1976). In *Beer*, we held that a reapportionment plan that created one majority-minority district where none existed before passed muster under section 5 because it improved the position of racial minorities.

Although the Court concluded that the redistricting scheme at issue in *Beer* was nonretrogressive, it did not hold that the plan, for that reason, was immune from constitutional challenge. The Court expressly declined to reach that question. [Thus], we do not read *Beer* or any of our other cases to give covered jurisdictions carte blanche to engage in racial gerrymandering in the name of nonretrogression. [Before] us, the state appellees contend that the General Assembly's revised plan was necessary not to prevent retrogression, but to avoid dilution of black voting strength in violation of section 2. [Appellants] maintain that the General Assembly's revised plan could not have been required by section 2. They contend that the State's black population is too dispersed to support two geographically compact majority-black districts, as the bizarre shape of District 12 demonstrates, and that there is no evidence of black political cohesion. They also contend that recent black electoral successes demonstrate the willingness of white voters in North Carolina to vote for black candidates. [These] arguments were not developed below, and the issues remain open for consideration on remand.

The state appellees alternatively argue that the General Assembly's plan advanced a compelling interest entirely distinct from the Voting Rights Act. We previously have recognized a significant state interest in eradicating the effects of past racial discrimination. But the State must have a "strong basis in evidence for [concluding] that remedial action [is] necessary." The state appellees submit that two pieces of evidence gave the General Assembly a strong basis for believing that remedial action was warranted here: the Attorney General's imposition of the section 5 preclearance requirement on 40 North Carolina counties, and the [District] Court's findings of a long history of official racial discrimination in North Carolina's political system and of pervasive racial bloc voting. The state appellees assert that the deliberate creation of majority-minority districts is the most precise way — indeed the only effective way — to overcome the effects of racially polarized voting. This question also need not be decided at this stage of the litigation. We note, however, that only three Justices in UJO were prepared to say that States have a significant interest in minimizing the consequences of racial bloc voting apart from the requirements of the Voting Rights Act. And those three Justices specifically concluded that race-based districting, as a response to racially polarized voting, is constitutionally permissible only when the State "employs sound districting principles," and only when the affected racial group's "residential patterns afford the opportunity of creating districts in which they will be in the majority." 430 U.S., at 167-168 (opinion of WHITE, J., joined by STEVENS and REHNQUIST, JJ.).

Racial classifications of any sort pose the risk of lasting harm to our society. They reinforce the belief, held by too many for too much of our history, that individuals should be judged by the color of their skin. Racial classifications with respect to voting carry particular dangers. Racial gerrymandering, even for remedial purposes, may balkanize us into competing racial factions; it threatens to carry us further from the goal of a political system in which race no longer matters — a goal that the Fourteenth and Fifteenth Amendments embody, and to which the Nation continues to aspire. It is for these reasons that race-based districting by our state legislatures demands close judicial scrutiny.

In this case, the Attorney General suggested that North Carolina could have created a reasonably compact second majority-minority district in the south-central to southeastern part of the State. We express no view as to whether appellants successfully could have challenged such a district under the Fourteenth Amendment. We also do not decide whether appellants' complaint stated a claim under constitutional provisions other than the Fourteenth Amendment. Today we hold only that appellants have stated a claim under the Equal Protection Clause by alleging that the North Carolina General Assembly adopted a reapportionment scheme so irrational on its face that it can be understood only as an effort to segregate voters into separate voting districts because of their race, and that the separation lacks sufficient justification. If the allegation of racial gerrymandering remains uncontradicted, the District Court further must determine whether the North Carolina plan is narrowly tailored to further a compelling governmental interest. Accordingly, we reverse the judgment of the District Court and remand the case for further proceedings consistent with this opinion.

It is so ordered.

JUSTICE WHITE, with whom JUSTICE BLACKMUN and JUSTICE STEVENS join, dissenting.

The facts of this case mirror those presented in United Jewish Organizations of Williamsburgh, Inc. v. Carey, 430 U.S. 144 (1977) (UJO), where the Court rejected a claim that creation of a majority-minority district violated the Constitution, either as a per se matter or in light of the circumstances leading to the creation of such a district. . . . On the same reasoning, I would affirm the district court's dismissal of appellants' claim in this instance.

The grounds for my disagreement with the majority are simply stated: Appellants have not presented a cognizable claim, because they have not alleged a cognizable injury. To date, we have held that only two types of state voting practices could give rise to a constitutional claim. The first involves direct and outright deprivation of the right to vote, for example by means of a poll tax or literacy test. See, e.g., Guinn v. United States, 238 U.S. 347 (1915). Plainly, this variety is not implicated by appellants' allegations and need not detain us further. The second type of unconstitutional practice is that which "affects the political strength of various groups," Mobile v. Bolden, 446 U.S. 55, 83 (1980) (STEVENS, J., concurring in judgment), in violation of the Equal Protection Clause. As for this latter category, we have insisted that members of the political or racial group demonstrate that the challenged action have the intent and effect of unduly diminishing their influence on the political process. Although this severe burden has limited the number of successful suits, it was adopted for sound reasons.

The central explanation has to do with the nature of the redistricting process. As the majority recognizes, "redistricting differs from other kinds of state decisionmaking in that the legislature always is aware of race when it draws district lines, just as it is aware of age, economic status, religious and political persuasion, and a variety of other demographic factors." "Being aware," in this context, is shorthand for "taking into account," and it hardly can be doubted that legislators routinely engage in the business of making electoral predictions based on group characteristics — racial, ethnic, and the like. . . .

Redistricting plans also reflect group interests and inevitably are conceived with partisan aims in mind. To allow judicial interference whenever this occurs would be to invite constant and unmanageable intrusion. Moreover, a group's power to affect the political process does not automatically dissipate by virtue of an electoral loss. Accordingly, we have asked that an identifiable group demonstrate more than mere lack of success at the polls to make out a successful gerrymandering claim.

With these considerations in mind, we have limited such claims by insisting upon a showing that "the political processes . . . were not equally open to participation by the group in question — that its members had less opportunity than did other residents in the district to participate in the political processes and to elect legislators of their choice."

To distinguish a claim that alleges that the redistricting scheme has discriminatory intent and effect from one that does not has nothing to do with dividing racial classifications between the "benign" and the malicious — an enterprise which, as the majority notes, the Court has treated with skepticism. Rather, the issue is whether the classification based on race discriminates against anyone by denying equal access to the political process.

The majority attempts to distinguish UJO by imagining a heretofore unknown type of constitutional claim. In its words, "UJO set forth a standard under which white voters can establish unconstitutional vote dilution. . . . Nothing in the decision precludes white voters (or voters of any other race) from bringing the analytically distinct claim that a reapportionment plan rationally cannot be understood as anything other than an effort to segregate citizens into separate voting districts on the basis of race without sufficient justification." There is no support for this distinction in UJO, and no authority in the cases relied on by the Court either. More importantly, the majority's submission does not withstand analysis. The logic of its theory appears to be that race-conscious redistricting that "segregates" by drawing odd-shaped lines is qualitatively different from race-conscious redistricting that affects groups in some other way. The distinction is without foundation.

Lacking support in any of the Court's precedents, the majority's novel type of claim also makes no sense. As I understand the theory that is put forth, a redistricting plan that uses race to "segregate" voters by drawing "uncouth" lines is harmful in a way that a plan that uses race to distribute voters differently is not, for the former "bears an uncomfortable resemblance to political apartheid." While district irregularities may provide strong indicia of a potential gerrymander, they do no more than that. In particular, they have no bearing on whether the plan ultimately is found to violate the Constitution. Given two districts drawn on similar, race-based grounds, the one does not become more injurious than the other simply by virtue of being snake-like, at least so far as the Constitution is concerned and absent any evidence of differential racial impact. . . .

When, as is the case here, the creation of a majority-minority district does not unfairly minimize the voting power of any other group, the Constitution does not justify, much less mandate, such obstruction.

JUSTICE STEVENS, dissenting.

For the reasons stated by JUSTICE WHITE, the decision of the District Court should be affirmed. I add these comments to emphasize that the two critical facts in this case are undisputed: first, the shape of District 12 is so bizarre that it must have been drawn for the purpose of either advantaging or disadvantaging a cognizable group of voters; and, second, regardless of that shape, it was drawn for the purpose of facilitating the election of a second black representative from North Carolina.

These unarguable facts, which the Court devotes most of its opinion to proving, give rise to three constitutional questions: Does the Constitution impose a requirement of contiguity or compactness on how the States may draw their electoral districts? Does the Equal Protection Clause prevent a State from drawing district boundaries for the purpose of facilitating the election of a member of an identifiable group of voters? And, finally, if the answer to the second question is generally "No," should it be different when the favored group is defined by race?

The first question is easy. There is no independent constitutional requirement of compactness or contiguity. The existence of bizarre and uncouth district boundaries is powerful evidence of an ulterior purpose behind the shaping of those boundaries — usually a purpose to advantage the political party in control of the districting process. Such evidence will always be useful in cases that lack other evidence of invidious intent. In this case, however, we know what the legislators' purpose was: The North Carolina Legislature drew District 12 to include a majority of African-American voters. Evidence of the district's shape is therefore convincing, but it is also cumulative, and, for our purposes, irrelevant.

As for the second question, I believe that the Equal Protection Clause is violated when the State creates the kind of uncouth district boundaries, for the sole purpose of making it more difficult for members of a minority group to win an election. The duty to govern impartially is abused when a group with power over the electoral process defines electoral boundaries solely to enhance its own political strength at the expense of any weaker group. That duty, however, is not violated when the majority acts to facilitate the election of a member of a group that lacks such power because it remains underrepresented in the state legislature — whether that group is defined by political affiliation, by common economic interests, or by religious, ethnic, or racial characteristics. The difference between constitutional and unconstitutional gerrymanders has nothing to do with whether they are based on assumptions about the groups they affect, but whether their purpose is to enhance the power of the group in control of the districting process at the expense of any minority group, and thereby to strengthen the unequal distribution of electoral power. When an assumption that people in particular a minority group (whether they are defined by the political party, religion, ethnic group, or race to which they belong) will vote in a particular way is used to benefit that group, no constitutional violation occurs. Politicians have always relied on assumptions that people in particular groups are likely to vote in a particular way when they draw new district lines, and I cannot believe that anything in today's opinion will stop them from doing so in the future.

Finally, we must ask whether otherwise permissible redistricting to benefit an underrepresented minority group becomes impermissible when the minority group is defined by its race. The Court today answers this question in the affirmative, and its answer is wrong. If it is permissible to draw boundaries to provide adequate representation for rural voters, for union members, for Hasidic Jews, for Polish Americans, or for Republicans, it necessarily follows that it is permissible to do the same thing for members of the very minority group whose history in the United States gave birth to the Equal Protection Clause.

JUSTICE SOUTER, dissenting.

[In] districting, the mere placement of an individual in one district instead of another denies no one a right or benefit provided to others. All citizens may register, vote, and be represented. In whatever district, the individual voter has a right to vote in each election, and the election will result in the voter's representation. . . .

There is thus no theoretical inconsistency in having two distinct approaches to equal protection analysis, one for cases of electoral districting and one for most other types of state governmental decisions. Nor, because of the distinctions between the two categories, is there any risk that Fourteenth Amendment districting law as such will be taken to imply anything for purposes of general Fourteenth Amendment scrutiny about "benign" racial discrimination, or about group entitlement as distinct from individual protection, or about the appropriateness of strict or other heightened scrutiny.

The Court offers no adequate justification for treating the narrow category of bizarrely shaped district claims differently from other districting claims. The only justification I can imagine would be the preservation of "sound districting principles," such as compactness and contiguity. But as JUSTICE WHITE points out, and as the Court acknowledges, we have held that such principles are not constitutionally required, with the consequence that their absence cannot justify the distinct constitutional regime put in place by the Court today. Since there is no justification for the departure here from the principles that continue to govern electoral districting cases generally in accordance with our prior decisions, I would not respond to the seeming egregiousness of the redistricting now before us by untethering the concept of racial gerrymander in such a case from the concept of harm exemplified by dilution.

In the absence of an allegation of such harm, I would affirm the judgment of the District Court. I respectfully dissent.

4. Welfare

Page 889. Before subsection 5, add the following:

8. The Court rejected a claim to governmental protection in Collins v. Texas, 112 S. Ct. 1061 (1992). Larry Collins, a municipal employee, died of asphyxia after entering a manhole to unstop a sewer line. His widow brought suit, claiming that her husband had a constitutional right to be free from unreasonable risks of harm, or at least to be protected from deliberate official indifference to employee safety. The Court concluded that the Constitution had not been violated, at least in the absence of an allegation of deliberate harm, or of willful violation of rights.

"Neither the text nor the history of the Due Process Clause supports petitioner's claim that the governmental employer's duty to provide its employees with a safe working environment is a substantive component of the Due Process Clause." Relying on the *DeShaney* case (see p. 1601) and the action/inaction distinction, the Court found "unprecedented" the suggestion that there is "a federal constitutional obligation to provide . . . employees with certain minimal levels of safety and security." Nor was a duty of training or warning implied by the Constitution. "Decisions concerning the allocation of resources to individual programs, such as sewer maintenance, and to particular aspects of those programs, such as the training and compensation of employees, involve a host of policy choices that must be made by locally elected representatives. . . ."

The *Collins* Court acknowledged that there might be a constitutional claim if the state had coerced a citizen by placing him in hazardous conditions — as, for example, if a facility in which a citizen confined for mental illness is not provided with "minimal custodial standards." What is the difference between such a case and *Collins* itself?

F. MODERN SUBSTANTIVE DUE PROCESS: PRIVACY, PERSONHOOD, AND FAMILY

2. Abortion

Page 932. Before section 4 of the Note, add the following:

For additional arguments to the effect that abortion restrictions should be seen as a form of sex discrimination, see MacKinnon, Reflections on Sex Equality Under Law, 100 Yale L.J. 1281, 1308-1324 (1991); Sunstein, Neutrality in Constitutional Law (with Special Reference to Pornography, Abortion, and Surrogacy), 92 Colum. L. Rev. 1 (1992).

For a detailed historical examination of abortion restrictions, with special reference to sex equality and equal protection, see Siegel, Reasoning from the Body: A Historical Perspective on Abortion Regulation and Questions of Equal Protection, 44 Stan. L. Rev. 261 (1992).

Page 936. At the end of section 6 of the Note, add the following:

Consider the following, suggested by Rosalind Hursthouse, Beginning Lives 189 (1987): Suppose that a dictatorial government has begun a program to exterminate its political opponents and their families. The government is a regional power, with influence over the governments of its neighbors. In some neighboring countries, however, a chain of "safe houses" was created to help refugees escape to neutral territory. Those who operate the safe houses risk arrest and, sometimes, execution if they are caught. Suppose that you buy a house that you know was used as a safe house in previous years. When it was used that way, the signal that a refugee could enter the house was that a specific window was left open. The house has not been used as a safe house for several years. The first summer you own it, you keep the signal window closed just in case, but you do not hear of any refugees trying to get through the area during the following year. By the second summer, the possibility that a refugee would try to use the house (and the risk that would pose to you) seems small, so you open the windows when it is very hot. Suppose that, one night, a physician whose family had been arrested and killed climbs in the open window, interpreting it as a signal that the house is still used as a safe house. Would you act wrongly in expelling the physician from your house, knowing that to do so would imperil the physician and that not doing so would imperil you? Would you act (more) wrongly if, to expel her, you had to call for assistance from a cousin?

Hursthouse uses her version of this hypothetical as an analogy to abortion. How, if at all, does the hypothetical differ from abortion? For an exchange on the use of Hursthouse's original hypothetical in a prior edition of this Supplement, see Reconstruction (forthcoming).

Page 942. At the end of section 3 of the Note, add the following:

The Court extended *Maher* and *Harris* in Rust v. Sullivan, 111 S. Ct. 1759 (1991). In that case, the government refused to fund speech that involved abortion; the refusal was challenged on both first and fifth amendment grounds. The first amendment issues are discussed in Chapter 7 at section F-1, infra this Supplement. On the fifth amendment issue, the Court said:

> We recently reaffirmed the long-recognized principle that "the Due Process Clauses generally confer no affirmative right to governmental aid, even where such aid may be necessary to secure life, liberty, or property interests of which the government itself may not deprive the individual.'" *Webster,* quoting DeShaney v. Winnebago County Dept. of Social Services, 489 U.S. 189, 196 (1989). The Government has no constitutional duty to subsidize an activity merely because the activity is constitutionally protected and may validly choose to fund childbirth over abortion and "implement that judgment by the allocation of public funds'" for medical services relating to childbirth but not to those relating to abortion. The Government has no affirmative duty to "commit any resources to facilitating abortions," *Webster,* and its decision to fund childbirth but not abortion "places no governmental obstacle in the path of a woman who chooses to terminate her pregnancy, but rather, by means of unequal subsidization of abortion and other medical services, encourages alternative activity deemed in the public interest."
>
> That the regulations do not impermissibly burden a woman's Fifth Amendment rights is evident from the line of cases beginning with *Maher* and *McRae* and culminating in our most recent decision in *Webster.* Just as Congress' refusal to fund abortions in McRae left "an indigent woman with at least the same range of choice in deciding whether to obtain a medically necessary abortion as she would have had if Congress had chosen to subsidize no health care costs at all," 448 U.S., at 317, and "Missouri's refusal to allow public employees to perform abortions in public hospitals leaves a pregnant woman with the same choices as if the State had chosen not to operate any public hospitals," Congress' refusal to fund abortion counseling and advocacy leaves a pregnant woman with the same choices as if the government had chosen not to fund family-planning services at all. The difficulty that a woman encounters when a Title X project does not provide abortion counseling or referral leaves her in no different position than she would have been if the government had not enacted Title X.
>
> In *Webster* we stated that "[h]aving held that the State's refusal [in *Maher*] to fund abortions does not violate Roe v. Wade, it strains logic to reach a contrary result for the use of public facilities and employees." It similarly would strain logic, in light of the more extreme restrictions in those cases, to find that the mere decision to exclude abortion-related services from a federally funded pre-conceptual family planning program, is unconstitutional.
>
> Petitioners also argue that by impermissibly infringing on the doctor/patient relationship and depriving a Title X client of information concerning abortion as a method of family planning, the regulations violate a woman's Fifth Amendment right to medical self-determination and to make informed medical decisions free of government-imposed harm. They argue that under our decisions in Akron v. Akron Center for Reproductive Health, Inc., 462 U.S. 416 (1983), and Thornburg v. American College of Obstetricians and Gynecologists, 476 U.S. 747 (1986), the government cannot interfere with a

woman's right to make an informed and voluntary choice by placing restrictions on the patient/doctor dialogue.

In *Akron,* we invalidated a city ordinance requiring all physicians to make specified statements to the patient prior to performing an abortion in order to ensure that the woman's consent was "truly informed." 462 U.S., at 423. Similarly, in *Thornburg,* we struck down a state statute mandating that a list of agencies offering alternatives to abortion and a description of fetal development be provided to every woman considering terminating her pregnancy through an abortion. Critical to our decisions in *Akron* and *Thornburg* to invalidate a governmental intrusion into the patient/doctor dialogue was the fact that the laws in both cases required all doctors within their respective jurisdictions to provide all pregnant patients contemplating an abortion a litany of information, regardless of whether the patient sought the information or whether the doctor thought the information necessary to the patient's decision. Under the Secretary's regulations, however, a doctor's ability to provide, and a woman's right to receive, information concerning abortion and abortion-related services outside the context of the Title X project remains unfettered. It would undoubtedly be easier for a woman seeking an abortion if she could receive information about abortion from a Title X project, but the Constitution does not require that the Government distort the scope of its mandated program in order to provide that information.

Petitioners contend, however, that most Title X clients are effectively precluded by indigency and poverty from seeing a health care provider who will provide abortion-related services. But once again, even these Title X clients are in no worse position than if Congress had never enacted Title X. "The financial constraints that restrict an indigent woman's ability to enjoy the full range of constitutionally protected freedom of choice are the product not of governmental restrictions on access to abortion, but rather of her indigency." *McRae,* supra, at 316.

The current Court has been increasingly insistent on the proposition that the Constitution only protects "negative" rights. Indeed, this insistence is a hallmark of contemporary doctrine. But is the basic claim right? Consider the following view:

The Constitution creates several positive rights. The contracts clause protects a "positive" right — the right to available courts, to enforce contractual agreements. The eminent domain clause protects a positive right — the right to governmental help to protect private property from invasions by others, including private persons. (Consider whether it would be unconstitutional for the state to repeal its trespass laws. If it would, the fifth amendment creates a right to affirmative protection. But cf. Prunyard Shopping Center v. Robins p.1584 of the main text (state law requirement that shopping centers allow access to picketers not an unconstitutional taking). Even the due process clause creates a right to governmental assistance against public and private invasions. It is thus false to say that the Constitution is only about negative rights.

On this view, the current Court, in *Rust* and elsewhere, is simply relying on a common law baseline (the common law interests in property and contract), or on existing distributions of assets, in deciding what counts as positive and what as negative. It is not truly distinguishing between positive and negative rights at all. A right is characterized as negative if it is the sort of right recognized at common law, or if it is a right that someone enjoys in the world before the welfare state; it is otherwise characterized as positive. And this view in turn replicates the errors of the Lochner era; indeed, it is the precise modern analogue to Lochner; and it is poorly adapted to constitutionalism in the world of the welfare state. On this and related questions, see Strauss, Due Process, Government Inaction, and Private Wrongs, 1989 Supreme Court Review 53; Sunstein, Neutrality in Constitutional Law (with Special Reference to Pornography, Abortion, and Surrogacy), 92 Colum. L. Rev. 1 (1992).

Page 955. Before subsection 3, add the following:

Would the case for abortion rights be weakened if America provided stronger social supports for women with small children? Has abortion turned out to be America's odd response to the problem of unwanted pregnancy? Might compromise on this matter be possible if social supports were offered as a kind of quid pro quo for social or legal limits on abortion? For an intriguing comparative discussion, see M. Glendon, Abortion and Divorce in Western Law (1987). For a discussion of some of the facts relating to the abortion problem, see R. Posner, Sex and Reason 272-290 (1992).

PLANNED PARENTHOOD OF SOUTHEASTERN PENNSYLVANIA v. CASEY

112 S. Ct 2791 (1992)

JUSTICE O'CONNOR, JUSTICE KENNEDY, and JUSTICE SOUTER announced the judgment of the Court and delivered the opinion of the Court with respect to Parts I, II, III, V-A, V-C, and VI, an opinion with respect to Part V-E, in which JUSTICE STEVENS joins, and an opinion with respect to Parts IV, V-B, and V-D.

I

Liberty finds no refuge in a jurisprudence of doubt. Yet 19 years after our holding that the Constitution protects a woman's right to terminate her pregnancy in its early stages, that definition of liberty is still questioned. Joining the respondents as amicus curiae, the United States, as it has done in five other cases in the last decade, again asks us to overrule *Roe*.

At issue in these cases are five provisions of the Pennsylvania Abortion Control Act of 1982 as amended in 1988 and 1989. [The] Act requires that a woman seeking an abortion give her informed consent prior to the abortion procedure, and specifies that she be provided with certain information at least 24 hours before the abortion is performed. For a minor to obtain an abortion, the Act requires the informed consent of one of her parents, but provides for a judicial bypass option if the minor does not wish to or cannot obtain a parent's consent. Another provision of the Act requires that, unless certain exceptions apply, a married woman seeking an abortion must sign a statement indicating that she has notified her husband of her intended abortion. The Act exempts compliance with these three requirements in the event of a "medical emergency." [In] addition to the above provisions regulating the performance of abortions, the Act imposes certain reporting requirements on facilities that provide abortion services.

Before any of these provisions took effect, the petitioners, who are five abortion clinics and one physician representing himself as well as a class of physicians who provide abortion services, brought this suit seeking declaratory and injunctive relief. . . .

[At] oral argument in this Court, the attorney for the parties challenging the statute took the position that none of the enactments can be upheld without overruling Roe v. Wade. We disagree with that analysis; but we acknowledge that our decisions after *Roe* cast doubt upon the meaning and reach of its holding. Further, The Chief Justice admits that he would overrule the central holding of *Roe* and adopt the rational relationship test as the sole criterion of constitutionality. State and federal courts as well as legislatures throughout the Union must have guidance as they seek to address this subject in conformance with the Constitution. Given these premises, we find it imperative to review once more the principles that define the rights of the woman and the legitimate authority of the State respecting the termination of pregnancies by abortion procedures.

After considering the fundamental constitutional questions resolved by *Roe*, principles of institutional integrity, and the rule of stare decisis, we are led to conclude this: the essential holding of Roe v. Wade should be retained and once again reaffirmed.

It must be stated at the outset and with clarity that *Roe*'s essential holding, the holding we reaffirm, has three parts. First is a recognition of the right of the woman to choose to have an abortion before viability and to obtain it without undue interference from the State. Before viability, the State's interests are not strong enough to support a prohibition of abortion or the imposition of a substantial obstacle to the woman's effective right to elect the procedure. Second is a confirmation of the State's power to restrict abortions after fetal viability, if the law contains exceptions for pregnancies which endanger a woman's life or health. And third is the principle that the State has legitimate interests from the outset of the pregnancy in protecting the health of the woman and the life of the fetus that may become a child. These principles do not contradict one another; and we adhere to each.

II

Constitutional protection of the woman's decision to terminate her pregnancy derives from the Due Process Clause of the Fourteenth Amendment. It declares that no State shall "deprive any person of life, liberty, or property, without due process of law." The controlling word in the case before us is "liberty." Although a literal reading of the Clause might suggest that it governs only the procedures by which a State may deprive persons of liberty, for at least 105 years, at least since Mugler v. Kansas, 123 U.S. 623, 660-661 (1887), the Clause has been understood to contain a substantive component as well, one "barring certain government actions regardless of the fairness of the procedures used to implement them." Daniels v. Williams, 474 U.S. 327, 331 (1986). As Justice Brandeis (joined by Justice Holmes) observed, "despite arguments to the contrary which had seemed to me persuasive, it is settled that the due process clause of the Fourteenth Amendment applies to matters of substantive law as well as to matters of procedure. Thus all fundamental rights comprised within the term liberty are protected by the Federal Constitution from invasion by the States." Whitney v. California, 274 U.S. 357, 373 (1927) (Brandeis, J., concurring). "The guaranties of due process, though having their roots in Magna Carta's 'per legem terrae' and considered as procedural safeguards 'against executive usurpation and tyranny,' have in this country 'become bulwarks also against arbitrary legislation.'" Poe v. Ullman, 367 U.S. 497, 541 (1961) (Harlan, J., dissenting from dismissal on jurisdictional grounds) (quoting Hurtado v. California, 110 U.S. 516, 532 (1884)).

The most familiar of the substantive liberties protected by the Fourteenth Amendment are those recognized by the Bill of Rights. We have held that the Due Process Clause of the Fourteenth Amendment incorporates most of the Bill of Rights against the States. See, e.g., Duncan v. Louisiana, 391 U.S. 145, 147-148 (1968). It is tempting, as a means of curbing the discretion of federal judges, to suppose that liberty encompasses no more than those rights already guaranteed to the individual against federal interference by the express provisions of the first eight amendments to the Constitution. See Adamson v. California, 332 U.S. 46, 68-92 (1947) (Black, J., dissenting). But of course this Court has never accepted that view.

It is also tempting, for the same reason, to suppose that the Due Process Clause protects only those practices, defined at the most specific level, that were protected against government interference by other rules of law when the Fourteenth Amendment was ratified. See Michael H. v. Gerald D., 491 U.S. 110, 127-128, n. 6 (1989) (opinion of Scalia, J.). But such a view would be inconsistent with our law. It is a promise of the Constitution that there is a realm of personal liberty which the government may not enter. We have vindicated this principle before. Marriage is mentioned nowhere in the Bill of Rights and interracial marriage was illegal in most States in the 19th century, but the Court was no doubt correct in finding it to be an aspect of liberty protected against state interference by the substantive component of the Due Process Clause in Loving v. Virginia, 388 U.S. 1, 12 (1967) (relying, in an opinion for eight Justices, on the Due Process Clause). Similar examples may be found in Turner v. Safley, 482 U.S. 78, 94-99 (1987); in Carey v. Population Services International, 431 U.S. 678, 684-686 (1977); in Griswold v. Connecticut, 381 U.S. 479, 481-482 (1965), as well as in the separate opinions of a majority of the Members of the Court in that case, id., at 486-488 (Goldberg, J., joined by Warren, C.J., and Brennan, J., concurring) (expressly relying on due process), id., at 500-502 (Harlan, J., concurring in judgment) (same), id., at 502-507 (White, J., concurring in judgment) (same); in Pierce v. Society of Sisters, 268 U.S. 510, 534-535 (1925); and in Meyer v. Nebraska, 262 U.S. 390, 399-403 (1923).

Neither the Bill of Rights nor the specific practices of States at the time of the adoption of the Fourteenth Amendment marks the outer limits of the substantive sphere of liberty which the Fourteenth Amendment protects. See U.S. Const., Amend. 9. As the second Justice Harlan recognized:

> The full scope of the liberty guaranteed by the Due Process Clause cannot be found in or limited by the precise terms of the specific guarantees elsewhere provided in the Constitution. This "liberty" is not a series of isolated points pricked out in terms of the taking of property; the freedom of speech, press, and religion; the right to keep and bear arms; the freedom from unreasonable searches and seizures; and so on. It is a rational continuum which, broadly speaking, includes a freedom from all substantial arbitrary impositions and purposeless restraints, . . . and which also recognizes, what a reasonable and sensitive judgment must, that certain interests require particularly careful scrutiny of the state needs asserted to justify their abridgment.

Poe v. Ullman, supra, at 543 (Harlan, J., dissenting from dismissal on jurisdictional grounds). . . .

The inescapable fact is that adjudication of substantive due process claims may call upon the Court in interpreting the Constitution to exercise that same capacity which by tradition courts always have exercised: reasoned judgment. Its boundaries are not susceptible of expression as a simple rule. That does not mean we are free to invalidate state policy choices with which we disagree; yet neither does it permit us to shrink from the duties of our office. As Justice Harlan observed:

> Due process has not been reduced to any formula; its content cannot be determined by reference to any code. The best that can be said is that through the course of this Court's decisions it has represented the balance which our Nation, built upon postulates of respect for the liberty of the individual, has struck between that liberty and the demands of organized society. If the supplying of content to this Constitutional concept has of necessity been a rational process, it certainly has not been one where judges have felt free to roam where unguided speculation might take them. The balance of which I speak is the balance struck by this country, having regard to what history teaches are the traditions from which it developed as well as the traditions from which it broke. That tradition is a living thing. A decision of this Court which radically departs from it could not long survive, while a decision which builds on what has survived is likely to be sound. No formula could serve as a substitute, in this area, for judgment and restraint.

Poe v. Ullman, 367 U.S., at 542 (Harlan, J., dissenting from dismissal on jurisdictional grounds). See also Rochin v. California, [342 U.S. 165], 171-172 [1952] (Frankfurter, J., writing for the Court) ("To believe that this judicial exercise of judgment could be avoided by freezing 'due process of law' at some fixed stage of time or thought is to suggest that the most important aspect of constitutional adjudication is a function for inanimate machines and not for judges").

Men and women of good conscience can disagree, and we suppose some always shall disagree, about the profound moral and spiritual implications of terminating a pregnancy, even in its earliest stage. Some of us as individuals find abortion offensive to our most basic principles of morality, but that cannot control our decision. Our obligation is to define the liberty of all, not to mandate our own moral code. The underlying constitutional issue is whether the State can resolve these philosophic questions in such a definitive way that a woman lacks all choice in the matter, except perhaps in those rare circumstances in which the pregnancy is itself a danger to her own life or health, or is the result of rape or incest. . . .

Our law affords constitutional protection to personal decisions relating to marriage, procreation, contraception, family relationships, child rearing, and education. [These] matters, involving the most intimate and personal choices a person may make in a lifetime, choices central to personal dignity and autonomy, are central to the liberty protected by the Fourteenth Amendment. At the heart of liberty is the right to define one's own concept of existence, of meaning, of the universe, and of the mystery of human life. Beliefs about these matters could not define the attributes of personhood were they formed under compulsion of the State.

These considerations begin our analysis of the woman's interest in terminating her pregnancy but cannot end it, for this reason: though the abortion decision may originate within the zone of conscience and belief, it is more than a philosophic exercise. Abortion is a unique act. It is an act fraught with consequences for others: for the woman who must live with the implications of her decision; for the persons who perform and assist in the procedure; for the spouse, family, and society which must confront the knowledge that these procedures exist, procedures some deem nothing short of an act of violence against innocent human life; and, depending on one's beliefs, for the life or potential life that is aborted. Though abortion is conduct, it does not follow that the State is entitled to proscribe it in all instances. That is because the liberty of the woman is at stake in a sense unique to the human condition and so unique to the law. The mother who carries a child to full term is subject to anxieties, to physical constraints, to pain that only she must bear. That these sacrifices have from the beginning of the human race been endured by woman with a pride that ennobles her in the eyes of others and gives to the infant a bond of love cannot alone be grounds for the State to insist she make the sacrifice. Her suffering is too intimate and personal for the State to insist, without more, upon its own vision of the woman's role, however dominant that vision has been in the course of our history and our culture. The destiny of the woman must be shaped to a large extent on her own conception of her spiritual imperatives and her place in society.

It should be recognized, moreover, that in some critical respects the abortion decision is of the same character as the decision to use contraception, to which Griswold v. Connecticut, Eisenstadt v. Baird, and Carey v. Population Services International, afford constitutional protection. We have no doubt as to the correctness of those decisions. They support the reasoning in *Roe* relating to the woman's liberty because they involve personal decisions concerning not only the meaning of procreation but also human responsibility and respect for it. As with abortion, reasonable people will have differences of opinion about these matters. One view is based on such reverence for the wonder of creation that any pregnancy ought to be welcomed and carried to full term no matter how difficult it will be to provide for the child and ensure its well-being. Another is that the inability to provide for the nurture and care of the infant is a cruelty to the child and an anguish to the parent. These are intimate views with infinite variations, and their deep, personal character underlay our decisions in *Griswold, Eisenstadt,* and *Carey*. The same concerns are present when the woman confronts the reality that, perhaps despite her attempts to avoid it, she has become pregnant.

It was this dimension of personal liberty that *Roe* sought to protect, and its holding invoked the reasoning and the tradition of the precedents we have discussed, granting protection to substantive liberties of the person. *Roe* was, of course, an extension of those cases and, as the decision itself indicated, the separate States could act in some degree to further their own legitimate interests in protecting pre-natal life. The extent to which the legislatures of the States might act to outweigh the interests of the woman in choosing to terminate her pregnancy was a subject of debate both in *Roe* itself and in decisions following it.

While we appreciate the weight of the arguments made on behalf of the State in the case before us, arguments which in their ultimate formulation conclude that *Roe* should be overruled, the reservations any of us may have in reaffirming the central holding of *Roe* are outweighed by the explication of individual liberty we have given combined with the force of stare decisis. We turn now to that doctrine.

III

A

The obligation to follow precedent begins with necessity, and a contrary necessity marks its outer limit. With Cardozo, we recognize that no judicial system could do society's work if it eyed each issue afresh in every case that raised it. See B. Cardozo, The Nature of the Judicial Process 149 (1921). Indeed, the very concept of the rule of law underlying our own Constitution requires such continuity over time that a respect for precedent is, by definition, indispensable. See Powell, Stare Decisis and Judicial Restraint, 1991 Journal of Supreme Court History 13, 16. At the other extreme, a different necessity would make itself felt if a prior judicial ruling should come to be seen so clearly as error that its enforcement was for that very reason doomed.

Even when the decision to overrule a prior case is not, as in the rare, latter instance, virtually foreordained, it is common wisdom that the rule of stare decisis is not an "inexorable command," and certainly it is not such in every constitutional case, see Burnet v. Coronado Oil Gas Co., 285 U.S. 393, 405-411 (1932) (Brandeis, J., dissenting). See also Payne v. Tennessee, 501 U.S. —, — (1991) (Souter, J., joined by Kennedy, J., concurring); Arizona v. Rumsey, 467 U.S. 203, 212 (1984). Rather, when this Court reexamines a prior holding, its judgment is customarily informed by a series of prudential and pragmatic considerations designed to test the consistency of overruling a prior decision with the ideal of the rule of law, and to gauge the respective costs of reaffirming and overruling a prior case. Thus, for example, we may ask whether the rule has proved to be intolerable simply in defying practical workability, Swift & Co. v. Wickham, 382 U.S. 111, 116 (1965); whether the rule is subject to a kind of reliance that would lend a special hardship to the consequences of overruling and add inequity to the cost of repudiation, e.g., United States v. Title Ins. & Trust Co., 265 U.S. 472, 486 (1924); whether related principles of law have so far developed as to have left the old rule no more than a remnant of abandoned doctrine, see Patterson v. McLean Credit Union, 491 U.S. 164, 173-174 (1989); or whether facts have so changed or come to be seen so differently, as to have robbed the old rule of significant application or justification, e.g., *Burnet,* supra, at 412 (Brandeis, J., dissenting).

So in this case we may inquire whether *Roe*'s central rule has been found unworkable; whether the rule's limitation on state power could be removed without serious inequity to those who have relied upon it or significant damage to the stability of the society governed by the rule in question; whether the law's growth in the intervening years has left *Roe*'s central rule a doctrinal anachronism discounted by society; and whether *Roe*'s premises of fact have so far changed in the ensuing two decades as to render its central holding somehow irrelevant or unjustifiable in dealing with the issue it addressed.

1

Although *Roe* has engendered opposition, it has in no sense proven "unworkable," see Garcia v. San Antonio Metropolitan Transit Authority, 469 U.S. 528, 546 (1985), representing as it does a simple limitation beyond which a state law is unenforceable. While *Roe* has, of course, required judicial assessment of state laws affecting the exercise of the choice guaranteed against government infringement, and although the need for such review will remain as a consequence of today's decision, the required determinations fall within judicial competence.

2

The inquiry into reliance counts the cost of a rule's repudiation as it would fall on those who have relied reasonably on the rule's continued application. . . .

While neither respondents nor their amici in so many words deny that the abortion right invites some reliance prior to its actual exercise, one can readily imagine an argument stressing the dissimilarity of this case to one involving property or contract. Abortion is customarily chosen as an unplanned response to the consequence of unplanned activity or to the failure of conventional birth control, and except on the assumption that no intercourse would have occurred but for *Roe*'s holding, such behavior may appear to justify no reliance claim. Even if reliance could be claimed on that unrealistic assumption, the argument might run, any reliance interest would be de minimis. This argument would be premised on the hypothesis that reproductive planning could take virtually immediate account of any sudden restoration of state authority to ban abortions.

To eliminate the issue of reliance that easily, however, one would need to limit cognizable reliance to specific instances of sexual activity. But to do this would be simply to refuse to face the fact that for two decades of economic and social developments, people have organized intimate relationships and made choices that define their views of themselves and their places in society, in reliance on the availability of abortion in the event that contraception should fail. The ability of women to participate equally in the economic and social life of the Nation has been facilitated by their ability to control their reproductive lives. See, e.g., R. Petchesky, Abortion and Woman's Choice 109, 133, n.7 (rev. ed. 1990). The Constitution serves human values, and while the effect of reliance on *Roe* cannot be exactly measured, neither can the certain cost of overruling *Roe* for people who have ordered their thinking and living around that case be dismissed.

3

No evolution of legal principle has left *Roe*'s doctrinal footings weaker than they were in 1973. No development of constitutional law since the case was decided has implicitly or explicitly left *Roe* behind as a mere survivor of obsolete constitutional thinking.

It will be recognized, of course, that *Roe* stands at an intersection of two lines of decisions, but in whichever doctrinal category one reads the case, the result for present purposes will be the same. The *Roe* Court itself placed its holding in the succession of cases most prominently exemplified by Griswold v. Connecticut, 381 U.S. 479 (1965), see *Roe*, 410 U.S., at 152-153. When it is so seen, *Roe* is clearly in no jeopardy, since subsequent constitutional developments have neither disturbed, nor do they threaten to diminish, the scope of recognized protection accorded to the liberty relating to intimate relationships, the family, and decisions about whether or not to beget or bear a child. See, e.g., Carey v. Population Services International, 431 U.S. 678 (1977); Moore v. East Cleveland, 431 U.S. 678 (1977).

Roe, however, may be seen not only as an exemplar of *Griswold* liberty but as a rule (whether or not mistaken) of personal autonomy and bodily integrity, with doctrinal affinity to cases recognizing limits on governmental power to mandate medical treatment or to bar its rejection. If so, our cases since *Roe* accord with *Roe*'s view that a State's interest in the protection of life falls short of justifying any plenary override of individual liberty claims. Cruzan v. Director, Missouri Dept. of Health[, 110 S. Ct. 2841 (1990)].

Finally, one could classify *Roe* as sui generis. If the case is so viewed, then there clearly has been no erosion of its central determination. The original holding resting on the concurrence of seven Members of the Court in 1973 was expressly affirmed by a majority of six in 1983, see Akron v. Akron Center for Reproductive Health, Inc., 462 U.S. 416 (1983) (*Akron I*), and by a majority of five in 1986, see Thornburgh v. American College of Obstetricians and Gynecologists, 476 U.S. 747 (1986), expressing adherence to the constitutional ruling despite legislative efforts in some States to test its limits. More recently, in Webster v. Reproductive Health Services, 492 U.S. 490 (1989), although two of the present authors questioned the trimester framework in a way consistent with our judgment today, see id., at 518 (Rehnquist, C.J., joined by White, and Kennedy, JJ.); id., at 529 (O'Connor, J., concurring in part and concurring in judgment), a majority of the Court either decided to reaffirm or declined to address the constitutional validity of the central holding of *Roe*. See Webster, 492 U. S., at 521 (Rehnquist, C.J., joined by White and Kennedy, JJ.); id., at 525-526 (O'Connor, J., concurring in part and concurring in judgment); id., at 537, 553 (Blackmun, J., joined by Brennan and Marshall, JJ., concurring in part and dissenting in part); id., at 561-563 (Stevens, J., concurring in part and dissenting in part).

Nor will courts building upon *Roe* be likely to hand down erroneous decisions as a consequence. Even on the assumption that the central holding of *Roe* was in error, that error would go only to the strength of the state interest in fetal protection, not to the recognition afforded by the Constitution to the woman's liberty. The latter aspect of the decision fits comfortably within the framework of the Court's prior decisions including Skinner v. Oklahoma ex rel. Williamson. . . .

The soundness of this prong of the *Roe* analysis is apparent from a consideration of the alternative. If indeed the woman's interest in deciding whether to bear and beget a child had not been recognized as in *Roe*, the State might as readily restrict a woman's right to choose to carry a pregnancy to term as to terminate it, to further asserted state interests in population control, or eugenics, for example. Yet *Roe* has been sensibly relied upon to counter any such suggestions. E.g., Arnold v. Board of Education of Escambia County, Ala., 880 F.2d 305, 311 (CA11 1989) (relying upon *Roe* and concluding that government officials violate the Constitution by coercing a minor to have an abortion); Avery v. County of Burke, 660 F. 2d 111, 115 (CA4 1981) (county agency inducing teenage girl to undergo unwanted sterilization on the basis of misrepresentation that she had sickle cell trait); see also In re Quinlan, 70 N.J. 10, 355 A.2d 647, cert. denied sub nom. Garger v. New Jersey, 429 U.S. 922 (1976) (relying on *Roe* in finding a right to terminate medical treatment). In any event, because *Roe*'s scope is confined by the fact of its concern with postconception potential life, a concern otherwise likely to be implicated only by some forms of contraception protected independently under *Griswold* and later cases, any error in *Roe* is unlikely to have serious ramifications in future cases.

4

We have seen how time has overtaken some of *Roe*'s factual assumptions: advances in maternal health care allow for abortions safe to the mother later in pregnancy than was true in 1973, see *Akron I,* supra, at 429, n.11, and advances in neonatal care have advanced viability to a point somewhat earlier. Compare *Roe*, 410 U.S., at 160, with *Webster,* supra, at 515-516 (opinion of Rehnquist, C.J.); see *Akron I,* supra, at 457, and n.5 (O'Connor, J., dissenting). But these facts go only to the scheme of time limits on the realization of competing interests, and the divergences from the factual premises of 1973 have no bearing on the validity of *Roe*'s central holding, that viability marks the earliest point at which the State's interest in fetal life is constitutionally adequate to justify a legislative ban on nontherapeutic abortions. The soundness or unsoundness of that constitutional judgment in no sense turns on whether viability occurs at approximately 28 weeks, as was usual at the time of *Roe,* at 23 to 24 weeks, as it sometimes does today, or at some moment even slightly earlier in pregnancy, as it may if fetal respiratory capacity can somehow be enhanced in the future. Whenever it may occur, the attainment of viability may continue to serve as the critical fact, just as it has done since *Roe* was decided; which is to say that no change in *Roe*'s factual underpinning has left its central holding obsolete, and none supports an argument for overruling it.

5

The sum of the precedential inquiry to this point shows *Roe*'s underpinnings unweakened in any way affecting its central holding. While it has engendered disapproval, it has not been unworkable. An entire generation has come of age free to assume *Roe*'s concept of liberty in defining the capacity of women to act in society, and to make reproductive decisions; no erosion of principle going to liberty or personal autonomy has left *Roe*'s central holding a doctrinal remnant; *Roe* portends no developments at odds with other precedent for the analysis of personal liberty; and no changes of fact have rendered viability more or less appropriate as the point at which the balance of interests tips. Within the bounds of normal stare decisis analysis, then, and subject to the considerations on which it customarily turns, the stronger argument is for affirming *Roe*'s central holding, with whatever degree of personal reluctance any of us may have, not for overruling it.

B

In a less significant case, stare decisis analysis could, and would, stop at the point we have reached. But the sustained and widespread debate *Roe* has provoked calls for some comparison between that case and others of comparable dimension that have responded to national controversies and taken on the impress of the controversies addressed. Only two such decisional lines from the past century present themselves for examination, and in each instance the result reached by the Court accorded with the principles we apply today.

The first example is that line of cases identified with Lochner v. New York, 198 U.S. 45 (1905), which imposed substantive limitations on legislation limiting economic autonomy in favor of health and welfare regulation, adopting, in Justice Holmes' view, the theory of laissez-faire. Id., at 75 (Holmes, J., dissenting). The *Lochner* decisions were exemplified by Adkins v. Children's Hospital of D.C., 261 U.S. 525 (1923), in which this Court held it to be an infringement of constitutionally protected liberty of contract to require the employers of adult women to satisfy minimum wage standards. Fourteen years later, West Coast Hotel Co. v. Parrish, 300 U.S. 379 (1937), signalled the demise of *Lochner* by overruling *Adkins*. In the meantime, the Depression had come and, with it, the lesson that seemed unmistakable to most people by 1937, that the interpretation of contractual freedom protected in *Adkins* rested on fundamentally false factual assumptions about the capacity of a relatively unregulated market to satisfy minimal levels of human welfare. See *West Coast Hotel Co.* [v. Parrish, 300 U.S. 379 (1937)]. As Justice Jackson wrote of the constitutional crisis of 1937 shortly before he came on the bench, "The older world of laissez faire was recognized everywhere outside the Court to be dead." R. Jackson, The Struggle for Judicial Supremacy 85 (1941). The facts upon which the earlier case had premised a constitutional resolution of social controversy had proved to be untrue, and history's demonstration of their untruth not only justified but required the new choice of constitutional principle that *West Coast Hotel* announced. Of course, it was true that the Court lost something by its misperception, or its lack of prescience, and the Court-packing crisis only magnified the loss; but the clear demonstration that the facts of economic life were different from those previously assumed warranted the repudiation of the old law.

The second comparison that 20th century history invites is with the cases employing the separate-but-equal rule for applying the Fourteenth Amendment's equal protection guarantee. They began with Plessy v. Ferguson, 163 U.S. 537 (1896), holding that legislatively mandated racial segregation in public transportation works no denial of equal protection, rejecting the argument that racial separation enforced by the legal machinery of American society treats the black race as inferior. The *Plessy* Court considered "the underlying fallacy of the plaintiff's argument to consist in the assumption that the enforced separation of the two races stamps the colored race with a badge of inferiority. If this be so, it is not by reason of anything found in the act, but solely because the colored race chooses to put that construction upon it." Whether, as a matter of historical fact, the Justices in the *Plessy* majority believed this or not, see id. (Harlan, J., dissenting), this understanding of the implication of segregation was the stated justification for the Court's opinion. But this understanding of the facts and the rule it was stated to justify were repudiated in Brown v. Board of Education, 347 U.S. 483 (1954). As one commentator observed, the question before the Court in *Brown* was "whether discrimination inheres in that segregation which is imposed by law in the twentieth century in certain specific states in the American Union. And that question has meaning and can find an answer only on the ground of history and of common knowledge about the facts of life in the times and places aforesaid." Black, The Lawfulness of the Segregation Decisions, 69 Yale L.J. 421, 427 (1960).

The Court in *Brown* addressed these facts of life by observing that whatever may have been the understanding in *Plessy*'s time of the power of segregation to stigmatize those who were segregated with a "badge of inferiority," it was clear by 1954 that legally sanctioned segregation had just such an effect, to the point that racially separate public educational facilities were deemed inherently unequal. Society's understanding of the facts upon which a constitutional ruling was sought in 1954 was thus fundamentally different from the basis claimed for the decision in 1896. While we think *Plessy* was wrong the day it was decided, see *Plessy* (Harlan, J., dissenting), we must also recognize that the *Plessy* Court's explanation for its decision was so clearly at odds with the facts apparent to the Court in 1954 that the decision to reexamine *Plessy* was on this ground alone not only justified but required.

West Coast Hotel and *Brown* each rested on facts, or an understanding of facts, changed from those which furnished the claimed justifications for the earlier constitutional resolutions. Each case was comprehensible as the Court's response to facts that the country could understand, or had come to understand already, but which the Court of an earlier day, as its own declarations disclosed, had not been able to perceive. As the decisions were thus comprehensible they were also defensible, not merely as the victories of one doctrinal school over another by dint of numbers (victories though they were), but as applications of constitutional principle to facts as they had not been seen by the Court before. In constitutional adjudication as elsewhere in life, changed circumstances may impose new obligations, and the thoughtful part of the Nation could accept each decision to overrule a prior case as a response to the Court's constitutional duty.

Because the case before us presents no such occasion it could be seen as no such response. Because neither the factual underpinnings of *Roe*'s central holding nor our understanding of it has changed (and because no other indication of weakened precedent has been shown) the Court could not pretend to be reexamining the prior law with any justification beyond a present doctrinal disposition to come out differently from the Court of 1973. To overrule prior law for no other reason than that would run counter to the view repeated in our cases, that a decision to overrule should rest on some special reason over and above the belief that a prior case was wrongly decided. . . .

C

The examination of the conditions justifying the repudiation of *Adkins* by *West Coast Hotel* and *Plessy* by *Brown* is enough to suggest the terrible price that would have been paid if the Court had not overruled as it did. In the present case, however, as our analysis to this point makes clear, the terrible price would be paid for overruling. Our analysis would not be complete, however, without explaining why overruling *Roe*'s central holding would not only reach an unjustifiable result under principles of stare decisis, but would seriously weaken the Court's capacity to exercise the judicial power and to function as the Supreme Court of a Nation dedicated to the rule of law. To understand why this would be so it is necessary to understand the source of this Court's authority, the conditions necessary for its preservation, and its relationship to the country's understanding of itself as a constitutional Republic.

The root of American governmental power is revealed most clearly in the instance of the power conferred by the Constitution upon the Judiciary of the United States and specifically upon this Court. As Americans of each succeeding generation are rightly told, the Court cannot buy support for its decisions by spending money and, except to a minor degree, it cannot independently coerce obedience to its decrees. The Court's power lies, rather, in its legitimacy, a product of substance and perception that shows itself in the people's acceptance of the Judiciary as fit to determine what the Nation's law means and to declare what it demands.

The underlying substance of this legitimacy is of course the warrant for the Court's decisions in the Constitution and the lesser sources of legal principle on which the Court draws. That substance is expressed in the Court's opinions, and our contemporary understanding is such that a decision without principled justification would be no judicial act at all. But even when justification is furnished by apposite legal principle, something more is required. Because not every conscientious claim of principled justification will be accepted as such, the justification claimed must be beyond dispute. The Court must take care to speak and act in ways that allow people to accept its decisions on the terms the Court claims for them, as grounded truly in principle, not as compromises with social and political pressures having, as such, no bearing on the principled choices that the Court is obliged to make. Thus, the Court's legitimacy depends on making legally principled decisions under circumstances in which their principled character is sufficiently plausible to be accepted by the Nation.

The need for principled action to be perceived as such is implicated to some degree whenever this, or any other appellate court, overrules a prior case. This is not to say, of course, that this Court cannot give a perfectly satisfactory explanation in most cases. . . .

In two circumstances, however, the Court would almost certainly fail to receive the benefit of the doubt in overruling prior cases. There is, first, a point beyond which frequent overruling would overtax the country's belief in the Court's good faith. Despite the variety of reasons that may inform and justify a decision to overrule, we cannot forget that such a decision is usually perceived (and perceived correctly) as, at the least, a statement that a prior decision was wrong. There is a limit to the amount of error that can plausibly be imputed to prior courts. If that limit should be exceeded, disturbance of prior rulings would be taken as evidence that justifiable reexamination of principle had given way to drives for particular results in the short term. The legitimacy of the Court would fade with the frequency of its vacillation.

That first circumstance can be described as hypothetical; the second is to the point here and now. Where, in the performance of its judicial duties, the Court decides a case in such a way as to resolve the sort of intensely divisive controversy reflected in *Roe* and those rare, comparable cases, its decision has a dimension that the resolution of the normal case does not carry. It is the dimension present whenever the Court's interpretation of the Constitution calls the contending sides of a national controversy to end their national division by accepting a common mandate rooted in the Constitution.

The Court is not asked to do this very often, having thus addressed the Nation only twice in our lifetime, in the decisions of *Brown* and *Roe*. But when the Court does act in this way, its decision requires an equally rare precedential force to counter the inevitable efforts to overturn it and to thwart its implementation. Some of those efforts may be mere unprincipled emotional reactions; others may proceed from principles worthy of profound respect. But whatever the premises of opposition may be, only the most convincing justification under accepted standards of precedent could suffice to demonstrate that a later decision overruling the first was anything but a surrender to political pressure, and an unjustified repudiation of the principle on which the Court staked its authority in the first instance. So to overrule under fire in the absence of the most compelling reason to reexamine a watershed decision would subvert the Court's legitimacy beyond any serious question.

The country's loss of confidence in the judiciary would be underscored by an equally certain and equally reasonable condemnation for another failing in overruling unnecessarily and under pressure. Some cost will be paid by anyone who approves or implements a constitutional decision where it is unpopular, or who refuses to work to undermine the decision or to force its reversal. The price may be criticism or ostracism, or it may be violence. An extra price will be paid by those who themselves disapprove of the decision's results when viewed outside of constitutional terms, but who nevertheless struggle to accept it, because they respect the rule of law. To all those who will be so tested by following, the Court implicitly undertakes to remain steadfast, lest in the end a price be paid for nothing. The promise of constancy, once given, binds its maker for as long as the power to stand by the decision survives and the understanding of the issue has not changed so fundamentally as to render the commitment obsolete. From the obligation of this promise this Court cannot and should not assume any exemption when duty requires it to decide a case in conformance with the Constitution. A willing breach of it would be nothing less than a breach of faith, and no Court that broke its faith with the people could sensibly expect credit for principle in the decision by which it did that.

It is true that diminished legitimacy may be restored, but only slowly. Unlike the political branches, a Court thus weakened could not seek to regain its position with a new mandate from the voters, and even if the Court could somehow go to the polls, the loss of its principled character could not be retrieved by the casting of so many votes. Like the character of an individual, the legitimacy of the Court must be earned over time. So, indeed, must be the character of a Nation of people who aspire to live according to the rule of law. Their belief in themselves as such a people is not readily separable from their understanding of the Court invested with the authority to decide their constitutional cases and speak before all others for their constitutional ideals. If the Court's legitimacy should be undermined, then, so would the country be in its very ability to see itself through its constitutional ideals. The Court's concern with legitimacy is not for the sake of the Court but for the sake of the Nation to which it is responsible.

The Court's duty in the present case is clear. In 1973, it confronted the already-divisive issue of governmental power to limit personal choice to undergo abortion, for which it provided a new resolution based on the due process guaranteed by the Fourteenth Amendment. Whether or not a new social consensus is developing on that issue, its divisiveness is no less today than in 1973, and pressure to overrule the decision, like pressure to retain it, has grown only more intense. A decision to overrule *Roe*'s essential holding under the existing circumstances would address error, if error there was, at the cost of both profound and unnecessary damage to the Court's legitimacy, and to the Nation's commitment to the rule of law. It is therefore imperative to adhere to the essence of *Roe*'s original decision, and we do so today.

IV

From what we have said so far it follows that it is a constitutional liberty of the woman to have some freedom to terminate her pregnancy. We conclude that the basic decision in *Roe* was based on a constitutional analysis which we cannot now repudiate. The woman's liberty is not so unlimited, however, that from the outset the State cannot show its concern for the life of the unborn, and at a later point in fetal development the State's interest in life has sufficient force so that the right of the woman to terminate the pregnancy can be restricted.

That brings us, of course, to the point where much criticism has been directed at *Roe*, a criticism that always inheres when the Court draws a specific rule from what in the Constitution is but a general standard. We conclude, however, that the urgent claims of the woman to retain the ultimate control over her destiny and her body, claims implicit in the meaning of liberty, require us to perform that function. Liberty must not be extinguished for want of a line that is clear. And it falls to us to give some real substance to the woman's liberty to determine whether to carry her pregnancy to full term.

We conclude the line should be drawn at viability, so that before that time the woman has a right to choose to terminate her pregnancy. We adhere to this principle for two reasons. First, as we have said, is the doctrine of stare decisis. Any judicial act of line-drawing may seem somewhat arbitrary, but *Roe* was a reasoned statement, elaborated with great care. . . .

The second reason is that the concept of viability, as we noted in *Roe*, is the time at which there is a realistic possibility of maintaining and nourishing a life outside the womb, so that the independent existence of the second life can in reason and all fairness be the object of state protection that now overrides the rights of the woman. . . .

The woman's right to terminate her pregnancy before viability is the most central principle of Roe v. Wade. It is a rule of law and a component of liberty we cannot renounce.

On the other side of the equation is the interest of the State in the protection of potential life. The *Roe* Court recognized the State's "important and legitimate interest in protecting the potentiality of human life." The weight to be given this state interest, not the strength of the woman's interest, was the difficult question faced in *Roe*. We do not need to say whether each of us, had we been Members of the Court when the valuation of the State interest came before it as an original matter, would have concluded, as the *Roe* Court did, that its weight is insufficient to justify a ban on abortions prior to viability even when it is subject to certain exceptions. The matter is not before us in the first instance, and coming as it does after nearly 20 years of litigation in *Roe*'s wake we are satisfied that the immediate question is not the soundness of *Roe*'s resolution of the issue, but the precedential force that must be accorded to its holding. And we have concluded that the essential holding of *Roe* should be reaffirmed.

Yet it must be remembered that Roe v. Wade speaks with clarity in establishing not only the woman's liberty but also the State's "important and legitimate interest in potential life." That portion of the decision in *Roe* has been given too little acknowledgement and implementation by the Court in its subsequent cases. Those cases decided that any regulation touching upon the abortion decision must survive strict scrutiny, to be sustained only if drawn in narrow terms to further a compelling state interest. Not all of the cases decided under that formulation can be reconciled with the holding in *Roe* itself that the State has legitimate interests in the health of the woman and in protecting the potential life within her. In resolving this tension, we choose to rely upon *Roe*, as against the later cases.

Roe established a trimester framework to govern abortion regulations. Under this elaborate but rigid construct, almost no regulation at all is permitted during the first trimester of pregnancy; regulations designed to protect the woman's health, but not to further the State's interest in potential life, are permitted during the second trimester; and during the third trimester, when the fetus is viable, prohibitions are permitted provided the life or health of the mother is not at stake. Most of our cases since *Roe* have involved the application of rules derived from the trimester framework.

The trimester framework no doubt was erected to ensure that the woman's right to choose not become so subordinate to the State's interest in promoting fetal life that her choice exists in theory but not in fact. We do not agree, however, that the trimester approach is necessary to accomplish this objective. A framework of this rigidity was unnecessary and in its later interpretation sometimes contradicted the State's permissible exercise of its powers. . . .

We reject the trimester framework, which we do not consider to be part of the essential holding of *Roe*. [The] trimester framework suffers from these basic flaws: in its formulation it misconceives the nature of the pregnant woman's interest; and in practice it undervalues the State's interest in potential life, as recognized in *Roe*. . . .

[Numerous] forms of state regulation might have the incidental effect of increasing the cost or decreasing the availability of medical care, whether for abortion or any other medical procedure. The fact that a law which serves a valid purpose, one not designed to strike at the right itself, has the incidental effect of making it more difficult or more expensive to procure an abortion cannot be enough to invalidate it. Only where state regulation imposes an undue burden on a woman's ability to make this decision does the power of the State reach into the heart of the liberty protected by the Due Process Clause. . . .

These considerations of the nature of the abortion right illustrate that it is an overstatement to describe it as a right to decide whether to have an abortion "without interference from the State," Planned Parenthood of Central Mo. v. Danforth, 428 U.S. 52, 61 (1976). [Not] all governmental intrusion is of necessity unwarranted; and that brings us to the other basic flaw in the trimester framework: even in *Roe*'s terms, in practice it undervalues the State's interest in the potential life within the woman. . . .

The very notion that the State has a substantial interest in potential life leads to the conclusion that not all regulations must be deemed unwarranted. Not all burdens on the right to decide whether to terminate a pregnancy will be undue. In our view, the undue burden standard is the appropriate means of reconciling the State's interest with the woman's constitutionally protected liberty. . . .

A finding of an undue burden is a shorthand for the conclusion that a state regulation has the purpose or effect of placing a substantial obstacle in the path of a woman seeking an abortion of a nonviable fetus. A statute with this purpose is invalid because the means chosen by the State to further the interest in potential life must be calculated to inform the woman's free choice, not hinder it. And a statute which, while furthering the interest in potential life or some other valid state interest, has the effect of placing a substantial obstacle in the path of a woman's choice cannot be considered a permissible means of serving its legitimate ends. [Understood] another way, we answer the question, left open in previous opinions discussing the undue burden formulation, whether a law designed to further the State's interest in fetal life which imposes an undue burden on the woman's decision before fetal viability could be constitutional. See, e.g., *Akron I,* supra, at 462-463 (O'Connor, J., dissenting). The answer is no.

Some guiding principles should emerge. What is at stake is the woman's right to make the ultimate decision, not a right to be insulated from all others in doing so. Regulations which do no more than create a structural mechanism by which the State, or the parent or guardian of a minor, may express profound respect for the life of the unborn are permitted, if they are not a substantial obstacle to the woman's exercise of the right to choose. Unless it has that effect on her right of choice, a state measure designed to persuade her to choose childbirth over abortion will be upheld if reasonably related to that goal. Regulations designed to foster the health of a woman seeking an abortion are valid if they do not constitute an undue burden.

Even when jurists reason from shared premises, some disagreement is inevitable. That is to be expected in the application of any legal standard which must accommodate life's complexity. We do not expect it to be otherwise with respect to the undue burden standard. We give this summary:

(a) To protect the central right recognized by Roe v. Wade while at the same time accommodating the State's profound interest in potential life, we will employ the undue burden analysis as explained in this opinion. An undue burden exists, and therefore a provision of law is invalid, if its purpose or effect is to place a substantial obstacle in the path of a woman seeking an abortion before the fetus attains viability.

(b) We reject the rigid trimester framework of Roe v. Wade. To promote the State's profound interest in potential life, throughout pregnancy the State may take measures to ensure that the woman's choice is informed, and measures designed to advance this interest will not be invalidated as long as their purpose is to persuade the woman to choose childbirth over abortion. These measures must not be an undue burden on the right.

(c) As with any medical procedure, the State may enact regulations to further the health or safety of a woman seeking an abortion. Unnecessary health regulations that have the purpose or effect of presenting a substantial obstacle to a woman seeking an abortion impose an undue burden on the right.

(d) Our adoption of the undue burden analysis does not disturb the central holding of Roe v. Wade, and we reaffirm that holding. Regardless of whether exceptions are made for particular circumstances, a State may not prohibit any woman from making the ultimate decision to terminate her pregnancy before viability.

(e) We also reaffirm *Roe*'s holding that "subsequent to viability, the State in promoting its interest in the potentiality of human life may, if it chooses, regulate, and even proscribe, abortion except where it is necessary, in appropriate medical judgment, for the preservation of the life or health of the mother."

These principles control our assessment of the Pennsylvania statute, and we now turn to the issue of the validity of its challenged provisions.

V

The Court of Appeals applied what it believed to be the undue burden standard and upheld each of the provisions except for the husband notification requirement. We agree generally with this conclusion, but refine the undue burden analysis in accordance with the principles articulated above. We now consider the separate statutory sections at issue.

A

Because it is central to the operation of various other requirements, we begin with the statute's definition of medical emergency. Under the statute, a medical emergency is

> that condition which, on the basis of the physician's good faith clinical judgment, so complicates the medical condition of a pregnant woman as to necessitate the immediate abortion of her pregnancy to avert her death or for which a delay will create serious risk of substantial and irreversible impairment of a major bodily function.

Petitioners argue that the definition is too narrow, contending that it forecloses the possibility of an immediate abortion despite some significant health risks. If the contention were correct, we would be required to invalidate the restrictive operation of the provision, for the essential holding of *Roe* forbids a State from interfering with a woman's choice to undergo an abortion procedure if continuing her pregnancy would constitute a threat to her health.

The District Court found that there were three serious conditions which would not be covered by the statute: preeclampsia, inevitable abortion, and premature ruptured membrane. Yet, as the Court of Appeals observed, it is undisputed that under some circumstances each of these conditions could lead to an illness with substantial and irreversible consequences. While the definition could be interpreted in an unconstitutional manner, the Court of Appeals construed the phrase "serious risk" to include those circumstances. It stated: "we read the medical emergency exception as intended by the Pennsylvania legislature to assure that compliance with its abortion regulations would not in any way pose a significant threat to the life or health of a woman." [We] conclude that, as construed by the Court of Appeals, the medical emergency definition imposes no undue burden on a woman's abortion right.

B

We next consider the informed consent requirement. Except in a medical emergency, the statute requires that at least 24 hours before performing an abortion a physician inform the woman of the nature of the procedure, the health risks of the abortion and of childbirth, and the "probable gestational age of the unborn child." The physician or a qualified nonphysician must inform the woman of the availability of printed materials published by the State describing the fetus and providing information about medical assistance for childbirth, information about child support from the father, and a list of agencies which provide adoption and other services as alternatives to abortion. An abortion may not be performed unless the woman certifies in writing that she has been informed of the availability of these printed materials and has been provided them if she chooses to view them. . . .

To the extent *Akron I* and *Thornburgh* find a constitutional violation when the government requires, as it does here, the giving of truthful, nonmisleading information about the nature of the procedure, the attendant health risks and those of childbirth, and the "probable gestational age" of the fetus, those cases go too far, are inconsistent with *Roe*'s acknowledgment of an important interest in potential life, and are overruled. [In] attempting to ensure that a woman apprehend the full consequences of her decision, the State furthers the legitimate purpose of reducing the risk that a woman may elect an abortion, only to discover later, with devastating psychological consequences, that her decision was not fully informed. If the information the State requires to be made available to the woman is truthful and not misleading, the requirement may be permissible.

We also see no reason why the State may not require doctors to inform a woman seeking an abortion of the availability of materials relating to the consequences to the fetus, even when those consequences have no direct relation to her health. . . .

All that is left of petitioners' argument is an asserted First Amendment right of a physician not to provide information about the risks of abortion, and childbirth, in a manner mandated by the State. To be sure, the physician's First Amendment rights not to speak are implicated, see Wooley v. Maynard, 430 U.S. 705 (1977), but only as part of the practice of medicine, subject to reasonable licensing and regulation by the State. Cf. Whalen v. Roe, 429 U.S. 589, 603 (1977). We see no constitutional infirmity in the requirement that the physician provide the information mandated by the State here.

The Pennsylvania statute also requires us to reconsider the holding in *Akron I* that the State may not require that a physician, as opposed to a qualified assistant, provide information relevant to a woman's informed consent. Since there is no evidence on this record that requiring a doctor to give the information as provided by the statute would amount in practical terms to a substantial obstacle to a woman seeking an abortion, we conclude that it is not an undue burden. . . .

Our analysis of Pennsylvania's 24-hour waiting period between the provision of the information deemed necessary to informed consent and the performance of an abortion under the undue burden standard requires us to reconsider the premise behind the decision in *Akron I* invalidating a parallel requirement. In *Akron I* we said: "Nor are we convinced that the State's legitimate concern that the woman's decision be informed is reasonably served by requiring a 24-hour delay as a matter of course." We consider that conclusion to be wrong. The idea that important decisions will be more informed and deliberate if they follow some period of reflection does not strike us as unreasonable, particularly where the statute directs that important information become part of the background of the decision. . . .

Whether the mandatory 24-hour waiting period is nonetheless invalid because in practice it is a substantial obstacle to a woman's choice to terminate her pregnancy is a closer question. The findings of fact by the District Court indicate that because of the distances many women must travel to reach an abortion provider, the practical effect will often be a delay of much more than a day because the waiting period requires that a woman seeking an abortion make at least two visits to the doctor. The District Court also found that in many instances this will increase the exposure of women seeking abortions to "the harassment and hostility of anti-abortion protestors demonstrating outside a clinic." As a result, the District Court found that for those women who have the fewest financial resources, those who must travel long distances, and those who have difficulty explaining their whereabouts to husbands, employers, or others, the 24-hour waiting period will be "particularly burdensome."

These findings are troubling in some respects, but they do not demonstrate that the waiting period constitutes an undue burden. We do not doubt that, as the District Court held, the waiting period has the effect of "increasing the cost and risk of delay of abortions," but the District Court did not conclude that the increased costs and potential delays amount to substantial obstacles. [As] we have stated, under the undue burden standard a State is permitted to enact persuasive measures which favor childbirth over abortion, even if those measures do not further a health interest. And while the waiting period does limit a physician's discretion, that is not, standing alone, a reason to invalidate it. In light of the construction given the statute's definition of medical emergency by the Court of Appeals, and the District Court's findings, we cannot say that the waiting period imposes a real health risk.

We also disagree with the District Court's conclusion that the "particularly burdensome" effects of the waiting period on some women require its invalidation. . . .

We are left with the argument that the various aspects of the informed consent requirement are unconstitutional because they place barriers in the way of abortion on demand. Even the broadest reading of *Roe*, however, has not suggested that there is a constitutional right to abortion on demand. Rather, the right protected by *Roe* is a right to decide to terminate a pregnancy free of undue interference by the State. Because the informed consent requirement facilitates the wise exercise of that right it cannot be classified as an interference with the right *Roe* protects. The informed consent requirement is not an undue burden on that right.

C

Section 3209 of Pennsylvania's abortion law provides, except in cases of medical emergency, that no physician shall perform an abortion on a married woman without receiving a signed statement from the woman that she has notified her spouse that she is about to undergo an abortion. The woman has the option of providing an alternative signed statement certifying that her husband is not the man who impregnated her; that her husband could not be located; that the pregnancy is the result of spousal sexual assault which she has reported; or that the woman believes that notifying her husband will cause him or someone else to inflict bodily injury upon her. A physician who performs an abortion on a married woman without receiving the appropriate signed statement will have his or her license revoked, and is liable to the husband for damages.

The District Court heard the testimony of numerous expert witnesses, and made detailed findings of fact regarding the effect of this statute. These included:

> 273. The vast majority of women consult their husbands prior to deciding to terminate their pregnancy. . . .
>
> 279. The "bodily injury" exception could not be invoked by a married woman whose husband, if notified, would, in her reasonable belief, threaten to (a) publicize her intent to have an abortion to family, friends or acquaint-

ances; (b) retaliate against her in future child custody or divorce proceedings; (c) inflict psychological intimidation or emotional harm upon her, her children or other persons; (d) inflict bodily harm on other persons such as children, family members or other loved ones; or (e) use his control over finances to deprive of necessary monies for herself or her children. . . .

281. Studies reveal that family violence occurs in two million families in the United States. This figure, however, is a conservative one that substantially understates (because battering is usually not reported until it reaches life-threatening proportions) the actual number of families affected by domestic violence. In fact, researchers estimate that one of every two women will be battered at some time in their life. . . .

282. A wife may not elect to notify her husband of her intention to have an abortion for a variety of reasons, including the husband's illness, concern about her own health, the imminent failure of the marriage, or the husband's absolute opposition to the abortion. . . .

284. Women of all class levels, educational backgrounds, and racial, ethnic and religious groups are battered. . . .

285. Wife-battering or abuse can take on many physical and psychological forms. The nature and scope of the battering can cover a broad range of actions and be gruesome and torturous. . . .

286. Married women, victims of battering, have been killed in Pennsylvania and throughout the United States. . . .

287. Battering can often involve a substantial amount of sexual abuse, including marital rape and sexual mutilation. . . .

288. In a domestic abuse situation, it is common for the battering husband to also abuse the children in an attempt to coerce the wife. . . .

289. Mere notification of pregnancy is frequently a flashpoint for battering and violence within the family. The number of battering incidents is high during the pregnancy and often the worst abuse can be associated with pregnancy. . . . The battering husband may deny parentage and use the pregnancy as an excuse for abuse. . . .

290. Secrecy typically shrouds abusive families. Family members are instructed not to tell anyone, especially police or doctors, about the abuse and violence. Battering husbands often threaten their wives or her children with further abuse if she tells an outsider of the violence and tells her that nobody will believe her. A battered woman, therefore, is highly unlikely to disclose the violence against her for fear of retaliation by the abuser. . . .

291. Even when confronted directly by medical personnel or other helping professionals, battered women often will not admit to the battering because they have not admitted to themselves that they are battered. . . .

294. A woman in a shelter or a safe house unknown to her husband is not reasonably likely to have bodily harm inflicted upon her by her batterer, however her attempt to notify her husband pursuant to section 3209 could accidentally disclose her whereabouts to her husband. Her fear of future ramifications would be realistic under the circumstances.

295. Marital rape is rarely discussed with others or reported to law enforcement authorities, and of those reported only few are prosecuted. . . .

> 296. It is common for battered women to have sexual intercourse with their husbands to avoid being battered. While this type of coercive sexual activity would be spousal sexual assault as defined by the Act, many women may not consider it to be so and others would fear disbelief. . . .
>
> 297. The marital rape exception to section 3209 cannot be claimed by women who are victims of coercive sexual behavior other than penetration. The 90-day reporting requirement of the spousal sexual assault statute, 18 Pa. Con. Stat. Ann. §3218(c), further narrows the class of sexually abused wives who can claim the exception, since many of these women may be psychologically unable to discuss or report the rape for several years after the incident. . . .
>
> 298. Because of the nature of the battering relationship, battered women are unlikely to avail themselves of the exceptions to section 3209 of the Act, regardless of whether the section applies to them.

These findings are supported by studies of domestic violence. The American Medical Association (AMA) has published a summary of the recent research in this field, which indicates that in an average 12-month period in this country, approximately two million women are the victims of severe assaults by their male partners. In a 1985 survey, women reported that nearly one of every eight husbands had assaulted their wives during the past year. The AMA views these figures as "marked underestimates," because the nature of these incidents discourages women from reporting them, and because surveys typically exclude the very poor, those who do not speak English well, and women who are homeless or in institutions or hospitals when the survey is conducted. According to the AMA, "researchers on family violence agree that the true incidence of partner violence is probably double the above estimates; or four million severely assaulted women per year. Studies suggest that from one-fifth to one-third of all women will be physically assaulted by a partner or ex-partner during their lifetime." AMA Council on Scientific Affairs, Violence Against Women 7 (1991). Thus on an average day in the United States, nearly 11,000 women are severely assaulted by their male partners. Many of these incidents involve sexual assault. Id., at 3-4; Shields & Hanneke, Battered Wives' Reactions to Marital Rape, in The Dark Side of Families: Current Family Violence Research 131, 144 (D. Finkelhor, R. Gelles, G. Hataling, & M. Straus eds. 1983). In families where wife-beating takes place, moreover, child abuse is often present as well. Violence Against Women, supra, at 12.

Other studies fill in the rest of this troubling picture. Physical violence is only the most visible form of abuse. Psychological abuse, particularly forced social and economic isolation of women, is also common. L. Walker, The Battered Woman Syndrome 27-28 (1984). Many victims of domestic violence remain with their abusers, perhaps because they perceive no superior alternative. Herbert, Silver, & Ellard, Coping with an Abusive Relationship: I. How and Why Do Women Stay?, 53 J. Marriage & the Family 311 (1991). Many abused women who find temporary refuge in shelters return to their husbands, in large part because they have no other source of income. Aguirre, Why Do They Return? Abused Wives in Shelters, 30 J. Nat. Assn. of Social Workers 350, 352 (1985). Returning to one's abuser can be dangerous. Recent Federal Bureau of Investigation statistics disclose that 8.8% of all homicide victims in the United States are killed by their spouse. Mercy & Saltzman, Fatal Violence Among Spouses in the United States, 1976-85, 79 Am. J. Public Health 595 (1989). Thirty percent of female homicide victims are killed by their male partners. Domestic Violence: Terrorism in the Home, Hearing before the Subcommittee on Children, Family, Drugs and Alcoholism of the Senate Committee on Labor and Human Resources, 101st Cong., 2d Sess., 3 (1990).

The limited research that has been conducted with respect to notifying one's husband about an abortion, although involving samples too small to be representative, also supports the District Court's findings of fact. The vast majority of women notify their male partners of their decision to obtain an abortion. In many cases in which married women do not notify their husbands, the pregnancy is the result of an extramarital affair. Where the husband is the father, the primary reason women do not notify their husbands is that the husband and wife are experiencing marital difficulties, often accompanied by incidents of violence. Ryan & Plutzer, When Married Women Have Abortions: Spousal Notification and Marital Interaction, 51 J. Marriage & the Family 41, 44 (1989).

This information and the District Court's findings reinforce what common sense would suggest. In well-functioning marriages, spouses discuss important intimate decisions such as whether to bear a child. But there are millions of women in this country who are the victims of regular physical and psychological abuse at the hands of their husbands. Should these women become pregnant, they may have very good reasons for not wishing to inform their husbands of their decision to obtain an abortion. Many may have justifiable fears of physical abuse, but may be no less fearful of the consequences of reporting prior abuse to the Commonwealth of Pennsylvania. Many may have a reasonable fear that notifying their husbands will provoke further instances of child abuse; these women are not exempt from §3209's notification requirement. Many may fear devastating forms of psychological abuse from their husbands, including verbal harassment, threats of future violence, the destruction of possessions, physical confinement to the home, the withdrawal of financial support, or the disclosure of the abortion to family and friends. These methods of psychological abuse may act as even more of a deterrent to notification than the possibility of physical violence, but women who are the victims of the abuse are not exempt from §3209's notification requirement. And many women who are pregnant as a result of sexual assaults by their husbands will be unable to avail themselves of the exception for spousal sexual assault, §3209(b)(3), because the exception requires that the woman have notified law enforcement authorities within 90 days of the assault, and her husband will be notified of her report once an investigation begins. §3128(c). If anything in this field is certain, it is that victims of spousal sexual assault are extremely reluctant to report the abuse to the government; hence, a great many spousal rape victims will not be exempt from the notification requirement imposed by §3209.

The spousal notification requirement is thus likely to prevent a significant number of women from obtaining an abortion. It does not merely make abortions a little more difficult or expensive to obtain; for many women, it will impose a substantial obstacle. We must not blind ourselves to the fact that the significant number of women who fear for their safety and the safety of their children are likely to be deterred from procuring an abortion as surely as if the Commonwealth had outlawed abortion in all cases.

Respondents attempt to avoid the conclusion that §3209 is invalid by pointing out that [the] effects of §3209 are felt by only one percent of the women who obtain abortions. [We] disagree with respondents' basic method of analysis.

The analysis does not end with one percent of women upon whom the statute operates; it begins there. Legislation is measured for consistency with the Constitution by its impact on those whose conduct it affects. For example, we would not say that a law which requires a newspaper to print a candidate's reply to an unfavorable editorial is valid on its face because most newspapers would adopt the policy even absent the law. The proper focus of constitutional inquiry is the group for whom the law is a restriction, not the group for whom the law is irrelevant. . . .

[The] unfortunate yet persisting conditions we document above will mean that in a large fraction of the cases in which §3209 is relevant, it will operate as a substantial obstacle to a woman's choice to undergo an abortion. It is an undue burden, and therefore invalid.

This conclusion is in no way inconsistent with our decisions upholding parental notification or consent requirements. Those enactments, and our judgment that they are constitutional, are based on the quite reasonable assumption that minors will benefit from consultation with their parents and that children will often not realize that their parents have their best interests at heart. We cannot adopt a parallel assumption about adult women. . . .

Before birth, however, the issue takes on a very different cast. It is an inescapable biological fact that state regulation with respect to the child a woman is carrying will have a far greater impact on the mother's liberty than on the father's. The effect of state regulation on a woman's protected liberty is doubly deserving of scrutiny in such a case, as the State has touched not only upon the private sphere of the family but upon the very bodily integrity of the pregnant woman. Cf. Cruzan v. Director, Missouri Dept. of Health. The Court has held that "when the wife and the husband disagree on this decision, the view of only one of the two marriage partners can prevail. Inasmuch as it is the woman who physically bears the child and who is the more directly and immediately affected by the pregnancy, as between the two, the balance weighs in her favor." *Danforth.* This conclusion rests upon the basic nature of marriage and the nature of our Constitution: "The marital couple is not an independent entity with a mind and heart of its own, but an association of two individuals each with a separate intellectual and emotional makeup. If the right of privacy means anything, it is the right of the individual, married or single, to be free from unwarranted governmental intrusion into matters so fundamentally affecting a person as the decision whether to bear or beget a child." Eisenstadt v. Baird[, 405 U.S. 438 (1972)]. The Constitution protects individuals, men and women alike, from unjustified state interference, even when that interference is enacted into law for the benefit of their spouses.

There was a time, not so long ago, when a different understanding of the family and of the Constitution prevailed. In Bradwell v. Illinois, 16 Wall. 130 (1873), three Members of this Court reaffirmed the common-law principle that "a woman had no legal existence separate from her husband, who was regarded as her head and representative in the social state; and, notwithstanding some recent modifications of this civil status, many of the special rules of law flowing from and dependent upon this cardinal principle still exist in full force in most States." Id., at 141 (Bradley J., joined by Swayne and Field, JJ., concurring in judgment). Only one generation has passed since this Court observed that "woman is still regarded as the center of home and family life," with attendant "special responsibilities" that precluded full and independent legal status under the Constitution. Hoyt v. Florida, 368 U.S. 57, 62 (1961). These views, of course, are no longer consistent with our understanding of the family, the individual, or the Constitution.

In keeping with our rejection of the common-law understanding of a woman's role within the family, the Court held in *Danforth* that the Constitution does not permit a State to require a married woman to obtain her husband's consent before undergoing an abortion. The principles that guided the Court in *Danforth* should be our guides today. For the great many women who are victims of abuse inflicted by their husbands, or whose children are the victims of such abuse, a spousal notice requirement enables the husband to wield an effective veto over his wife's decision. Whether the prospect of notification itself deters such women from seeking abortions, or whether the husband, through physical force or psychological pressure or economic coercion, prevents his wife from obtaining an abortion until it is too late, the notice requirement will often be tantamount to the veto found unconstitutional in *Danforth*. The women most affected by this law — those who most reasonably fear the consequences of notifying their husbands that they are pregnant — are in the gravest danger.

The husband's interest in the life of the child his wife is carrying does not permit the State to empower him with this troubling degree of authority over his wife. The contrary view leads to consequences reminiscent of the common law. A husband has no enforceable right to require a wife to advise him before she exercises her personal choices. If a husband's interest in the potential life of the child outweighs a wife's liberty, the State could require a married woman to notify her husband before she uses a postfertilization contraceptive. Perhaps next in line would be a statute requiring pregnant married women to notify their husbands before engaging in conduct causing risks to the fetus. After all, if the husband's interest in the fetus' safety is a sufficient predicate for state regulation, the State could reasonably conclude that pregnant wives should notify their husbands before drinking alcohol or smoking. Perhaps married women should notify their husbands before using contraceptives or before undergoing any type of surgery that may have complications affecting the husband's interest in his wife's reproductive organs. And if a husband's interest justifies notice in any of these cases, one might reasonably argue that it justifies exactly what the *Danforth* Court held it did not justify — a requirement of the husband's consent as well. A State may not give to a man the kind of dominion over his wife that parents exercise over their children.

Section 3209 embodies a view of marriage consonant with the common-law status of married women but repugnant to our present understanding of marriage and of the nature of the rights secured by the Constitution. Women do not lose their constitutionally protected liberty when they marry. The Constitution protects all individuals, male or female, married or unmarried, from the abuse of governmental power, even where that power is employed for the supposed benefit of a member of the individual's family. These considerations confirm our conclusion that §3209 is invalid.

D

We next consider the parental consent provision. Except in a medical emergency, an unemancipated young woman under 18 may not obtain an abortion unless she and one of her parents (or guardian) provides informed consent as defined above. If neither a parent nor a guardian provides consent, a court may authorize the performance of an abortion upon a determination that the young woman is mature and capable of giving informed consent and has in fact given her informed consent, or that an abortion would be in her best interests. . . .

The only argument made by petitioners respecting this provision and to which our prior decisions do not speak is the contention that the parental consent requirement is invalid because it requires informed parental consent. For the most part, petitioners' argument is a reprise of their argument with respect to the informed consent requirement in general, and we reject it for the reasons given above. . . .

E

Under the recordkeeping and reporting requirements of the statute, every facility which performs abortions is required to file a report stating its name and address as well as the name and address of any related entity, such as a controlling or subsidiary organization. In the case of state-funded institutions, the information becomes public. . . .

In *Danforth*, we held that recordkeeping and reporting provisions "that are reasonably directed to the preservation of maternal health and that properly respect a patient's confidentiality and privacy are permissible." We think that under this standard, all the provisions at issue here except that relating to spousal notice are constitutional. Although they do not relate to the State's interest in informing the woman's choice, they do relate to health. The collection of information with respect to actual patients is a vital element of medical research, and so it cannot be said that the requirements serve no purpose other than to make abortions more difficult. Nor do we find that the requirements impose a substantial obstacle to a woman's choice. At most they might increase the cost of some abortions by a slight amount. While at some point increased cost could become a substantial obstacle, there is no such showing on the record before us. . . .

VI

Our Constitution is a covenant running from the first generation of Americans to us and then to future generations. It is a coherent succession. Each generation must learn anew that the Constitution's written terms embody ideas and aspirations that must survive more ages than one. We accept our responsibility not to retreat from interpreting the full meaning of the covenant in light of all of our precedents. We invoke it once again to define the freedom guaranteed by the Constitution's own promise, the promise of liberty.

JUSTICE BLACKMUN, concurring in part, concurring in the judgment in part, and dissenting in part. . . .

Three years ago, in Webster v. Reproductive Health Serv., 492 U.S. 490 (1989), four Members of this Court appeared poised to "cast into darkness the hopes and visions of every woman in this country" who had come to believe that the Constitution guaranteed her the right to reproductive choice. Id., at 557 (Blackmun, J., dissenting). See id., at 499 (opinion of Rehnquist, C.J.); id., at 532 (opinion of Scalia, J.). All that remained between the promise of *Roe* and the darkness of the plurality was a single, flickering flame. Decisions since *Webster* gave little reason to hope that this flame would cast much light. See, e.g., Ohio v. Akron Center for Reproductive Health, 497 U.S. 502, 524 (1990) (opinion of Blackmun, J.). But now, just when so many expected the darkness to fall, the flame has grown bright.

I do not underestimate the significance of today's joint opinion. Yet I remain steadfast in my belief that the right to reproductive choice is entitled to the full protection afforded by this Court before *Webster*. And I fear for the darkness as four Justices anxiously await the single vote necessary to extinguish the light. . . .

Today, no less than yesterday, the Constitution and decisions of this Court require that a State's abortion restrictions be subjected to the strictest of judicial scrutiny. Our precedents and the joint opinion's principles require us to subject all non-de minimis abortion regulations to strict scrutiny. Under this standard, the Pennsylvania statute's provisions requiring content-based counseling, a 24-hour delay, informed parental consent, and reporting of abortion-related information must be invalidated. . . .

State restrictions on abortion violate a woman's right of privacy in two ways. First, compelled continuation of a pregnancy infringes upon a woman's right to bodily integrity by imposing substantial physical intrusions and significant risks of physical harm. During pregnancy, women experience dramatic physical changes and a wide range of health consequences. Labor and delivery pose additional health risks and physical demands. In short, restrictive abortion laws force women to endure physical invasions far more substantial than those this Court has held to violate the constitutional principle of bodily integrity in other contexts. See, e.g., Winston v. Lee, 470 U.S. 753 (1985) (invalidating surgical removal of bullet from murder suspect); Rochin v. California, 342 U.S. 165 (1952) (invalidating stomach-pumping).

Further, when the State restricts a woman's right to terminate her pregnancy, it deprives a woman of the right to make her own decision about reproduction and family planning — critical life choices that this Court long has deemed central to the right to privacy. The decision to terminate or continue a pregnancy has no less an impact on a woman's life than decisions about contraception or marriage. Because motherhood has a dramatic impact on a woman's educational prospects, employment opportunities, and self-determination, restrictive abortion laws deprive her of basic control over her life. For these reasons, "the decision whether or not to beget or bear a child" lies at "the very heart of this cluster of constitutionally protected choices."

A State's restrictions on a woman's right to terminate her pregnancy also implicate constitutional guarantees of gender equality. State restrictions on abortion compel women to continue pregnancies they otherwise might terminate. By restricting the right to terminate pregnancies, the State conscripts women's bodies into its service, forcing women to continue their pregnancies, suffer the pains of childbirth, and in most instances, provide years of maternal care. The State does not compensate women for their services; instead, it assumes that they owe this duty as a matter of course. This assumption — that women can simply be forced to accept the "natural" status and incidents of motherhood — appears to rest upon a conception of women's role that has triggered the protection of the Equal Protection Clause. See, e.g., Mississippi Univ. for Women v. Hogan, 458 U.S. 718, 724-726 (1982); Craig v. Boren, 429 U.S. 190, 198-199 (1976). The joint opinion recognizes that these assumptions about women's place in society "are no longer consistent with our understanding of the family, the individual, or the Constitution." . . .

Roe's trimester framework does not ignore the State's interest in prenatal life. Like Justice Stevens, I agree that the State may take steps to ensure that a woman's choice "is thoughtful and informed," and that "States are free to enact laws to provide a reasonable framework for a woman to make a decision that has such profound and lasting meaning." But "serious questions arise when a State attempts to 'persuade the woman to choose childbirth over abortion.' " Decisional autonomy must limit the State's power to inject into a woman's most personal deliberations its own views of what is best. The State may promote its preferences by funding childbirth, by creating and maintaining alternatives to abortion, and by espousing the virtues of family, but it must respect the individual's freedom to make such judgments." As the joint opinion recognizes, "the means chosen by the State to further the interest in potential life must be calculated to inform the woman's free choice, not hinder it."

In sum, *Roe*'s requirement of strict scrutiny as implemented through a trimester framework should not be disturbed. No other approach has gained a majority, and no other is more protective of the woman's fundamental right. Lastly, no other approach properly accommodates the woman's constitutional right with the State's legitimate interests. . . .

Measured against these principles, some aspects of the Pennsylvania informed-consent scheme are unconstitutional. While it is unobjectionable for the Commonwealth to require that the patient be informed of the nature of the procedure, the health risks of the abortion and of childbirth, and the probable gestational age of the unborn child, I remain unconvinced that there is a vital state need for insisting that the information be provided by a physician rather than a counselor. . . .

Sections 3205(a)(2)(i)-(iii) of the Act further require that the physician or a qualified non-physician inform the woman that printed materials are available from the Commonwealth that describe the fetus and provide information about medical assistance for childbirth, information about child support from the father, and a list of agencies which provide adoption and other services as alternatives to abortion. *Thornburgh* invalidated biased patient-counseling requirements virtually identical to the one at issue here. . . .

The 24-hour waiting period following the provision of the foregoing information is also clearly unconstitutional. The District Court found that the mandatory 24-hour delay could lead to delays in excess of 24 hours, thus increasing health risks, and that it would require two visits to the abortion provider, thereby increasing travel time, exposure to further harassment, and financial cost. Finally, the District Court found that the requirement would pose especially significant burdens on women living in rural areas and those women that have difficulty explaining their whereabouts. In *Akron* this Court invalidated a similarly arbitrary or inflexible waiting period because, as here, it furthered no legitimate state interest. . . .

Finally, the Pennsylvania statute requires every facility performing abortions to report its activities to the Commonwealth. Pennsylvania contends that this requirement is valid under *Danforth*, in which this Court held that recordkeeping and reporting requirements that are reasonably directed to the preservation of maternal health and that properly respect a patient's confidentiality are permissible. The Commonwealth attempts to justify its required reports on the ground that the public has a right to know how its tax dollars are spent. A regulation designed to inform the public about public expenditures does not further the Commonwealth's interest in protecting maternal health. Accordingly, such a regulation cannot justify a legally significant burden on a woman's right to obtain an abortion.

The confidential reports concerning the identities and medical judgment of physicians involved in abortions at first glance may seem valid, given the State's interest in maternal health and enforcement of the Act. The District Court found, however, that, notwithstanding the confidentiality protections, many physicians, particularly those who have previously discontinued performing abortions because of harassment, would refuse to refer patients to abortion clinics if their names were to appear on these reports. The Commonwealth has failed to show that the name of the referring physician either adds to the pool of scientific knowledge concerning abortion or is reasonably related to the Commonwealth's interest in maternal health. I therefore agree with the District Court's conclusion that the confidential reporting requirements are unconstitutional insofar as they require the name of the referring physician and the basis for his or her medical judgment. . . .

At long last, The Chief Justice admits it. Gone are the contentions that the issue need not be (or has not been) considered. There, on the first page, for all to see, is what was expected: "We believe that *Roe* was wrongly decided, and that it can and should be overruled consistently with our traditional approach to stare decisis in constitutional cases." If there is much reason to applaud the advances made by the joint opinion today, there is far more to fear from The Chief Justice's opinion.

The Chief Justice's criticism of *Roe* follows from his stunted conception of individual liberty. While recognizing that the Due Process Clause protects more than simple physical liberty, he then goes on to construe this Court's personal-liberty cases as establishing only a laundry list of particular rights, rather than a principled account of how these particular rights are grounded in a more general right of privacy. This constricted view is reinforced by The Chief Justice's exclusive reliance on tradition as a source of fundamental rights. He argues that the record in favor of a right to abortion is no stronger than the record in Michael H. v. Gerald D., 491 U.S. 110 (1989), where the plurality found no fundamental right to visitation privileges by an adulterous father, or in Bowers v. Hardwick, 478 U.S. 186 (1986), where the Court found no fundamental right to engage in homosexual sodomy, or in a case involving the "firing of a gun . . . into another person's body." In The Chief Justice's world, a woman considering whether to terminate a pregnancy is entitled to no more protection than adulterers, murderers, and so-called "sexual deviates." Given The Chief Justice's exclusive reliance on tradition, people using contraceptives seem the next likely candidate for his list of outcasts.

Even more shocking than The Chief Justice's cramped notion of individual liberty is his complete omission of any discussion of the effects that compelled childbirth and motherhood have on women's lives. The only expression of concern with women's health is purely instrumental — for The Chief Justice, only women's psychological health is a concern, and only to the extent that he assumes that every woman who decides to have an abortion does so without serious consideration of the moral implications of their decision. In short, The Chief Justice's view of the State's compelling interest in maternal health has less to do with health than it does with compelling women to be maternal.

Nor does The Chief Justice give any serious consideration to the doctrine of stare decisis. . . .

But, we are reassured, there is always the protection of the democratic process. While there is much to be praised about our democracy, our country since its founding has recognized that there are certain fundamental liberties that are not to be left to the whims of an election. A woman's right to reproductive choice is one of those fundamental liberties. Accordingly, that liberty need not seek refuge at the ballot box.

In one sense, the Court's approach is worlds apart from that of The Chief Justice and Justice Scalia. And yet, in another sense, the distance between the two approaches is short — the distance is but a single vote.

I am 83 years old. I cannot remain on this Court forever, and when I do step down, the confirmation process for my successor well may focus on the issue before us today. That, I regret, may be exactly where the choice between the two worlds will be made.

JUSTICE STEVENS, concurring in part and dissenting in part. . . .

[The] societal costs of overruling *Roe* at this late date would be enormous. *Roe* is an integral part of a correct understanding of both the concept of liberty and the basic equality of men and women. . . .

My disagreement with the joint opinion begins with its understanding of the trimester framework established in *Roe*. [It] is not a "contradiction" to recognize that the State may have a legitimate interest in potential human life and, at the same time, to conclude that that interest does not justify the regulation of abortion before viability (although other interests, such as maternal health, may). The fact that the State's interest is legitimate does not tell us when, if ever, that interest outweighs the pregnant woman's interest in personal liberty. It is appropriate, therefore, to consider more carefully the nature of the interests at stake.

First, it is clear that, in order to be legitimate, the State's interest must be secular; consistent with the First Amendment the State may not promote a theological or sectarian interest. . . .

Identifying the State's interests — which the States rarely articulate with any precision — makes clear that the interest in protecting potential life is not grounded in the Constitution. It is, instead, an indirect interest supported by both humanitarian and pragmatic concerns. Many of our citizens believe that any abortion reflects an unacceptable disrespect for potential human life and that the performance of more than a million abortions each year is intolerable; many find third-trimester abortions performed when the fetus is approaching personhood particularly offensive. The State has a legitimate interest in minimizing such offense. The State may also have a broader interest in expanding the population, believing society would benefit from the services of additional productive citizens — or that the potential human lives might include the occasional Mozart or Curie.

In counterpoise is the woman's constitutional interest in liberty. One aspect of this liberty is a right to bodily integrity, a right to control one's person. . . .

The woman's constitutional liberty interest also involves her freedom to decide matters of the highest privacy and the most personal nature. [The] authority to make such traumatic and yet empowering decisions is an element of basic human dignity. As the joint opinion so eloquently demonstrates, a woman's decision to terminate her pregnancy is nothing less than a matter of conscience. . . .

[Under] these principles, §§3205(a)(2)(i)-(iii) of the Pennsylvania statute are unconstitutional. Those sections require a physician or counselor to provide the woman with a range of materials clearly designed to persuade her to choose not to undergo the abortion. While the State is free, pursuant to §3208 of the Pennsylvania law, to produce and disseminate such material, the State may not inject such information into the woman's deliberations just as she is weighing such an important choice.

Under this same analysis, §§3205(a)(1)(i) and (iii) of the Pennsylvania statute are constitutional. Those sections, which require the physician to inform a woman of the nature and risks of the abortion procedure and the medical risks of carrying to term, are neutral requirements comparable to those imposed in other medical procedures. Those sections indicate no effort by the State to influence the woman's choice in any way. If anything, such requirements enhance, rather than skew, the woman's decisionmaking.

The 24-hour waiting period required by §§3205(a)(1)-(2) of the Pennsylvania statute raises even more serious concerns. Such a requirement arguably furthers the State's interests in two ways, neither of which is constitutionally permissible.

First, it may be argued that the 24-hour delay is justified by the mere fact that it is likely to reduce the number of abortions, thus furthering the

State's interest in potential life. But such an argument would justify any form of coercion that placed an obstacle in the woman's path. The State cannot further its interests by simply wearing down the ability of the pregnant woman to exercise her constitutional right.

Second, it can more reasonably be argued that the 24-hour delay furthers the State's interest in ensuring that the woman's decision is informed and thoughtful. But there is no evidence that the mandated delay benefits women or that it is necessary to enable the physician to convey any relevant information to the patient. The mandatory delay thus appears to rest on outmoded and unacceptable assumptions about the decisionmaking capacity of women. While there are well-established and consistently maintained reasons for the State to view with skepticism the ability of minors to make decisions, see Hodgson v. Minnesota, 497 U.S. 417, 449 (1990), none of those reasons applies to an adult woman's decisionmaking ability. Just as we have left behind the belief that a woman must consult her husband before undertaking serious matters, so we must reject the notion that a woman is less capable of deciding matters of gravity. Cf. Reed v. Reed, 404 U.S. 71 (1971).

In the alternative, the delay requirement may be premised on the belief that the decision to terminate a pregnancy is presumptively wrong. . . .

In my opinion, a correct application of the "undue burden" standard leads to the same conclusion concerning the constitutionality of these requirements. A state-imposed burden on the exercise of a constitutional right is measured both by its effects and by its character: A burden may be "undue" either because the burden is too severe or because it lacks a legitimate, rational justification.

The 24-hour delay requirement fails both parts of this test. . . .

The counseling provisions are similarly infirm. Whenever government commands private citizens to speak or to listen, careful review of the justification for that command is particularly appropriate. In this case, the Pennsylvania statute directs that counselors provide women seeking abortions with information concerning alternatives to abortion, the availability of medical assistance benefits, and the possibility of child-support payments. The statute requires that this information be given to all women seeking abortions, including those for whom such information is clearly useless, such as those who are married, those who have undergone the procedure in the past and are fully aware of the options, and those who are fully convinced that abortion is their only reasonable option. Moreover, the statute requires physicians to inform all of their patients of "the probable gestational age of the unborn child." This information is of little decisional value in most cases, because 90% of all abortions are performed during the first trimester when fetal age has less relevance than when the fetus nears viability. . . .

CHIEF JUSTICE REHNQUIST, with whom JUSTICE WHITE, JUSTICE SCALIA, and JUSTICE THOMAS join, concurring in the judgment in part and dissenting in part.

The joint opinion, following its newly-minted variation on stare decisis, retains the outer shell of Roe v. Wade, 410 U.S. 113 (1973), but beats a wholesale retreat from the substance of that case. We believe that *Roe* was wrongly decided, and that it can and should be overruled consistently with our traditional approach to stare decisis in constitutional cases. We would adopt the approach of the plurality in Webster v. Reproductive Health Services, 492 U.S. 490 (1989), and uphold the challenged provisions of the Pennsylvania statute in their entirety.

I

[In] construing the phrase "liberty" incorporated in the Due Process Clause of the Fourteenth Amendment, we have recognized that its meaning extends beyond freedom from physical restraint. In Pierce v. Society of Sisters, 268 U.S. 510 (1925), we held that it included a parent's right to send a child to private school; in Meyer v. Nebraska, 262 U.S. 390 (1923), we held that it included a right to teach a foreign language in a parochial school. Building on these cases, we have held that that the term "liberty" includes a right to marry, Loving v. Virginia, 388 U.S. 1 (1967); a right to procreate, Skinner v. Oklahoma ex rel. Williamson, 316 U.S. 535 (1942); and a right to use contraceptives, Griswold v. Connecticut, 381 U.S. 479 (1965); Eisenstadt v. Baird, 405 U.S. 438 (1972). But a reading of these opinions makes clear that they do not endorse any all-encompassing "right of privacy."

In Roe v. Wade, the Court recognized a "guarantee of personal privacy" which "is broad enough to encompass a woman's decision whether or not to terminate her pregnancy." 410 U. S., at 152-153. We are now of the view that, in terming this right fundamental, the Court in *Roe* read the earlier opinions upon which it based its decision much too broadly. Unlike marriage, procreation and contraception, abortion "involves the purposeful termination of potential life." Harris v. McRae, 448 U.S. 297, 325 (1980). The abortion decision must therefore "be recognized as sui generis, different in kind from the others that the Court has protected under the rubric of personal or family privacy and autonomy." Thornburgh v. American College of Obstetricians and Gynecologists, supra, at 792 (White, J., dissenting). One cannot ignore the fact that a woman is not isolated in her pregnancy, and that the decision to abort necessarily involves the destruction of a fetus.

Nor do the historical traditions of the American people support the view that the right to terminate one's pregnancy is "fundamental." The common law which we inherited from England made abortion after "quickening" an offense. At the time of the adoption of the Fourteenth Amendment, statutory prohibitions or restrictions on abortion were commonplace; in 1868, at least 28 of the then-37 States and 8 Territories had statutes banning or limiting abortion. J. Mohr, Abortion in America 200 (1978). By the turn of the century virtually every State had a law prohibiting or restricting abortion on its books. By the middle of the present century, a liberalization trend had set in. But 21 of the restrictive abortion laws in effect in1868 were still in effect in 1973 when *Roe* was decided, and an overwhelming majority of the States prohibited abortion unless necessary to preserve the life or health of the mother. Roe v. Wade, 410 U.S., at 139-140; id., at 176-177, n. 2 (Rehnquist, J., dissenting). On this record, it can scarcely be said that any deeply rooted tradition of relatively unrestricted abortion in our history supported the classification of the right to abortion as "fundamental" under the Due Process Clause of the Fourteenth Amendment.

We think, therefore, both in view of this history and of our decided cases dealing with substantive liberty under the Due Process Clause, that the Court was mistaken in *Roe* when it classified a woman's decision to terminate her pregnancy as a "fundamental right" that could be abridged only in a manner which withstood "strict scrutiny." In so concluding, we repeat the observation made in Bowers v. Hardwick, 478 U.S. 186 (1986):

> Nor are we inclined to take a more expansive view of our authority to discover new fundamental rights imbedded in the Due Process Clause. The Court is most vulnerable and comes nearest to illegitimacy when it deals with judge-made constitutional law having little or no cognizable roots in the language or design of the Constitution.

Id., at 194.

We believe that the sort of constitutionally imposed abortion code of the type illustrated by our decisions following *Roe* is inconsistent "with the notion of a Constitution cast in general terms, as ours is, and usually speaking in general principles, as ours does." Webster v. Reproductive Health Services, 492 U.S., at 518 (plurality opinion). The Court in *Roe* reached too far when it analogized the right to abort a fetus to the rights involved in *Pierce, Meyer, Loving*, and *Griswold*, and thereby deemed the right to abortion fundamental.

II

The joint opinion [cannot] bring itself to say that *Roe* was correct as an original matter, but the authors are of the view that "the immediate question is not the soundness of *Roe*'s resolution of the issue, but the precedential force that must be accorded to its holding." Instead of claiming that *Roe* was correct as a matter of original constitutional interpretation, the opinion therefore contains an elaborate discussion of stare decisis. This discussion of the principle of stare decisis appears to be almost entirely dicta, because the joint opinion does not apply that principle in dealing with *Roe*. *Roe* decided that a woman had a fundamental right to an abortion. The joint opinion rejects that view. *Roe* decided that abortion regulations were to be subjected to "strict scrutiny" and could be justified only in the light of "compelling state interests." The joint opinion rejects that view. *Roe* analyzed abortion regulation under a rigid trimester framework, a framework which has guided this Court's decisionmaking for 19 years. The joint opinion rejects that framework.

Stare decisis is defined in Black's Law Dictionary as meaning "to abide by, or adhere to, decided cases." Whatever the "central holding" of *Roe* that is left after the joint opinion finishes dissecting it is surely not the result of that principle. While purporting to adhere to precedent, the joint opinion instead revises it. *Roe* continues to exist, but only in the way a storefront on a western movie set exists: a mere facade to give the illusion of reality. Decisions following *Roe*, such as Akron v. Akron Center for Reproductive Health, Inc., 462 U.S. 416 (1983), and Thornburgh v. American College of Obstetricians and Gynecologists, 476 U.S. 747 (1986), are frankly overruled in part under the "undue burden" standard expounded in the joint opinion.

In our view, authentic principles of stare decisis do not require that any portion of the reasoning in *Roe* be kept intact. "Stare decisis is not . . . a universal, inexorable command," especially in cases involving the interpretation of the Federal Constitution. Burnet v. Coronado Oil & Gas Co., 285 U.S. 393, 405 (1932) (Brandeis, J., dissenting). Erroneous decisions in such constitutional cases are uniquely durable, because correction through legislative action, save for constitutional amendment, is impossible. . . .

The joint opinion discusses several stare decisis factors which, it asserts, point toward retaining a portion of *Roe*. Two of these factors are that the main "factual underpinning" of *Roe* has remained the same, and that its doctrinal foundation is no weaker now than it was in 1973. Of course, what might be called the basic facts which gave rise to *Roe* have remained the same — women become pregnant, there is a point somewhere, depending on medical technology, where a fetus becomes viable, and women give birth to children. But this is only to say that the same facts which gave rise to *Roe* will continue to give rise to similar cases. It is not a reason, in and of itself, why those cases must be decided in the same incorrect manner as was the first case to deal with the question. . . .

The joint opinion also points to the reliance interests involved in this context in its effort to explain why precedent must be followed for precedent's sake. Certainly it is true that where reliance is truly at issue, as in the case of judicial decisions that have formed the basis for private decisions, "considerations in favor of stare decisis are at their acme." But, as the joint opinion apparently agrees, ante, any traditional notion of reliance is not applicable here. The Court today cuts back on the protection afforded by *Roe*, and no one claims that this action defeats any reliance interest in the disavowed trimester framework. Similarly, reliance interests would not be diminished were the Court to go further and acknowledge the full error of *Roe*, as "reproductive planning could take virtually immediate account of" this action. . . .

In the end, having failed to put forth any evidence to prove any true reliance, the joint opinion's argument is based solely on generalized assertions about the national psyche, on a belief that the people of this country have grown accustomed to the *Roe* decision over the last 19 years and have "ordered their thinking and living around" it. As an initial matter, one might inquire how the joint opinion can view the "central holding" of *Roe* as so deeply rooted in our constitutional culture, when it so casually uproots and disposes of that same decision's trimester framework. Furthermore, at various points in the past, the same could have been said about this Court's erroneous decisions that the Constitution allowed "separate but equal" treatment of minorities, see Plessy v. Ferguson, 163 U.S. 537 (1896), or that "liberty" under the Due Process Clause protected "freedom of contract." See Adkins v. Children's Hospital of D.C., 261 U.S. 525 (1923); Lochner v. New York, 198 U.S. 45 (1905). The "separate but equal" doctrine lasted 58 years after *Plessy*, and *Lochner*'s protection of contractual freedom lasted 32 years. However, the simple fact that a generation or more had grown used to these major decisions did not prevent the Court from correcting its errors in those cases, nor should it prevent us from correctly interpreting the Constitution here.

Apparently realizing that conventional stare decisis principles do not support its position, the joint opinion advances a belief that retaining a portion of *Roe* is necessary to protect the "legitimacy" of this Court. Because the Court must take care to render decisions "grounded truly in principle," and not simply as political and social compromises, the joint opinion properly declares it to be this Court's duty to ignore the public criticism and protest that may arise as a result of a decision. Few would quarrel with this statement, although it may be doubted that Members of this Court, holding their tenure as they do during constitutional "good behavior," are at all likely to be intimidated by such public protests.

But the joint opinion goes on to state that when the Court "resolves the sort of intensely divisive controversy reflected in *Roe* and those rare, comparable cases," its decision is exempt from reconsideration under established principles of stare decisis in constitutional cases. This is so, the joint opinion contends, because in those "intensely divisive" cases the Court has "called the contending sides of a national controversy to end their national division by accepting a common mandate rooted in the Constitution," and must therefore take special care not to be perceived as "surrendering to political pressure" and continued opposition. This is a truly novel principle, one which is contrary to both the Court's historical practice and to the Court's traditional willingness to tolerate criticism of its opinions. Under this principle, when the Court has ruled on a divisive issue, it is apparently prevented from overruling that decision for the sole reason that it was incorrect, unless opposition to the original decision has died away.

The first difficulty with this principle lies in its assumption that cases which are "intensely divisive" can be readily distinguished from those that are not. The question of whether a particular issue is "intensely divisive" enough to qualify for special protection is entirely subjective and dependent on the individual assumptions of the members of this Court. In addition, because the Court's duty is to ignore public opinion and criticism on issues that come before it, its members are in perhaps the worst position to judge whether a decision divides the Nation deeply enough to justify such uncommon protection. . . .

The joint opinion picks out and discusses two prior Court rulings that it believes are of the "intensely divisive" variety, and concludes that they are of comparable dimension to *Roe*. It appears to us very odd indeed that the joint opinion chooses as benchmarks two cases in which the Court chose not to adhere to erroneous constitutional precedent, but instead enhanced its stature by acknowledging and correcting its error, apparently in violation of the joint opinion's "legitimacy" principle. . . .

The joint opinion agrees that the Court's stature would have been seriously damaged if in *Brown* and *West Coast Hotel* it had dug in its heels and refused to apply normal principles of stare decisis to the earlier decisions. But the opinion contends that the Court was entitled to overrule *Plessy* and *Lochner* in those cases, despite the existence of opposition to the original decisions, only because both the Nation and the Court had learned new lessons in the interim. This is at best a feebly supported, post hoc rationalization for those decisions.

For example, the opinion asserts that the Court could justifiably overrule its decision in *Lochner* only because the Depression had convinced "most people" that constitutional protection of contractual freedom contributed to an economy that failed to protect the welfare of all. Surely the joint opinion does not mean to suggest that people saw this Court's failure to uphold minimum wage statutes as the cause of the Great Depression! In any event, the *Lochner* Court did not base its rule upon the policy judgment that an unregulated market was fundamental to a stable economy; it simply believed, erroneously, that "liberty" under the Due Process Clause protected the "right to make a contract." Lochner v. New York, 198 U.S., at 53. Nor is it the case that the people of this Nation only discovered the dangers of extreme laissez faire economics because of the Depression. . . .

When the Court finally recognized its error in *West Coast Hotel,* it did not engage in the post hoc rationalization that the joint opinion attributes to it today; it did not state that *Lochner* had been based on an economic view that had fallen into disfavor, and that it therefore should be overruled. Chief Justice Hughes in his opinion for the Court simply recognized what Justice Holmes had previously recognized in his *Lochner* dissent, that "the Constitution does not speak of freedom of contract." West Coast Hotel Co. v. Parrish, 300 U.S., at 391; Lochner v. New York, supra, at 75 (Holmes, J., dissenting) ("[A] Constitution is not intended to embody a particular economic theory, whether of paternalism and the organic relation of the citizen to the State or of laissez faire"). Although the Court did acknowledge in the last paragraph of its opinion the state of affairs during the then-current Depression, the theme of the opinion is that the Court had been mistaken as a matter of constitutional law when it embraced "freedom of contract" 32 years previously.

The joint opinion also agrees that the Court acted properly in rejecting the doctrine of "separate but equal" in *Brown.* In fact, the opinion lauds *Brown* in comparing it to *Roe.* This is strange, in that under the opinion's "legitimacy" principle the Court would seemingly have been forced to adhere to its erroneous decision in *Plessy* because of its "intensely divisive" character. To us, adherence to *Roe* today under the guise of "legitimacy" would seem to resemble more closely adherence to *Plessy* on the same ground. Fortunately, the Court did not choose that option in *Brown,* and instead frankly repudiated *Plessy.* The joint opinion concludes that such repudiation was justified only because of newly discovered evidence that segregation had the effect of treating one race as inferior to another. But it can hardly be argued that this was not urged upon those who decided *Plessy,* as Justice Harlan observed in his dissent that the law at issue "puts the brand of servitude and degradation upon a large class of our fellow-citizens, our equals before the law." Plessy v.

Ferguson (Harlan, J., dissenting). It is clear that the same arguments made before the Court in *Brown* were made in *Plessy* as well. The Court in *Brown* simply recognized, as Justice Harlan had recognized beforehand, that the Fourteenth Amendment does not permit racial segregation. The rule of *Brown* is not tied to popular opinion about the evils of segregation; it is a judgment that the Equal Protection Clause does not permit racial segregation, no matter whether the public might come to believe that it is beneficial. On that ground it stands, and on that ground alone the Court was justified in properly concluding that the *Plessy* Court had erred.

There is also a suggestion in the joint opinion that the propriety of overruling a "divisive" decision depends in part on whether "most people" would now agree that it should be overruled. Either the demise of opposition or its progression to substantial popular agreement apparently is required to allow the Court to reconsider a divisive decision. How such agreement would be ascertained, short of a public opinion poll, the joint opinion does not say. But surely even the suggestion is totally at war with the idea of "legitimacy" in whose name it is invoked. The Judicial Branch derives its legitimacy, not from following public opinion, but from deciding by its best lights whether legislative enactments of the popular branches of Government comport with the Constitution. The doctrine of stare decisis is an adjunct of this duty, and should be no more subject to the vagaries of public opinion than is the basic judicial task. . . .

The end result of the joint opinion's paeans of praise for legitimacy is the enunciation of a brand new standard for evaluating state regulation of a woman's right to abortion — the "undue burden" standard. As indicated above, Roe v. Wade adopted a "fundamental right" standard under which state regulations could survive only if they met the requirement of "strict scrutiny." While we disagree with that standard, it at least had a recognized basis in constitutional law at the time *Roe* was decided. The same cannot be said for the "undue burden" standard, which is created largely out of whole cloth by the authors of the joint opinion. It is a standard which even today does not command the support of a majority of this Court. And it will not, we believe, result in the sort of "simple limitation," easily applied, which the joint opinion anticipates. In sum, it is a standard which is not built to last.

In evaluating abortion regulations under that standard, judges will have to decide whether they place a "substantial obstacle" in the path of a woman seeking an abortion. In that this standard is based even more on a judge's subjective determinations than was the trimester framework, the standard will do nothing to prevent "judges from roaming at large in the constitutional field" guided only by their personal views. Griswold v.

Connecticut, 381 U.S., at 502 (Harlan, J., concurring in judgment). Because the undue burden standard is plucked from nowhere, the question of what is a "substantial obstacle" to abortion will undoubtedly engender a variety of conflicting views. For example, in the very matter before us now, the authors of the joint opinion would uphold Pennsylvania's 24-hour waiting period, concluding that a "particular burden" on some women is not a substantial obstacle. But the authors would at the same time strike down Pennsylvania's spousal notice provision, after finding that in a "large fraction" of cases the provision will be a substantial obstacle. And, while the authors conclude that the informed consent provisions do not constitute an "undue burden," Justice Stevens would hold that they do.

Furthermore, while striking down the spousal notice regulation, the joint opinion would uphold a parental consent restriction that certainly places very substantial obstacles in the path of a minor's abortion choice. The joint opinion is forthright in admitting that it draws this distinction based on a policy judgment that parents will have the best interests of their children at heart, while the same is not necessarily true of husbands as to their wives. This may or may not be a correct judgment, but it is quintessentially a legislative one. The "undue burden" inquiry does not in any way supply the distinction between parental consent and spousal consent which the joint opinion adopts. Despite the efforts of the joint opinion, the undue burden standard presents nothing more workable than the trimester framework which it discards today. Under the guise of the Constitution, this Court will still impart its own preferences on the States in the form of a complex abortion code. . . .

We have stated above our belief that the Constitution does not subject state abortion regulations to heightened scrutiny. Accordingly, we think that the correct analysis is that set forth by the plurality opinion in *Webster*. A woman's interest in having an abortion is a form of liberty protected by the Due Process Clause, but States may regulate abortion procedures in ways rationally related to a legitimate state interest. With this rule in mind, we examine each of the challenged provisions. . . .

The question before us is therefore whether the spousal notification requirement rationally furthers any legitimate state interests. We conclude that it does. First, a husband's interests in procreation within marriage and in the potential life of his unborn child are certainly substantial ones. See Planned Parenthood of Central Mo. v. Danforth, 428 U.S., at 69 ("We are not unaware of the deep and proper concern and interest that a devoted and protective husband has in his wife's pregnancy and in the growth and development of the fetus she is carrying"); id., at 93 (White, J., concurring in part and dissenting in part); Skinner v. Oklahoma ex rel. Williamson, 316 U.S., at 541. The State itself has legitimate interests both in protecting these interests of the father and in protecting the potential life of the fetus, and the spousal notification requirement is reasonably related to advancing those state interests. By providing that a husband will usually know of his spouse's intent to have an abortion, the provision makes it more likely that the husband will participate in deciding the fate of his unborn child, a possibility that might otherwise have been denied him. This participation might in some cases result in a decision to proceed with the pregnancy. As Judge Alito observed in his dissent below, "the Pennsylvania legislature could have rationally believed that some married women are initially inclined to obtain an abortion without their husbands' knowledge because of perceived problems — such as economic constraints, future plans, or the husbands' previously expressed opposition — that may be obviated by discussion prior to the abortion." 947 F.2d, at 726 (Alito, J., concurring in part and dissenting in part).

The State also has a legitimate interest in promoting "the integrity of the marital relationship." [In] our view, the spousal notice requirement is a rational attempt by the State to improve truthful communication between spouses and encourage collaborative decisionmaking, and thereby fosters marital integrity. See Labine v. Vincent, 401 U.S. 532, 538 (1971) ("The power to make rules to establish, protect, and strengthen family life" is committed to the state legislatures). Petitioners argue that the notification requirement does not further any such interest; they assert that the majority of wives already notify their husbands of their abortion decisions, and the remainder have excellent reasons for keeping their decisions a secret. In the first case, they argue, the law is unnecessary, and in the second case it will only serve to foster marital discord and threats of harm. Thus, petitioners see the law as a totally irrational means of furthering whatever legitimate interest the State might have. But, in our view, it is unrealistic to assume that every husband-wife relationship is either (1) so perfect that this type of truthful and important communication will take place as a matter of course, or (2) so imperfect that, upon notice, the husband will react selfishly, violently, or contrary to the best interests of his wife. See Planned Parenthood of Central Mo. v. Danforth, supra, at 103-104 (Stevens, J., concurring in part and dissenting in part) (making a similar point in the context of a parental consent statute). The spousal notice provision will admittedly be unnecessary in some circumstances, and possibly harmful in others, but "the existence of particular cases in which a feature of a statute performs no function (or is even counterproductive) ordinarily does not render the statute unconstitutional or even constitutionally suspect." Thornburgh v. American College of Obstetricians and Gynecologists, 476 U.S., at 800 (White, J., dissenting). The Pennsylvania Legislature was in a position to weigh the likely benefits of the provision against its likely adverse effects, and presumably concluded, on balance, that the provision would be beneficial. Whether this was a wise decision or not, we cannot say that it was irrational. We therefore conclude that the spousal notice provision comports with the Constitution. See Harris v. McRae, 448 U.S., at 325-326 ("It is not the mission of this Court or any other to decide whether the balance of competing interests . . . is wise social policy"). . . . .

[We would] hold that each of the challenged provisions of the Pennsylvania statute is consistent with the Constitution. It bears emphasis that our conclusion in this regard does not carry with it any necessary approval of these regulations. Our task is, as always, to decide only whether the challenged provisions of a law comport with the United States Constitution. If, as we believe, these do, their wisdom as a matter of public policy is for the people of Pennsylvania to decide.

JUSTICE SCALIA, with whom THE CHIEF JUSTICE, JUSTICE WHITE, and JUSTICE THOMAS join, concurring in the judgment in part and dissenting in part. . . .

[A] State's choice between two positions on which reasonable people can disagree is constitutional even when (as is often the case) it intrudes upon a "liberty" in the absolute sense. Laws against bigamy, for example — which entire societies of reasonable people disagree with — intrude upon men and women's liberty to marry and live with one another. But bigamy happens not to be a liberty specially "protected" by the Constitution.

That is, quite simply, the issue in this case: not whether the power of a woman to abort her unborn child is a "liberty" in the absolute sense; or even whether it is a liberty of great importance to many women. Of course it is both. The issue is whether it is a liberty protected by the Constitution of the United States. I am sure it is not. I reach that conclusion not because of anything so exalted as my views concerning the "concept of existence, of meaning, of the universe, and of the mystery of human life." Rather, I reach it for the same reason I reach the conclusion that bigamy is not constitutionally protected — because of two simple facts: (1) the Constitution says absolutely nothing about it, and (2) the longstanding traditions of American society have permitted it to be legally proscribed.

The Court destroys the proposition, evidently meant to represent my position, that "liberty" includes "only those practices, defined at the most specific level, that were protected against government interference by other rules of law when the Fourteenth Amendment was ratified." That is not, however, what *Michael H.* says; it merely observes that, in defining "liberty," we may not disregard a specific, "relevant tradition protecting, or denying protection to, the asserted right." But the Court does not wish to be fettered by any such limitations on its preferences. The Court's statement that it is "tempting" to acknowledge the authoritativeness of tradition in order to "curb the discretion of federal judges," is of course rhetoric rather than reality; no government official is "tempted" to place restraints upon his own freedom of action, which is why Lord Acton did not say "Power tends to purify." The Court's temptation is in the quite opposite and more natural direction — towards systematically eliminating checks upon its own power; and it succumbs.

Beyond that brief summary of the essence of my position, I will not swell the United States Reports with repetition of what I have said before; and applying the rational basis test, I would uphold the Pennsylvania statute in its entirety. I must, however, respond to a few of the more outrageous arguments in today's opinion, which it is beyond human nature to leave unanswered. I shall discuss each of them under a quotation from the Court's opinion to which they pertain.

> The inescapable fact is that adjudication of substantive due process claims may call upon the Court in interpreting the Constitution to exercise that same capacity which by tradition courts always have exercised: reasoned judgment. . . .

The emptiness of the "reasoned judgment" that produced *Roe* is displayed in plain view by the fact that, after more than 19 years of effort by some of the brightest (and most determined) legal minds in the country, after more than 10 cases upholding abortion rights in this Court, and after dozens upon dozens of amicus briefs submitted in this and other cases, the best the Court can do to explain how it is that the word "liberty" must be thought to include the right to destroy human fetuses is to rattle off a collection of adjectives that simply decorate a value judgment and conceal a political choice. . . .

"Liberty finds no refuge in a jurisprudence of doubt."

One might have feared to encounter this august and sonorous phrase in an opinion defending the real Roe v. Wade, rather than the revised version fabricated today by the authors of the joint opinion. The shortcomings of *Roe* did not include lack of clarity: Virtually all regulation of abortion before the third trimester was invalid. But to come across this phrase in the joint opinion — which calls upon federal district judges to apply an "undue burden" standard as doubtful in application as it is unprincipled in origin — is really more than one should have to bear. . . .

[Defining] an "undue burden" as an "undue hindrance" (or a "substantial obstacle") hardly "clarifies" the test. Consciously or not, the joint opinion's verbal shell game will conceal raw judicial policy choices concerning what is "appropriate" abortion legislation.

The ultimately standardless nature of the "undue burden" inquiry is a reflection of the underlying fact that the concept has no principled or coherent legal basis. . . .

> While we appreciate the weight of the arguments . . . that *Roe* should be overruled, the reservations any of us may have in reaffirming the central holding of *Roe* are outweighed by the explication of individual liberty we have given combined with the force of stare decisis.

The Court's reliance upon stare decisis can best be described as contrived. It insists upon the necessity of adhering not to all of *Roe*, but only to what it calls the "central holding." It seems to me that stare decisis ought to be applied even to the doctrine of stare decisis, and I confess never to have heard of this new, keep-what-you-want-and-throw-away-the-rest version. I wonder whether, as applied to Marbury v. Madison, 1 Cranch 137 (1803), for example, the new version of stare decisis would be satisfied if we allowed courts to review the constitutionality of only those statutes that (like the one in *Marbury*) pertain to the jurisdiction of the courts.

I am certainly not in a good position to dispute that the Court has saved the "central holding" of *Roe*, since to do that effectively I would have to know what the Court has saved, which in turn would require me to understand (as I do not) what the "undue burden" test means. I must confess, however, that I have always thought, and I think a lot of other people have always thought, that the arbitrary trimester framework, which the Court today discards, was quite as central to *Roe* as the arbitrary viability test, which the Court today retains. . . .

> Where, in the performance of its judicial duties, the Court decides a case in such a way as to resolve the sort of intensely divisive controversy reflected in *Roe* . . . ., its decision has a dimension that the resolution of the normal case does not carry. It is the dimension present whenever the Court's interpretation of the Constitution calls the contending sides of a national controversy to end their national division by accepting a common mandate rooted in the Constitution.

The Court's description of the place of *Roe* in the social history of the United States is unrecognizable. Not only did *Roe* not, as the Court suggests, resolve the deeply divisive issue of abortion; it did more than anything else to nourish it, by elevating it to the national level where it is infinitely more difficult to resolve. National politics were not plagued by abortion protests, national abortion lobbying, or abortion marches on Congress, before Roe v. Wade was decided. Profound disagreement existed among our citizens over the issue — as it does over other issues, such as the death penalty — but that disagreement was being worked out at the state level. As with many other issues, the division of sentiment within each State was not as closely balanced as it was among the population of the Nation as a whole, meaning not only that more people would be satisfied with the results of state-by-state resolution, but also that those results would be more stable. Pre-*Roe*, moreover, political compromise was possible.

Roe's mandate for abortion-on-demand destroyed the compromises of the past, rendered compromise impossible for the future, and required the entire issue to be resolved uniformly, at the national level. At the same time, *Roe* created a vast new class of abortion consumers and abortion proponents by eliminating the moral opprobrium that had attached to the act. ("If the Constitution guarantees abortion, how can it be bad?" — not an accurate line of thought, but a natural one.) Many favor all of those developments, and it is not for me to say that they are wrong. But to portray *Roe* as the statesmanlike "settlement" of a divisive issue, a jurisprudential Peace of Westphalia that is worth preserving, is nothing less than Orwellian. *Roe* fanned into life an issue that has inflamed our national politics in general, and has obscured with its smoke the selection of Justices to this Court in particular, ever since. And by keeping us in the abortion-umpiring business, it is the perpetuation of that disruption, rather than of any pax *Roe*ana, that the Court's new majority decrees.

[It] is particularly difficult, in the circumstances of the present decision, to sit still for the Court's lengthy lecture upon the virtues of "constancy," of "remaining steadfast," of adhering to "principle." Among the five Justices who purportedly adhere to *Roe*, at most three agree upon the principle that constitutes adherence (the joint opinion's "undue burden" standard) — and that principle is inconsistent with *Roe*. To make matters worse, two of the three, in order thus to remain steadfast, had to abandon previously stated positions. It is beyond me how the Court expects these accommodations to be accepted "as grounded truly in principle, not as compromises with social and political pressures having, as such, no bearing on the principled choices that the Court is obliged to make." The only principle the Court "adheres" to, it seems to me, is the principle that the Court must be seen as standing by *Roe*. That is not a principle of law (which is what I thought the Court was talking about), but a principle of Realpolitik — and a wrong one at that.

I cannot agree with, indeed I am appalled by, the Court's suggestion that the decision whether to stand by an erroneous constitutional decision must be strongly influenced — against overruling, no less — by the substantial and continuing public opposition the decision has generated. . . .

What makes all this relevant to the bothersome application of "political pressure" against the Court are the twin facts that the American people love democracy and the American people are not fools. As long as this Court thought (and the people thought) that we Justices were doing essentially lawyers' work up here — reading text and discerning our society's traditional understanding of that text — the public pretty much left us alone. Texts and traditions are facts to study, not convictions to demonstrate about. But if in reality our process of constitutional adjudication consists primarily of making value judgments; if we can ignore a long and clear tradition clarifying an ambiguous text, as we did, for example, five days ago in declaring unconstitutional invocations and benedictions at public-high-school graduation ceremonies, Lee v. Weisman, 505 U.S. — (1992); if, as I say, our pronouncement of constitutional law rests primarily on value judgments, then a free and intelligent people's attitude towards us can be expected to be (ought to be) quite different. The people know that their value judgments are quite as good as those taught in any law school — maybe better. If, indeed, the "liberties" protected by the Constitution are, as the Court says, undefined and unbounded, then the people should demonstrate, to protest that we do not implement their values instead of ours. Not only that, but confirmation hearings for new Justices should deteriorate into question-and-answer sessions in which Senators go through a list of their constituents' most favored and most disfavored alleged constitutional rights, and seek the nominee's commitment to support or oppose them. Value judgments, after all, should be voted on, not dictated; and if our Constitution has somehow accidentally committed them to the Supreme Court, at least we can have a sort of plebiscite each time a new nominee to that body is put forward. Justice Blackmun not only regards this prospect with equanimity, he solicits it.

There is a poignant aspect to the Court's opinion. Its length, and what might be called its epic tone, suggest that its authors believe they are bringing to an end a troublesome era in the history of our Nation and of our Court. "It is the dimension" of authority, they say, to "call the contending sides of national controversy to end their national division by accepting a common mandate rooted in the Constitution."

There comes vividly to mind a portrait by Emanuel Leutze that hangs in the Harvard Law School: Roger Brooke Taney, painted in 1859, the 82d year of his life, the 24th of his Chief Justiceship, the second after his opinion in *Dred Scott.* He is all in black, sitting in a shadowed red armchair, left hand resting upon a pad of paper in his lap, right hand hanging limply, almost lifelessly, beside the inner arm of the chair. He sits facing the viewer, and staring straight out. There seems to be on his face, and in his deep-set eyes, an expression of profound sadness and disillusionment. Perhaps he always looked that way, even when dwelling upon the happiest of thoughts. But those of us who know how the lustre of his great Chief Justiceship came to be eclipsed by *Dred Scott* cannot help believing that he had that case — its already apparent consequences for the Court, and its soon-to-be-played-out consequences for the Nation — burning on his mind. I expect that two years earlier he, too, had thought himself "calling the contending sides of national controversy to end their national division by accepting a common mandate rooted in the Constitution."

It is no more realistic for us in this case, than it was for him in that, to think that an issue of the sort they both involved — an issue involving life and death, freedom and subjugation — can be "speedily and finally settled" by the Supreme Court, as President James Buchanan in his inaugural address said the issue of slavery in the territories would be. Quite to the contrary, by foreclosing all democratic outlet for the deep passions this issue arouses, by banishing the issue from the political forum that gives all participants, even the losers, the satisfaction of a fair hearing and an honest fight, by continuing the imposition of a rigid national rule instead of allowing for regional differences, the Court merely prolongs and intensifies the anguish.

We should get out of this area, where we have no right to be, and where we do neither ourselves nor the country any good by remaining.

Note: A New Era: The Casey *Case and the Role of the Court*

1. *Politics and judicial independence*. The *Casey* case raises a number of important issues about stare decisis, liberty, equality, and the role of the Court in general. Note first that five of the justices on the *Casey* Court were appointed by Presidents Reagan and Bush, both sharp critics of *Roe*. Does the decision contain lessons about the power of the President to remake the Court? Does it suggest that law does indeed operate in a way that is independent of politics?

2. *Stare decisis and constitutional history*. Consider the intriguing discussion in the lead opinion of what happened between *Lochner* and *West Coast Hotel*, and between *Plessy* and *Brown*. Exactly what, in the authors' opinions, changed in the relevant period? Much, in their view, appears to have turned on some change in "the facts," or in social understandings of "the facts." Do you think that this is an accurate description of the change? Consider the following views:

(a) The justices are really saying something deeply true: that *Lochner* was wrong because the system of laissez-faire disserved human liberty, and that

Plessy was wrong because the social stigma of segregation was misattributed to black people when it should have been attributed to the law. Both of the cases thus depended on judgments that could not long be supported. *West Coast Hotel* and *Brown* were important corrections here. They saw that regulatory improvements on laissez-faire could serve human liberty, and that segregation was a system of second-class citizenship for blacks.

(b) The justices are really just dressing up the fact that there was an ideological change between *Lochner* and *West Coast Hotel*, and between *Plessy* and *Brown*. By the time of the latter decisions, people simply saw things differently. And if all we have is ideological change, then overruling *Roe* would indeed have been appropriate.

(c) In discussing *Lochner* and *Plessy*, the justices are not thinking enough about whether the specific constitutional provision justified these decisions. The problem with *Lochner* was the Court's creation of aggressive substantive due process (the same problem as in *Roe*). The problem with *Plessy* was that the Court wrongly allowed racial segregation under the equal protection clause. None of this has to do with changes or with new facts. See in this regard the views on *Lochner* and *Plessy* in dissenting opinions.

3. *Abortion and gender equality*. Note that Justice Blackmun, Justice Stevens, and the joint opinion all refer to equality on the basis of gender and to the relationship between the *Roe* right and gender equality. Is there now an argument that restrictions on abortion implicate the equal protection clause? What is it, and what implications might it have for other areas of constitutional law? See in this regard Strauss, Abortion, Toleration, and Moral Uncertainty, 1993 Supreme Court Review 1, 27: "The Court in Casey addressed, essentially for the first time, the issues that ought to be central to the legal debate over abortion: not whether there are 'unenumerated rights' in the Constitution, but how to deal with fetal life, on the one hand, and the effect of abortion laws on the status of women, on the other. [T]he Court adopted [a] plausible and coherent justification for a regime of toleration in the area of abortion. That justification is premised on, first, fundamental moral uncertainty about the status of fetal life; and, second, the danger that the political process will subordinate women, a danger that is the basis of the well-established constitutional principles governing gender discrimination." Strauss grounds this argument on a claim for tolerance in the face of moral uncertainty — a claim that, on his view, is analogous to the claim for tolerance in the religious setting. The question of the role of religion in this setting is taken up in detail in R. Dworkin, Life's Dominion (1993), which argues on behalf of the abortion right on the basis of the "essentially religious" nature of the key question, which is the sanctity of human life.

4. Roe *and the democratic process*. Has the experience with *Roe* really been healthy for the country, for democracy, or for women? Is it appropriate for the confirmation hearings to focus a great deal on likely votes on *Roe*? Is it appropriate for presidential elections to turn a great deal on the likely votes of Supreme Court nominees? Might social fragmentation have been produced, not alleviated, by *Roe* and (now) *Casey*?

5. *The future*. Consider the implications of *Casey* for the future trends and likely character of the newly remade Supreme Court of the United States.

3. Family and Other "Privacy" Interests

Page 965. Before Stanley v. Illinois, add the following:

For an attack on Justice Scalia's footnote, see L. Tribe & M. Dorf, On Reading the Constitution 98 (1991):

> [W]e argue that Justice Scalia's claim is false on several grounds; first, . . . the extraction of fundamental rights from societal traditions is no more value-neutral than is the extraction of fundamental rights from legal precedent; second, . . . there is no universal metric of specificity against which to measure an asserted right; and third, [e]ven if Justice Scalia's program were workable, it would achieve a semblance of judicial neutrality only at the unacceptably high cost of near-complete abdication of the judicial responsibility to protect individual rights.

The argument is set out in more detail in Tribe & Dorf, Levels of Generality in Constitutional Law, 57 U. Chi. L. Rev. 1057 (1991).

See also Balkin, Tradition, Betrayal, and the Politics of Deconstruction, 11 Cardozo L. Rev. 1613, 1615-1616:

> [Justice Scalia's] test assumes that [for] each asserted right there either is or is not a specific tradition associated with its protection. Yet there are many ways of describing a liberty, and many different ways of characterizing a tradition. [There] has been no established tradition in California for protecting Justice Scalia's own rights to visit his children, since there is no tradition of affording protection to fathers who are children of Italian immigrants and who graduated from Ivy League law schools before 1965, were appointed to the United States Supreme Court by former governors of the state of California and have more than two children but less than thirteen. Indeed, the question has hardly ever come up. [To] be sure, Justice Scalia has a plausible response. When Justice Scalia claims parental rights to his children, the liberty he claims is the parental rights of fathers with respect to biological children born while the father was married to the child's mother. This has been traditionally protected. The rights of adulterous fathers, however, have not been traditionally protected. But this answer reveals that Justice Scalia's theory is not simply a preference for narrower traditions over broader traditions. It rests upon an important metaphysical set of assumptions — that traditions or (more impor-

> tantly) the absences of traditions, come in discrete units with discrete boundaries. [Like] glass bottles, traditions and liberties come in premade sizes. [Thus,] there is a tradition of protecting marital privacy but not a tradition of protecting the marital privacy of a narrower class — for example, middle class persons, and certainly not a tradition of protecting the privacy of a broader class of persons that would include unmarried couples. Yet, under this logic, it is also historically clear that there is a tradition of protecting married couples' privacy, but not a historical tradition of protecting married couples' right to purchase contraceptives. Griswold v. Connecticut is thus a potential embarrassment for Justice Scalia.

In Reno v. Flores, 61 USLW 4237 (1993), the Court upheld against substantive due process challenge an Immigration and Naturalization Service (INS) regulation authorizing the arrest and holding of alien juveniles unaccompanied by parents or other related adults. The juveniles claimed a right to be released to "responsible adults," even if they were not family members. The Court doubted that "a child has a constitutional right not to be placed in a decent and humane custodial institution if there is available a responsible person unwilling to become the child's legal guardian but willing to undertake temporary legal custody." Because no fundamental right was involved — merely "the lesser" interest in being released into the custody of strangers" — the Court required only a reasonable fit between the government purposes and the restriction in question. The Court said that the purpose of protecting juveniles was adequately advanced by the regulation in question, especially in light of the INS' lack of child-placement expertise and the fact that aliens were involved.

Justice O'Connor, joined by Justice Souter, wrote a lengthy concurring opinion, stressing that children have a "core liberty interest in remaining free from institutional confinement," that this freedom "is no narrower than an adult's," but that in this case, "normal forms of custody," such as parents, close relatives, or legal guardians, have been unavailable, and therefore the INS program survives constitutional scrutiny. Justice Stevens, joined by Justice Blackmun, dissented on the ground that the "interest in minimizing administrative costs is a patently inadequate justification for the detention of harmless children."

Page 967. Before the Note, add the following:

Does the criminal prosecution of drug-addicted mothers, for harms to their fetuses, violate the Constitution? For an affirmative answer, drawing on principles of due process and equal protection, see Roberts, Punishing Drug Addicts Who Have Babies: Women of Color, Equality, and the Right of Privacy, 104 Harv. L. Rev. 1419 (1991). Consider in particular the suggestion that the appropriate "concept of privacy includes not only the negative prosecution against government coercion, but also the affirmative duty of government to protect the individual's personhood from degradation and to facilitate the processes of choice and self-determination. This approach shifts the focus of privacy theory from state nonintervention to an affirmative guarantee of personhood and autonomy. Under this post-liberal doctrine, the government is not only prohibited from punishing crack-addicted women for choosing to bear children; it is also required to provide drug treatment and prenatal care." Id. at 1479. Might Professor Roberts's use of the words "coercion" and "affirmative" be building on a theory that she is attempting to repudiate? And is it plausible to think that provision of these things should be a judicially enforceable right?

4. The Right to Die

Page 985. Before section 3 of the Note, add the following:

Consider, Seidman, Confusion at the Border: Cruzan, "The Right to Die," and the Public/Private Distinction, 1992 Sup. Ct. Rev. 47, 68-70:

> [Justice Scalia] may be correct when he asserts that there is little support for the claim that a right to suicide is rooted in our traditions, but, as Justice Brennan forcefully argued, there is considerable support for a traditional right to avoid unwanted medical treatment. Whether the Constitution speaks to Ms. Cruzan's predicament therefore depends upon which tradition one chooses to emphasize. . . .
>
> Unfortunately, in *Cruzan,* it is far from clear which tradition is more specific and which more general. If one looks at the matter from a certain angle, one might say that Ms. Cruzan is not asserting a generalized right to end her life in all circumstances, but only a narrow, specific right to do so in circumstances where death results from abstinence from medical treatment. [On] the other hand, an opponent of such a right might plausibly respond that the narrow prohibition against suicide is more specific than a generalized right to determine medical treatment in all circumstances, including those not involving death. . . .
>
> The analysis is further complicated by the fact that some traditions are permissive, while others are restrictive. Thus, there is a tradition permitting state regulation of suicide in tension with a tradition restricting state interference with private decisions to refuse treatment. . . .
>
> Some of Justice Scalia's writing suggest that [when] a permissive and restrictive tradition conflict, the permissive tradition should prevail, whether or not it is more specific. Thus, because the state has traditionally been permitted to regulate suicide, there cannot be a constitutional right to refuse medical treatment even if the nonrecognition of this right would interfere with a restrictive tradition concerning state imposed medical treatment.

But this explanation for the *Cruzan* result only begs the central question. Justice Scalia never explains why permissive traditions are favored over restrictive traditions. This preference amounts to a privileging of the domain of collective public policy over the domain of private individual rights. We are still left with the need to explain or justify the decision to place the decision in one sphere rather than the other.

Page 985. After section 3 of the Note, add the following:

Consider the following hypothetical: *X*, a 55-year-old, is feeling under the weather. He goes to his doctor for an examination. The doctor does a blood test and informs *X* that he has good news and he has bad news. First, the bad news. The doctor tells *X* that he is suffering from a rare disease that will cause his death, peacefully and in his sleep, in about a month. Second, the good news. There is a cure. All the doctor need do is shine a newly developed cosmic ray at *X* and the disease will be gone. There is, however, a catch. The cosmic ray has a side effect. It will do permanent damage to *X*'s head, spine, and alimentary system and thus render him a quadriplegic, permanently immobile, strapped to a hospital bed for the remainder of his life, perhaps 20 years, connected to a maze of hydration and nutrition hoses and pumps, in severe, unrelenting, and untreatable physical and emotional pain and suffering.

After consulting with his family, *X* calls the doctor and says he will pass on the ray and let nature take its course. Two days later, an agent of the State's Life Preservation Patrol appears at *X*'s house. When *X* opens the door, the agent shines the cosmic ray at *X*, effecting the "cure." *X* awakens to find himself strapped to a hospital bed, paralyzed from head to toe, connected to a variety of machines, in grievous physical pain.

Page 985. After section 4 of the Note, add the following:

5. In Foucha v. Louisiana, 112 S. Ct. 1780 (1992), the Court invalidated a state law allowing someone acquitted of crime by reason of insanity to be confined indefinitely to a mental institution unless he is able to demonstrate that he is not dangerous to himself or to others. The Court concluded that under the due process clause, someone deprived of liberty in this way must have procedural safeguards requiring the state to show mental illness and dangerousness by clear and convincing evidence. Justice Thomas dissented, joined by the Chief Justice and Justice Scalia.

Chapter Seven

Freedom of Expression

A. INTRODUCTION

Page 1020. Before subsection 2d of the Note, add the following:

c-1. Sunstein, Free Speech Now, 59 U. Chi. L. Rev. 255, 301, 304-306 (1992):

> [T]he First Amendment is principally about political deliberation. The fact that words or pictures are involved is not, standing by itself, a sufficient reason for full constitutional protection. [We should] treat speech as political when it is both intended and received as a contribution to public deliberation about some issue. [An] approach that affords special protection to political speech, thus defined, is justified on numerous grounds. [It] receives firm support from history — not only from the Framer's theory of free expression, but also from the development of that principle through the history of American law. There can be little doubt that suppression by the government of political ideas that it disapproved, or found threatening, was the central motivation for the clause. [This] approach seems likely as well to accord with our initial or considered judgments about particular free speech problems. [It] seems clear that such forms of speech as perjury, bribery, threats, misleading or false commercial advertising, criminal solicitation, and libel of private persons — or at least most of these — are not entitled to the highest degree of constitutional protection. In addition, an insistence that government's burden is greatest when political speech is at issue responds well to the fact that here government is most likely to be biased. The presumption of distrust of government is strongest when politics are at issue. It is far weaker when government is regulating (say) commercial speech, bribery, private libel, or obscenity. [Finally], this approach protects speech when regulation is most likely to be harmful. Restrictions on political speech have the distinctive feature of impairing the ordinary channels for political [change]. If there are controls on commercial advertising, it always remains possible to argue that such controls should be lifted. [But] if the government forecloses political argument, the democratic corrective is unavailable. [Taken] in concert, these considerations suggest that government should be under a special burden of justification

when it seeks to control speech intended and received as a contribution to public deliberation.

Page 1023. At the end of subsection 4c of the Note, add the following:

For further elaboration of this view, see Bollinger, The Tolerant Society: A Response to Critics, 90 Colum. L. Rev. 979 (1990).

d. *A public choice perspective.* Consider Farber, Free Speech Without Romance: Public Choice and the First Amendment, 105 Harv. L. Rev. 554, 558-561 (1991):

> Over the past twenty years, economists have become increasingly interested in the economics of information. Their most basic finding [is] that markets are likely to produce too little information because information [has] many of the attributes of a public good. That is, the benefits of information cannot be restricted to direct purchasers but inevitably spread to larger groups. [Because] the producer does not consider these benefits in his production decision, less information is produced than is socially optimal.
>
> [Moreover,] the political system is likely to overregulate information [because] consumers of information, like all large, diffuse groups of individuals with small personal stakes, face serious organizational problems in lobbying and other political activities. [When] the product in question is information, this effect is exacerbated because the benefits of improved information are so diffuse. Hence, [consumers] of information are [especially] likely to be dismal failures in preventing government from limiting information production. [Thus], information is likely not only to be underproduced in the private market, but also [to] be insufficiently protected by the political system. It is [this] tendency to overregulate speech activities that requires constitutional protection for speech.

B. CONTENT-BASED RESTRICTIONS: DANGEROUS IDEAS AND INFORMATION

1. *Expression That Induces Unlawful Conduct*

Page 1039. Before section 3 of the Note, add the following:

The recently discovered, unpublished dissent by Holmes in Baltzer v. United States casts doubt on the "transformation" theory. *Baltzer* was the first of the wartime first amendment cases considered by the Court. In *Baltzer*, the defendants wrote the governor of South Dakota demanding reforms in the selective service process. They threatened to vote the governor out of office if the demands were not met. For writing these letters, the defendants were prosecuted and convicted for attempting to obstruct the enlistment service.

In conference, several months before argument in *Schenck*, the Justices voted seven-to-two to uphold the convictions. A few days later, Justice Holmes circulated a dissenting opinion:

> It seems to me that this petition to an official by ignorant persons who suppose him to possess power [he lacks] was nothing [but] the foolish exercise of a right. [From] beginning to end the changes advocated are changes by law, not in resistance to it, the only threat being that which every citizen may utter, that if his wishes are not followed his vote will be lost. [Our] intention to put out all our powers in aid of success in war should not hurry us into intolerance of opinions and speech that could not be imagined to do harm, though opposed to our own. It is better for those who have unquestioned and almost unlimited power in their hands to err on the side of freedom. We have enjoyed so much freedom for so long that perhaps we are in danger of forgetting that the bill of rights which cost so much blood to establish is still worth fighting for, and that no tittle of it should be abridged. [The] emergency would have to be very great before I could be persuaded that an appeal for political action through legal channels, addressed to those supposed to have power to take such action, was an act that the Constitution did not protect. . . .

Shortly after Holmes circulated this dissent, the Government confessed error and the case was remanded "for further proceedings in accordance with law." Sheldon Novick, who discovered this opinion, concludes that it shows that Holmes did not change his view from *Schenck* to *Abrams*, but was in fact "stubbornly consistent" in his insistence that the first amendment "required that two things be proven before criminal liability could be imposed for speech or publication: foreseeability of harm of a kind Congress had power to forbid; and a subjective intent to bring about the specific, forbidden harm." Novick, The Unrevised Holmes and Freedom of Expression, 1991 Sup. Ct. Rev. 303, 305. For the full text of Holmes's opinion in *Baltzer*, see Novick, supra, at 388-390.

Page 1051. Before section 2 of the Note, add the following:

1A. *The persuasion principle.* Consider Strauss, Persuasion, Autonomy, and Freedom of Expression, 91 Colum. L. Rev. 334-336, 346-347, 353-356 (1991):

> The government may not suppress speech on the ground that it is too persuasive. Except, perhaps, in extraordinary circumstances, the government may not restrict speech because it fears, however justifiably, that the speech will persuade those who hear it to do something of which the government disapproves. [This] principle [unifies] much of first amendment law.

> [T]he persuasion principle can[not] be justified on consequentialist grounds. [Brandeis's] opinion in *Whitney* [argues that "good counsels"] are a "remedy" for "evil counsels." [The] suggestion is that "more" speech can accomplish practically everything that suppression could accomplish. [If] this were true, the persuasion principle would be easy to justify. [But] there will be many occasions on which this optimistic view is an illusion. The problem with the "more speech" approach is that it is not unusual for people to be persuaded to do bad things, and it will not always be possible to talk them out of it. . . .
>
> Brandeis's opinion in *Whitney*, in addition to suggesting a consequentialist argument, uses terms that we would today say reflect a conception of human autonomy: "the final end of the State" is to make people "free to develop their faculties," and liberty is valuable "both as an end and as a means." [T]he persuasion principle can be defended on autonomy grounds in the following way: Violations of the persuasion principle are similar in kind [to] lies that are told for the purpose of influencing behavior. Violating the persuasion principle is wrong for some of the reasons that lies of this kind are wrong: both involve a denial of autonomy in the sense that they interfere with a person's control over her own reasoning processes. [When] the government violates the persuasion principle, it has determined that people [will] pursue [the government's] objectives, instead of their own.

Page 1054. Before section 2 of the Note, add the following:

For an interesting "cultural history" of the political events that led to the Court's decision in *Herndon*, see Thomas, *Rouge et Noir* Reread: A Popular Constitutional History of the Angelo Herndon Case, 65 So. Cal. L. Rev. 2599 (1992).

Page 1076. At the end of section 5 of the Note, add the following:

5A. *Additional Variations.* Consider Herceg v. Hustler Magazine, Inc., 814 F.2d 1017 (5th Cir. 1987), in which a fourteen-year-old boy was found hanging in his closet with a copy of Hustler on the floor beneath his feet, opened to an article entitled "Orgasms of Death," which detailed the procedures for autoerotic asphyxiation. The court invalidated a civil jury verdict against Hustler, awarding damages of $169,000, because Brandenburg was not satisfied. Consider also Olivia N. v. National Broadcasting Co., 178 Cal. Rptr. 888 (Ct. App. 1981), in which the court held that even though the television movie Born Innocent, which described a rape using a "plumber's helper," had caused just such a rape of a nine-year-old girl by a group of teenage boys who had seen Born Innocent shortly before, the rule in Brandenburg immunized NBC because no intent to injure could be shown.

Page 1077. At the end of section 6 of the Note, add the following:

Suppose the defendant in a capital case is a member of a white racist organization. May the jury consider this membership in determining guilt or innocence? Suppose the crime involves racial overtones? Consider Dawson v. Delaware, 112 S. Ct. 1093 (1992), in which the Court held that it was a violation of the first amendment for a court to admit evidence in a capital sentencing proceeding of the defendant's membership in the Aryan Brotherhood, a white racist prison gang, because "the evidence was not relevant to any issue being decided at the proceeding." At the same time, however, the Court expressly rejected the contention that evidence of a defendant's constitutionally protected association or expression is per se inadmissible at such a proceeding. To the contrary, the Court indicated that "we would have a much different case" if the prosecution had shown, for example, that the murder committed by the defendant had had racial overtones, or that the Aryan Brotherhood had "committed or endorsed unlawful or violent acts," which would have shown that the defendant "represents a future danger to society," or if the prosecution had otherwise demonstrated that the defendant's "abstract beliefs" had a "bearing on the issue being tried." In this case, however, "the inference which the jury was invited to draw" was based on nothing more than the defendant's "abstract beliefs" and invited the jury to act on the ground that it found those beliefs "morally reprehensible." The Court held that this was impermissible. Justice Thomas dissented on the ground that the evidence gave rise to the inference that the defendant had committed unlawful acts while in prison and thus was relevant to "rebut mitigating character evidence introduced" by the defendant that tended to show he had been "kind to others." See also United States v. Abel, 469 U.S. 45 (1984) (the government may impeach a defense witness by showing that both the defendant and the witness were members of the Aryan Brotherhood and that members were sworn to lie on behalf of each other).

Suppose defendant is charged with bombing a government building. Can the state constitutionally attempt to prove that defendant was the culprit by introducing into evidence prior statements of the defendant advocating such conduct? Consider Wisconsin v. Mitchell, — S. Ct. — (1993), in which the Court upheld a statute enhancing the maximum penalty for an offense whenever the defendant "intentionally selects the person against whom the crime [is committed] because of the race, religion, color, disability, sexual orientation, national origin or ancestry of that person." The Court rejected the defendant's claim that the statute was invalid because "evidence of the defendant's prior speech or associations may be used to prove that the defendant intentionally selected his victim on account of the victim's protected status," thus chilling "free expression with respect to such matters by those concerned about the possibility of enhanced sentences if they should in the future commit a criminal offense covered by the statute." The Court found "no merit in this contention." The Court reasoned that "the sort of chill envisioned here" is highly attenuated because to make sense of it "we must conjure up a vision of [an individual] suppressing his unpopular bigoted opinions for fear that if he later commits an offense covered by the statute, these opinions will be offered at trial to establish that he selected his victim on account of the victim's protected status, thus qualifying him for penalty-enhancement." The Court concluded that this "is simply too speculative" to warrant invalidation of the statute. The Court added that the first amendment "does not prohibit the evidentiary use of speech to establish the elements of a crime or to prove motive or intent." To the contrary, evidence "of a defendant's previous declarations or statements is commonly admitted in criminal trials."

2. *Criticism of the Judicial Process*

Page 1082. Before section 3 of the Note, add the following:

5. *Restricting the speech of lawyers.* In Gentile v. State Bar of Nevada, 111 S. Ct. 2720 (1991), petitioner, an attorney, held a press conference the day after his client was indicted on criminal charges. The case was highly publicized and, at the press conference, petitioner proclaimed his client's innocence, asserted that his client was being used as a scapegoat by the police, maintained that the real culprit was a police detective, and cast doubt on the credibility of several government witnesses. Although petitioner's client ultimately was acquitted of all charges, petitioner received an official reprimand by the state bar on the ground that his press conference violated Nevada Supreme Court Rule 177, which prohibits a lawyer from making extrajudicial statements to the press that the lawyer knows or reasonably should know will have a "substantial likelihood of materially prejudicing" an adjudicative proceeding. The Court, in a 5-to-4 decision, concluded that this was a constitutionally permissible standard for regulating the speech of lawyers in this context.

Relying on cases like *Bridges, Craig,* and *Pennekamp*, petitioner argued that the first amendment requires a state "to demonstrate a 'clear and present danger' of 'actual prejudice or an imminent threat' " to the administration of justice "before any discipline may be imposed on a lawyer who initiates a press conference such as occurred here." In an opinion by Chief Justice Rehnquist, the Court rejected this claim. The Court observed that none of the cases relied on by petitioner "involved lawyers who represented parties to a pending proceeding in court" and maintained that there is a sharp "distinction between participants in the litigation and strangers to it." Because lawyers "representing clients in pending cases are key participants in the criminal justice system" and "have special access to information," their speech "may be regulated under a less demanding standard than that established for regulation of the press" and other nonparticipants in the process.

The Court explained that Rule 177 was "aimed at two principal evils: (1) comments that are likely to influence the actual outcome of the trial, and (2) comments that are likely to prejudice the jury venire, even if an untainted panel can ultimately be found." With respect to (2), the Court added that "even if a fair trial can ultimately be ensured through voir dire, change of venue, or some other device," the state "has a substantial interest in preventing officers of the court, such as lawyers, from imposing such costs on the judicial system and on the litigants." The Court therefore concluded that Rule 177 struck an appropriate "balance," for "it is designed to protect the integrity and fairness of a state's judicial system, and it imposes only narrow and necessary limitations on lawyers' speech." Justice Kennedy, joined by Justices Marshall, Blackmun, and Stevens, dissented from this conclusion.

3. Expression That Provokes a Hostile Audience Reaction

Page 1090. After section 3 of the Note, add the following:

3A. *Permit fees and the hostile audience.* In Forsyth County, Georgia v. The Nationalist Movement, 112 S. Ct. 2395 (1992), the Court invalidated a municipal ordinance that authorized permit fees for parades, demonstrations, marches, and similar activities, up to a maximum of $1,000, based in part upon the anticipated expense necessary to maintain the public order. The Court, in an opinion by Justice Blackmun, explained:

> The county envisions that the administrator [will] assess a fee to cover "the cost of necessary and reasonable protection of persons participating or observing [said] activity." [To perform this function, the administrator] "must necessarily examine the content of the message that is conveyed," [estimate] the response of others to that content, and judge the number of police necessary to meet that response. The fee assessed will depend on the administrator's measure of the amount of hostility likely to be created by the speech based on its content. Those wishing to express views unpopular with bottle throwers, for example, may have to pay more for their permit. [Speech] cannot be financially burdened, any more than it can be punished or banned, simply

> because it might offend a hostile mob. ["Regulations] which permit the Government to discriminate on the basis of the content of the message cannot be tolerated under the First Amendment." [The county] contends that the $1,000 cap on the fee [saves] its constitutionality. [But neither] the $1,000 cap on the fee charged, nor even some lower nominal cap, could save the ordinance because in this context, the level of the fee is irrevelant. A tax based on the content of speech does not become more constitutional because it is a small tax.

Chief Justice Rehnquist, joined by Justices White, Scalia, and Thomas, dissented on other grounds.

Consider the following situation, described by the Court in *Forsyth County* as part of the background of the case: In 1987, a civil rights march took place involving some 20,000 marchers. There were more than 1,000 counterdemonstrators along the parade route, and some 3,000 state and local police and National Guardsmen were necessary to keep the peace. The police protection for the demonstration cost more than $670,000. After *Forsyth County*, could the government sue the demonstrators to recoup this cost? Could it sue the counterdemonstrators?

Page 1090. After section 4 of the Note, add the following:

5. *Victim compensation.* Suppose *X* makes a public speech that causes a riot. Several bystanders who are injured in the melee sue *X* for the tort of reckless endangerment. The court finds that *X* cannot constitutionally be held liable although he was negligent, because he did not undertake "incitement to riot." In such circumstances, does it make sense to require the bystanders to bear the cost of their injuries? Consider Schauer, Uncoupling Free Speech, 92 Colum. L. Rev. 1321, 1322 (1992):

> [E]xisting understandings of the First Amendment are based on the assumption that, because a price must be paid for free speech, it must be the victims of harmful speech who are to pay it. This assumption, however, seems curious. It ought to be troubling whenever the cost of a general societal benefit must be borne exclusively or disproportionately by a small subset of the beneficiaries. [If] free speech belongs to us all, then ideally we ought to pay for it. . . .

Schauer suggests that in such circumstances a government-funded "victim compensation scheme" might be a more appropriate way to reconcile the competing interests. Do you see any objections to such an approach?

Page 1100. At the end of section 3 of the Note, add the following:

3A. *The problem of underinclusion.* Suppose a law restricts only a subset of fighting words, such as (a) fighting words directed against blacks or (b) fighting words uttered in bars. Are such restrictions necessarily constitutional because the category of fighting words is "unprotected" by the first amendment? Are such restrictions subject to scrutiny even though the category is "unprotected" because of the inequalities posed by the failure to restrict the entire category? The issue is addressed in R.A.V. v. City of St. Paul, infra section D2 this Supplement, in which the Court invalidated a law restricting only those fighting words that are directed at "race, color, creed, religion or gender" as an impermissible content-based restriction.

Page 1100. After section 4 of the Note, add the following:

5. *Street harassment.* Consider the constitutionality of the following statute, proposed in Bowman, Street Harassment and the Informal Ghettoization of Women, 106 Harv. L. Rev. 517, 575 (1993):

> It shall be a misdemeanor [to] engage in street harassment. Street harassment occurs when one or more unfamiliar men accost one or more women in a public place [and] intrude or attempt to intrude upon the woman's attention in a manner that is unwelcome to the woman, with language that is explicitly or implicitly sexual. Such language includes, but is not limited to, references to male or female genitalia or to female body parts or to sexual activities, solicitation of sex, or reference by word or action to the target of the harassment as the object of sexual desire, or similar words that by their very utterance inflict injury or naturally tend to provoke violent resentment, even if the woman did not herself react with violence. The harasser's intent, except his intent to say the words or engage in the conduct, is not an element of this offense. This section does not apply to any peaceable activity intended to express political views or provide public information to others.

4. Expression That Discloses Confidential Information

Page 1115. At the end of section 2 of the Note, add the following:

Should the state have greater power to restrict extrajudicial speech by attorneys in pending cases than it has to restrict speech by the press about such cases? See Gentile v. State Bar of Nevada, 111 S. Ct. 2720 (1991) (although the state may not restrict speech by the press about pending criminal cases without meeting the "clear and present danger" standard, it may restrict speech by an attorney about pending cases if the attorney knows or reasonably should know that the speech will have a "substantial likelihood of materially prejudicing" the proceeding). Thus, in some circumstances, an attorney could be disciplined for commenting to the press about a pending case, but the press could not be restricted from publishing those comments. Is this sensible? For a fuller account of *Gentile*, see this chapter, section F.3.b, infra this Supplement.

C. OVERBREADTH, VAGUENESS, AND PRIOR RESTRAINT

1. *Overbreadth and Vagueness*

Page 1127. After the citation to Redish, add the following:

Fallon, Making Sense of Overbreadth, 100 Yale L.J. 853, 894 (1991) (in deciding when overbreadth is "intolerably substantial," courts "should weigh (a) the state's substantive interest in being able to "employ a standard that is broader than less restrictive substitutes" against "(b) the First Amendment interest [in] avoiding [the] chilling of constitutionally protected conduct" — the "farther [the] chilled conduct lies from the central concerns of the First Amendment [the] more [a] court should hesitate about declaring a [statute] void for overbreadth").

Page 1128. At the end of section 6 of the Note on Overbreadth, add the following:

7. *Overbreadth v. the requirement that a law be "narrowly tailored."* Is there a difference between invalidating a law for overbreadth and invalidating it because it is not "narrowly tailored"? In Simon & Schuster, Inc. v. New York Crime Victims Board, 112 S. Ct. 501 (1991), the Court invalidated New York's Son of Sam law, which requires any entity contracting with a criminal to publish any depiction of the crime to turn over any income under the contract to the Crime Victims Board, which then deposits the payment in an escrow account "for the benefit of and payable to any victim." The Court justified its result on the ground that the law was not "narrowly tailored" to further the State's "compelling" interest in compensating victims from the profits of crime because it "applies to works on *any* subject, provided that they express the author's thought or recollections about his crime, however tangentially or incidentally," and because it "enables the Board to escrow the income of any author who admits in his work to having committed a crime, whether or not the author was ever actually accused or convicted." The Court noted that such a law would reach such works as Thoreau's Civil Disobedience, the Confessions of Saint Augustine, and the autobiographies of such figures as Emma Goldman, Martin Luther King, Jr., Sir Walter Raleigh, and Bertrand Russell. Is this merely overbreadth analysis by another name?

Page 1130. At the end of section 3 of the Note, add the following:

Consider Fallon, Making Sense of Overbreadth, 100 Yale L.J. 853, 904-905 (1991):

> First Amendment vagueness doctrine [is] best conceptualized as a subpart of First Amendment overbreadth doctrine. [Imagine] a statute that defines a class of publications as "obscene" and therefore prohibitable by means of a test that satisfies all pertinent constitutional requirements concerning the definition of obscenity, but prohibits the sale of only a smaller subclass, defined to encompass those obscene publications "that would be found to be exceptionally repugnant by persons of ordinary sensibilities." [I] assume that the criminal prohibition is vague (since it would be uncertain in many cases whether a magazine or film would be regarded as "exceptionally morally repugnant"), but not overbroad (since no publication could fall within the prohibition unless it were "obscene." [Imagine] further that someone is prosecuted under the statute for selling a film that depicts acts so outrageously repugnant that the statute could not reasonably be held vague as applied to her. Is she entitled to invoke "First Amendment vagueness" [doctrine?] It seems clear that she should not be [because] in this type of case [there] is no substantial threat of chilling constitutionally protected speech. [This] suggests that vagueness is especially troubling in the free speech area only insofar as a vague statute is susceptible of being so construed as to be constitutionally overbroad.

2. *Prior Restraint*

Page 1133. After the reference to Saia v. New York at the end of section 1 of the Note, add the following:

Forsyth County, Georgia v. The Nationalist Movement, 112 S. Ct. 2395 (1992) (even nominal permit fees for marches, demonstrations, parades, and similar activities cannot be imposed in the absence of clear standards governing the setting of fees).

Page 1144. After section 6 of the Note, add the following:

Note: Forfeiture as Prior Restraint

In Alexander v. United States, — S. Ct. — (1993), petitioner, the owner of more than a dozen stores and theaters dealing in sexually explicit materials, was convicted of violating federal obscenity laws and the Racketeer Influenced and Corrupt Organizations Act (RICO). The obscenity convictions, which were based on a finding that four magazines and three videotapes sold in petitioner's stores were obscene, served as the predicate for the RICO convictions. In addition to sentencing petitioner to a prison term of six years and a fine of $100,000, the trial court ordered the forfeiture under RICO of all of petitioner's businesses because they had "been used to conduct his racketeering enterprise." (Because the government did not wish to go into the business of selling sexually explicit materials itself, it destroyed the forfeited, but nonobscene, books, magazines, and movies that made up petitioner's inventory rather than sell them to the public.) Petitioner claimed that the forfeiture of these nonobscene, constitutionally protected materials constituted an impermissible prior restraint. The Court, in an opinion by Chief Justice Rehnquist, disagreed:

"According to petitioner, forfeiture of expressive materials and the assets of businesses engaged in expressive activity, when predicated solely upon previous obscenity violations, operates as a prior restraint because it prohibits future presumptively protected expression in retaliation for prior unprotected speech. Practically speaking, petitioner argues, the effect of the RICO forfeiture order here was no different from the injunction prohibiting the publication of expressive material found to be a prior restraint in Near v. Minnesota. [We] disagree. . . .

"The term prior restraint is used to 'to describe administrative and judicial orders forbidding certain communications when issued in advance of the time that such communications are to occur. [By] contrast, the RICO forfeiture order in this case does not forbid petitioner from engaging in any expressive activities in the future, nor does it require him to obtain prior approval for any expressive activities. It only deprives him of specific assets that were found to be related to his previous racketeering violations. [He] can go back into the adult entertainment business tomorrow, and sell as many sexually explicit magazines and videotapes as he likes, without any risk of being held in contempt for violating a court order. Unlike the [injunction in *Near*], the forfeiture in this case imposes no legal impediment to — no prior restraint on — petitioner's ability to engage in any expressive activity he chooses. . . .

"The constitutional infirmity in nearly all of our prior restraint cases [was] that Government had seized or otherwise restrained material [without] a prior judicial determination that they were [unprotected by the first amendment]. In this case, however, the assets in question were not ordered forfeit because they were believed to be [unprotected by the first amendment]. but because they were directly related to petitioner's past racketeering violations. The RICO forfeiture statute calls for the forfeiture of assets because of the financial role they play in the operation of the racketeering enterprise. The statute is oblivious to the expressive or nonexpressive nature of the assets forfeited; books, sports cars, narcotics, and cash are all forfeitable alike under RICO. . . .

"Nor were the assets in question order forfeited without according petitioner the requisite procedural safeguards, another recurring theme in our prior restraint cases. [Here], the seizure was not premature, because the Government established beyond a reasonable doubt the basis for the forfeiture. [Petitioner's] claim falls short of the mark."

Justice Kennedy, joined by Justices Blackmun and Stevens, dissented on the prior restraint issue: "As governments try new ways to subvert essential freedoms, legal and constitutional systems respond by making more explicit the nature and the extent of the liberty in question. [In *Near*], faced with official action which did not fall within the traditional meaning [of] prior restraint, yet posed many of the same censorship dangers, [the Court held that] the doctrine not only includes licensing schemes requiring speech to be submitted to a censor for review prior to dissemination, but also encompasses injunctive systems which threaten or bar future speech based on some past infraction. Although we consider today a new method of government control with unmistakable dangers of official censorship, the majority concludes that First Amendment freedoms are not endangered because forfeiture follows a lawful conviction [for] obscenity offenses. But this explanation does not suffice. . . .

"The operation and effect of RICO's forfeiture remedies is different from a heavy fine or a severe jail sentence because RICO's forfeiture provisions are different in purpose and kind from ordinary criminal sanctions. The government's stated purpose under RICO, to destroy or incapacitate the offending enterprise, bears a striking resemblance to the motivation for the state nuisance statute the Court struck down as an impermissible prior restraint in *Near*. [As the Court noted in *Near*, the] purpose of the state statute [in that case] was 'not punishment, in the ordinary sense, but suppression of the offending newspaper or periodical.' . . .

"What is happening here is simple: Books and films are condemned and destroyed not for their own content but for the content of their owner's prior speech. Our law does not permit the government to burden future speech for this sort of taint. [RICO] requires trial courts to forfeit not only the unlawful items and any proceeds from their sale, but also the defendant's entire interest in the enterprise involved. [Though] perhaps not in the form of a classic prior restraint, the application of the forfeiture statute here bears its censorial cast. [The] operation of RICO's forfeiture provisions is an exercise of government censorship and control over protected speech as condemned in our prior restraint cases."

Justice Souter dissented on the ground that, even if this is not a prior restraint, the government is nonetheless prohibited by the first amendment from forfeiting nonobscene, constitutionally protected materials.

D. CONTENT-BASED RESTRICTIONS: "LOW" VALUE SPEECH

1. False Statements of Fact

Page 1145. At the end of the carryover paragraph, add the following:

Is a "two-level" theory essential to "any well-functioning system of free expression" because without it one of two "unacceptable" results would follow — either (1) "the burden of justification imposed on government" when it regulates high value speech, such as pure political expression, "would have to be lowered," or (2) "the properly stringent standards applied to efforts to regulate" high value speech would have to be applied to low value speech, with the result that government would not be able to regulate speech "that in all probability should be regulated"? C. Sunstein, The Partial Constitution 233-234 (1993).

Page 1154. Before section 6 of the Note, add the following:

5A. *Victim compensation.* Is the proper resolution of cases like *New York Times* for the government to establish publicly funded victim compensation programs to ensure that the cost of free speech is borne by all members of society, rather than only by those who happen to be injured? Under such a program, L.B. Sullivan could receive compensation from the state or federal government for libel that would have been actionable under the common law, but is not actionable because of the first amendment. See Schauer, Uncoupling Free Speech, 92 Colum. L. Rev. 1321 (1992).

Page 1154. In section 6 of the Note, before the reference to Harte-Hanks Communications v. Connaughton, add the following:

Masson v. New Yorker Magazine, 111 S. Ct. 2419 (1991) (in a public figure's action for libel based on the publication of altered quotations, the first amendment precludes liability even for deliberate alteration unless the plaintiff proves that the alteration "results in a material change in the meaning conveyed by the statements" and that the alteration has a defamatory character);

2. *Group Defamation*

Page 1176. Before the citation to Doe v. University of Michigan in section 3 of the Note, add the following:

Byrne, Racial Insults and Free Speech Within the University, 79 Georgetown L.J. 399 (1991); Symposium, Free Speech and Religious, Racial, and Sexual Harassment, 32 Wm. & Mary L. Rev. 207 (1991).

Page 1176. At the end of section 3 of the Note, add the following:

On the issue of "street harassment" of women, see Bowman, Street Harassment and the Informal Ghettoization of Women, 106 Harv. L. Rev. 517 (1993). For a model "street harassment" statute, see supra p. 1100, this Supplement.

Page 1176. Before section 4 of the Note, add the following:

3A. *Further reflections on "hate speech."* Consider the following:

a. Lawrence, supra, at 439-440:

> The key [to] understanding [Brown v. Board of Education] is that the practice of segregation [was] speech. *Brown* held that segregation is unconstitutional [primarily] because of the message [it] conveys — the message that black children are an untouchable caste, unfit to be educated with white children. Segregation serves its purpose by conveying an idea. It stamps a badge of inferiority upon blacks, and this badge communicates a message [that] is injurious to blacks. Therefore, *Brown* can be read as regulating the content of racist speech. As [such], the decision is an exception to the usual rule that regulation of speech content is presumed unconstitutional.

b. Post, Racist Speech, Democracy, and the First Amendment, 32 Wm. & Mary L. Rev. 267, 312-317 (1991):

> [If] representations in the current literature are accepted as true, [the members of victim groups] confront in public discourse an undifferentiated complex of circumstances in which they are systematically demeaned, stigmatized, ignored; in which the very language of debate resists the articulation of their claims; in which they are harassed, abused, intimidated, and systematically [injured] both individually and collectively. The question [posed is whether these liabilities], when taken together as a complex whole, [render] public discourse unfit as an instrument of collective self-determination for members of minority groups, and whether this unacceptable situation would be cured by restraints on speech. [The claim is] that racist speech ought to be censored so as to open up public discourse to victim groups. [In effect], society's willing-

ness to circumscribe public discourse is transformed into a touchstone of the esteem with which it regards victim groups. . . .

Bluntly expressed, the argument requires us to balance the integrity of public discourse as a general structure [against] the importance of enhancing the experience of political participation by members of victim groups. The argument thus reiterates the position that public discourse ought to be subordinated to the egalitarian ideals of the fourteenth amendment. [This] invitation to balance ought to be declined. This is not because balancing can be ruled out in advance by some "absolutist" algorithm, [but because] the temptation to balance rests on what might be termed the fallacy of immaculate isolation. The effect on public discourse is acceptable only if it is de minimis, and it is arguably de minimis only when a specific claim is evaluated in isolation from other, similar claims. But no claim is in practice immaculately isolated in this manner. As the flag burning [issue] suggests, there is no shortage of powerful groups contending that uncivil speech [ought] to be "minimally" regulated for highly pressing symbolic reasons. [The] point I want to press does not depend upon the intellectual difficulty of drawing lines to separate similar claims. It is rather that the remedial and political logic of equal participation applies with analogous force to a broad and growing spectrum of group claims. [This] is already plain in the regulations that have proliferated on college campuses, which commonly proscribe not merely speech that degrades persons on the basis of their race, but also [on] the basis of their "color, national origin, religion, sex, sexual orientation, age, handicap, or veteran's status." The claim of de minimis impact loses credibility as the list of claimants to special protection grows longer.

c. Consider the code adopted by Stanford University:

Speech or other expression constitutes [prohibited] harassment by personal vilification if it:

(a) is intended to insult or stigmatize an individual or a small number of individuals on the basis of their sex, race, color, handicap, religion, sexual orientation, or national and ethnic origin; and

(b) is addressed directly to the individual or individuals whom it insults or stigmatizes; and

(c) makes use of insulting or "fighting" words or non-verbal symbols . . . "which by their very utterance inflict injury . . ." [and] are commonly understood to convey direct and visceral hatred or contempt for human beings on the basis of their sex, race, color, handicap, religion, sexual orientation, or national and ethnic origin.

Is such a regulation, which is narrower than the invalidated University of Michigan regulation, consistent with first amendment principles? Is it defensible by analogy to the fighting-words doctrine? See Lawrence, supra, at 451-457; Strossen, supra, at 508-514.

d. Fried, A New First Amendment Jurisprudence: A Threat to Liberty, 59 U. Chi. L. Rev. 225, 245-255 (1992):

The ideas the [university hate speech regulations] condemn are false and offensive, but the universities do not condemn all false and offensive ideas. For example, an invective condemning the United States as an oppressor nation or condemning capitalism as a form of exploitation may be repeated with impunity. The same impunity would extend to invectives directed against students and professors seen as agents, apologists or running dogs of an oppressor nation and of capitalism. Individuals within the community may not espouse some forms of race and gender superiority, but may espouse others. [And] none of these codes would condemn burning the American flag, even to affront a gathering of veterans or the widows and orphans of soldiers killed in battle. [This] discrimination makes clear that those who promulgate these regulations assign to themselves the authority to determine which ideas are false and which false ideas people may not express as they choose. [Indeed], some of the proponents of these codes scorn the idea of content-neutrality. The ban is an exercise of power. It shows who is boss. Thus the holders of noxious ideas are suppressed and the rest of the community is impressed and intimidated by this display of political might.

Page 1176. Before Section 3, add the following.

R.A.V. v. CITY OF ST. PAUL
112 S. Ct. 2538 (1992)

JUSTICE SCALIA delivered the opinion of the Court.

[After allegedly burning a cross on a black family's lawn, petitioner, a teenager, was charged under the St. Paul, Minnesota, Bias-Motivated Crime Ordinance, which prohibits the display of a burning cross, a swastika, or other symbol which one knows or has reason to know "arouses anger, alarm or resentment in others" on the basis of race, color, creed, religion or gender. The State Supreme Court rejected a claim that the ordinance was unconstitutinally overbroad because the phrase "arouses anger, alarm or resentment in others" had been construed in earlier state cases to limit the ordinance's reach to fighting words within the meaning of *Chaplinsky*. It also rejected the claim that the ordinance was impermissibly content-based because it was narrowly tailored to serve a compelling governmental interest. The United States Supreme Court reversed.]

I

[We] accept the Minnesota Supreme Court's authoritative statement that the ordinance reaches only those expressions that constitute "fighting words" within the meaning of *Chaplinsky*. Petitioner [urges] us to modify the scope of the *Chaplinsky* formulation, thereby invalidating the ordinance as "substantially overbroad." We find it unnecessary to consider this issue. Assuming, arguendo, that all of the expression reached by the ordinance is proscribable under the "fighting words" doctrine, we nonetheless conclude that the ordinance is facially unconstitutional in that it prohibits otherwise permitted speech solely on the basis of the subjects the speech addresses.

The First Amendment generally prevents government from proscribing speech [or] expressive conduct because of disapproval of the ideas expressed. Content-based regulations are presumptively invalid. From 1791 to the present, however, our society [has] permitted restrictions upon the content of speech in a few limited areas, which are "of such slight social value as a step to truth that any benefit that may be derived from them is clearly outweighed by the social interest in order and morality." [*Chaplinsky*, supra section B3]. We have recognized that "the freedom of speech" referred to by the First Amendment does not include a freedom to disregard these traditional limitations. [Citing Roth v. United States, infra section D5 (obscenity); *Beauharnais*, supra section D2 (defamation); *Chaplinsky*, supra ("fighting words").]

[We] have sometimes said that these categories of expression are "not within the area of constitutionally protected speech." [Such] statements must be taken in context, however. [What] they mean is that these areas of speech can, consistently with the First Amendment, be regulated because of their constitutionally proscribable content (obscenity, defamation, etc.) — not that they are categories of speech entirely invisible to the Constitution, so that they may be made the vehicles for content discrimination unrelated to their distinctively proscribable content. Thus, the government may proscribe libel; but it may not make the further content discrimination of proscribing only libel critical of the government. . . .

Our cases surely do not establish the proposition that the First Amendment imposes no obstacle whatsoever to regulation of particular instances of such proscribable expression, so that the government "may regulate [them] freely." That would mean that a city council could enact an ordinance prohibiting only those legally obscene works that contain criticism of the city government or, indeed, that do not include endorsement of the city government. Such a simplistic, all-or-nothing-at-all approach to First Amendment protection is at odds with common sense and with our jurisprudence as well. It is not true that "fighting words" have at most a "de minimis" expressive content, or that their content is in all respects "worthless and undeserving of constitutional protection"; sometimes they are quite expressive indeed. We have not said that they constitute "no part of the expression of ideas," but only that they constitute "no essential part of any exposition of ideas."

The proposition that a particular instance of speech can be proscribable on the basis of one feature (e.g., obscenity) but not on the basis of another (e.g., opposition to the city government) is commonplace, and has found application in many contexts. We have long held, for example, that nonverbal expressive activity can be banned because of the action it entails, but not because of the ideas it expresses — so that burning a flag in violation of an ordinance against outdoor fires could be punishable, whereas burning a flag in violation of an ordinance against dishonoring the flag is not. [Citing Texas v. Johnson, infra section E3.] Similarly, we have upheld reasonable "time, place, or manner" restrictions, but only if they are "justified without reference to the content of the regulated speech." [See infra sections E1 and F1.] And just as the power to proscribe particular speech on the basis of a noncontent element (e.g., noise) does not entail the power to proscribe the same speech on the basis of a content element; so also, the power to proscribe it on the basis of one content element (e.g., obscenity) does not entail the power to proscribe it on the basis of other content elements.

In other words, the exclusion of "fighting words" from the scope of the First Amendment simply means that, for purposes of that Amendment, the unprotected features of the words are, despite their verbal character, essentially a "nonspeech" element of communication. Fighting words are thus analogous to a noisy sound truck: Each is [a] "mode of speech"; both can be used to convey an idea; but neither has, in and of itself, a claim upon the First Amendment. As with the sound truck, however, so also with fighting words: The government may not regulate use based on hostility — or favoritism — towards the underlying message expressed.

The concurrences describe us as setting forth a new First Amendment principle that prohibition of constitutionally proscribable speech cannot be "underinclusive." [But in] our view, the First Amendment imposes not an "underinclusiveness" limitation but a "content discrimination" limitation upon a State's prohibition of proscribable speech. There is no problem whatever, for example, with a State's prohibiting obscenity (and other forms of proscribable expression) only in certain media or markets, for although that prohibition would be "underinclusive," it would not discriminate on the basis of content.

Even the prohibition against content discrimination that we assert the First Amendment requires is not absolute. It applies differently in the context of proscribable speech than in the area of fully protected speech. The rationale of the general prohibition, after all, is that content discrimination "raises the specter that the Government may effectively drive certain ideas or viewpoints from the marketplace." But content discrimination among various instances of a class of proscribable speech often does not pose this threat.

When the basis for the content discrimination consists entirely of the very reason the entire class of speech at issue is proscribable, no significant danger of idea or viewpoint discrimination exists. Such a reason, having been adjudged neutral enough to support exclusion of the entire class of speech from First Amendment protection, is also neutral enough to form the basis of distinction within the class. To illustrate: A State might choose to prohibit only that obscenity which is the most patently offensive in its prurience — i.e., that which involves the most lascivious displays of sexual activity. But it may not prohibit, for example, only that obscenity which includes offensive political messages. And the Federal Government can criminalize only those threats of violence that are directed against the President — since the reasons why threats of violence are outside the First Amendment (protecting individuals from the fear of violence, from the disruption that fear engenders, and from the possibility that the threatened violence will occur) have special force when applied to the person of the President. But the Federal Government may not criminalize only those threats against the President that mention his policy on aid to inner cities. And to take a final example, [a] State may choose to regulate price advertising in one industry but not in others, because the risk of fraud (one of the characteristics of commercial speech that justifies depriving it of full First Amendment protection, see [infra section E4]) is in its view greater there. But a State may not prohibit only that commercial advertising that depicts men in a demeaning fashion.

Another valid basis for according differential treatment to even a content-defined subclass of proscribable speech is [that] words can in some circumstances violate laws directed not against speech but against conduct (a law against treason, for example, is violated by telling the enemy the nation's defense secrets), [and] a particular content-based subcategory of a proscribable class of speech can be swept up incidentally within the reach of a statute directed at conduct rather than speech. Thus, for example, sexually derogatory "fighting words," among other words, may produce a violation of Title VII's general prohibition against sexual discrimination in employment practices. Where the government does not target conduct on the basis of its expressive content, acts are not shielded from regulation merely because they express a discriminatory idea or philosophy. [See infra section E3.] [Indeed], to validate such selectivity (where totally proscribable speech is at issue) it may not even be necessary to identify any particular "neutral" basis, so long as the nature of the content discrimination is such that there is no realistic possibility that official suppression of ideas is afoot. (We cannot think of any First

Amendment interest that would stand in the way of a State's prohibiting only those obscene motion pictures with blue-eyed actresses.) Save for that limitation, the regulation of "fighting words," like the regulation of noisy speech, may address some offensive instances and leave other, equally offensive, instances alone.

II

Applying these principles to the St. Paul ordinance, we conclude that, even as narrowly construed by the Minnesota Supreme Court, the ordinance is facially unconstitutional. Although the phrase in the ordinance, "arouses anger, alarm or resentment in others," has been limited by the Minnesota Supreme Court's construction to reach only those symbols or displays that amount to "fighting words," the remaining, unmodified terms make clear that the ordinance applies only to "fighting words" that insult, or provoke violence, "on the basis of race, color, creed, religion or gender." Displays containing abusive invective, no matter how vicious or severe, are permissible unless they are addressed to one of the specified disfavored topics. Those who wish to use "fighting words" in connection with other ideas — to express hostility, for example, on the basis of political affiliation, union membership, or homosexuality — are not covered. The First Amendment does not permit St. Paul to impose special prohibitions on those speakers who express views on disfavored subjects.

In its practical operation, moreover, the ordinance goes even beyond mere content discrimination, to actual viewpoint discrimination. Displays containing some words — odious racial epithets, for example — would be prohibited to proponents of all views. But "fighting words" that do not themselves invoke race, color, creed, religion, or gender — aspersions upon a person's mother, for example — would seemingly be usable ad libitum in the placards of those arguing in favor of racial, color, etc. tolerance and equality, but could not be used by that speaker's opponents. One could hold up a sign saying, for example, that all "anti-Catholic bigots" are misbegotten; but not that all "papists" are, for that would insult and provoke violence "on the basis of religion." St. Paul has no such authority to license one side of a debate to fight freestyle, while requiring the other to follow Marquis of Queensbury Rules.

What we have here, it must be emphasized, is not a prohibition of fighting words that are directed at certain persons or groups (which would be facially valid if it met the requirements of the Equal Protection Clause); but rather, a prohibition of fighting words that contain (as the Minnesota Supreme Court repeatedly emphasized) messages of "bias-motivated" hatred and in particular, as applied to this case, messages "based on virulent notions of racial supremacy." One must wholeheartedly agree with the Minnesota Supreme Court that "it is the responsibility, even the obligation, of diverse communities to confront such notions in whatever form they appear," but the manner of that confrontation cannot consist of selective limitations upon speech. St. Paul's brief asserts that a general "fighting words" law would not meet the city's needs because only a content-specific measure can communicate to minority groups that the "group hatred" aspect of such speech "is not condoned by the majority." Brief for Respondent 25. The point of the First Amendment is that majority preferences must be expressed in some fashion other than silencing speech on the basis of its content.

Despite the fact that the Minnesota Supreme Court and St. Paul acknowledge that the ordinance is directed at expression of group hatred, Justice Stevens suggests that this "fundamentally misreads" the ordinance. It is directed, he claims, not to speech of a particular content, but to particular "injuries" that are "qualitatively different" from other injuries. This is word-play. What makes the anger, fear, sense of dishonor, etc. produced by violation of this ordinance distinct from the anger, fear, sense of dishonor, etc. produced by other fighting words is nothing other than the fact that it is caused by a distinctive idea, conveyed by a distinctive message. The First Amendment cannot be evaded that easily. . . .

The content-based discrimination reflected in the St. Paul ordinance [does] not fall within the exception for content discrimination based on the very reasons why the particular class of speech at issue (here, fighting words) is proscribable. [The] reason why fighting words are categorically excluded from the protection of the First Amendment is not that their content communicates any particular idea, but that their content embodies a particularly intolerable (and socially unnecessary) mode of expressing whatever idea the speaker wishes to convey. St. Paul has not singled out an especially offensive mode of expression — it has not, for example, selected for prohibition only those fighting words that communicate ideas in a threatening (as opposed to a merely obnoxious) manner. Rather, it has proscribed fighting words of whatever manner that communicate messages of racial, gender, or religious intolerance. Selectivity of this sort creates the possibility that the city is seeking to handicap the expression of particular ideas. . . .

Finally, St. Paul [argues] that, even if the ordinance regulates expression based on hostility towards its protected ideological content, this discrimination is nonetheless justified because it is narrowly tailored to serve compelling state interests. Specifically, [it asserts] that the ordinance helps to ensure the basic human rights of members of groups that have historically been subjected to discrimination, including the right of such group members to live in peace where they wish. We do not doubt that these interests are compelling, and that the ordinance can be said to promote them. But the "danger of censorship" presented by a facially content-based statute, requires that that weapon be employed only where it is "necessary to serve the asserted [compelling] interest." The existence of adequate content-neutral alternatives thus "undercuts significantly" any defense of such a statute, casting considerable doubt on the government's protestations that "the asserted justification is in fact an accurate description of the purpose and effect of the law." The dispositive question in this case, therefore, is whether content discrimination is reasonably necessary to achieve St. Paul's compelling interests; it plainly is not. An ordinance not limited to the favored topics, for example, would have precisely the same beneficial effect. In fact the only interest distinctively served by the content limitation is that of displaying the city council's special hostility towards the particular biases thus singled out. That is precisely what the First Amendment forbids. . . .

Let there be no mistake about our belief that burning a cross in someone's front yard is reprehensible. But St. Paul has sufficient means at its disposal to prevent such behavior[1] without adding the First Amendment to the fire.

The judgment of the Minnesota Supreme Court is reversed. . . .

JUSTICE WHITE, with whom JUSTICE BLACKMUN and JUSTICE O'CONNOR join, and with whom JUSTICE STEVENS joins except as to Part I(A), concurring in the judgment. . . .

I

A

This Court's decisions have plainly stated that expression falling within certain limited categories so lacks the values the First Amendment was designed to protect that the Constitution affords no protection to that expression. [*Chaplinsky*.] [Today], however, the Court announces that earlier Courts did not mean their repeated statements that certain categories of expression are "not within the area of constitutionally protected speech." The present Court submits that such clear statements "must be taken in context" and are not "literally true." [To] the contrary, those statements meant precisely what they said: The categorical approach is a firmly entrenched part of our First Amendment jurisprudence. . . .

[Nevertheless], the majority holds that the First Amendment protects those narrow categories of expression long held to be undeserving of First Amendment protection — at least to the extent that lawmakers may

1. The conduct might have violated Minnesota statutes [prohibiting "terrorist threats," arson, or criminal damage to property]. [Relocated footnote — EDS.]

not regulate some fighting words more strictly than others because of their content. The Court announces that such content-based distinctions violate the First Amendment because "the government may not regulate use based on hostility — or favoritism — towards the underlying message expressed." Should the government want to criminalize certain fighting words, the Court now requires it to criminalize all fighting words. [It] is inconsistent to hold that the government may proscribe an entire category of speech because the content of that speech is evil; but that the government may not treat a subset of that category differently without violating the First Amendment; the content of the subset is by definition worthless and undeserving of constitutional protection. [Fighting] words are not a means of exchanging views, rallying supporters, or registering a protest; they are directed against individuals to provoke violence or to inflict injury. Therefore, a ban on all fighting words or on a subset of the fighting words category would restrict only the social evil of hate speech, without creating the danger of driving viewpoints from the marketplace. . . .

B

In a second break with precedent, the Court refuses to sustain the ordinance even though it would survive under the strict scrutiny applicable to other protected expression. Assuming, arguendo, that the St. Paul ordinance is a content-based regulation of protected expression, it nevertheless would pass First Amendment review under settled law upon a showing that the regulation "is necessary to serve a compelling state interest and is narrowly drawn to achieve that end." St. Paul has urged that its ordinance, in the words of the majority, "helps to ensure the basic human rights of members of groups that have historically been subjected to discrimination. . . ." The Court expressly concedes that this interest is compelling and is promoted by the ordinance. Nevertheless, [under] the majority's view, a narrowly drawn, content-based ordinance could never pass constitutional muster if the object of that legislation could be accomplished by banning a wider category of speech. This appears to be a general renunciation of strict scrutiny review, a fundamental tool of First Amendment analysis.

This abandonment of the doctrine is inexplicable in light of our decision in Burson v. Freeman [infra Section F1 of this Supplement], which was handed down just a month ago. In *Burson*, seven of the eight participating members of the Court agreed that the strict scrutiny standard applied in a case involving a First Amendment challenge to a content-based statute [that] prohibited the solicitation of votes and the display or distribution of campaign materials within 100 feet of the entrance to a polling place. The plurality concluded that the legislation survived strict scrutiny because the State had asserted a compelling interest in regulating electioneering near polling places and because the statute at issue was narrowly tailored to accomplish that goal. [Significantly], the statute in *Burson* did not proscribe all speech near polling places; it restricted only political speech. The *Burson* plurality [concluded] that the distinction between types of speech required application of strict scrutiny, but it squarely rejected the proposition that the legislation failed First Amendment review because it could have been drafted in broader, content-neutral terms: "States adopt laws to address the problems that confront them. The First Amendment does not require States to regulate for problems that do not exist." This reasoning is in direct conflict with the majority's analysis in the present case. . . .

As with its rejection of the Court's categorical analysis, the majority offers no reasoned basis for discarding our firmly established strict scrutiny analysis at this time. The majority appears to believe that its doctrinal revisionism is necessary to prevent our elected lawmakers from prohibiting libel against members of one political party but not another and from enacting similarly preposterous laws. The majority is misguided. [Although] the First Amendment does not apply to categories of unprotected speech, such as fighting words, the Equal Protection Clause requires that the regulation of unprotected speech be rationally related to a legitimate government interest. A defamation statute that drew distinctions on the basis of political affiliation or "an ordinance prohibiting only those legally obscene works that contain criticism of the city government" would unquestionably fail rational basis review.

Turning to the St. Paul ordinance and assuming arguendo, as the majority does, that the ordinance is not constitutionally overbroad (but see Part II, infra), there is no question that it would pass equal protection review. The ordinance proscribes a subset of "fighting words," those that injure "on the basis of race, color, creed, religion or gender." This selective regulation reflects the City's judgment that harms based on race, color, creed, religion, or gender are more pressing public concerns than the harms caused by other fighting words. In light of our Nation's long and painful experience with discrimination, this determination is plainly reasonable. Indeed, as the majority concedes, the interest is compelling.

C

The Court has patched up its argument with an apparently nonexhaustive list of ad hoc [exceptions]. For instance, if the majority were to give general application to the rule on which it decides this case, today's decision would call into question the constitutionality of the statute making it illegal to threaten the life of the President. Surely, this statute, by singling out certain threats, incorporates a content-based distinction; it indicates that the Government especially disfavors threats against the President as opposed to threats against all others. But because the Government could prohibit all threats and not just those directed against the President, under the Court's theory, the compelling reasons justifying the enactment of special legislation to safeguard the President would be irrelevant, and the statute would fail First Amendment review.

To save the statute, the majority has engrafted the following exception onto its newly announced First Amendment rule: Content-based distinctions may be drawn within an unprotected category of speech if the basis for the distinctions is the very reason the entire class of speech at issue is proscribable. Thus, the argument goes, the statute making it illegal to threaten the life of the President is constitutional, since the reasons why threats of violence are outside the First Amendment (protecting individuals from the fear of violence, from the disruption that fear engenders, and from the possibility that the threatened violence will occur) have special force when applied to the person of the President. [The] exception swallows the majority's rule. Certainly, it should apply to the St. Paul ordinance, since "the reasons why [fighting words] are outside the First Amendment . . . have special force when applied to [groups that have historically been subjected to discrimination]." . . .

As I see it, the Court's theory does not work and will do nothing more than confuse the law. Its selection of this case to rewrite First Amendment law is particularly inexplicable, because the whole problem could have been avoided by deciding this case under settled First Amendment principles.

II

Although I disagree with the Court's analysis, I do agree with its conclusion: The St. Paul ordinance is unconstitutional. However, I would decide the case on overbreadth grounds. [In] construing the St. Paul ordinance, the Minnesota Supreme Court drew upon the definition of fighting words that appears in *Chaplinsky* — words "which by their very utterance inflict injury or tend to incite an immediate breach of the peace." [The court also stated, however,] "the ordinance censors only those displays that one knows or should know will create anger, alarm or resentment based on racial, ethnic, gender or religious bias." [Our] fighting words cases have made clear, however, that such generalized reactions are not sufficient to strip expression of its constitutional protection. The mere fact that expressive activity causes hurt feelings, offense, or resentment does not render the expression unprotected. [Citing, e.g., Cohen v. California, infra section D6, Street v. New York, infra section D6, and Terminiello v. Chicago, supra section B3.] [Thus, although] the ordinance reaches conduct that is unprotected, it also makes criminal expressive conduct that causes only hurt feelings, offense, or resentment, and is protected by the First Amendment. The ordinance is therefore fatally overbroad and invalid on its face. . . .

JUSTICE BLACKMUN, concurring in the judgment.

I regret what the Court has done in this case. [I] fear that the Court has been distracted from its proper mission by the temptation to decide the issue over "politically correct speech" and "cultural diversity," neither of which is presented here. [I] see no First Amendment values that are compromised by a law that prohibits hoodlums from driving minorities out of their homes by burning crosses on their lawns, but I see great harm in preventing the people of Saint Paul from specifically punishing the race-based fighting words that so prejudice their community.

I concur in the judgment, however, because I agree with Justice White that this particular ordinance reaches beyond fighting words to speech protected by the First Amendment.

JUSTICE STEVENS, with whom JUSTICE WHITE and JUSTICE BLACKMUN join as to Part I, concurring in the judgment.

Conduct that creates special risks or causes special harms may be prohibited by special rules. Lighting a fire near an ammunition dump or a gasoline storage tank is especially dangerous; such behavior may be punished more severely than burning trash in a vacant lot. Threatening someone because of her race or religious beliefs may cause particularly severe trauma or touch off a riot, and threatening a high public official may cause substantial social disruption; such threats may be punished more severely than threats against someone based on, say, his support of a particular athletic team. There are legitimate, reasonable, and neutral justifications for such special rules. [This] case involves the constitutionality of one such ordinance. . . .

I

[Drawing] on broadly worded dicta, the Court establishes a near-absolute ban on content-based regulations of [expression]. Thus, while the Court rejects the "all-or-nothing-at-all" nature of the categorical approach, it promptly embraces an absolutism of its own: within a particular "proscribable" category of expression, the Court holds, a government must either proscribe all speech or no speech at all. This aspect of the Court's ruling fundamentally misunderstands the role and constitutional status of content-based regulations on [speech, for] our decisions demonstrate that content-based distinctions, far from being presumptively invalid, are an inevitable and indispensable aspect of a coherent understanding of the First Amendment. [Citing, e.g., New York Times v. Sullivan, supra section D1; Young v. American Mini-Theatres, infra section D6; and Lehman v. City of Shaker Heights, infra section F1.] [The Court's] new absolutism in the prohibition of content-based regulations severely contorts the fabric of settled First Amendment law. . . .

[Perhaps] because the Court recognizes [the perversity of its analysis], it quickly offers some ad hoc limitations on its newly extended prohibition on content-based regulations. [For example, using threats against the President as an illustration the majority], states that a content-based regulation is valid "when the content discrimination is based upon the very reason the entire class of speech . . . is proscribable." [Precisely] this same reasoning, however, compels the conclusion that St. Paul's ordinance is constitutional. Just as Congress may determine that threats against the President entail more severe consequences than other threats, so St. Paul's City Council may determine that threats based on the target's race, religion, or gender cause more severe harm to both the target and to society than other threats. . . .

II

Although I agree with much of Justice White's analysis, I do not join Part I-A of his opinion because I have reservations about the "categorical approach" to the First Amendment. These concerns [lead] me to find Justice White's response to the Court's analysis unsatisfying.

Admittedly, the categorical approach to the First Amendment has some appeal: either expression is protected or it is not — the categories create safe harbors for governments and speakers alike. But this approach sacrifices subtlety for clarity and is, I am convinced, ultimately unsound. As an initial matter, the concept of "categories" fits poorly with the complex reality of expression. Few dividing lines in First Amendment law are straight and unwavering, and efforts at categorization inevitably give rise only to fuzzy boundaries. Our definitions of "obscenity" and "public forum" illustrate this all too well. [See infra sections D4, E2, and F1.] The quest for doctrinal certainty through the definition of categories and subcategories is, in my opinion, destined to fail [and I am therefore persuaded] the categorical approach presented in Part I-A of Justice White's opinion is not an adequate response to the novel "underbreadth" analysis the Court sets forth today.

III

[I] believe our decisions establish a more complex and subtle analysis, one that considers the content and context of the regulated speech, and the nature and scope of the restriction on speech. Applying this analysis and assuming arguendo (as the Court does) that the St. Paul ordinance is not overbroad, I conclude that such a selective, subject-matter regulation on proscribable speech is constitutional.

Not all content-based regulations are alike; our decisions clearly recognize that some content-based restrictions raise more constitutional questions than others. Although the Court's analysis of content-based regulations cannot be reduced to a simple formula, we have considered a number of factors in determining the validity of such regulations. [The] scope of protection provided expressive activity depends in part upon its content and character. We have long recognized that when government regulates political speech or "the expression of editorial opinion on matters of public importance," "First Amendment protection is at its zenith." In comparison, we have recognized that "commercial speech receives a limited form of First Amendment protection," and that "society's interest in protecting [sexually explicit films] is of a wholly different, and lesser magnitude than [its] interest in untrammeled political debate." [Citing Posadas De Puerto Rico Assocs. v. Tourism Co. of Puerto Rico, infra section D5, and FCC v. Pacifica Foundation, infra section D6.] The character of expressive activity also weighs in our consideration of its constitutional status. As we have frequently noted, "the government generally has a freer hand in restricting expressive conduct than it has in restricting the written or spoken word." [Citing Texas v. Johnson and United States v. O'Brien, infra section E3.]

The protection afforded expression turns as well on the context of the regulated speech. [The] distinctive character of a university environment, or a secondary school environment, influences our First Amendment analysis. [Citing Widmar v. Vincent and Hazelwood School Dist. v. Kuhlmier, infra section F2.] The same is true of the presence of a "captive audience." [Citing Lehman v. City of Shaker Heights, infra section F1.] Perhaps the most familiar embodiment of the relevance of context is our "fora" jurisprudence, differentiating the levels of protection afforded speech in different locations. [See infra sections E2 and F1.]

The nature of a contested restriction of speech also informs our evaluation of its constitutionality. Thus, for example, "any system of prior restraints of expression comes to this Court bearing a heavy presumption against its constitutional validity." More particularly to the matter of content-based regulations, we have implicitly distinguished between restrictions on expression based on subject matter and restrictions based on viewpoint, indicating that the latter are particularly pernicious. ["Viewpoint] discrimination is censorship in its purest form," and requires particular scrutiny, in part because such regulation often indicates a legislative effort to skew public debate on an issue. [Thus,] in general, viewpoint-based restrictions on expression require greater scrutiny than subject-matter based restrictions.

Finally, in considering the validity of content-based regulations we have also looked more broadly at the scope of the restrictions. For example, in Young v. American Mini Theatres, [infra section D6], we found significant the fact that "what [was] ultimately at stake [was] nothing more than a limitation on the place where adult films may be exhibited." . . .

All of these factors play some role in our evaluation of content-based regulations on expression. Such a multi-faceted analysis cannot be conflated into two dimensions. Whatever the allure of absolute doctrines, it is just too simple to declare expression "protected" or "unprotected" or to proclaim a regulation "content-based" or "content-neutral."

In applying this analysis to the St. Paul ordinance, I assume arguendo — as the Court does — that the ordinance regulates only fighting words and therefore is not overbroad. Looking to the content and character of the regulated activity, two things are clear. First, by hypothesis the ordinance bars only low-value speech, namely, fighting words. [Second], the ordinance regulates "expressive conduct [rather] than . . . the written or spoken word." [Looking] to the context of the regulated activity, it is again significant that the statute (by hypothesis) regulates [speech only] in confrontational and potentially violent situations. The case at hand is illustrative. The cross-burning in this case — directed as it was to a single African-American family trapped in their home — was nothing more than a crude form of physical intimidation. . . .

Significantly, the St. Paul ordinance regulates speech not on the basis of its subject matter or the viewpoint expressed, but rather on the basis of the harm the speech causes. In this regard, the Court fundamentally misreads the St. Paul ordinance. The Court describes the St. Paul ordinance as regulating expression addressed to one of [several] specified disfavored topics." Contrary to the Court's suggestion, the ordinance regulates only a subcategory of expression that causes injuries based on race, color, creed, religion or gender," not a subcategory that involves discussions that concern those characteristics. [Moreover], even if the St. Paul ordinance did regulate fighting words based on its subject matter, such a regulation would, in my opinion, be constitutional. As noted above, subject-matter [restrictions] generally do not raise the same concerns of government censorship and the distortion of public discourse presented by viewpoint regulations. [Contrary] to the suggestion of the majority, the St. Paul ordinance does not regulate expression based on viewpoint. [The] St. Paul ordinance is even-handed. In a battle between advocates of tolerance and advocates of intolerance, the ordinance does not prevent either side from hurling fighting words at the other on the basis of their conflicting ideas, but it does bar both sides from hurling such words on the basis of the target's "race, color, creed, religion or gender." To extend the Court's pugilistic metaphor, the St. Paul ordinance simply bans punches "below the belt" — by either party. It does not, therefore, favor one side of any debate.

Finally, it is noteworthy that the St. Paul ordinance is, as construed by the Court today, quite narrow. [It] does not ban all "hate speech," nor does it ban, say, all cross-burnings or all swastika displays. Rather it only bans a subcategory of the already narrow category of fighting words. Such a limited ordinance leaves open and protected a vast range of expression on the subjects of racial, religious, and gender equality. As construed by the Court today, the ordinance certainly does not "raise the specter that the Government may effectively drive certain ideas or viewpoints from the marketplace.'" Petitioner is free to burn a cross to announce a rally or to express his views about racial supremacy, he may do so on private property or public land, at day or at night, so long as the burning is not so threatening and so directed at an individual as to "by its very [execution] inflict injury." Such a limited proscription scarcely offends the First Amendment.

In sum, the St. Paul ordinance (as construed by the Court) regulates expressive activity that is wholly proscribable and does so not on the basis of viewpoint, but rather in recognition of the different harms caused by such activity. Taken together, these several considerations persuade me that the St. Paul ordinance is not an unconstitutional content-based regulation of speech. Thus, were the ordinance not overbroad, I would vote to uphold it.

34. Commercial Speech

Page 1191. Before section 2 of the Note, add the following:

h. Collins & Skover, Commerce & Communication, 71 Tex. L. Rev. 697, 707, 710, 727-728, 737-738, 745 (1993):

> On the eve of the twenty-first century, America's marketplace of ideas has largely become a junkyard of commodity ideology. Each day of our lives, twelve billion display ads, two and one-half million radio commercials, and over three hundred thousand television commercials are dumped into the collective consciousness. Advertising consumes almost "sixty percent of newspaper space, 52 percent of magazine pages, 18 percent of radio time, [and] 17

percent of network television prime time." [Today's] mass advertising often has less to do with products than lifestyles, less to do with facts than image, and less to do with reason than romance. . . .

Justice Harry Blackmun's assurance that commercial expression will serve the high purpose of intelligent and well-informed decisionmaking is best exemplified by [traditional classified advertising. But today's] advertising industry stands in stark contrast to the romanticized world of classified communication. [In modern mass advertising, simple] text about product and price is easily overshadowed by metaphorical images and lifestyle messages. [Entire] categories of commercial communication are essentially bereft of any real informational content. For cosmetics, fragrances, alcohol, tobacco, clothes, and other products, billions of advertising dollars say much about image and little about information. [Mass] advertisers [have] embraced the reality of commercial communication: there is no place for the mind in the marketplace. . . .

If commercial communication is safe [in the free speech marketplace], it is not because it *actually* furthers the First Amendment's traditional values of rational decisionmaking and self-realization. Rather, it is because it has effectively co-opted the marketplace metaphor. Meanwhile, Justice Blackmun and his allies have ignored the dissonance between today's commercial expression and the noble purposes of the First Amendment. If they were to be frank, they would concede that the real reason for constitutional protection of modern mass advertising is less enobling: It is speech in the service of selling.

Page 1192. After section 1 of the Note, add the following:

1A. *Direct, in-person solicitation of business.* In Ohralik v. Ohio State Bar, supra, an attorney personally contacted two young women who had been injured in a car accident and arranged to represent them in subsequent litigation. The Court held that the attorney could constitutionally be suspended for violating a state disciplinary rule prohibiting any "attorney who has given unsolicited advice to a layman that he should obtain counsel" to accept "employment resulting from that advice." The Court explained that the disciplinary rule could constitutionally be applied whenever, as in *Ohralik,* an attorney for remunerative purposes "personally solicits an unsophisticated, injured, or distressed lay person," for in such circumstances there is present a "potential for overreaching."

The Court distinguished *Ohralik* in Edenfield v. Fane, — S. Ct. — (1993), in which the Court invalidated a state rule providing that certified public accountants "shall not by any direct, in-person, uninvited solicitation solicit an engagement to perform public accounting services . . . where the engagement would be for a person or entity not already a client of [the CPA], unless such person or entity has invited such a communication." The CPA challenged the rule because it prevented him from "making unsolicited telephone calls [to] executives and arranging meetings to explain his services and expertise." The Court explained that "this type of personal solicitation is commercial expression" and "may have considerable value." Although conceding the substantiality of the state's interests in "protecting consumers from fraud or overreaching by CPAs" and in maintaining "both the fact and appearance of CPA independence in auditing a business," the Court concluded that the state had not carried its burden of proving that "the ban on CPA solicitation advances its asserted interests in any direct and material way." The Court distinguished CPA from lawyer solicitation on the grounds that "unlike a lawyer, a CPA is not 'a professional trained in the art of persuasion' " and that "the typical client of a CPA is far less susceptible to manipulation than the young accident victims in *Ohralik*." Thus, unlike the situation in *Ohralik*, "it cannot be said that [personal] solicitation by CPAs 'more often than not will be injurious to the person solicited.' "

Page 1197. After the Note, add the following:

CITY OF CINCINNATI v. DISCOVERY NETWORK, INC., 113 S. Ct. 1505 (1993): In 1989, Cincinnati authorized respondent companies to place 62 freestanding newsracks on public property for the purpose of distributing free magazines that consisted primarily of advertisements for respondents' services. In 1990, motivated by its interest in the safety and attractive appearance of its streets and sidewalks, Cincinnati revoked respondents' permits on the ground that the magazines were "commercial handbills" whose distribution on public property was prohibited by a pre-existing ordinance.

The Court, in an opinion by Justice Stevens, invalidated the restriction: "[R]espondents do not challenge their characterization as 'commercial speech.' Nor do respondents question the substantiality of the city's interest in safety and aesthetics. [The critical issue is therefore whether the city has met its burden under *Central Hudson* and *Fox*] to establish a 'reasonable fit' between its legitimate interests [and] its choice of a limited and selective prohibition of newsracks as the means chosen to serve those interests.

"[The] city did not 'establish the reasonable fit we require.' The [pre-existing] ordinance on which it relied was an outdated prohibition against the distribution of any commercial handbills on public property. It was enacted long before any concern about newsracks developed. Its apparent purpose was to prevent the kind of visual blight caused by littering, rather than any harm associated with permanent, freestanding dispensing devices. The fact that the city failed to address its recently developed concern about newsracks by regulating their size, shape, appearance, or number indicates that it has not 'carefully calculated' the costs and benefits associated with the burden on speech imposed by its prohibition. The benefit to be derived from the removal of 62 newsracks while about 1,500-2,000 remain in place [was] 'paltry'. . . .

"The city argues that there is a close fit between its ban on newsracks dispensing 'commercial handbills' and its interest in safety and esthetics because every decrease in the number of such dispensing devices necessarily effects an increase in safety and an improvement in the attractiveness of the cityscape. [This is] an insufficient justification for the discrimination against respondents' use of newsracks that are no more harmful than the permitted newsracks. . . . The major premise supporting the city's argument is the proposition that commercial speech has only a low value. Based on that premise, the city contends that the fact that assertedly more valuable publications are allowed to use newsracks does not undermine its judgment that its esthetic and safety interests are stronger than the interest in allowing commercial speakers to have similar access to the reading public.

"We cannot agree. [In] this case, the distinction [between commercial and noncommercial speech] bears no relationship whatsoever to the particular interests that the city has asserted. It is therefore an impermissible means of responding to the city's admittedly legitimate interests. [Respondents'] newsracks are no greater an eyesore than the newsracks permitted to remain on Cincinnati's sidewalks. Each newsrack, whether containing 'newspapers' or 'commercial handbills' is equally unattractive. [The] city's primary concern [is] with the aggregate number of newsracks on its streets. On that score, however, all newsracks, regardless of whether they contain commercial or noncommercial publications, are equally at fault. In fact, the newspapers are arguably the greater culprit because of their superior number. [In] the absence of some basis for distinguishing between 'newspapers' and 'commercial handbills' that is relevant to an interest asserted by the city, we are unwilling to recognize Cincinnati's bare assertion that the 'low value' of commercial speech is a sufficient justification for its selective and categorical ban on newsracks dispensing 'commercial handbills.'"

Justice Blackmun filed a concurring opinion.

Chief Justice Rehnquist, joined by Justices White and Thomas, dissented: "[This case turns] on the application of the last part of the *Central Hudson* analysis. Although the Court does not say so, there can be no question that Cincinnati's prohibition against respondents' newsracks 'directly advances' its safety and esthetic interests because, if enforced, the city's policy will decrease the number of newsracks on its street corners. This leaves the question whether the city's prohibition is 'more extensive than necessary' to serve its interests, or, as we elaborated in *Fox*, whether there is a 'reasonable fit' between the city's desired ends and the means it has chosen to accomplish those ends. [The Court's analysis] rests on the discredited notion that the availability of 'less restrictive means' to accomplish the city's objectives renders its regulation of commercial speech unconstitutional. [As is clear from our precedents in the area of commercial speech, that] there may be other — less restrictive — means by which Cincinnati could have gone about addressing its safety and esthetic concerns [does] not render its prohibition against respondents' newsracks unconstitutional. . . .

"The Court offers an alternative rationale for invalidating the city's policy: viz., the distinction Cincinnati has drawn (between commercial and noncommercial speech) in deciding which newsracks to regulate "bears no relationship whatsoever to the particular interests that the city has asserted.' [I] am at a loss to understand why [Cincinnati's] scheme is unconstitutional because it does not also regulate newsracks that disseminate noncommercial speech. One would have thought that the city, perhaps even following the teachings of our commercial speech jurisprudence, could have decided to place the burden of its regulatory scheme on less protected speech (i.e., commercial handbills) without running afoul of the First Amendment. Today's decision, though, places the city in the position of having to decide between restricting more speech — fully protected speech — and allowing the proliferation of newsracks on its street corners to continue unabated. It seems scarcely logical that the First Amendment compels such a result."

Page 1198. Before section 2 of the Note, add the following:

1A. *Interstate advertising of state-run lotteries.* In United States v. Edge Broadcasting Co., — S. Ct. — (1993), the Court considered the constitutionality of federal legislation prohibiting the broadcast of lottery advertisements, but exempting the broadcast of advertisements for state-run lotteries by stations licensed to a state that conducts such a lottery. Edge Broadcasting operates a radio station that is located in and licensed to North Carolina but that broadcasts primarily in Virginia. Because North Carolina is a nonlottery state, the effect of the federal legislation is to prohibit the radio station from broadcasting advertisements for the Virginia state lottery. Edge argued that this violated the first amendment. The Court, in an opinion by Justice White, rejected this claim and upheld the legislation:

"In *Central Hudson* we set out the general scheme for assessing government restrictions on commercial speech. [We] assume that Edge, if allowed to, would air nonmisleading advertisements about the Virginia lottery, a legal activity. As to the second *Central Hudson* factor, we are quite sure that the Government has a substantial interest in supporting the policy of nonlottery States, as well as not interfering with the policy of States that permit lotteries. As in *Posadas*, the activity underlying the relevant advertising — gambling — implicates no constitutionally protected right; rather, it falls into a category of "vice" activity that could be, and frequently has been, banned altogether. . . .

"The third *Central Hudson* factor asks whether the 'regulation directly advances the governmental interest asserted.' [We] have no doubt that the statutes directly advanced the governmental interest at stake in this case. In response to the appearance of state-sponsored lotteries, Congress might have continued to ban all radio or television advertisements, even by stations in States that have legalized lotteries. This it did not do. Neither did it permit stations such as Edge, located in a nonlottery State, to carry lottery ads if their signals reached into a State that sponsors lotteries; similarly, it did not forbid stations in a lottery State such as Virginia from carrying lottery ads if their signals reached into an adjoining State such as North Carolina where lotteries were illegal. Instead of favoring either the lottery or the nonlottery State, Congress opted to support the antigambling policy of a State like North Carolina by forbidding stations in such a State from airing lottery advertising. At the same time it sought not to unduly interfere with the policy of a lottery sponsoring State such as Virginia. Virginia could advertise its lottery through radio and television stations licensed to Virginia locations, even if their signals reached deep into North Carolina. [This] congressional policy of balancing the interests of lottery and nonlottery States is the substantial governmental interest that satisfies *Central Hudson*. . . .

"[The] fourth *Central Hudson* factor [is] whether the regulation is more extensive than is necessary to serve the governmental interest. [We] made clear in *Fox* that [the] fit between the restriction and the governmental interest [must be] reasonable. [That test is satisfied here.] Allowing [Edge] to carry lottery ads reaching over 90% of its listeners, all in Virginia, would surely enhance its revenues. But just as surely, because Edge's signals with lottery ads would be heard in the nine counties in North Carolina that its broadcasts reach, this would be in derogation of the substantial federal interest in supporting North Carolina's laws making lotteries illegal. In this posture, to prevent Virginia's lottery policy from dictating what stations in a neighboring State air, it is reasonable to require Edge to comply with the restriction against carrying lottery advertising.

"[Moreover,] this would be the case even if it were true, which it is not, that applying the general statutory restriction to Edge, in isolation, would no more than marginally insulate the North Carolinians in the North Carolina counties served by Edge from hearing lottery ads. [This is so because, in the commercial speech context,] 'the validity of the regulation depends on the relation it bears to the overall problem the government seeks to correct, not on the extent to which it further the government's interest in an individual case.'

Edge argued that application of the federal law to its activities has only a trivial effect in terms of shielding North Carolina residents from information about the Virginia lottery, for North Carolina residents routinely receive such information from Virginia-based radio and television stations and newspapers. The Court responded that the federal legislation was designed, not to keep North Carolina residents "ignorant of the Virginia lottery for ignorance's sake, but to accommodate nonlottery States' interest in discouraging public participation in lotteries." Because "advertising of gambling serves to increase the demand," Congress "was entitled to determine that broadcast of promotional advertising of lotteries undermines North Carolina's policy against gambling, even if the North Carolina audience" is exposed to such advertising from Virginia-based sources."

Justice Stevens, joined by Justice Blackmun, dissented: "I would hold that suppressing truthful advertising regarding a neighboring State's lottery, an activity which is, of course, perfectly legal, is a patently unconstitutional means of effectuating the Government's asserted interest in protecting the policies of nonlottery States. [Citing Bigelow v. Virginia]. The United States has selected the most intrusive, and dangerous, form of regulation possible — a ban on truthful information regarding a lawful activity imposed for the purpose of manipulating, through ignorance, the consumer choices of some of its citizens. Unless justified by a truly substantial governmental interest, this extreme, and extremely paternalistic, measure surely cannot withstand scrutiny under the First Amendment. [There is no such interest here, for while] a State may have an interest in discouraging its citizens from participating in state-run lotteries, it does not necessarily follow that its interest is 'substantial' enough to justify an infringement on constitutionally protected speech, especially one as draconian as the regulation at issue in this case. [Indeed, the] sea change in public attitudes toward state-run lotteries that this country has witnessed in recent years undermines any claim that a State's interest in discouraging its citizens from participating in state-run lotteries is so substantial as to outweigh [Edge's] First Amendment right to distribute, and the public's right to receive, truthful, nonmisleading information about a perfectly legal activity conducted in a neighboring State."

Page 1200. Before the Note on Labor Disputes and the First Amendment, add the following:

6. *Limiting Advertising to Promote Freedom of the Press.* Consider, Baker, Advertising and a Democratic Press, 140 U. Pa. L. Rev. 2097, 2139, 2178, 2180-81 (1992):

Organized private power is today the most serious threat to a free and democratic press [and] although advertising can be viewed as the life blood of free media, paying most of the costs and thus making the media widely available, [advertisers are also] the most consistent and the most pernicious "censors" of media content. [Advertising] directly affects media's [content] in at least four systematic ways. These effects can be characterized either as media's response to market pressures to increase and maintain advertising revenues or as advertisers "purchasing" content favorable to their interests. [T]he incentive of advertising revenue encourages media to tailor media content: 1) to treat advertisers' products and their broader interests charitably in both news reports and editorials; 2) to create a buying mood that will induce readers or viewers to have more favorable reactions to advertisements; 3) to make content less partisan and often less controversial, in order to avoid offending advertisers' potential customers and to increase the media's potential reach; and 4) to favor particular audiences, usually the middle-to-higher income audiences whose greater purchasing power advertisers value most.

[In light of these concerns], one might propose banning advertising in the media. Such a move would be as undesirable as it is untenable. [Such a] proposal ignores the significant positive contributions of advertising in the media, the two most important being advertising's financial support of media communications and advertising's provision of information that media consumers desire. Nevertheless, targeted policies that reduce specific objectionable effects of advertising may provide net social [benefits]. [Under one such approach government could] tax advertising and [use] the tax revenues to subsidize readers. [For] example, the government could impose a 10% sales tax on newspapers' advertising revenue, and redistribute this money back as a subsidy based on the paper's circulation revenue. [The] immediate result would be to reduce papers' incentive to respond to advertisers' wishes concerning editorial content and to encourage papers to provide a product for which readers are willing to pay.

WISCONSIN v. MITCHELL, — S. Ct. — (1993): After viewing the motion picture "Mississippi Burning," in which a white man beat a young black who was praying, Mitchell, who is black, urged a group of blacks to assault a young white boy who happened to be walking by. The group, including Mitchell, beat the white boy severely. Mitchell was convicted of aggravated battery, which ordinarily carries a maximum sentence of two years' imprisonment. But because the jury found that Mitchell had intentionally selected his victim because of the boy's race, the maximum sentence for his offense was increased to seven years under the State's hate-crime penalty enhancement statute, which enhances the maximum penalty for an offense whenever the defendant "intentionally selects the person against whom the crime . . . is committed . . . because of the race, religion, color, disability, sexual orientation, national origin or ancestry of that person." The Court overturned the holding of the Wisconsin

Supreme Court that the statute violated the first amendment. Chief Justice Rehnquist delivered the opinion for a unanimous Court:

"[A] physical assault is not by any stretch of the imagination expressive conduct protected by the First Amendment. [But this does not end the matter, for] although the statute punishes criminal conduct, it enhances the maximum penalty for conduct motivated by a discriminatory point of view more severely than the same conduct engaged in for some other reason or for no reason at all. Because the only reason for the enhancement is the defendant's discriminatory motive for selecting his victim, Mitchell argues (and the Wisconsin Supreme Court held) that the statute violates the First Amendment by punishing offenders' bigoted beliefs. [But] motive plays the same role under the Wisconsin statute as it does under federal and state antidiscrimination [laws]. Title VII, for example, makes it unlawful for an employer to discriminate against an employee 'because of such individual's race, color, religion, sex, or national origin.' [In Hishon v. King & Spalding, 467 U.S. 69 (1984), we] rejected the argument that Title VII infringed employers' First Amendment rights. And more recently, in R.A.V. v. St. Paul, we cited Title VII [as] an example of a permissible content-neutral regulation of conduct.

"Nothing in our decision last Term in *R.A.V.* compels a different result here, [for] whereas the ordinance struck down in *R.A.V.* was explicitly directed at expression (i.e., 'speech' or 'messages'), the statute in this case is aimed at conduct unprotected by the First Amendment. Moreover, the Wisconsin statute singles out for enhancement bias-inspired conduct because this conduct is thought to inflict greater individual and societal harm. For example, according to the [State], bias-motivated crimes are more likely to provoke retaliatory crimes, inflict distinct emotional harms on their victims, and incite community unrest. The State's desire to redress these perceived harms provides an adequate explanation for its penalty-enhancement provision over and above mere disagreement with offenders' beliefs or biases. . . ."

5. Obscenity

Page 1228. Before New York v. Ferber, add the following:

For a rejoinder, consider Sunstein, Neutrality in Constitutional Law (with Special Reference to Pornography, Abortion, and Surrogacy), 92 Colum. L. Rev. 1, 28-29 (1992):

> [F]irst Amendment law contains several categories of [low value] speech that are subject to ban or regulation even though they are nonneutral in precisely the same way as antipornography legislation. Consider, for example, labor law, where courts have held that government may ban employers from speaking unfavorably about the effects of unionization in the period before a union

election if the unfavorable statements might be interpreted as a threat. [Citing *Gissel,* casebook page 1201.] Regulation of such speech is unquestionably nonneutral, since employer speech favorable to unionization is not proscribed. Similarly, the State may prohibit truthful television and radio advertisements for casinos and cigarettes. [Citing *Posadas,* casebook page 1195.] This is so even though speech that takes the opposite side is freely permitted, in advertisements or elsewhere. Even regulation of bribery is nonneutral. One may not offer $100 to tempt a person to commit a tort, although a $100 offer to refrain from committing a tort is permissible. In all of the cases, the partisanship of the regulation is not apparent because there is so firm a consensus on the presence of real-world harms that the objection from neutrality does not even register. [Similarly,] we could imagine a society in which the harms produced by pornography were so widely acknowledged and so generally condemned that an antipornography ordinance would not be regarded as viewpoint-based at all.

i. For an empirical study of the overbreadth, underbreadth and vagueness problems involved in actually applying the various obscenity and pornography definitions, see Lindgren, Defining Pornography, 141 U. Pa. L. Rev. 1153 (1993).

Page 1233. Before section 5 of the Note, add the following:

4A. *Forfeiture.* In Alexander v. United States, — S. Ct. — (1993), petitioner, the owner of more than a dozen stores and theaters dealing in sexually explicit materials, was convicted of violating federal obscenity laws and the Racketeer Influenced and Corrupt Organizations Act (RICO). The obscenity convictions, which were based on a finding that four magazines and three videotapes sold in petitioner's stores were obscene, served as the predicate for the RICO convictions. In addition to sentencing petitioner to a prison term of six years and a fine of $100,000, the trial court ordered the forfeiture under RICO of all of petitioner's businesses because they had "been used to conduct his racketeering enterprise." (Because the government did not wish to go into the business of selling sexually explicit materials itself, it destroyed the forfeited, but nonobscene books, magazines and movies that made up petitioner's inventory, rather than sell them to the public.) In a five-to-four decision, the Court rejected petitioner's claim that the forfeiture of these nonobscene, constitutionally protected materials violated the first amendment. Chief Justice Rehnquist, writing for the Court, noted that petitioner "does not challenge either his 6-year jail sentence or his $100,000 fine as violative of the First Amendment." This being so, the Chief Justice asked "why, if incarceration for six years and a fine of $100,000 are permissible forms of punishment under the RICO statute, the challenged, forfeiture of certain assets directly related to petitioner's racketeering activity is not."

In dissent, Justice Kennedy, joined by Justices Blackmun, Stevens and Souter, argued: "The destruction of books and films that were not obscene [is] a remedy with no parallel in our cases. [Even] when interim pretrial seizures are used, we have been careful to say that First Amendment materials cannot be taken out of circulation until they have been determined to be unlawful. [It] follows from [cases like Marcus v. Search Warrant] that one title does not become seizable or tainted because of its proximity of the shelf to another. And if that is the rule for interim seizures, it follows with even greater force that protected materials cannot be destroyed altogether for some alleged taint from an owner who committed a speech violation."

Chief Justice Rehnquist responded: "The constitutional infirmity [in cases like Marcus v. Search Warrant] was that Government had seized or otherwise restrained materials suspected of being obscene without a prior judicial determination that they were in fact so. In this case, however, the assets in question were not ordered forfeit because they were believed to be obscene, but because they were directly related to petitioner's past racketeering violations. The RICO forfeiture statute calls for the forfeiture of assets because of the financial role they play in the operation of the racketeering enterprise. The statute is oblivious to the expressive or nonexpressive nature of the assets forfeited; books, sports cars, narcotics, and cash are all forfeitable alike under RICO."

6. Offensive Speech

Page 1255. Before section 5 of the Note, add the following:

4A. *Nude dancing: the* Barnes *case.* In Barnes v. Glen Theatre, Inc., 111 S. Ct. 2456 (1991), the Court, in a 5-to-4 decision, upheld an Indiana statute prohibiting any person to appear "in a state of nudity" in any "public place," as applied to establishments that present nude dancing as entertainment. Although there was no opinion of the Court, a majority of the justices concluded that nude performance dancing "is expressive conduct within the outer perimeters of the First Amendment." A majority also concluded, however, that the requirement that such dancers wear pasties and a G-string does not violate the first amendment because the public nudity statute was not directed at nude dancing and thus had only an "incidental effect" on constitutionally protected activity. Only Justice Souter, in a separate concurring opinion, rested his analysis on *Young* and *Renton*. In Souter's view, the public nudity statute was constitutional as applied to respondents' establishments because of "the State's substantial interest in combating the secondary effects of [such] adult establishments." Souter explained that, under this analysis, the public nudity statute might be constitutional as applied to nude dancing in adult establishments, but not to other uses of nudity in expressive activity, for "it is difficult to see, for example, how the enforcement of Indiana's statute against nudity in a production of 'Hair' or 'Equus' somewhere other than an 'adult' theater would further the State's interest in avoiding harmful secondary effects." For a fuller account of *Barnes,* see this chapter, section E, infra this Supplement.

Page 1256. Before the paragraph beginning at the very bottom of the page, add the following:

Should the Court define the high value/low value distinction more explicitly in terms of the distinction between political and nonpolitical expression? Consider C. Sunstein, The Partial Constitution 237-238 (1993):

> An approach that affords special protection to political speech [receives] firm support from history, [corresponds] to our [considered] judgments about particular free speech problems, [responds] well to the fact that it is in the political setting that government is most likely to be biased or to be acting on the basis of illegitimate considerations, [and] protects speech [against government regulation when such regulation] is most likely to be harmful, [for restrictions] on political speech have the distinctive feature of impairing the ordinary channels for political change.

E. CONTENT-NEUTRAL RESTRICTIONS: LIMITATIONS ON THE MEANS OF COMMUNICATION

1. General Principles

Page 1263. After the citation to Stone at the top of the page, add the following:

Williams, Content Discrimination and the First Amendment, 139 U. Pa. L. Rev. 615 (1991).

Page 1263. Before section 2 of the Note, add the following:

Consider C. Sunstein, The Partial Constitution 227-228 (1993):

> [A] familiar justification for skepticism about content-based regulation [is] that such regulation "skews" the marketplace of ideas. This idea has two problems. First, we do not have a full idea of what a well-functioning marketplace of ideas would look like. [Second], the idea of skewing depends on taking the marketplace as unobjectionable in its current form. [But it would be] exceptionally surprising [if] there were no such skewing [already built into the existing marketplace of ideas, for that marketplace is itself] a function of

existing law, including property law, which is responsible for the allocation of rights that can be turned into speech.

[On the other hand], the existence of an unjust status quo should probably not be a reason to allow regulation of the content of speech. [This is so because] the inquiry, for First Amendment purposes, is probably beyond governmental capacity. There is a serious risk that judicial or legislative decisions about the relative power of various groups [will] be biased or unreliable. [And what] is distinctive about regulation of speech [and distinguishes it from regulation of economics] is that [regulation of speech] forecloses the channels of change; it prevents other views from being presented at all.

Page 1265. Before subsection 4c of the Note, add the following:

In Simon & Schuster, Inc. v. New York Crime Victims Board, 112 S. Ct. 501 (1991), the Court invalidated New York's Son of Sam law, which requires any entity contracting with a person convicted of a crime to publish any depiction of the crime to turn over any income under the contract to the Crime Victims Board, which then deposits the payment in an escrow account "for the benefit of and payable to any victim." The law was designed to compensate victims from the profits of crime. Is such a law "content-neutral" under the theory advanced in *Renton*? The Court found it unnecessary to decide that question.

In Cincinnati v. Discovery Network, — S. Ct. — (1993), the Court invalidated a prohibition on the use of newsracks on public property to distribute commercial handbills. The prohibition was designed to further the city's interests in promoting the safety and attractive appearance of its streets. Although conceding that newsracks containing commercial handbills posed no greater threat to these interests than newsracks containing newspapers, which were allowed, the city argued that its distinction was permissible because commercial speech is of only "low" first amendment value. In response to the contention that the prohibition was an impermissible content-based restriction, the city argued that the challenged prohibition was content-neutral "because the interests in safety and esthetics [are] entirely unrelated to the content of [the] publications." The Court, in an opinion by Justice Stevens, rejected this argument:

> The argument is unpersuasive because the very basis for the regulation is the difference in content between ordinary newspapers and commercial speech. [Under] the city's newsrack policy, whether any particular newsrack falls within the ban is determined by the content of the publication resting inside the newsrack. Thus, by any commonsense understanding of the term, the ban [is] "content-based." Nor are we persuaded that our statements that the test for whether a regulation is content-based turns on the "justification" for the regulation [compel] a different conclusion. [The city's] reliance on

Renton is misplaced. [We] upheld the regulation [in *Renton*] largely because it was justified not by an interest in suppressing adult films, but by the city's concern for the "secondary effects" of such theaters on the surrounding neighborhoods. In contrast to the speech at issue in *Renton*, there are no secondary effects attributable to newsracks [containing commercial handbills] that distinguish them from the newsracks Cincinnati permits to remain on its sidewalks.

Page 1265. At the end of subsection 4c of the Note, add the following:

d. A fourth situation concerns those laws that are content-neutral on their face but have sharply content-differential effects. Recall, for example, Justice Black's observation in *Martin* that "door to door distribution of circulars is essential to the poorly financed causes of little people." To what extent should this be a factor in content-neutral analysis? To what extent should it be a factor that converts a content-neutral regulation into one that is content-based? See Williams, Content Discrimination and the First Amendment, 139 U. Pa. L. Rev. 615 (1991) (suggesting that such disparate impact may appropriately trigger content-based analysis); Stone, Content-Neutral Restrictions, 54 U. Chi. L. Rev. 46, 81-86 (1987) (suggesting that this should be a factor in content-neutral analysis).

2. *Speech on Public Property: The Public Forum*

a. The Public Forum: Streets and Parks

Page 1275. At the end of the Note, add the following:

In Forsyth County, Georgia v. The Nationalist Movement, 112 S. Ct. 2395 (1992), the Court invalidated a municipal ordinance that authorized permit fees for parades, demonstrations, marches, and similar activities, up to a maximum of $1,000, based in part upon the anticipated expense necessary to maintain the public order. The Court, in an opinion by Justice Blackmun, explained that, under this scheme, the fee "will depend on the administrator's measure of the amount of hostility likely to be created by the speech." As a result, those "wishing to express views unpopular with bottle throwers [may] have to pay more for their permit." The Court emphasized, however, that speech "cannot be financially burdened, any more than it can be punished or banned, simply because it might offend a hostile mob," and "regulations which permit the Government to discriminate on the basis of the content of the message cannot be tolerated under the First Amendment." Chief Justice Rehnquist, joined by Justices White, Scalia, and Thomas, dissented on other grounds.

After *Forsyth County*, how would you rule on the constitutionality of the Skokie insurance requirements?

b. The Public Forum: Other Publicly Owned Property

Page 1285. Before the Note, add the following:

INTERNATIONAL SOCIETY FOR KRISHNA CONSCIOUSNESS, INC. v. LEE, 112 S. Ct. 2701 (1992): The Port Authority of New York and New Jersey, which owns and operates three major airports in the New York City area, forbids within the airport terminals the repetitive solicitation of money and the repetitive sale or distribution of any merchandise, "including but not limited to jewelry, food stuffs, candles, flowers, . . . flyers, brochures, pamphlets, books or any other printed or written material." The regulation governs only the terminal buildings. It does not restrict such activities on the public sidewalks outside the buildings. In a bewildering array of opinions, the Court upheld the ban on solicitation, but invalidated the ban on the sale or distribution of literature.

Solicitation. Chief Justice Rehnquist delivered the opinion of the Court upholding the ban on solicitation. (On solicitation as "speech," see pages 1308-1310 of the main text.) At the outset, Rehnquist noted that "where the government is acting as a proprietor, managing its internal operations, rather than acting as lawmaker with the power to regulate or license, its actions will not be subjected to the heightened review to which its actions as lawmaker may be subject." With this in mind, Rehnquist concluded that "the terminals are nonpublic fora and that the regulation reasonably limits solicitation." Rehnquist explained that airport terminals are not traditional public fora because "given the lateness with which the modern air terminal has made its appearance, it hardly qualifies for the description of having 'immemorially . . . time out of mind' been held in the public trust and used for purposes of expressive activity." Moreover, such terminals have not "been intentionally opened by their operators to such activity." To the contrary, "the frequent and continuing litigation evidencing the operators' objections belies any such claim." Rehnquist also rejected the argument that airport terminals should be treated as public fora because other "transportation modes," such as rail stations, bus stations, and wharves, have traditionally been open to expressive activity. Rehnquist explained that such "evidence is irrelevant to public forum analysis, because [such sites] traditionally have had private ownership," and "the practices of privately held transportation centers do not bear on the government's regulatory authority over a publicly owned airport." In addition, "to make a category of 'transportation modes' [would] unjustifiably elide what may be critical differences," such as the fact that "airports are commercial establishments funded by use fees and designed to make a regulated profit." In sum, because "it cannot fairly be said that an airport terminal has as a principal purpose 'promoting the free exchange of ideas,'" it is not a public forum.

This being so, the prohibition on solicitation "need only satisfy a requirement of reasonableness," a standard Rehnquist held is easily satisfied because of "the disruptive effect that solicitation may have on business." Specifically, Rehnquist observed that solicitation impedes "the normal flow of traffic" and that such "delays may be particularly costly in this setting, as a flight missed by only a few minutes can result in hours worth of subsequent inconvenience." Moreover, "face-to-face solicitation presents risks of duress" and "fraud," and it may be especially difficult for airport authorities to enforce rules against such abuses because passengers "frequently are on tight schedules" and are "unlikely to stop and formally complain." Finally, the prohibition is reasonable because solicitation is permitted on the "sidewalk areas outside the terminals," where the "overwhelming" majority of airport users can be reached.

Justice O'Connor concurred with the Court's conclusion that airport terminals are not public fora. O'Connor emphasized, however, that this conclusion, "does not mean that the government can restrict speech in whatever way it likes." To the contrary, in order for a restriction on speech in a nonpublic forum to be "reasonable," it must be " 'consistent with the [government's] legitimate interest in "preserving the property . . . for the use to which it is lawfully dedicated.' " O'Connor pointed out that "ordinarily this inquiry is relatively straightforward, because we have almost always been confronted with cases where the fora at issue were discrete, single-purpose facilities." [Citing, e.g., *Adderly, Kokinda, Vincent,* and *Greenburgh,* supra.] O'Connor explained that this case is different because "the Port Authority is operating a shopping mall as well as an airport." As a result, the "reasonableness inquiry [is] not whether the restrictions on speech are 'consistent with preserving the property' for air travel, but whether they are reasonably related to maintaining the multipurpose environment that the Port Authority has deliberately created." Applying that standard, O'Connor agreed with the Court that the ban on face-to-face solicitation was "reasonable" because " '[s]olicitation impedes the normal flow of traffic,' " is "more intrusive and intimidating than an encounter with a person giving our information" and poses problems of "congestion and fraud."

Justice Kennedy, joined by Justices Blackmun, Stevens, and Souter, offered a very different approach to the public forum issue and, contrary to the majority, concluded that airport terminals are public fora. Kennedy complained that "our public forum doctrine ought [not] convert what was once an analysis protective of expression into one which grants the government authority to restrict speech by fiat." Kennedy observed that the Court's analysis, which "holds that traditional public forums are limited to public property which have as 'principal purpose . . . the free exchange of ideas' " as "evidenced by a longstanding historical practice of permitting speech," leaves "the government with almost unlimited authority to restrict speech on its property," for "the critical step in the Court's analysis is "the government's own definition or decision, unconstrained by an independent duty to respect the speech its citizens can voice" on public property. Kennedy argued that this view "is contrary to the underlying purposes of the public forum doctrine," for "at the heart of our jurisprudence lies the principle that in a free nation citizens must have the right to gather and speak with other persons in public places." Indeed, Kennedy pointed out that, if the Court's view were taken seriously, even streets, sidewalks and parks would not be public fora, for their "principal purpose" is not public discourse.

Kennedy therefore argued that the purposes of the public forum doctrine "cannot be given effect unless we recognize that open, public spaces and thoroughfares which are suitable for discourse may be public forums, whatever their historical pedigree and without concern for a precise classification of the property." Indeed, "without this recognition our forum doctrine retains no relevance in times of fast-changing technology and increasing insularity," and the Court's failure to "recognize the possibility that new types of government property may be appropriate forums for speech will lead to a serious curtailment of our expressive activity." Kennedy thus maintained that "if the objective, physical characteristics of the property at issue and the actual public access and uses which have been permitted by the government indicate that expressive activity would be appropriate and compatible with those uses, the property is a public forum." Kennedy emphasized that, "in conducting this last inquiry, courts must consider the consistency of those uses with expressive activities in general, rather than the specific sort of speech at issue in the case before it," and that "the possibility of some theoretical inconsistency between expressive activities and the property's uses should not bar a finding of a public forum, if those inconsistencies can be avoided through simple and permissible regulations."

Turning to the issue of airport terminals, Kennedy observed that "in these days an airport is one of the few government-owned spaces where many places have extensive contact with other members of the public," and given "that private spaces of similar character are not subject to the dictates of the First Amendment, it is critical that we preserve these areas for protected speech." Although an "airport corridor [is] not a street," it bears important "physical similarities" to a street, the relevant areas "are open to the public without restriction," and "the recent history of airports [demonstrates] that when adequate time, place, and manner regulations are in place, expressive activity is quite compatible with the uses of major airports." Kennedy thus found that the public areas of an airport terminal constitute a public forum.

Despite this disagreement with the Court, Justice Kennedy, writing only for himself, nonetheless concluded that the ban on solicitation funds was constitutional as "a reasonable time, place, and manner restriction" because of the risks of fraud and duress. (In reaching this result, Kennedy emphasized that, as he interpreted the regulation, it restricted only solicitation for immediate contributions, and not solicitation for subsequent contributions, as by the distribution of preaddressed envelopes.)

Justice Souter, joined by Justices Blackmun and Stevens, adopted Justice Kennedy's analysis of the general public forum issue, but dissented on the constitutionality of the ban on solicitation. In Souter's view, "the claim to be preventing coercion is weak" because "while a solicitor can be insistent, a pedestrian on the street or airport concourse can simply walk away." Moreover, Souter found the claim to be preventing fraud unpersuasive because the absolute ban on solicitation does not meet "the requirement of narrow tailoring." Finally, Souter maintained that the regulation did not leave open "ample" alternative channels of communication. Specifically, Souter disagreed that the distribution of preaddressed envelopes is "much of an alternative," and maintained that the regulation "shuts off a uniquely powerful avenue of communication [and] may, in effect, completely prohibit unpopular or poorly funded groups from receiving funds in response to protected solicitation."

Sale of Distribution of Literature. In a plurality opinion, Justice Kennedy, joined by Justices Blackmun, Stevens and Souter, concluded that the ban on the sale or distribution of literature violated the First Amendment. After finding, for the reasons set forth above, that airport terminals are public fora, Kennedy explained that the ban was invalid because "the right to distribute flyers and literature lies at the heart of the liberties guaranteed" by the First Amendment, the challenged "regulation is not drawn in narrow terms [and] does not leave open ample alternative channels for communication," and the "Port Authority's concerns with the problem of congestion can be addressed through narrow restrictions on the time and place of expressive activity."

Justice O'Connor concurred in the result. Although agreeing with the dissent that airport terminals are not public fora, she nonetheless concluded that the ban on the sale or distribution of literature was invalid because it was an "unreasonable" restriction. O'Connor explained that "leafletting does not necessarily entail the same kinds of problems presented by face-to-face solicitation." Indeed, "with the possible exception of avoiding litter, it is difficult to point to any problems intrinsic to the act of leafletting that would make it naturally incompatible with a large, multipurpose forum such as those at issue here." O'Connor emphasized, however, that the Port Authority may "promulgate regulations of the time, place, and manner of leafletting," and offered as an example of a permissible restriction the practice in some airports of limiting leafletting "to a relatively uncongested part of the airport terminal, the same part that houses the airport chapel."

Chief Justice Rehnquist, joined by Justices White, Scalia and Thomas, dissented. Having found that airport terminals are not public fora, Rehnquist reasoned that "the distribution ban, no less than the solicitation ban, is reasonable." Rehnquist argued that "the weary, harried or hurried traveler may have no less desire and need to avoid the delays generated by having literature foisted upon him than he does to avoid delays from a financial solicitation." Moreover, like solicitation, leafletting can cause congestion to the extend individuals choose "to stop and engage the leafletter in debate." Finally, leafletting is even worse than solicitation insofar as leafletting may produce litter, thereby "creating an eyesore, a safety hazard, and additional clean-up work for the airport staff."

Page 1286. Before section 3 of the Note, add the following:

For the view that "the Court's goal in developing the law of the public forum has not been to promote 'uninhibited, robust, wide-open' debate but to craft a doctrinal structure that will reduce the systemic opportunities for public forum regulators to abuse their governmental power," see BeVier, Rehabilitating Public Forum Doctrine: In Defense of Categories, 1992 Sup. Ct. Rev. 79, 81.

Page 1288. Before section 3 of the Note, add the following:

Consider also C. Sunstein, The Partial Constitution 208 (1993):

> The [Court] has said that the First Amendment is not implicated [in cases like *Hudgens* because] no government regulation of speech is involved. All that has happened is that private property owners have barred people from their land. [But] this is a poor way to understand the situation. [The] owners of the shopping center are able to exclude the protestors only because government has conferred on them a legal right to do so. The conferral of that right is an exercise of state power. It is this action that restricts the speech of the protestors. Surely it is a real question whether the grant of exclusionary power violates the First Amendment.

Page 1289. At the end of the Note, add the following:

For an interesting twist on this problem, consider *Simon & Schuster*:

SIMON & SCHUSTER, INC. v. MEMBERS OF THE NEW YORK STATE CRIME VICTIMS BOARD, 112 S. Ct. 501 (1992): In 1977, New York was terrorized by a serial killer popularly known as Son of Sam. By the time David Berkowitz was identified as the killer and apprehended, the rights to his story were worth a substantial amount. Berkowitz's chance to profit from his notoriety while his victims and their families remained uncompensated led the State to enact the Son of Sam law, which requires any entity contracting with a person convicted of a crime or a person who has voluntarily and intelligently admitted the commission of a crime to publish any depiction of the crime to turn over any income under the contract to the Crime Victims Board, which is then required to deposit the payment in an escrow account "for the benefit of and payable to any victim" within five years. This case began in 1986 when the Board became aware of a contract between Simon & Schuster and admitted organized crime figure Henry Hill. This contract resulted in the publication of the highly successful book, Wiseguy, which depicts in colorful detail the day-to-day existence of organized crime, and the equally successful movie, Goodfellas, which won a host of awards as the best film of 1990. Simon & Schuster filed this action challenging the constitutionality of the Son of Sam law. The Court, in an unanimous decision, held the law unconstitutional. Justice O'Connor delivered the opinion of the Court.

At the outset, the Court observed that "a statute is presumptively inconsistent with the First Amendment if it imposes a financial burden on speakers because of the content of their speech" because such a restriction "raises the specter that the Government may effectively drive certain ideas or viewpoints from the marketplace." The Court explained that the Son of Sam law "is such a content-based statute" because it "singles out income derived from expressive activity for a burden the State places on no other income, and it is directed only at works with a specified content." The Court declared that, to justify such a law, "the State must show that its regulation is necessary to serve a compelling state interest and is narrowly drawn to achieve that end."

Applying that standard, the Court rejected the Board's assertion that the State has a compelling interest in "ensuring that criminals do not profit from storytelling about their crimes before their victims have a meaningful opportunity to be compensated for their injuries" because the State does not "have any greater interest in compensating victims from the proceeds of such 'storytelling' than from any of the criminal's other assets" and because there is no justification for the "distinction between this expressive activity and any other activity in connection with its interest in transferring the fruits of crime from criminals to their victims." On the other hand, the Court found that the State does have "a compelling interest in depriving criminals of the profits of their crimes, and in using these funds to compensate victims." The Court concluded, however, that the Son of Sam law was not "narrowly tailored" to achieve this objective. Rather, the law "is significantly overinclusive" because it "applies to works on *any* subject, provided that they express the author's thought or recollections about his crime, however, tangentially or incidentally," and because it "enables the Board to escrow the income of any author who admits in his work to having committed a crime, whether or not the author was ever actually accused or convicted." The Court noted that such a law would reach such works as Thoreau's Civil Disobedience, the Confessions of Saint Augustine, and the autobiographies of such figures as Emma Goldman, Martin Luther King, Jr., Sir Walter Raleigh and Bertrand Russell. The Court thus concluded that the Son of Sam law is "inconsistent with the First Amendment" because it is not "narrowly tailored" to serve the State's compelling interest in compensating victims from the profits of crime. Justices Blackmun and Kennedy filed concurring opinions. Justice Thomas did not participate.

In concluding that the Son of Sam law was not "narrowly tailored," the Court seems to suggest a more narrowly drawn law would be constitutional. Suppose the law governed only works by persons (a) convicted of a serious crime, (b) that are published within three years of the crime and (c) that focus substantially on the criminal conduct. Would such a law satisfy the Court? Do you agree with the Court that the State's interest "in compensating victims from the profits of crime" is sufficiently "compelling" to justify the deterrent effect such a law might have on the production of such expression? Even if such a law is "narrowly drawn" to serve a "compelling interest," wouldn't it still be objectionable on grounds of "underinclusion" on the theory that the State cannot constitutionally take assets produced by a criminal's speech if it does not take *all* of his assets, and that the State cannot constitutionally penalize a criminal's speech as a "fruit" of the crime if it does not penalize *all* of the fruits of the crime? Can the State constitutionally "discriminate" against speech in this manner? Might the State avoid this problem by declaring that the victim of a crime "owns" the rights to any publication or other depiction of the crime by the criminal up to an amount necessary to compensate the victim? Consider the analogy to *Zacchini*.

Suppose a State enacts a law providing that all assets owned by a person convicted of a crime and all assets thereafter earned by a person convicted of a crime must be deposited with the Crime Victims Board to compensate victims of the crime. After *Simon & Schuster*, would such a law violate the First Amendment, as applied to royalties for a book written by a person convicted of a crime that only briefly discusses the crime in passing? For discussion of "incidental" restrictions of speech, see pages 1289-1299 in the main text.

3. Symbolic Content

Page 1296. At the end of section 2 of the Note, add the following:

For the argument that the law upheld in *O'Brien* should be understood as content-based rather than content-neutral because the prohibited act is "a symbolic representation of the message," rather than merely a means of communicating the message, see Williams, Content Discrimination and the First Amendment, 139 U. Pa. L. Rev. 615, 659-662 (1991).

Page 1297. Before section 4 of the Note, add the following:

In Wisconsin v. Mitchell, — S. Ct. — (1993), the Court upheld a state statute enhancing the maximum penalty for an offense whenever the defendant "intentionally selects the person against whom the crime [is committed] because of the race, religion, color, disability, sexual orientation, national origin or ancestry of that person." The Court noted that "a physical assault is not by any stretch of the imagination expressive conduct protected by the First Amendment." The Court recognized, however, that this did not necessarily end the matter, for "although the statute punishes criminal conduct, it enhances the maximum penalty for conduct motivated by a discriminatory point of view more severely than the same conduct engaged in for some other reason or for no reason at all." In upholding the statute, the Court observed that "the statute singles out for enhancement bias-inspired conduct because this conduct is thought to inflict greater individual and societal harm. For example, according to the [State], bias-motivated crimes are more likely to provoke retaliatory crimes, inflict distinct emotional harms on their victims, and incite community unrest." The Court concluded that the "State's desire to redress these perceived harms provides an adequate explanation for its penalty-enhancement provision over and above mere disagreement with offenders' beliefs or biases." Is this statute "related" or "unrelated" to the suppression of free expression? Note that the harms identified by the Court arise only if the victim knows that the defendant has committed a hate crime. In such circumstances, can one say that the law is "related" to the suppression of free expression because the harm sought to be prevented occurs only if the defendant has in some way communicated his motive to the victim of the crime?

Page 1305. Before the Note, add the following:

For additional views on the flag desecration debate, consider the following:

a. Kmiec, In the Aftermath of *Johnson* and *Eichman*, 1990 Brigham Young U.L. Rev. 577, 617, 620, 624, 634:

> Because of the lineage and unique design of the flag, the government may be able to protect the design of the flag as a matter of copyright law. [Although] government property is generally thought not to be copyrightable, [government] in all likelihood has inherent sovereign authority to declare a property interest in the flag's design. [In] applying the First Amendment, a number of cases recognize that the government has greater leeway to restrict access as property owner or proprietor than it would as sovereign or regulator. [Moreover, in] light of the Court's express recognition of the legitimacy of government speech, [it] seems likely that [the Court would] treat subsidized private speech comparably to direct government speech.

For more on this view, see Rust v. Sullivan, this chapter, section F, infra this Supplement.

b. Michelman, Saving Old Glory: On Constitutional Iconography, 42 Stan. L. Rev. 1337, 1338-1339, 1344, 1356-1359 (1990):

> [Several] civil libertarians offered expert testimony [to Congress arguing that the Flag Protection Act of 1989 had] a reasonable chance of surviving a constitutional test in the Supreme Court. Those who did so had reasons quite apart from any liking for the statute. [Rather, showing] that the Act stood a fair chance of passing muster before the Court gave a basis upon which to argue *against* resort to the amendment process [to overrule *Johnson*. That] argument's unspoken premise is that constitutional amendment on the subject of flag abuse is a worse alternative for civil liberties than a congressional enactment later accepted by the Supreme Court as consonant with the Constitution as it stands. [But] a well-drafted flag amendment need encompass nothing more than a local defeat for civil liberties, strictly confined to that specific form of symbolic speech consisting of mutilation of American [flags, whereas] judicial acceptance of even the most carefully crafted flag-protection law must to some degree jeopardize civil libertarian aims across the whole sweep of first amendment jurisprudence. [The civil libertarian view may be explained by their concern about what one] might call the theory of addictive amendment. [What they] seem to fear is that if the country [amends the first amendment] this time, and finds the heavens don't fall in consequence, the country won't be so automatically reticent in the future as it has been in the past. [This view is difficult] to square [with] the conventional wisdom's picture of a self-governing American People, sovereignly free to make their funda-

mental law whatever they resolve to make it. [This] all seems dangerously close to declaring that the People cannot be trusted with self-government. . . .

c. Tushnet, The Flag-Burning Episode: An Essay on the Constitution, 61 U. Colo. L. Rev. 39, 47-48 (1990):

Bruce Ackerman has argued that many of the conceptual difficulties of judicial review can be dispelled by distinguishing between times of ordinary politics [and] what he calls "constitutional moments." During constitutional moments, the public is attentive to fundamental issues of constitutional government — we consider what sort of government we want to have, we consider what kinds of limits we want to place on that government, and, most important, we recognize that the arrangements we put in place will persist for a relatively long time. Because of our attention to the long run, the courts can invoke our decisions in constitutional moments against us, and our successors, as they consider the constitutionality of legislation adopted during times of ordinary politics. I suggest that we ought to consider the [failure to enact a flag-burning amendment such] a constitutional moment. . . .

BARNES v. GLEN THEATRE, INC., 111 S. Ct. 2456 (1991): Respondents, two Indiana establishments that present nude dancing as entertainment, brought suit to enjoin enforcement of Indiana's public indecency statute, which prohibits any person to appear "in a state of nudity" in any "public place." The state courts have interpreted the statute as requiring nude dancers in such establishments to wear pasties and a G-string. The Court, in a 5-to-4 decision, rejected the claim that this statute, as applied in such circumstances, violates the first amendment.

Chief Justice Rehnquist, joined by Justices O'Connor and Kennedy, delivered the plurality opinion: "[N]ude dancing of the kind sought to be performed here is expressive conduct within the outer perimeters of the First Amendment, though we view it as only marginally so. [Indiana], of course, has not banned nude dancing as such, but has proscribed public nudity across the board. [Applying] the four-part *O'Brien* test, we find that Indiana's public indecency statute is justified despite its incidental limitations on some expressive activity. The public indecency statute is clearly within the constitutional power of the State and furthers substantial governmental interests. [Such statutes, which] are of ancient origin, and presently exist in at least 47 States, [reflect] moral disapproval of people appearing in the nude among strangers in public places. [The] traditional police power of the States is defined as the authority to provide for the public health, safety, and morals, and we have upheld such a basis for legislation. [Citing Roth v. United States, page 1203 of the text;

Paris Adult Theatre I v. Slaton, page 1216 of the text; Bowers v. Hardwick, page 968 of the text.]

"This interest is unrelated to the suppression of free expression. [Respondents contend] that even though prohibiting nudity in public generally may not be related to suppressing expression, prohibiting the performance of nude dancing is related to expression because the state seeks to prevent its erotic message. [But] we do not think that when Indiana applies its statute to the nude dancing in these nightclubs it is proscribing nudity because of the erotic message conveyed by the dancers. Presumably numerous other erotic performances are presented at these establishments [without] any interference from the state, so long as the performers wear a scant amount of clothing. Likewise, the requirement that the dancers don pasties and a G-string does not deprive the dance of whatever erotic message it conveys; it simply makes the message slightly less graphic. The perceived evil that Indiana seeks to address is not erotic dancing, but public nudity. The appearance of people of all shapes and sizes in the nude at a beach, for example, would convey little if any erotic message, yet the state still seeks to prevent it. Public nudity is the evil the state seeks to prevent, whether or not it is combined with expressive activity. . . .

"The fourth part of the *O'Brien* test requires that the incidental restriction on First Amendment freedom be no greater than is essential to the furtherance of the governmental interest. [Here], the governmental interest [is] societal disapproval of nudity in public places and among strangers. The statutory prohibition is not a means to some greater end, but an end in itself. It is without cavil that the public indecency statute is 'narrowly tailored;' Indiana's requirement that the dancers wear at least pasties and a G-string is modest, and the bare minimum necessary to achieve the state's purpose."

Justice Scalia filed a separate concurring opinion: "[T]he challenged regulation must be upheld [because], as a general law regulating conduct and not specifically directed at expression, it is not subject to First Amendment scrutiny at all. [The] First Amendment explicitly protects 'the freedom of speech [and] of the press' — oral and written speech — not 'expressive conduct.' When any law restricts speech, even for a purpose that has nothing to do with the suppression of communication (for instance, to reduce noise, see Saia v. New York, [page 1260 of the text], to regulate election campaigns, see Buckley v. Valeo, [page 1310 of the text], or to prevent littering, see Schneider v. State, [page 1257 of the text]), we insist that it meet the high, First Amendment standard of justification. But virtually every law restricts conduct, and virtually any prohibited conduct can be performed for an expressive purpose — if only expressive of the fact that the actor disagrees with the prohibition. It cannot reasonably be demanded, therefore, that every restriction of expression incidentally produced by a general law regulating conduct pass normal First Amendment scrutiny, or even — as some of our cases have suggested, see, e.g., *O'Brien* — that it be justified by an 'important or substantial' government interest. . . .

"This is not to say that the first Amendment affords no protection to expressive conduct. Where the government prohibits conduct precisely because of its communicative attributes, we hold the regulation unconstitutional. See, e.g., United States v. Eichman; Texas v. Johnson; Spence v. Washington. [In] each of the foregoing cases, we explicitly found that suppressing communication was the object of the regulation of conduct. Where that has not been the case, however — where suppression of communicative use of the conduct was merely the incidental effect of forbidding the conduct for other reasons — we have allowed the regulation to stand. [All] our holdings (though admittedly not some of our discussion) support the conclusion that 'the only First Amendment analysis applicable to laws that do not directly or indirectly impede speech is the threshold inquiry of whether the purpose of the law is to suppress communication. If not, that is the end of the [matter].' We have explicitly adopted such a regime in another First Amendment context: that of Free Exercise. [Citing Employment Division v. Smith, page 1519 of the text.] I think we should avoid wherever possible [a] mode of analysis that requires judicial assessment of the 'importance' of government interests — and especially of government interests in various aspects of morality."

Justice Souter also filed a separate concurring opinion: "[D]ancing as a performance [gives] expression at least to generalized emotion or feeling. [Although such] dancing is inherently expressive, nudity per se is not. [But] when nudity is combined with expressive activity, its stimulative and attractive value certainly can enhance the force of [expression]. I therefore agree [that] an interest in freely engaging in the nude dancing at issue here is subject to a degree of First Amendment protection. I also agree with the plurality that the appropriate analysis to determine the actual protection required by the First Amendment is the four-part enquiry described in *O'Brien*. [I rest my concurrence, however,] not on the possible sufficiency of society's moral views [but] on the State's substantial interest in combating the secondary effects of adult establishments of the sort typified by respondents' establishments. [In] my view, the interest [in] preventing prostitution, sexual assault, and other criminal activity, although presumably not a justification for all applications of the statute, is sufficient under *O'Brien* to justify the State's enforcement of the statute against the type of adult entertainment at issue here. [Citing *Renton*, page 1253 of the text; *Young*, page 1248 of the text.] [This] justification of the statute may not be ignored merely because it is unclear to what extent this purpose motivated the Indiana Legislature in enacting the statute. Our appropriate focus is not an empirical enquiry into the actual intent of the enacting legislature, but rather the existence or not of a current governmental interest in the service of which the challenged application of the statute may be constitutional. [Because] there is no overbreadth challenge before us, we are not called upon to decide whether the application of the statute would be valid in other contexts. It is enough, then, to say that the secondary effects rationale on which I rely would be open to question if the State were to seek to enforce the statute by barring expressive nudity in classes of productions that could not readily be analogized to the adult films at issue in *Renton*. It is difficult to see, for example, how the enforcement of Indiana's statute against nudity in a production of 'Hair' or 'Equus' somewhere other in an 'adult' theater would further the State's interest in avoiding harmful secondary effects. . . ."

Justice White, joined by Justices Marshall, Blackmun and Stevens, dissented: "The Court's analysis is erroneous in several respects. [None] of the cases they rely [upon] involved anything less than truly general proscriptions on individual conduct. In *O'Brien*, for example, individuals were prohibited from destroying their draft cards at any time and in any place, even in completely private places such as the home. [By] contrast, in this case Indiana does not suggest that its statute applies to, or could be applied to, nudity wherever it occurs, including the home. [Thus], the Indiana statute is not a general prohibition of the type we have upheld in prior cases. [In such circumstances], we are obligated to carefully examine the reasons the State has chosen to regulate this expressive conduct in a less than general statute. In other words, when the State enacts a law which draws a line between expressive conduct which is regulated and nonexpressive conduct of the same type which is not regulated, *O'Brien* places the burden on the State to justify the distinctions it has made. . . .

"The purpose of forbidding people from appearing nude in parks, beaches, hot dog stands, and like public places is to protect others from offense. But that could not possibly be the purpose of preventing nude dancing in theaters and barrooms since the viewers are exclusively consenting adults who pay money to see these dances. The purpose of the proscription in these contexts is to protect the viewers from what the State believes is the harmful message that nude dancing communicates. [This] being the case, it cannot be that the statutory prohibition is unrelated to expressive conduct. [It] is only because nude dancing performances may generate emotions and feelings of eroticism and sensuality among the spectators that the State seeks to regulate such expressive activity, apparently on the assumption that creating or emphasizing such thoughts and ideas in the minds of the spectators may lead to increased prostitution and the degradation of women. But generating thoughts, ideas, and emotions is the essence of communication. The nudity element of nude dancing performances cannot be neatly pigeonholed as mere 'conduct' independent of any expressive component of the dance. That fact dictates the level of First Amendment protection to be accorded the performances at issue here. [Content] based restrictions 'will be upheld only if narrowly drawn to accomplish a compelling governmental interest.' [Neither] the Court nor the State suggests that the statute could withstand scrutiny under that standard. [That] the performances in the Kitty Kat Lounge may not be high art, to say the least, and may not appeal to the Court, is hardly an excuse for distorting and ignoring settled doctrine. The Court's assessment of the artistic merits of nude dancing performances should not be the determining factor in deciding this case."

Consider Justice Scalia's response to Justice White's dissent: "The dissent confidently asserts that the purpose of restricting nudity in public places in general is to protect nonconsenting parties from offense; and argues that since only consenting, admission-paying patrons see respondents dance, that purpose cannot apply and the only remaining purpose must relate to the communicative elements of the performance. Perhaps the dissenters believe that 'offense to others' ought to be the only reason for restricting nudity in public places generally, but there is no basis for thinking that our society has ever shared that Thoreauvian 'you-may-do-what-you-like-so-long-as-it-does-not-injure-someone-else' beau ideal — much less for thinking that it was written into the Constitution. The purpose of Indiana's nudity law would be violated, I think, if 60,000 fully consenting adults crowded into the Hoosierdome to display their genitals to one another, even if there were not an offended innocent in the crowd. Our society prohibits, and all human societies have prohibited, certain activities not because they harm others but because they are considered in the traditional phrase, 'contra bonos mores,' i.e., immoral. [The] purpose of the Indiana statute [is] to enforce the traditional moral belief that people should not expose their private parts indiscriminately, regardless of whether those who see them are disedified. Since that is so, the dissent has no basis for positing that, where only thoroughly edified adults are present, the purpose must be repression of communication."

In light of this disagreement, consider the constitutionality, after *Barnes*, of the application of Indiana's public nudity statute to movies, art exhibits, and television productions depicting nudity.

Consider also Justice Souter's response to Justice White's dissent: "To say that pernicious secondary effects are associated with nude dancing establishments is not necessarily to say that such effects result from the persuasive effect of the expression inherent in nude dancing. It is to say, rather, only that the effects are correlated with the existence of establishments offering such dancing, without deciding what the precise causes of the correlation actually are. It is possible, for example, that the higher incidence of prostitution and sexual assault in the vicinity of adult entertainment locations results from the concentration of crowds of men predisposed to such activities, or from the simple viewing of nude bodies regardless of whether those bodies are engaged in expression or not. In neither case would the chain of causation run through the persuasive effect of the expressive component of nude dancing. Because the state's interest in banning nude dancing results from a simple correlation of such dancing with the other evils, rather than from a relationship between the other evils and the expressive component of dancing, the interest is unrelated to the suppression of free expression." [Citing *Renton.*]

4. Money and Free Expression: Regulation of Solicitation, Contribution, and Expenditure

Page 1310. At the end of paragraph before Buckley v. Valeo, add the following:

International Society for Krishna Consciousness, Inc. v. Lee, 112 S. Ct. 2701 (1992) (upholding a ban on solicitation in airport terminals).

Page 1319. Before the quotation from Wright, add the following:

For an elaboration of this view, consider Sunstein, Free Speech Now, 59 U. Chi. L. Rev. 255, 263-267, 272, 291-292 (1992):

> Perhaps we need a New Deal for speech, one that would parallel what the New Deal provided to property rights during the 1930's, and that would be rooted in substantially similar concerns. Before the New Deal, the Constitution was often understood as a constraint on government "regulation." In practice, this meant that the Constitution was often invoked to prohibit governmental interference with existing distributions of rights and entitlements. Hence minimum wage and maximum hour laws were seen as unjustifiable exactions — takings — from employers for the benefit of employees and the public at large. [The] New Deal reformers [understood] that this [framework] was built on fictions. [The] pre-New Deal framework treated the existing distribution of resources and opportunities as prepolitical, when in fact it was not. It saw minimum wage and maximum hour laws as introducing government into a private or voluntary sphere. But the New Dealers pointed out that this sphere was actually a creation of law. Rules of property, contract, and tort produced the set of entitlements that ultimately yielded market hours and wages. [Thus, rather] than superimposing regulation on a realm of purely voluntary interactions, minimum wage laws substituted one form of regulation for another. . . .
>
> These ideas have played little role in the law of free speech. For purposes of speech, contemporary understandings of neutrality and partisanship [are]

identical to those that predate the New Deal. [It is time for us to recognize that,] in some circumstances, what seems to be government regulation of speech actually might promote free speech, and should not be treated as an abridgment at all. [Consider, for example,] a case in which a network decides not to sell advertising time to a group that wants [to] express some dissident view. Under current law, the refusal raises no First Amendment question, in part because [we would say] there is no "state action." But government gives broadcasters property rights in their licenses, and their exercise of those rights is a function of law in no subtle sense. [The] exclusion of the would-be speakers is made possible by the law of civil and criminal trespass [and] is thus the product of a governmental decision. . . .

[Similarly], *Buckley* reflects pre-New Deal understandings. We should view it as the modern-day analogue of *Lochner*: a decision to take the market status quo as just and prepolitical, and to use that decision to invalidate democratic efforts at reform. Reliance on markets is governmental neutrality. Use of existing distributions for political expenditures marks out government inactions. [But] it should be clear that elections based on those distributions are actually subject to a regulatory system, made possible and constituted through law. That law consists, first, in legal rules protecting the present distribution of wealth, and more fundamentally, in legal rules allowing candidates to buy speech rights through markets.

Because it involves speech, *Buckley* is even more striking than *Lochner*. Efforts to redress economic inequalities, or to ensure that they do not translate into political inequalities, should not be seen as impermissible redistribution, or as the introduction of government regulation where it did not exist before. Instead, we should evaluate campaign finance laws pragmatically in terms of their consequences for the system of free expression.

Consider in this connection Balkin, Some Realism about Pluralism: Legal Realist Approaches to the First Amendment, 1990 Duke L.J. 375, 410-412:

Speech rights depend upon access to communicative technologies, which are forms of private property. The effective exercise of speech rights thus both depends upon one's own property rights, and is potentially in conflict with the property rights of others. [Whenever] the state enforces an advertising contract, allows a person to own and run a newspaper, or grants a broadcast license, it is sanctioning a grant of access to the means of communication. Whenever the state ejects a protestor from private property, or enforces the right of CBS to refuse to broadcast the views of [dissidents], it is sanctioning a denial of access to the means of communication. [In such circumstances,] it is difficult to argue that the state is neutral when some persons have vastly greater access to the means of communication than others because of vastly more economic power. [The] government is responsible for inequalities in access to the means of communication because it has created the system of property rights that makes such inequalities possible. Therefore, it is not only wrong but also incoherent for opponents of campaign finance reform to contend that the government should not regulate access to the political process. Government already regulates access to the political process — the first amendment simply demands that it do so fairly.

Page 1328. After the citation to Eu v. San Francisco Democratic Central Committee in section 6 of the Note, add the following:

Burdick v. Takushi, 112 S. Ct. 2059 (1992) (upholding Hawaii's prohibition on write-in voting).

F. ADDITIONAL PROBLEMS

1. *Equality and Free Expression*

Page 1337. At the bottom of the page, add the following:

Consider Kagan, The Changing Faces of First Amendment Neutrality, 1992 Sup. Ct. Rev. 29, 38-40:

> What, precisely, is content-based underinclusion? Suppose that the government, consistent with the First Amendment, may limit — by prohibiting or by refusing to subsidize — either an entire category of speech or all speech within a particular context. Now suppose that the government declines to go so far: rather than limiting speech to the full extent of its constitutional power, the government chooses to limit only some expression — and that on the basis of content. The resulting government action is, in the ordinary sense, narrower than the action stipulated to be constitutional. That is, the merely partial limitation allows more expression. Yet this "narrower" action incorporates a content-based distinction: it picks and chooses among expression on the basis of what is said. The question thus becomes whether and when a government that has the power to restrict speech generally may instead limit select kinds of expression. . . .
>
> Such underinclusion [is] a particular kind of content-based restriction, by no means equivalent to all government actions falling with the broad content-based category. In many — indeed, most — cases of content-based speech restrictions, the question [is] the permissibility of the burden placed on the speech affected. Consider, for example, a case arising from a statute that [criminalizes] seditious advocacy. In deciding such a case, the Court usually will not ask whether the government has a sufficient reason to treat speech of one kind (seditious advocacy) differently from speech of another; rather, the Court will ask merely whether the government has a sufficient reason to restrict the speech actually affected. [In] such a case, the issue is not underinclusion, for the government could not cure the constitutional flaw by ex-

tending the restriction to all speech regardless of its content. By contrast, in a content-based underinclusion case, equality is all that is at issue.

Page 1343. Before section 6 of the Note, add the following:

See also Lamb's Chapel v. Center Moriches Union Free School District, — S. Ct. — (1993) (relying upon *Widmar* to invalidate a school district rule permitting school property to be used after school for social, civic, and recreational uses, but prohibiting the use of such property for religious purposes).

Page 1343. At the end of section 6 of the Note, add the following:

7. *The reach of* Mosley: *The "careful scrutiny" standard.* Are there circumstances in which a content-based law, like the ones invalidated in *Mosley, Carey* and *Widmar,* can withstand "careful scrutiny"? In Burson v. Freeman, 112 S. Ct. 1846 (1992), the Court upheld a Tennessee law prohibiting the solicitation of votes and the display or distribution of campaign materials within 100 feet of the entrance to a polling place. Justice Blackmun announced the judgment of the Court and delivered an opinion in which Chief Justice Rehnquist, Justice White, and Justice Kennedy joined:

> The Tennessee statute implicates three central concerns in our First Amendment jurisprudence: regulation of political speech, regulation of speech in a public forum, and regulation based on the content of the speech. [As] a facially content-based restriction on political speech in a public forum, [the statute] must be subjected to exacting scrutiny. [Tennessee] asserts that its campaign-free zone serves [its] compelling interest in protecting the rights of its citizens to vote freely for the candidates of their choice [and in protecting] the right to vote in an election conducted with integrity and reliability. [These interests] obviously are compelling. . . .
>
> To survive strict scrutiny, however, a State must [also] demonstrate that its law is necessary to serve the asserted interest. While we readily acknowledge that a law rarely survives such scrutiny, an examination of the evolution of election reform [demonstrates] the necessity of the restricted areas in and around polling places. [Indeed], an examination of the history of election regulation [reveals] a persistent battle against two evils: voter intimidation and election fraud. [Today], all 50 States, together with numerous other Western democracies, [have] settled on the same solution: a secret ballot secured in part by a restricted zone around the voting compartments. We find that this wide-spread and time-tested consensus demonstrates that some restricted zone is necessary in order to serve the States' compelling interest in preventing voter intimidation of election fraud.

In dissent, Justice Stevens, joined by Justices O'Connor and Souter, agreed with the plurality's statement of the governing standard but disagreed with the plurality's conclusion that Tennessee had "made anything approaching such a showing":

> Campaign-free zones are noteworthy for their broad, antiseptic sweep. The Tennessee zone encompassed at least 30,000 square feet around each polling [place]. Moreover, the Tennessee statute does not merely regulate conduct that might inhibit voting; it bars the simple "display of campaign posters, signs, or other campaign materials." [The] notion that such sweeping restrictions on speech are necessary to maintain the freedom to vote and the integrity of the ballot box borders on the absurd. The evidence introduced at trial to demonstrate the necessity for Tennessee's campaign-free zone was exceptionally thin. [Perhaps] in recognition of the poverty of the record, the plurality — without briefing, or legislative or judicial factfinding — looks to history to assess whether Tennessee's statute is in fact necessary to serve the State's interests. [But the plurality's] analysis is deeply flawed; it confuses history with necessity, and mistakes the traditional for the indispensable. [We] have never regarded tradition as a proxy for necessity where necessity must be demonstrated [citing, for example, the Court's invalidation of poll taxes, durational residence requirements for voting, petition requirements for ballot access, onerous filing fees, and malaportioned legislatures, all of which are addressed in Chapter VI, E1]. [Courts] that have [made] findings with regard to campaign-free zones have, without exception, found such zones unnecessary. [All] of these courts [have] concluded that such suppression of expression [is] something of a social atavism. [W]hatever the original historical basis for campaign-free zones may have been, their continued "necessity" has not been established. [In] sum, what the plurality [calls] "exacting scrutiny" appears by the end of its analysis to be neither exacting nor scrutiny. To borrow a mixed metaphor, the plurality's scrutiny is "toothless."
>
> In addition to sweeping too broadly in its reach, [the Tennessee law] selectively prohibits speech based on content. [Within] the zone, [it] silences all campaign-related expression, but allows expression on any other subject: religious, artistic speech, even political debate and solicitation concerning issues or candidates not on the day's ballot. [This] content-based discrimination is particularly problematic because such a regulation will inevitably favor certain groups of candidates. [Candidates] with fewer resources, candidates for lower visibility offices, and "grassroots" candidates benefit disproportionately from last-minute campaigning near the polling place. [In] Carey v. Brown, [we] acknowledged Illinois' interest in "residential privacy" but invalidated [the] ban on picketing because the distinction between labor and non-labor picketing could not be "justified by reference to the State's interest in maintaining domestic tranquility." In this case, the same is true: [Tennessee] has failed to point to any legitimate interest that would justify its selective regulation of campaign-related expression. [In] my opinion, the presence of campaign workers outside a polling place [may] be a nuisance, but it is also the sound of a vibrant democracy.

In his plurality opinion, Justice Blackmun rejected the dissent's argument that the restricted zones are "overinclusive" because states could secure their compelling interests with narrower "statutes that make it a [crime] to interfere with an election or to use violence or intimidation to prevent voting," arguing that such laws would address "only the most blatant and specific attempts to impede elections." Justice Blackmun also rejected the dissent's argument that the challenged statute is "underinclusive" because "it does not restrict other types of speech [within] the 100-foot zone," arguing that such content discrimination requires strict scrutiny, but is not necessarily fatal. "States adopt laws to address the problems that confront them. The First Amendment does not require States to regulate for problems that do not exist."

Does it make sense to treat the law in *Burson* as content-based? Why is the content distinction in *Burson* problematic? Would the first amendment concerns be any less if the law eliminated the content distinction by prohibiting *all* speech within 100 feet of a polling place? Wouldn't such a law be vulnerable to overbreadth challenge? Consider whether *Burson* is any different from *Mosley, Carey* or *Widmar* in this respect. Does Justice Stevens' concern that the challenged "regulation will inevitably favor certain groups of candidates" have anything to do with the fact that the regulation is content-based?

In Mills v. Alabama, 384 U.S. 214 (1966), the Court invalidated a state law prohibiting election day editorial endorsements, denouncing the law as an "obvious and flagrant abridgment" of the first amendment. Is *Burson* reconcilable with *Mills*?

Justice Thomas did not participate in *Burson.* Justice Scalia filed a concurring opinion in which he argued that "[b]ecause restrictions on speech around polling places on election day are [a] venerable [part] of the American tradition, [the challenged law] does not restrict speech in a traditional public forum, and the 'exacting scrutiny' that the Court purports to apply is inappropriate." In Scalia's view, the Tennessee statute, "though content-based, is constitutional because it is a reasonable, viewpoint-neutral regulation of a nonpublic forum." Is there anything to this approach? Consider the *Lehman* case that follows:

Page 1353. Before section 6 of the Note, add the following:

5A. Widmar *revisited: the meaning of viewpoint neutrality.* Lamb's Chapel v. Moriches Union Free School District, — S. Ct. — (1993), concerned the constitutionality of a school district rule that permitted after-school social, civic, and recreational uses of school property, but prohibited the use of such property for religious purposes. Applying this rule, the school district rejected Lamb's Chapel's request to show religious-oriented films on family values and childrearing on school property. The lower courts upheld the rule on the theory that the school property was "a limited public forum open only for designated purposes" and that access to such a forum "can be based on subject matter [so] long as the distinctions drawn are reasonable [and] viewpoint neutral." The Supreme Court accepted this analysis, but nonetheless invalidated the rule because it was not "viewpoint neutral."

In reaching this result, the Court rejected the lower courts' conclusion that the challenged rule was based on subject matter rather than viewpoint "because it [would] be applied in the same way to all uses of school property for religious purposes." Although conceding that "all religions and all uses for religious purposes are treated alike" under the rule, the Court observed that this "does not answer the critical question" whether it constitutes discrimination "on the basis of viewpoint to permit the school property to be used for the presentation of all views about family issues [except] those dealing with the subject matter from a religious standpoint." The Court reasoned that the "film involved here [dealt] with a subject otherwise permissible under [the rule], and its exhibition was denied solely because the film dealt with the subject from a religious standpoint." The Court therefore concluded that the rule "violates the First Amendment" because it denied "access to a speaker solely to suppress the point of view he espouses on an otherwise included subject."

Consider Stone, The Equal Access Controversy: The Religion Clauses and the Meaning of "Neutrality," 81 Nw. U. L. Rev. 168, 169-170 (1986):

> The protection of political speech, like religious speech, lies at the very core of the first amendment. The Court often has recognized, however, that government may grant special benefits to nonpolitical speech without extending those benefits to political speech, so long as it does not expressly favor any particular political viewpoint. [Citing Lehman, Greer and Cornelius]. This is so because policies that disadvantage political speech as a class are less threatening to first amendment values than laws that expressly disadvantage specific points of view.
>
> A similar principle governs religious expression. As the Supreme Court has long recognized, the "clearest command" of the religion clauses is that "one religious denomination cannot be officially preferred over another." [Denominational] discrimination in the religious context is the analog of viewpoint discrimination in the political context. [The] corollary is also true, however. Governmental policies that grant special benefits to nonreligious expression as a class should be tested by the same — less demanding — standards that the Court uses to test the constitutionality of governmental policies that grant special benefits to nonpolitical expression as a class. In the religious, as in the political, realm the broader subject-matter classification is less threatening to core first amendment values.

Lamb's Chapel also applied for permission to use school rooms for its Sunday morning services. What result after *Lamb's Chapel?*

Page 1362. Before Section 2, add the following citation to the list of "additional commentary" at the top of the page.

Cole, Beyond Unconstitutional Conditions: Charting Spheres of Neutrality in Government-Funded Speech, 67 N.Y.U. L. Rev. 675 (1992).

Page 1362. Before Section 2, add the following:

RUST v. SULLIVAN, 111 S. Ct. 1759 (1991): Title X of the Public Health Service Act, enacted in 1970, provides that none of the federal funds appropriated under the Act for family planning services "shall be used in programs where abortion is a method of family planning." In 1988, Respondent, the Secretary of Health and Human Services, issued new regulations attaching three conditions on the grant of federal funds for Title X projects. First, a "Title X project may not provide counseling concerning the use of abortion as a method of family planning or provide referral for abortion as a method of family planning," even upon request. Second, a Title X project may not engage in activities that "encourage, promote or advocate abortion as a method of family planning." Forbidden activities include lobbying for legislation and disseminating materials, providing speakers, or using legal action to increase the availability of abortion. Third, Title X projects must be organized so that they are "physically and financially separate" from prohibited abortion activities. Petitioners, Title X grantees and doctors suing on behalf of themselves and their patients, challenged the validity of these regulations. The Court, in a 5 to 4 decision, upheld the regulations. After rejecting the contention that the regulations exceeded the Secretary's authority under the statute, the Court turned to the question whether the regulations were invalid "on their face" under the first amendment. Chief Justice Rehnquist delivered the opinion of the Court:

"Petitioners contend that the regulations violate the first amendment by impermissibly discriminating based on viewpoint because they prohibit 'all discussion about abortion as a lawful option — including counseling, referral, and the provision of neutral and accurate information about ending a pregnancy — while compelling the clinic or counselor to provide information that promotes continuing a pregnancy to term' [In] Maher v. Roe [page 937 of the text], we upheld a state welfare regulation under which Medicaid recipients received payments for services related to childbirth, but not for nontherapeutic abortions. The Court rejected the claim that this unequal subsidization worked a violation of the Constitution. We held that the government may 'make a value judgment favoring childbirth over abortion, and . . . implement that judgment by the allocation of public funds.' Here the Government is exercising the authority it possesses under *Maher* [to] subsidize family planning services [while] declining to 'promote or encourage abortion.' The Government can, without violating the Constitution, selectively fund a program to encourage certain activities it believes to be in the public interest, without at the same time funding an alternate program which seeks to deal with the problem in another way. In so doing, the Government has not discriminated on the basis of viewpoint; it has merely chosen to fund one activity to the exclusion of the other. '[A governmental] decision not to subsidize the exercise of a fundamental right does not infringe the right.' [quoting *Taxation with Representation*.] The challenged regulations [are] designed to ensure that the limits of the federal program are observed. [This] is not a case of the Government 'suppressing a dangerous idea,' but of a prohibition on a project grantee or its employees from engaging in activities outside of its scope.

"To hold that the Government unconstitutionally discriminates on the basis of viewpoint when it chooses to fund a program dedicated to advance certain permissible goals, because the program in advancing those goals necessarily discourages alternate goals, would render numerous government programs constitutionally suspect. When Congress established a National Endowment for Democracy to encourage other countries to adopt democratic principles, it was not constitutionally required to fund a program to encourage competing lines of political philosophy such as Communism and Fascism. Petitioners' assertions ultimately boil down to the position that if the government chooses to subsidize one protected right, it must subsidize analogous counterpart rights. But the Court has soundly rejected that proposition. [Citing *Taxation with Representation; Maher*]. Within far broader limits than petitioners are willing to concede, when the government appropriates public funds to establish a program it is entitled to define the limits of that program. [We] have here not the case of a general law singling out a disfavored group on the basis of speech content, but a case of the Government refusing to fund activities, including speech, which are specifically excluded from the scope of the project funded.

"[Relying on *League of Women Voters*, petitioners] contend that the restrictions on the subsidization of abortion-related speech [are] impermissible because they condition the receipt of a benefit [on] the relinquishment of [the constitutional] right to engage in abortion advocacy and counseling. [Petitioners'] reliance on [this case] is unavailing, however, because here the government is not denying a benefit to anyone, but is instead simply insisting that public funds be spent for the purposes for which they were authorized. The [regulations] do not force the Title X grantee to give up abortion-related speech; they merely require that the grantee keep such activities separate and distinct from Title X activities. [By] requiring that the Title X grantee engage in abortion-related activity separately from activity receiving federal funding, Congress has, consistent with our teachings in *League of Women Voters* and *Taxation with Representation,* not denied it the right to engage in abortion-related activities. Congress has merely refused to fund such activities out of the public fisc. . . .

"This is not to suggest that funding by the Government, even when coupled with the freedom of the fund recipients to speak outside the scope of the Government-funded project, is invariably sufficient to justify government control over the content of expression. For example, this Court has recognized that the existence of a Government 'subsidy,' in the form of Government-owned property, does not justify the restriction of speech in areas that have 'been traditionally open to the public for expressive activity' [or] have been 'expressly dedicated to speech activity.' [Citing *Kokinda, Hague,* and *Perry*]. [It might also be argued] that traditional relationships such as that between doctor and patient should enjoy protection under the First Amendment from government regulation, even when subsidized by the Government. We need not resolve that question here, however, because the Title X program regulations do not significantly impinge upon the doctor-patient relationship. Nothing in them requires a doctor to represent as his own any opinion that he does not in fact hold. [The] doctor is always free to make clear that advice regarding abortion is simply beyond the scope of the program. In these circumstances, the general rule that the Government may choose not to subsidize speech applies with full force." The Court also rejected the claim that the regulations violate a woman's due process right to choose whether to terminate a pregnancy. See Chapter 6, section F, supra this Supplement.

Justice Blackmun, joined by Justices Marshall and Stevens, dissented: "Until today, the Court has never upheld viewpoint-based suppression of speech simply because that suppression was a condition upon the acceptance of public funds. [Nothing in *Taxation with Representation*] can be said to challenge this long-settled understanding. In [*Taxation with Representation*], the Court upheld a content-neutral provision [and emphasized that the] 'case would be different if Congress were to discriminate invidiously in its subsidies in such a way as to "[aim] at the suppression of dangerous ideas." ' [The regulations at issue here are] clearly viewpoint-based. [Indeed, if] a client asks directly about abortion, a Title X physician or counselor is required to say, in essence, that the project does not consider abortion to be an appropriate method of family planning. [The] Regulations pertaining to 'advocacy' are even more explicitly viewpoint-based. [The] majority's reliance on the fact that the Regulations pertain solely to funding decisions simply begs the question. Clearly, there are some bases upon which government may not rest its decision to fund or not to fund. For example, the Members of the majority surely would agree that government may not base its decision to support an activity upon considerations of race. [Our] cases make clear that ideological viewpoint is a similarly repugnant ground upon which to base funding decisions. . . .

"In the cases at bar, the speaker's interest in the communication is both clear and vital. In addressing the family planning needs of their clients, the physicians and counselors who staff Title X projects seek to provide them with the full range of information and options regarding their health and reproductive freedom. Indeed, the legitimate expectations of the patient and the ethical responsibilities of the medical profession demand no less. [When] a client becomes pregnant, the full range of therapeutic alternatives includes the abortion option, and Title X counselors' interest in providing this information is compelling. The Government's articulated interest in distorting the doctor/patient dialogue — ensuring that federal funds are not spent for a purpose outside the scope of the program — falls far short of that necessary to justify suppression of truthful information and professional medical opinion regarding constitutionally protected conduct. [Indeed], it is of no small significance that the speech the Secretary would suppress is truthful information regarding constitutionally protected conduct of vital importance to the listener. One can imagine no legitimate governmental interest that might be served by suppressing such information."

Justice O'Connor dissented on statutory grounds.

For another twist on the problem of underinclusive, content-based restrictions, see R.A.V. v. City of St. Paul, supra section D2, this Supplement. Although it may seem that *R.A.V.* and *Rust* pose quite different questions, consider Kagan, The Changing Faces of First Amendment Neutrality, 1992 Sup. Ct. Rev. 29, 31-32:

> *Rust* and *R.A.V.* both raise the same question: If, in a certain setting, the government need not protect or promote any speech at all, may the government choose to protect or promote only speech with a certain content? *Rust* is easily seen in this light. The government, we believe is not constitutionally required to promote speech through the use of federal funds. May the government then fund whatever speech it wants? [The] question is similar in *R.A.V.* The government is not constitutionally required to tolerate any "fighting words" at all. May the government then permit some but not all fighting words? The question posed in each case is in an important sense the question

of First Amendment neutrality in its starkest form: when speech [has] no claim to government promotion or protection, what limitations does the government face in voluntarily advancing some messages, but not all? [Although] the cases have a similar structure, implicate an identical question, and fall within a single [category] of First Amendment [cases, the Justices deciding them saw no connection at all].

3. Public Employment

b. Criticizing Government Policy

Page 1378. At the end of the Note, add the following:

To what extent, if any, should the free speech rights of government licensees, such as attorneys and doctors, be subject to greater restriction than the speech of other citizens? Consider the following:

GENTILE v. STATE BAR OF NEVADA, 111 S. Ct. 2720 (1991): Petitioner, an attorney, held a press conference the day after his client was indicted on criminal charges. The case was highly publicized and, at the press conference, petitioner proclaimed his client's innocence, asserted that his client was being used as a scapegoat by the police, maintained that the real culprit was a police detective, and cast doubt on the credibility of several government witnesses. Although petitioner's client ultimately was acquitted of all charges, petitioner received an official reprimand by the state bar on the ground that his press conference violated Nevada Supreme Court Rule 177, which prohibits a lawyer from making extrajudicial statements to the press that the lawyer knows or reasonably should know will have a "substantial likelihood of materially prejudicing" an adjudicative proceeding. The Court, in a 5-to-4 decision, concluded that this is a constitutionally permissible standard for regulating the speech of lawyers in this context.

Chief Justice Rehnquist delivered the opinion of the Court:

"In the United States, the courts have historically regulated admission to the practice of law before them, and exercised the authority to discipline and ultimately to disbar lawyers whose conduct departed from prescribed standards. 'Membership in the bar is a privilege burdened with conditions.' [In] the last quarter-century, the legal profession has reviewed its ethical limitations on extrajudicial statements by lawyers in the context of this Court's cases interpreting the First Amendment. [Currently, thirty-two states have adopted the "substantial likelihood of material prejudice" standard, eleven states have adopted the less speech-protective "reasonable likelihood of prejudice" standard, and five states and the District of Columbia have adopted the "clear and present danger" standard, or some variation thereof.]

"[Relying on cases like *Bridges, Nebraska Press,* and *Landmark Communications,* this chapter, section B, supra this Supplement, petitioner maintains] that the First Amendment requires a State to demonstrate a 'clear and present danger' of 'actual prejudice or an imminent threat' before any discipline may be imposed on a lawyer who initiates a press conference such as occurred here. [But] none of those cases involved lawyers who represented parties to a pending proceeding in court. [The] question we must answer in this case is whether a lawyer who represents a defendant involved with the criminal justice system may insist on the same standard before he is disciplined for public pronouncements about the case, or whether the State instead may penalize that sort of speech upon a lesser showing.

"It is unquestionable that in the courtroom itself, during a judicial proceeding, whatever right to 'free speech' an attorney has is extremely circumscribed. [Moreover, even] in an area far removed from the courtroom and the pendency of a case, our decisions dealing with a lawyer's right [to] solicit business and advertise [have] not suggested that lawyers are protected by the First Amendment to the same extent as those engaged in other businesses. [To the contrary, such cases as *Bates* and *Ohralik*, supra page 1192 of the text] recognized the long-established principle stated in In re Cohen, 7 N.Y.2d 488 (1960): 'Appellant as a citizen could not be denied any of the common rights of citizens. But he stood before the inquiry [in a] quite different capacity, also. As a lawyer, he was "an officer of the court, and, like the court itself, an instrument . . . of justice. . . ." '

"We think [that] the speech of lawyers representing clients in pending cases may be regulated under a less demanding standard than that established for regulation of the press [and other nonparticipants in the system]. Lawyers representing clients in pending cases are key participants in the criminal justice system, and the State may demand some adherence to the precepts of that system in regulating their [speech]. Because lawyers have special access to information through discovery and client communications, their extrajudicial statements pose a threat to the fairness of a pending proceeding since lawyers' statements are likely to be received as especially authoritative. [We] agree with the majority of the States that the 'substantial likelihood of material prejudice' standard constitutes a constitutionally permissible balance between the First Amendment rights of attorneys in pending cases and the State's interest in fair trials, [for this standard] imposes only narrow and necessary limitations on lawyers' speech. The limitations are aimed at two principal evils: (1) comments that are likely to influence the actual outcome of the trial, and (2) comments that are likely to prejudice the jury venire, even if an untainted panel can ultimately be found. Few, if any, interests under the Constitution are more fundamental than the right to a fair trial by 'impartial' jurors, and an outcome affected by extrajudicial statements would violate that fundamental right. [Moreover, even] if a fair trial can ultimately be ensured through voir dire, change of venue, or some other device, these measures entail serious costs to the system. [The] State has a substantial interest in preventing officers of the court, such as lawyers, from imposing such costs on the judicial system and on the litigants."

Justice Kennedy, joined by Justices Marshall, Blackmun, and Stevens, dissented: "[O]ne central fact must dominate the analysis: [at] issue here is the constitutionality of a ban on political speech critical of the government and its officials. [Such speech] lies at the very center of the First Amendment. [The] judicial system, and in particular our criminal justice courts, play a vital part in a democratic state, and the public has a legitimate interest in their operations. [The Court] argues speech by an attorney is subject to greater regulation than speech by others, and restrictions on an attorney's speech should be assessed under a balancing [test]. Wide-open balancing of interests is not appropriate in this context. [The Court] would justify a substantial limitation on speech by attorneys because 'lawyers have special access to [information]' so lawyers' statements 'are likely to be received as especially authoritative.' [But there is no claim here] that petitioner revealed client confidences or [released] information received through court proceedings or special access afforded attorneys.

"[The Court also] uses the 'officer of the court' label to imply that attorney contact with the press somehow is inimical to the attorney's proper role. [Because] attorneys participate in the criminal justice system and are trained in its complexities, they hold unique qualifications as a source of information about pending cases. [To] the extent the press and public rely upon attorneys for information because attorneys are well-informed, this may prove the value to the public of speech by members of the bar. If the dangers of their speech arise from its persuasiveness, from their ability to explain judicial proceedings, or from the likelihood the speech will be believed, these are not the sort of dangers that can validate restrictions. The First Amendment does not permit suppression of speech because of its power to command assent.

"One may concede the proposition that an attorney's speech about pending cases may present dangers that could not arise from statements by a nonparticipant, and that an attorney's duty to cooperate in the judicial process may prevent him or her from taking actions with an intent to frustrate that process. The role of attorneys in the criminal justice system subjects them to fiduciary obligations to the court and the parties. [This] case is a poor vehicle for defining with precision the outer limits under the Constitution of a court's ability to regulate an attorney's statements about ongoing adjudicative proceedings. At the very least, however, we can say that the Rule which punished petitioner's statement represents a limitation of First Amendment freedoms greater than is necessary [and] does not protect a danger of the necessary gravity, imminence, or likelihood."

The Court ultimately overturned the reprimand, by a 5-to-4 vote, on grounds of vagueness.

c. Patronage

Page 1384. At the end of Rutan v. Republican Party of Illinois, add the following:

For analysis of the consequences of the elimination of patronage, see Bowman, "We Don't Want Anybody Anybody Sent": The Death of Patronage Hiring in Chicago, 86 Nw. U.L. Rev. 57 (1991) (concluding that predictions "that dire consequences will flow from the prohibition of patronage" are "mistaken").

4. Compelled Affirmation, Expression, and Association: The Right Not *to Speak*

Page 1402. Before the Note, add the following:

In Lehnert v. Ferris Faculty Association, 111 S. Ct. 1950 (1991), the Court divided sharply over the constitutionality of a union's use of compelled public employee contributions to support union activities falling between the two extremes — ideological activities not directly related to the collective bargaining process and nonideological activities directly related to collective bargaining — addressed in *Abood.* The Court, in an opinion by Justice Blackmun, held that a union may constitutionally charge dissenting employees only for those activities that are (1) "germane" to collective bargaining; (2) justified by the government's interests in labor peace and avoiding free riders; and (3) not significantly burdening of free speech. Applying this standard, the Court concluded that the public university faculty union involved in this case could constitutionally use dissenting employees' contributions to fund (a) the national union's "non-political" information services concerning teaching, professional development, and job opportunities, even though they do not relate directly to the members of the particular local union at issue. On the other hand, Justice Blackmun, joined only by Chief Justice Rehnquist and Justices White and Stevens, concluded that, under the three-part test, the union could not constitutionally use dissenting employees' contributions to fund (b) lobbying, electoral, or other union political activities outside the limited context of contract ratification or implementation; (c) union programs designed to secure additional state funds for public education; or (d) union public relations efforts designed to enhance the reputation of the teaching profession.

In a separate opinion, Justice Marshall, who joined the Court's opinion with respect to the three-part test and outcome (a), dissented with respect to (b), (c), and (d). Marshall argued that to represent their members effectively, public sector unions must necessarily concern themselves not only with negotiations at the bargaining table, but also with advancing their members' interests in legislative and other political arenas, and that to require dissenting employees to pay for such activities as (b), (c), and (d) does not violate their right "to refrain from speaking," but merely requires them to pay a pro rata share of the legitimate costs incurred by the union to further its general "collective-bargaining goals."

Justice Scalia, joined by Justices O'Connor, Kennedy, and Souter, agreed with the plurality with respect to (b), (c), and (d), but rejected the three-part test and dissented with respect to (a). Scalia argued that the Court's three-part test "provides little guidance" and that a "more administrable test" would permit a union to compel contributions from dissenting members only for the costs of performing the union's statutory duties as exclusive bargaining agent, which in this case does not include (a), (b), (c), or (d).

Page 1417. Before the Note, add the following:

For a full exploration of the conflict between the constitutional interest in maintaining the privacy of such information to enable individuals to engage in unpopular political activities and the constitutional interest in disclosing such information to promote an informed public, see Kreimer, Sunlight, Secrets, and Scarlet Letters: The Tension Between Privacy and Disclosure in Constitutional Law, 140 U. Pa. L. Rev. 1 (1991) (concluding that the only practical way to resolve the most difficult conflicts is through a process of ad hoc balancing).

6. *Freedom of the Press*

a. A "Preferred" Status for the Press?

Page 1419. Before Section b, add the following:

COHEN v. COWLES MEDIA CO., 111 S. Ct. 2513 (1991): During the 1982 Minnesota gubernatorial race, petitioner, who was associated with one party's campaign, gave court records disclosing derogatory information about another party's candidate to respondent newspapers after receiving a promise of confidentiality from their reporters. Despite this promise of confidentiality, the newspapers identified him in their stories and petitioner was thereafter fired from his job. In a 5-to-4 decision, the Court held that the first amendment does not bar petitioner's state law action for damages on a theory of promissory estoppel. Justice White delivered the opinion of the Court:

"Respondents rely on the proposition that 'if a newspaper lawfully obtains truthful information about a matter of public significance then state officials may not constitutionally punish publication of the information, absent a need to further a state interest of the highest order.' [Citing Smith v. Daily Mail and Landmark Communications v. Virginia, this chapter, section B, subsection 4, supra main text.] This case, however, is not controlled by this line of cases but rather by the equally well-established line of decisions holding that generally applicable laws do not offend the First Amendment simply because their enforcement against the press has incidental effects on its ability to gather and report the news. [Citing *Associated Press, Citizen Publishing,* and *Oklahoma Press Publishing*.] As [even] the cases relied on by respondents recognize, the truthful information sought to be published must have been lawfully acquired. The press may not with impunity break and enter an office or dwelling to gather news. [Similarly], the media must obey the National Labor Relations Act; may not restrain trade in violation of the antitrust laws; and must pay nondiscriminatory taxes. It is therefore beyond dispute [that] enforcement of such general laws against the press is not subject to stricter scrutiny than would be applied to enforcement against other persons or organizations. There can be little doubt that the Minnesota doctrine of promissory estoppel is a law of general applicability. It does not target or single out the press. [The] First Amendment does not forbid its application to the press."

Justice Blackmun, joined by Justices Marshall and Souter, dissented: "[The cases relied upon by the Court, such as *Associated Press, Citizen Publishing,* and *Oklahoma Press Publishing,*] did not involve the imposition of liability based upon the content of speech. [I] regard our decision in *Hustler* [page 1169 of the text] to be precisely on point. There, we found that the use of a claim of intentional infliction of emotional distress to impose liability for the publication of a satirical critique violated the First Amendment. There was no doubt that Virginia's tort of intentional infliction of emotional distress was 'a law of general applicability' unrelated to the suppression of speech. Nonetheless, a unanimous Court found that, when used to penalize the expression of opinion, the law was subject to the strictures of the First Amendment. [As] in *Hustler*, the operation of Minnesota's doctrine of promissory estoppel in this case cannot be said to have a merely 'incidental' burden on speech; the publication of important political speech is the claimed violation. Thus, as in *Hustler*, the law may not be enforced to punish the expression of truthful information or opinion."

Is Justice Blackmun's invocation of *Hustler* persuasive? Is *Hustler* distinguishable on the ground that there the state's interest was triggered directly by the communicative impact of the expression, whereas in *Cohen* the state's interest was triggered by the breach of promise?

Justice Souter, joined by Justices Marshall, Blackmun, and O'Connor, also filed a dissenting opinion: "I agree with Justice Blackmun that this case does not fall within the line of authority holding the press to laws of general applicability where commercial activities and relationships, not the content of publication, are at issue. [Moreover], '[t]here is nothing talismanic about neutral laws of general applicability,' for such laws may restrict First Amendment rights just as effectively as those directed specifically at speech itself. Because I do not believe the fact of general applicability to be dispositive, I find it necessary to articulate, measure, and compare the competing interests involved in any given case to determine the legitimacy of burdening constitutional interests. [In this case, there] can be no doubt that the fact of [petitioner's] identity expanded the universe of information relevant to the choice faced by Minnesota voters in that State's 1982 gubernatorial election, the publication of which was thus of the sort quintessentially subject to strict First Amendment protection. The propriety of his leak to respondents could be taken to reflect on his character, which in turn could be taken to reflect on the character of the candidate who had retained him as an adviser. An election could turn on just such a factor; if it should, I am ready to assume that it would be to the greater public good, at least over the long run. This is not to say that the breach of such a promise of confidentiality could never give rise to liability. One can conceive of situations in which the injured party is a private individual, whose identity is of less public concern than that of petitioner; liability there might not be constitutionally prohibited. [But because] I believe the State's interest in enforcing a newspaper's promise of confidentiality insufficient to outweigh the interest in unfettered publication of the information revealed in this case, I respectfully dissent."

Justice Souter also rejected the claim that there was no need to balance in this case "because the burden on publication [was] 'self-imposed' by the newspaper's voluntary promise of confidentiality." Souter explained: "This suggests both the possibility of waiver, the requirements for which have not been met here, as well as a conception of First Amendment rights as those of the speaker alone, with a value that may be measured without reference to the importance of the information to public discourse. But freedom of the press is ultimately founded on the value of enhancing such discourse for the sake of a citizenry better informed and thus more prudently self-governed."

b. Differential Treatment of the Press

Page 1422. Before Section c, add the following:

In Leathers v. Medlock, 111 S. Ct. 1438 (1991), the Court considered the constitutionality of the Arkansas Gross Receipts Act, which imposes a 4 percent tax on receipts from the sale of all tangible personal property. The Act expressly exempts receipts from subscription and over-the-counter newspaper and magazine sales, but was amended in 1987 to impose the sales tax on cable television. The Court, in an opinion by Justice O'Connor, rejected a claim that the 1987 amendment violated the first amendment. At the outset, the Court observed that "a tax that discriminates among speakers is constitutionally suspect only in certain circumstances." Specifically, the Court explained that such a tax is "suspect" only if it "threatens to suppress the expression of particular ideas or viewpoints," "singles out the press," "targets a small group of speakers," or "discriminates on the basis of the content of the taxpayer speech." The Court concluded that the "Arkansas tax [presents] none of these types of discrimination." In reaching this result, the Court added that "there is no indication [that] Arkansas has targeted cable television in a purposeful attempt to interfere with its First Amendment activities" and there is no evidence in the record that the material presented by cable television "differs systematically in its message from that communicated" by other media.

The Court next turned to petitioners' argument "that [the] tax discriminates among media and [that such] intermedia discrimination, even in the absence of any evidence of intent to suppress speech or of any effect on the expression of particular ideas, violates the First Amendment." Citing *Taxation with Representation*, supra page 1360 of the text, the Court reiterated that there is a "strong presumption in favor of duly enacted taxation schemes" and declared that "a tax scheme that discriminates among speakers does not implicate the First Amendment unless it discriminates on the basis of ideas." The Court thus concluded that Arkansas's "extension of its generally applicable sales tax to cable television [service], while exempting the print media, does not violate the First Amendment."

Justice Marshall, joined by Justice Blackmun, dissented: "The majority's [conclusion] — that the State is free to discriminate between otherwise like-situated media so long as the more heavily taxed medium is not too 'small' in number — [calls] into question whether any general obligation to treat media actors even-handedly survives today's decision. [Because] cable competes with members of the print and electronic media in the larger information market, the power to discriminate between these media triggers the central concern underlying the nondiscrimination principle: the risk of covert censorship. [By] imposing tax burdens that disadvantage one information medium relative to another, the State can favor those media that it likes and punish those that it dislikes. [In such circumstances], the State bears the burden of demonstrating that 'differential treatment' of cable television is justified by some 'special characteristic' of that particular information medium or by some other 'counterbalancing interest of compelling importance that [the State] cannot achieve without differential taxation.' [The] only justification that the State asserts for taxing cable operators more heavily than newspapers, magazines, television broadcasters and radio stations is its interest in raising revenue. This interest is not sufficiently compelling to overcome the presumption of unconstitutionality under the nondiscrimination principle."

c. Regulating the Press to "Improve" the Marketplace of Ideas

Page 1426. At the end of section 1 of the Note, add the following:

For discussion of this question, see Sunstein, Free Speech Now, 59 U. Chi. L. Rev. 255 (1992) (approving *Red Lion,* criticizing *Buckley,* and calling for even greater regulation of the media to promote free expression).

Page 1429. Before section 5 of the Note, add the following:

e. Consider L. Bollinger, Images of a Free Press 133-145 (1991):

> [Under the image of freedom of the press established in New York Times v. Sullivan], the goal of press freedom [was] viewed as the creation of a vast space for "uninhibited, robust, and wide-open" public discussion [and it was] assumed that the role of the Supreme Court is to stand guard against government intervention. [This approach is] insensitive to problems affecting the quality of public discussion that are posed by a laissez-faire system of modern mass media. [What is needed is a] more fundamental understanding [of press freedom].
>
> [To achieve this more fundamental understanding, we] must address the nature of our own behavior in the discussion of public questions [and we must] be concerned about the character of our demands in the market. [We must] be wary of ourselves [and of] our own failure of intellect, [for a] democratic society, like an individual, should strive to remain conscious of the biases that

skew, distort, and corrupt its own thinking about public issues. [Even] in a world in which the press is entirely free and open to all voices, with a perfect market in that sense, human nature would still see to it that quality public debate and decisionmaking would not rise naturally to the surface but would [need] the buoyant support of some form of collective action [involving] public institutions. [In our criminal justice system, for example,] we go to great lengths to ensure the decisionmaking process is purified of biases, and we recognize that an entire laissez-faire system is likely to produce great injustice. [We accept the constraints in this context, exemplified by the rules of evidence], because we understand that the stakes are so high for the individual defendant. [We should think the same way about democracy. Indeed, it] should be considered a sign of high intellectual development when a society is able to take steps to correct those problems within itself that interfere with quality decisionmaking. . . .

[Thus, although the mass media may] give viewers and readers what they "want," or demand, through the expression of their preferences in the marketplace, [it is nonetheless imaginable] that we — the same "we" that issue our marketplace votes for what we get — might be very concerned about how we are behaving, about what choices we are making, in that system. [Accordingly, we may] decide together, through public regulation, that we would like to alter or modify the demands we find ourselves making in that market context, [for we may] recognize that if we are left to choose on our own whether and how to inform ourselves, too many will neglect to undertake the burdens of self-education, choosing instead to pursue more pleasant things. [It] would be a more advanced society, a more advanced democratic society, that could act to correct deficiencies arising out of [the] citizens themselves.

Consider also Stone, Imagining a Free Press, 90 Mich. L. Rev. 1246, 1262-1263 (1992):

Bollinger's analogy to the criminal justice system is especially powerful. As Bollinger notes, we exclude all sorts of evidence from the consideration of the jury in its decision of important questions of fact, [and we often do so because we believe] jurors are more likely to reach a fair and accurate result if they are denied access to the evidence completely. Consider the following extension of the analogy. Traditionally, the press did not report information about the private sexual conduct of political candidates. In exercising such discretion, the press acted like a judge in a criminal trial, preventing the people — the jurors — from learning information that arguably would distort their judgment and distract their attention from more important matters. Today, however, as part of a general breakdown of journalistic standards, the press, driven by rampant commercialism, routinely sensationalizes such information to the (arguable) detriment of the political process.

In its defense, the press argues that it would be irresponsible not to report such information, pointing to polls indicating that perhaps fifteen percent of the public would not vote for a candidate who engaged in such activity. But on the same theory, the press presumably would have to argue that because seven percent of the public would not vote for a candidate who engaged in oral sex with his spouse, it must disclose that information, too. [There] must be some limit, however, and this limit must be designed not only to respect the legitimate privacy interests of candidates, but also to reflect our right, as a society, to decide that some matters simply should not play a significant role in our political process, even if some of our fellow citizens disagree. And our right to make such a decision should be strongest when, as in the trial context, the information has a great potential to distract and distort than to inform our better judgment. As in the trial context, we should be able to protect the political process against our own failures of judgment.

Chapter Eight

The Constitution and Religion

A. INTRODUCTION: HISTORICAL AND ANALYTICAL OVERVIEW

Page 1455. The correct date for the Everson decision is 1947.

Page 1458. Replace the first two paragraphs of note 1 on page 1458, and pages 1471-87, the discussion of Marsh v. Chambers on pages 1489-90, and note 5 on page 1491 with the following:

LEE v. WEISMAN

112 S. Ct. 2649 (1992)

JUSTICE KENNEDY delivered the opinion of the Court.

School principals in the public school system of the city of Providence, Rhode Island, are permitted to invite members of the clergy to offer invocation and benediction prayers as part of the formal graduation ceremonies for middle schools and for high schools. The question before us is whether including clerical members who offer prayers as part of the official school graduation ceremony is consistent with the Religion Clauses of the First Amendment, provisions the Fourteenth Amendment makes applicable with full force to the States and their school districts.

I

A

[Following the school district's custom, a middle school principal invited a member of the clergy, Rabbi Leslie Gutterman, to deliver prayers at the school's graduation exercises. The principal gave Rabbi Gutterman a pamphlet, "Guidelines for Civic Occasions," prepared by the National Conference of Christians and Jews. The pamphlet recommended that prayers at civic ceremonies be "inclusive[ ]" and "sensitiv[e]." Rabbi Gutterman's invocation was:

> God of the Free, Hope of the Brave. For the legacy of America where diversity is celebrated and the rights of minorities are protected, we thank You. May these young men and women grow up to enrich it. For the liberty of America, we thank You. May these new graduates grow up to guard it. For the political process of America in which all its citizens may participate, for its court system where all may seek justice we thank You. May those we honor this morning always turn to it in trust. For the destiny of America we thank You. May the graduates of Nathan Bishop Middle School so live that they might help to share it. May our aspirations for our country and for these young people, who are our hope for the future, be richly fulfilled.

The benediction was:

> O God, we are grateful to You for having endowed us with the capacity for learning which we have celebrated on this joyous commencement. Happy families give thanks for seeing their children achieve an important milestone. Send Your blessings upon the teachers and administrators who helped prepare them. The graduates now need strength and guidance for the future, help them to understand that we are not complete with academic knowledge alone. We must each strive to fulfill what You require of us all: To do justly, to love mercy, to walk humbly. We give thanks to You, Lord, for keeping us alive, sustaining us and allowing us to reach this special, happy occasion.

Deborah Weisman, a student at the school, challenged the practice of having prayers at public school graduations.]

The school board (and the United States, which supports it as amicus curiae) argued that [short] prayers and others like them at graduation exercises are of profound meaning to many students and parents throughout this country who consider that due respect and acknowledgement for divine guidance and for the deepest spiritual aspirations of our people ought to be expressed at an event as important in life as a graduation. . . .

II

These dominant facts mark and control the confines of our decision: State officials direct the performance of a formal religious exercise at promotional and graduation ceremonies for secondary schools. Even for those students who object to the religious exercise, their attendance and participation in the state-sponsored religious activity are in a fair and real sense obligatory, though the school district does not require attendance as a condition for receipt of the diploma.

This case does not require us to revisit the difficult questions dividing us in recent cases, questions of the definition and full scope of the principles governing the extent of permitted accommodation by the State for the religious beliefs and practices of many of its citizens. See Allegheny County v. Greater Pittsburgh ACLU, 492 U.S. 573 (1989); Wallace v. Jaffree, 472 U.S. 38 (1985); Lynch v. Donnelly, 465 U.S. 668 (1984). For without reference to those principles in other contexts, the controlling precedents as they relate to prayer and religious exercise in primary and secondary public schools compel the holding here that the policy of the city of Providence is an unconstitutional one. We can decide the case without reconsidering the general constitutional framework by which public schools' efforts to accommodate religion are measured. Thus we do not accept the invitation of petitioners and amicus the United States to reconsider our decision in Lemon v. Kurtzman. The government involvement with religious activity in this case is pervasive, to the point of creating a state-sponsored and state-directed religious exercise in a public school. Conducting this formal religious observance conflicts with settled rules pertaining to prayer exercises for students, and that suffices to determine the question before us.

The principle that government may accommodate the free exercise of religion does not supersede the fundamental limitations imposed by the Establishment Clause. It is beyond dispute that, at a minimum, the Constitution guarantees that government may not coerce anyone to support or participate in religion or its exercise, or otherwise act in a way which "establishes a [state] religion or religious faith, or tends to do so." *Lynch.* The State's involvement in the school prayers challenged today violates these central principles.

That involvement is as troubling as it is undenied. A school official, the principal, decided that an invocation and a benediction should be given; this is a choice attributable to the State, and from a constitutional perspective it is as if a state statute decreed that the prayers must occur. The principal chose the religious participant, here a rabbi, and that choice is also attributable to the State. The reason for the choice of a rabbi is not disclosed by the record, but the potential for divisiveness over the choice of a particular member of the clergy to conduct the ceremony is apparent.

Divisiveness, of course, can attend any state decision respecting religions, and neither its existence nor its potential necessarily invalidates the State's attempts to accommodate religion in all cases. The potential for divisiveness is of particular relevance here though, because it centers around an overt religious exercise in a secondary school environment where, as we discuss below, subtle coercive pressures exist and where the student had no real alternative which would have allowed her to avoid the fact or appearance of participation.

The State's role did not end with the decision to include a prayer and with the choice of clergyman. Principal Lee provided Rabbi Gutterman with a copy of the "Guidelines for Civic Occasions," and advised him that his prayers should be nonsectarian. Through these means the principal directed and controlled the content of the prayer. "[It] is a cornerstone principle of our Establishment Clause jurisprudence that it is no part of the business of government to compose official prayers for any group of the American people to recite as a part of a religious program carried on by government," Engel v. Vitale, 370 U.S. 421, 425 (1962), and that is what the school officials attempted to do.

Petitioners argue, and we find nothing in the case to refute it, that the directions for the content of the prayers were a good-faith attempt by the school to ensure that the sectarianism which is so often the flashpoint for religious animosity be removed from the graduation ceremony. The concern is understandable, as a prayer which uses ideas or images identified with a particular religion may foster a different sort of sectarian rivalry than an invocation or benediction in terms more neutral. The school's explanation, however, does not resolve the dilemma caused by its participation. The question is not the good faith of the school in attempting to make the prayer acceptable to most persons, but the legitimacy of its undertaking that enterprise at all when the object is to produce a prayer to be used in a formal religious exercise which students, for all practical purposes, are obliged to attend.

We are asked to recognize the existence of a practice of nonsectarian prayer, prayer within the embrace of what is known as the Judeo-Christian tradition, prayer which is more acceptable than one which, for example, makes explicit references to the God of Israel, or to Jesus Christ, or to a patron saint. There may be some support, as an empirical observation, to the statement [that] there has emerged in this country a civic religion, one which is tolerated when sectarian exercises are not. Note, Civil Religion and the Establishment Clause, 95 Yale L.J. 1237 (1986). If common ground can be defined which permits once conflicting faiths to express the shared conviction that there is an ethic and a morality which transcend human invention, the sense of community and purpose sought by all decent societies might be advanced. But though the First Amendment does not allow the government to stifle prayers which aspire to these ends, neither does it permit the government to undertake that task for itself.

The First Amendment's Religion Clauses mean that religious beliefs and religious expression are too precious to be either proscribed or prescribed by the State. The design of the Constitution is that preservation and transmission of religious beliefs and worship is a responsibility and a choice committed to the private sphere, which itself is promised freedom to pursue that mission. It must not be forgotten then, that while concern must be given to define the protection granted to an objector or a dissenting non-believer, these same Clauses exist to protect religion from government interference. James Madison, the principal author of the Bill of Rights, did not rest his opposition to a religious establishment on the sole ground of its effect on the minority. A principal ground for his view was: "Experience witnesseth that ecclesiastical establishments, instead of maintaining the purity and efficacy of Religion, have had a contrary operation." Memorial and Remonstrance Against Religious Assessments (1785).

These concerns have particular application in the case of school officials, whose effort to monitor prayer will be perceived by the students as inducing a participation they might otherwise reject. Though the efforts of the school officials in this case to find common ground appear to have been a good-faith attempt to recognize the common aspects of religions and not the divisive ones, our precedents do not permit school officials to assist in composing prayers as an incident to a formal exercise for their students. And these same precedents caution us to measure the idea of a civic religion against the central meaning of the Religion Clauses of the First Amendment, which is that all creeds must be tolerated and none favored. The suggestion that government may establish an official or civic religion as a means of avoiding the establishment of a religion with more specific creeds strikes us as a contradiction that cannot be accepted.

The degree of school involvement here made it clear that the graduation prayers bore the imprint of the State and thus put school-age children who objected in an untenable position. . . .

To endure the speech of false ideas or offensive content and then to counter it is part of learning how to live in a pluralistic society, a society which insists upon open discourse towards the end of a tolerant citizenry. And tolerance presupposes some mutuality of obligation. It is argued that our constitutional vision of a free society requires confidence in our own ability to accept or reject ideas of which we do not approve, and that prayer at a high school graduation does nothing more than offer a choice. By the time they are seniors, high school students no doubt have been required to attend classes and assemblies and to complete assignments exposing them to ideas they find distasteful or immoral or absurd or all of these. Against this background, students may consider it an odd measure of justice to be subjected during the course of their educations to ideas deemed offensive and irreligious, but to be denied a brief, formal prayer ceremony that the school offers in return. This argument cannot prevail, however. It overlooks a fundamental dynamic of the Constitution.

The First Amendment protects speech and religion by quite different mechanisms. Speech is protected by insuring its full expression even when the government participates, for the very object of some of our most important speech is to persuade the government to adopt an idea as its own. The method for protecting freedom of worship and freedom of conscience in religious matters is quite the reverse. In religious debate or expression the government is not a prime participant, for the Framers deemed religious establishment antithetical to the freedom of all. The Free Exercise Clause embraces a freedom of conscience and worship that has close parallels in the speech provisions of the First Amendment, but the Establishment Clause is a specific prohibition on forms of state intervention in religious affairs with no precise counterpart in the speech provisions. The explanation lies in the lesson of history that was and is the inspiration for the Establishment Clause, the lesson that in the hands of government what might begin as a tolerant expression of religious views may end in a policy to indoctrinate and coerce. A state-created orthodoxy puts at grave risk that freedom of belief and conscience which are the sole assurance that religious faith is real, not imposed.

The lessons of the First Amendment are as urgent in the modern world as in the 18th Century when it was written. One timeless lesson is that if citizens are subjected to state-sponsored religious exercises, the State disavows its own duty to guard and respect that sphere of inviolable conscience and belief which is the mark of a free people. To compromise that principle today would be to deny our own tradition and forfeit our standing to urge others to secure the protections of that tradition for themselves.

As we have observed before, there are heightened concerns with protecting freedom of conscience from subtle coercive pressure in the elementary and secondary public schools. [What] to most believers may seem nothing more than a reasonable request that the nonbeliever respect their religious practices, in a school context may appear to the nonbeliever or dissenter to be an attempt to employ the machinery of the State to enforce a religious orthodoxy.

We need not look beyond the circumstances of this case to see the phenomenon at work. The undeniable fact is that the school district's supervision and control of a high school graduation ceremony places public pressure, as well as peer pressure, on attending students to stand as a group or, at least, maintain respectful silence during the Invocation and Benediction. This pressure, though subtle and indirect, can be as real as any overt compulsion. Of course, in our culture standing or remaining silent can signify adherence to a view or simple respect for the views of others. And no doubt some persons who have no desire to join a prayer have little objection to standing as a sign of respect for those who do. But for the dissenter of high school age, who has a reasonable perception that she is being forced by the State to pray in a manner her conscience will not allow, the injury is no less real. There can be no doubt that for many, if not most, of the students at the graduation, the act of standing or remaining silent was an expression of participation in the Rabbi's prayer. That was the very point of the religious exercise. It is of little comfort to a dissenter, then, to be told that for her the act of standing or remaining in silence signifies mere respect, rather than participation. What matters is that, given our social conventions, a reasonable dissenter in this milieu could believe that the group exercise signified her own participation or approval of it.

Finding no violation under these circumstances would place objectors in the dilemma of participating, with all that implies, or protesting. We do not address whether that choice is acceptable if the affected citizens are mature adults, but we think the State may not, consistent with the Establishment Clause, place primary and secondary school children in this position. Research in psychology supports the common assumption that adolescents are often susceptible to pressure from their peers towards conformity, and that the influence is strongest in matters of social convention. To recognize that the choice imposed by the State constitutes an unacceptable constraint only acknowledges that the government may no more use social pressure to enforce orthodoxy than it may use more direct means.

The injury caused by the government's action, and the reason why Daniel and Deborah Weisman object to it, is that the State, in a school setting, in effect required participation in a religious exercise. It is, we concede, a brief exercise during which the individual can concentrate on joining its message, meditate on her own religion, or let her mind wander. But the embarrassment and the intrusion of the religious exercise cannot be refuted by arguing that these prayers, and similar ones to be said in the future, are of a de minimis character. To do so would be an affront to the Rabbi who offered them and to all those for whom the prayers were an essential and profound recognition of divine authority. And for the same reason, we think that the intrusion is greater than the two minutes or so of time consumed for prayers like these. Assuming, as we must, that the prayers were offensive to the student and the parent who now object, the intrusion was both real and, in the context of a secondary school, a violation of the objectors' rights. That the intrusion was in the course of promulgating religion that sought to be civic or nonsectarian rather than pertaining to one sect does not lessen the offense or isolation to the objectors. At best it narrows their number, at worst increases their sense of isolation and affront.

There was a stipulation in the District Court that attendance at graduation and promotional ceremonies is voluntary. [Law] reaches past formalism. And to say a teenage student has a real choice not to attend her high school graduation is formalistic in the extreme. True, Deborah could elect not to attend commencement without renouncing her diploma; but we shall not allow the case to turn on this point. Everyone knows that in our society and in our culture high school graduation is one of life's most significant occasions. A school rule which excuses attendance is beside the point. Attendance may not be required by official decree, yet it is apparent that a student is not free to absent herself from the graduation exercise in any real sense of the term "voluntary," for absence would require forfeiture of those intangible benefits which have motivated the student through youth and all her high school years. Graduation is a time for family and those closest to the student to celebrate success and express mutual wishes of gratitude and respect, all to the end of impressing upon the young person the role that it is his or her right and duty to assume in the community and all of its diverse parts.

The importance of the event is the point the school district and the United States rely upon to argue that a formal prayer ought to be permitted, but it becomes one of the principal reasons why their argument must fail. Their contention, one of considerable force were it not for the constitutional constraints applied to state action, is that the prayers are an essential part of these ceremonies because for many persons an occasion of this significance lacks meaning if there is no recognition, however brief, that human achievements cannot be understood apart from their spiritual essence. We think the Government's position that this interest suffices to force students to choose between compliance or forfeiture demonstrates fundamental inconsistency in its argumentation. It fails to acknowledge that what for many of Deborah's classmates and their parents was a spiritual imperative was for Daniel and Deborah Weisman religious conformance compelled by the State. While in some societies the wishes of the majority might prevail, the Establishment Clause of the First Amendment is addressed to this contingency and rejects the balance urged upon us. The Constitution forbids the State to exact religious conformity from a student as the price of attending her own high school graduation. This is the calculus the Constitution commands.

The Government's argument gives insufficient recognition to the real conflict of conscience faced by the young student. The essence of the Government's position is that with regard to a civic, social occasion of this importance it is the objector, not the majority, who must take unilateral and private action to avoid compromising religious scruples, here by electing to miss the graduation exercise. This turns conventional First Amendment analysis on its head. It is a tenet of the First Amendment that the State cannot require one of its citizens to forfeit his or her rights and benefits as the price of resisting conformance to state-sponsored religious practice. To say that a student must remain apart from the ceremony at the opening invocation and closing benediction is to risk compelling conformity in an environment analogous to the classroom setting, where we have said the risk of compulsion is especially high. . . .

We do not hold that every state action implicating religion is invalid if one or a few citizens find it offensive. People may take offense at all manner of religious as well as nonreligious messages, but offense alone does not in every case show a violation. We know too that sometimes to endure social isolation or even anger may be the price of conscience or nonconformity. But, by any reading of our cases, the conformity required of the student in this case was too high an exaction to withstand the test of the Establishment Clause. The prayer exercises in this case are especially improper because the State has in every practical sense compelled attendance and participation in an explicit religious exercise at an event of singular importance to every student, one the objecting student had no real alternative to avoid.

Our jurisprudence in this area is of necessity one of line-drawing, of determining at what point a dissenter's rights of religious freedom are infringed by the State.

> The First Amendment does not prohibit practices which by any realistic measure create none of the dangers which it is designed to prevent and which do not so directly or substantially involve the state in religious exercises or in the favoring of religion as to have meaningful and practical impact. It is of course true that great consequences can grow from small beginnings, but the measure of constitutional adjudication is the ability and willingness to distinguish between real threat and mere shadow. Abington School District v. Schempp (Goldberg, J., concurring).

Our society would be less than true to its heritage if it lacked abiding concern for the values of its young people, and we acknowledge the profound belief of adherents to many faiths that there must be a place in the student's life for precepts of a morality higher even than the law we today enforce. We express no hostility to those aspirations, nor would our oath permit us to do so. A relentless and all-pervasive attempt to exclude religion from every aspect of public life could itself become inconsistent with the Constitution. We recognize that, at graduation time and throughout the course of the educational process, there will be instances when religious values, religious practices, and religious persons will have some interaction with the public schools and their students. But these matters, often questions of accommodation of religion, are not before us. The sole question presented is whether a religious exercise may be conducted at a graduation ceremony in circumstances where, as we have found, young graduates who object are induced to conform. No holding by this Court suggests that a school can persuade or compel a student to participate in a religious exercise. That is being done here, and it is forbidden by the Establishment Clause of the First Amendment.

For the reasons we have stated, the judgment of the Court of Appeals is affirmed.

JUSTICE BLACKMUN, with whom JUSTICE STEVENS and JUSTICE O'CONNOR join, concurring.

Nearly half a century of review and refinement of Establishment Clause jurisprudence has distilled one clear understanding: Government may neither promote nor affiliate itself with any religious doctrine or organization, nor may it obtrude itself in the internal affairs of any religious institution. The application of these principles to the present case mandates the decision reached today by the Court.

I

This Court first reviewed a challenge to state law under the Establishment Clause in Everson v. Board of Education, 330 U.S. 1 (1947). Relying on the history of the Clause, and the Court's prior analysis, Justice Black outlined the considerations that have become the touchstone of Establishment Clause jurisprudence: Neither a State nor the Federal Government can pass laws which aid one religion, aid all religions, or prefer one religion over another. Neither a State nor the Federal Government, openly or secretly, can participate in the affairs of any religious organization and vice versa.[2] "In the words of Jefferson, the clause

2. The Court articulated six examples of paradigmatic practices that the Establishment Clause prohibits: "The establishment of religion clause of the First Amendment means at least this: Neither a state nor the Federal Government can set up a church. Neither can pass laws which aid one religion, aid all religions, or prefer one religion over another. Neither can force or influence a person to go to or to remain away from church against his will or force him to profess a belief or disbelief in any religion. No person can be punished for entertaining or professing religious beliefs or disbeliefs, for church attendance or non-attendance. No tax in any amount, large or small, can be levied to support any religious activities or institutions, whatever they may be called, or whatever form they may adopt to teach or practice religion. Neither a state nor the Federal Government can, openly or secretly, participate in the affairs of any religious organizations or groups and vice versa." Everson v. Board of Ed., 330 U.S. 1, 15 (1947).

against establishment of religion by law was intended to erect 'a wall of separation between church and State.'" *Everson*, quoting Reynolds v. United States, 98 U.S. 145, 164 (1879). The dissenters agreed: "The Amendment's purpose ... was to create a complete and permanent separation of the spheres of religious activity and civil authority by comprehensively forbidding every form of public aid or support for religion." (Rutledge, J., dissenting, joined by Frankfurter, Jackson, and Burton, JJ.).

In Engel v. Vitale, 370 U.S. 421 (1962), the Court considered for the first time the constitutionality of prayer in a public school. Students said aloud a short prayer selected by the State Board of Regents: "Almighty God, we acknowledge our dependence upon Thee, and we beg Thy blessings upon us, our parents, our teachers and our Country." Justice Black, writing for the Court, again made clear that the First Amendment forbids the use of the power or prestige of the government to control, support, or influence the religious beliefs and practices of the American people. Although the prayer was "denominationally neutral" and "its observance on the part of the students [was] voluntary," the Court found that it violated this essential precept of the Establishment Clause.

A year later, the Court again invalidated government-sponsored prayer in public schools in Abington School District v. Schempp, 374 U.S. 203 (1963). In *Schempp*, the school day for Baltimore, Maryland, and Abington Township, Pennsylvania, students began with a reading from the Bible, or a recitation of the Lord's Prayer, or both. After a thorough review of the Court's prior Establishment Clause cases, the Court concluded:

> The Establishment Clause has been directly considered by this Court eight times in the past score of years and, with only one Justice dissenting on the point, it has consistently held that the clause withdrew all legislative power respecting religious belief or the expression thereof. The test may be stated as follows: what are the purpose and the primary effect of the enactment? If either is the advancement or inhibition of religion, then the enactment exceeds the scope of legislative power as circumscribed by the Constitution.

Because the schools' opening exercises were government-sponsored religious ceremonies, the Court found that the primary effect was the advancement of religion and held, therefore, that the activity violated the Establishment Clause. . . .

In 1971, Chief Justice Burger reviewed the Court's past decisions and found: "Three ... tests may be gleaned from our cases." Lemon v. Kurtzman, 403 U.S. 602, 612. In order for a statute to survive an Establishment Clause challenge, "first, the statute must have a secular legislative purpose; second, its principal or primary effect must be one that neither advances nor inhibits religion; finally the statute must not foster an excessive government entanglement with religion." . . .

Application of these principles to the facts of this case is straightforward. There can be "no doubt" that the "invocation of God's blessings" delivered at Nathan Bishop Middle School "is a religious activity." *Engel.* In the words of *Engel,* the Rabbi's prayer "is a solemn avowal of divine faith and supplication for the blessings of the Almighty. The nature of such a prayer has always been religious." The question then is whether the government has "placed its official stamp of approval" on the prayer. As the Court ably demonstrates, when the government "composes official prayers," selects the member of the clergy to deliver the prayer, has the prayer delivered at a public school event that is planned, supervised and given by school officials, and pressures students to attend and participate in the prayer, there can be no doubt that the government is advancing and promoting religion. As our prior decisions teach us, it is this that the Constitution prohibits.

II

I join the Court's opinion today because I find nothing in it inconsistent with the essential precepts of the Establishment Clause developed in our precedents. The Court holds that the graduation prayer is unconstitutional because the State "in effect required participation in a religious exercise." Although our precedents make clear that proof of government coercion is not necessary to prove an Establishment Clause violation, it is sufficient. Government pressure to participate in a religious activity is an obvious indication that the government is endorsing or promoting religion.

But it is not enough that the government restrain from compelling religious practices: it must not engage in them either. . . .[6]

Our decisions have gone beyond prohibiting coercion, [because] the Court has recognized that "the fullest possible scope of religious liberty," *Schempp,* (Goldberg, J., concurring), entails more than freedom from coercion. The Establishment Clause protects religious liberty on a grand scale; it is a social compact that guarantees for generations a democracy and a strong religious community — both essential to safeguarding religious liberty. "Our fathers seem to have been perfectly sincere in their

6. As a practical matter, of course, anytime the government endorses a religious belief there will almost always be some pressure to conform. "When the power, prestige and financial support of government is placed behind a particular religious belief, the indirect coercive pressure upon religious minorities to conform to the prevailing officially approved religion is plain." Engel v. Vitale, 370 U.S. 421, 431 (1962). [Relocated footnote — EDS.]

belief that the members of the Church would be more patriotic, and the citizens of the State more religious, by keeping their respective functions entirely separate." Religious Liberty, in Essays and Speeches of Jeremiah S. Black 53 (C. Black ed. 1885) (Chief Justice of the Commonwealth of Pennsylvania).

The mixing of government and religion can be a threat to free government, even if no one is forced to participate. When the government puts its imprimatur on a particular religion, it conveys a message of exclusion to all those who do not adhere to the favored beliefs.[9] A government cannot be premised on the belief that all persons are created equal when it asserts that God prefers some. Only "anguish, hardship and bitter strife" result "when zealous religious groups struggle with one another to obtain the Government's stamp of approval." *Engel.*[10] Such a struggle can "strain a political system to the breaking point." Walz v. Tax Commission, 397 U.S. 664, 694 (1970) (opinion of Harlan, J.).

When the government arrogates to itself a role in religious affairs, it abandons its obligation as guarantor of democracy. Democracy requires the nourishment of dialogue and dissent, while religious faith puts its trust in an ultimate divine authority above all human deliberation. When the government appropriates religious truth, it "transforms rational debate into theological decree." Nuechterlein, Note, The Free Exercise Boundaries of Permissible Accommodation Under the Establishment Clause, 99 Yale L.J. 1127, 1131 (1990). Those who disagree no longer are questioning the policy judgment of the elected but the rules of a higher authority who is beyond reproach.

Madison warned that government officials who would use religious authority to pursue secular ends "exceed the commission from which they derive their authority and are Tyrants. The People who submit to it are governed by laws made neither by themselves, nor by an authority

9. "The Establishment Clause is infringed when the government makes adherence to religion relevant to a person's standing in the political community. Direct government action endorsing religion or a particular religious practice is invalid under this approach because it sends a message to nonadherents that they are outsiders, not full members of the political community, and an accompanying message to adherents that they are insiders, favored members of the political community." Wallace v. Jaffree, 472 U.S., at 69 (O'Connor, J., concurring) (internal quotations omitted).

10. Sigmund Freud expressed it this way: "a religion, even if it calls itself the religion of love, must be hard and unloving to those who do not belong to it." S. Freud, Group Psychology and the Analysis of the Ego 51 (1922). James Madison stated the theory even more strongly in his "Memorial and Remonstrance" against a bill providing tax funds to religious teachers: "It degrades from the equal rank of Citizens all those whose opinions in Religion do not bend to those of the Legislative authority. Distant as it may be, in its present form, from the Inquisition it differs from it only in degree. The one is the first step, the other the last in the career of intolerance." . . .

derived from them, and are slaves." Memorial and Remonstrance against Religious Assessments. Democratic government will not last long when proclamation replaces persuasion as the medium of political exchange.

Likewise, we have recognized that "religion flourishes in greater purity, without than with the aid of Government."[11] To "make room for as wide a variety of beliefs and creeds as the spiritual needs of man deem necessary," Zorach v. Clauson, 343 U.S. 306, 313 (1952), the government must not align itself with any one of them. When the government favors a particular religion or sect, the disadvantage to all others is obvious, but even the favored religion may fear being "tainted . . . with a corrosive secularism." Grand Rapids School Dist. v. Ball, 473 U.S. 373, 385 (1985). The favored religion may be compromised as political figures reshape the religion's beliefs for their own purposes; it may be reformed as government largesse brings government regulation. Keeping religion in the hands of private groups minimizes state intrusion on religious choice and best enables each religion to "flourish according to the zeal of its adherents and the appeal of its dogma." *Zorach*, 343 U.S., at 313.

It is these understandings and fears that underlie our Establishment Clause jurisprudence. We have believed that religious freedom cannot exist in the absence of a free democratic government, and that such a government cannot endure when there is fusion between religion and the political regime. We have believed that religious freedom cannot thrive in the absence of a vibrant religious community and that such a community cannot prosper when it is bound to the secular. And we have believed that these were the animating principles behind the adoption of the Establishment Clause. To that end, our cases have prohibited government endorsement of religion, its sponsorship, and active involvement in religion, whether or not citizens were coerced to conform.

I remain convinced that our jurisprudence is not misguided, and that it requires the decision reached by the Court today. Accordingly, I join the Court in affirming the judgment of the Court of Appeals.

JUSTICE SOUTER, with whom JUSTICE STEVENS and JUSTICE O'CONNOR join, concurring.

I join the whole of the Court's opinion, and fully agree that prayers at public school graduation ceremonies indirectly coerce religious observance. I write separately nonetheless on two issues of Establishment Clause analysis that underlie my independent resolution of this case:

11. The view that the Establishment Clause was primarily a vehicle for protecting churches was expounded initially by Roger Williams. "Worldly corruptions . . . might consume the churches if sturdy fences against the wilderness were not maintained." M. Howe, The Garden and the Wilderness 6 (1965).

whether the Clause applies to governmental practices that do not favor one religion or denomination over others, and whether state coercion of religious conformity, over and above state endorsement of religious exercise or belief, is a necessary element of an Establishment Clause violation.

I

Forty-five years ago, this Court announced a basic principle of constitutional law from which it has not strayed: the Establishment Clause forbids not only state practices that "aid one religion . . . or prefer one religion over another," but also those that "aid all religions." Everson v. Board of Education of Ewing, 330 U.S. 1, 15 (1947). [In] barring the State from sponsoring generically Theistic prayers where it could not sponsor sectarian ones, we hold true to a line of precedent from which there is no adequate historical case to depart.

A

Since *Everson*, we have consistently held the Clause applicable no less to governmental acts favoring religion generally than to acts favoring one religion over others. . . .

B

Some have challenged this precedent by reading the Establishment Clause to permit "nonpreferential" state promotion of religion. The challengers argue that, as originally understood by the Framers, "the Establishment Clause did not require government neutrality between religion and irreligion nor did it prohibit the Federal Government from providing nondiscriminatory aid to religion." *Wallace*, (Rehnquist, J., dissenting); see also R. Cord, Separation of Church and State: Historical Fact and Current Fiction (1988). While a case has been made for this position, it is not so convincing as to warrant reconsideration of our settled law; indeed, I find in the history of the Clause's textual development a more powerful argument supporting the Court's jurisprudence following *Everson*.

When James Madison arrived at the First Congress with a series of proposals to amend the National Constitution, one of the provisions read that "the civil rights of none shall be abridged on account of religious belief or worship, nor shall any national religion be established, nor shall the full and equal rights of conscience be in any manner, or on any pretext, infringed." Madison's language did not last long. It was sent to a Select Committee of the House, which, without explanation, changed it to read that "no religion shall be established by law, nor shall the equal rights of conscience be infringed." Thence the proposal went to the

Committee of the Whole, which was in turn dissatisfied with the Select Committee's language and adopted an alternative proposed by Samuel Livermore of New Hampshire: "Congress shall make no laws touching religion, or infringing the rights of conscience." Livermore's proposal would have forbidden laws having anything to do with religion and was thus not only far broader than Madison's version, but broader even than the scope of the Establishment Clause as we now understand it. See, e.g., Corporation of Presiding Bishop of Church of Jesus Christ of Latter-Day Saints v. Amos, 483 U.S. 327 (1987) (upholding legislative exemption of religious groups from certain obligations under civil rights laws).

The House rewrote the amendment once more before sending it to the Senate, this time adopting, without recorded debate, language derived from a proposal by Fisher Ames of Massachusetts: "Congress shall make no law establishing Religion, or prohibiting the free exercise thereof, nor shall the rights of conscience be infringed." Perhaps, on further reflection, the Representatives had thought Livermore's proposal too expansive, or perhaps, as one historian has suggested, they had simply worried that his language would not "satisfy the demands of those who wanted something said specifically against establishments of religion." L. Levy, The Establishment Clause 81 (1986). We do not know; what we do know is that the House rejected the Select Committee's version, which arguably ensured only that "no religion" enjoyed an official preference over others, and deliberately chose instead a prohibition extending to laws establishing "religion" in general.

The sequence of the Senate's treatment of this House proposal, and the House's response to the Senate, confirm that the Framers meant the Establishment Clause's prohibition to encompass nonpreferential aid to religion. In September 1789, the Senate considered a number of provisions that would have permitted such aid, and ultimately it adopted one of them. First, it briefly entertained this language: "Congress shall make no law establishing One Religious Sect or Society in preference to others, nor shall the rights of conscience be infringed." After rejecting two minor amendments to that proposal, the Senate dropped it altogether and chose a provision identical to the House's proposal, but without the clause protecting the "rights of conscience." With no record of the Senate debates, we cannot know what prompted these changes, but the record does tell us that, six days later, the Senate went half circle and adopted its narrowest language yet: "Congress shall make no law establishing articles of faith or a mode of worship, or prohibiting the free exercise of religion." The Senate sent this proposal to the House along with its versions of the other constitutional amendments proposed.

Though it accepted much of the Senate's work on the Bill of Rights, the House rejected the Senate's version of the Establishment Clause and called for a joint conference committee, to which the Senate agreed. The House conferees ultimately won out, persuading the Senate to accept this as the final text of the Religion Clauses: "Congress shall make no law respecting an establishment of religion, or prohibiting the free exercise thereof." What is remarkable is that, unlike the earliest House drafts or the final Senate proposal, the prevailing language is not limited to laws respecting an establishment of "a religion," "a national religion," "one religious sect," or specific "articles of faith."[2] The Framers repeatedly considered and deliberately rejected such narrow language and instead extended their prohibition to state support for "religion" in general.

Implicit in their choice is the distinction between preferential and nonpreferential establishments, which the weight of evidence suggests the Framers appreciated. Of particular note, the Framers were vividly familiar with efforts in the colonies and, later, the States to impose general, nondenominational assessments and other incidents of ostensibly ecumenical establishments. The Virginia Statute for Religious Freedom, written by Jefferson and sponsored by Madison, captured the separationist response to such measures. Condemning all establishments, however nonpreferentialist, the Statute broadly guaranteed that "no man shall be compelled to frequent or support any religious worship, place, or ministry whatsoever," including his own. Act for Establishing Religious Freedom (1785). Forcing a citizen to support even his own church would, among other things, deny "the ministry those temporary rewards, which proceeding from an approbation of their personal conduct, are an additional incitement to earnest and unremitting labours for the instruction of mankind." In general, Madison later added, "religion & Govt. will both exist in greater purity, the less they are mixed together." Letter from J. Madison to E. Livingston, 10 July 1822.

What we thus know of the Framers' experience underscores the observation of one prominent commentator, that confining the Establishment Clause to a prohibition on preferential aid "requires a premise that the Framers were extraordinarily bad drafters — that they believed one thing but adopted language that said something substantially different,

2. Some commentators have suggested that by targeting laws respecting "an" establishment of religion, the Framers adopted the very nonpreferentialist position whose much clearer articulation they repeatedly rejected. See, e.g., R. Cord, Separation of Church and State: Historical Fact and Current Fiction 11-12 (1988). Yet the indefinite article before the word "establishment" is better seen as evidence that the Clause forbids any kind of establishment, including a nonpreferential one. If the Framers had wished, for some reason, to use the indefinite term to achieve a narrow meaning for the Clause, they could far more aptly have placed it before the word "religion." See Laycock, "Nonpreferential" Aid to Religion: A False Claim About Original Intent, 27 Wm. & Mary L. Rev. 875, 884-885 (1986).

and that they did so after repeatedly attending to the choice of language." Laycock, "Nonpreferential" Aid. We must presume, since there is no conclusive evidence to the contrary, that the Framers embraced the significance of their textual judgment.[3] Thus, on balance, history neither contradicts nor warrants reconsideration of the settled principle that the Establishment Clause forbids support for religion in general no less than support for one religion or some.

C

While these considerations are, for me, sufficient to reject the nonpreferentialist position, one further concern animates my judgment. In many contexts, including this one, nonpreferentialism requires some distinction between "sectarian" religious practices and those that would be, by some measure, ecumenical enough to pass Establishment Clause muster. Simply by requiring the enquiry, nonpreferentialists invite the courts to engage in comparative theology. I can hardly imagine a subject less amenable to the competence of the federal judiciary, or more deliberately to be avoided where possible. . . .

[At] some undefinable point, the similarities between a state-sponsored prayer and the sacred text of a specific religion would so closely identify the former with the latter that even a nonpreferentialist would have to concede a breach of the Establishment Clause. [Many] Americans who consider themselves religious are not Theistic; some, like several of the Framers, are Deists who would question Rabbi Gutterman's plea for divine advancement of the country's political and moral good. Thus, a nonpreferentialist who would condemn subjecting public school graduates to, say, the Anglican liturgy would still need to explain why the government's preference for Theistic over non-Theistic religion is constitutional.

Nor does it solve the problem to say that the State should promote a "diversity" of religious views; that position would necessarily compel the government and, inevitably, the courts to make wholly inappropri-

3. In his dissent in Wallace v. Jaffree, 472 U.S. 38 (1985), the Chief Justice rested his nonpreferentialist interpretation partly on the post-ratification actions of the early national government. Aside from the willingness of some (but not all) early Presidents to issue ceremonial religious proclamations, which were at worst trivial breaches of the Establishment Clause, he cited such seemingly preferential aid as a treaty provision, signed by Jefferson, authorizing federal subsidization of a Roman Catholic priest and church for the Kaskaskia Indians. But this proves too much, for if the Establishment Clause permits a special appropriation of tax money for the religious activities of a particular sect, it forbids virtually nothing. See Laycock, "Nonpreferential" Aid 915. Although evidence of historical practice can indeed furnish valuable aid in the interpretation of contemporary language, acts like the one in question prove only that public officials, no matter when they serve, can turn a blind eye to constitutional principle.

ate judgments about the number of religions the State should sponsor and the relative frequency with which it should sponsor each. In fact, the prospect would be even worse than that. As Madison observed in criticizing religious presidential proclamations, the practice of sponsoring religious messages tends, over time, "to narrow the recommendation to the standard of the predominant sect." Madison's "Detached Memoranda," 3 Wm. & Mary Q. 534, 561 (E. Fleet ed. 1946). We have not changed much since the days of Madison, and the judiciary should not willingly enter the political arena to battle the centripetal force leading from religious pluralism to official preference for the faith with the most votes.

II

Petitioners rest most of their argument on a theory that, whether or not the Establishment Clause permits extensive nonsectarian support for religion, it does not forbid the state to sponsor affirmations of religious belief that coerce neither support for religion nor participation in religious observance. I appreciate the force of some of the arguments supporting a "coercion" analysis of the Clause. McConnell, Coercion: The Lost Element of Establishment, 27 Wm. & Mary L. Rev. 933 (1986). But we could not adopt that reading without abandoning our settled law, a course that, in my view, the text of the Clause would not readily permit. Nor does the extratextual evidence of original meaning stand so unequivocally at odds with the textual premise inherent in existing precedent that we should fundamentally reconsider our course.

A

Over the years, this Court has declared the invalidity of many noncoercive state laws and practices conveying a message of religious endorsement. For example, in *Allegheny County*, we forbade the prominent display of a nativity scene on public property; without contesting the dissent's observation that [no one was coerced] into accepting or supporting whatever message [was] proclaimed, five Members of the Court found [the] display unconstitutional as a state endorsement of Christianity. Likewise, in Wallace v. Jaffree, 472 U.S. 38 (1985), we struck down a state law requiring a moment of silence in public classrooms not because the statute coerced students to participate in prayer (for it did not), but because the manner of its enactment "conveyed a message of state approval of prayer activities in the public schools." . . .

Our precedents may not always have drawn perfectly straight lines. They simply cannot, however, support the position that a showing of coercion is necessary to a successful Establishment Clause claim.

B . . .

While some argue that the Framers added the word "respecting" simply to foreclose federal interference with State establishments of religion, see, e.g., Amar, The Bill of Rights as a Constitution, 100 Yale L.J. 1131, 1157 (1991), the language sweeps more broadly than that. In Madison's words, the Clause in its final form forbids "everything like" a national religious establishment, see Madison's "Detached Memoranda" 558, and, after incorporation, it forbids "everything like" a State religious establishment. The sweep is broad enough that Madison himself characterized congressional provisions for legislative and military chaplains as unconstitutional "establishments." Madison's "Detached Memoranda" 558-559.

While petitioners insist that the prohibition extends only to the "coercive" features and incidents of establishment, they cannot easily square that claim with the constitutional text. The First Amendment forbids not just laws "respecting an establishment of religion," but also those "prohibiting the free exercise thereof." Yet laws that coerce nonadherents to "support or participate in any religion or its exercise," *Allegheny County*, (opinion of Kennedy, J.), would virtually by definition violate their right to religious free exercise. [Thus], a literal application of the coercion test would render the Establishment Clause a virtual nullity. . . .

C

Petitioners argue from the political setting in which the Establishment Clause was framed, and from the Framers' own political practices following ratification, that government may constitutionally endorse religion so long as it does not coerce religious conformity. The setting and the practices warrant canvassing, but while they yield some evidence for petitioners' argument, they do not reveal the degree of consensus in early constitutional thought that would raise a threat to stare decisis by challenging the presumption that the Establishment Clause adds something to the Free Exercise Clause that follows it.

The Framers adopted the Religion Clauses in response to a long tradition of coercive state support for religion, particularly in the form of tax assessments, but their special antipathy to religious coercion did not exhaust their hostility to the features and incidents of establishment. Indeed, Jefferson and Madison opposed any political appropriation of religion, and, even when challenging the hated assessments, they did not always temper their rhetoric with distinctions between coercive and noncoercive state action. When, for example, Madison criticized Virginia's general assessment bill, he invoked principles antithetical to all state efforts to promote religion. An assessment, he wrote, is improper not simply because it forces people to donate "three pence" to religion, but, more broadly, because "it is itself a signal of persecution. It degrades from the equal rank of Citizens all those whose opinions in Religion do not bend to those of the Legislative authority." J. Madison, Memorial and Remonstrance Against Religious Assessments. Madison saw that, even without the tax collector's participation, an official endorsement of religion can impair religious liberty.

Petitioners contend that because the early Presidents included religious messages in their inaugural and Thanksgiving Day addresses, the Framers could not have meant the Establishment Clause to forbid noncoercive state endorsement of religion. The argument ignores the fact, however, that Americans today find such proclamations less controversial than did the founding generation, whose published thoughts on the matter belie petitioners' claim. President Jefferson, for example, steadfastly refused to issue Thanksgiving proclamations of any kind, in part because he thought they violated the Religion Clauses. Letter from Thomas Jefferson to Rev. S. Miller (Jan. 23, 1808). In explaining his views to the Reverend Samuel Miller, Jefferson effectively anticipated, and rejected, petitioners' position:

> It is only proposed that I should recommend, not prescribe a day of fasting & prayer. That is, that I should indirectly assume to the U.S. an authority over religious exercises which the Constitution has directly precluded from them. It must be meant too that this recommendation is to carry some authority, and to be sanctioned by some penalty on those who disregard it; not indeed of fine and imprisonment, but of some degree of proscription perhaps in public opinion.

By condemning such noncoercive state practices that, in "recommending" the majority faith, demean religious dissenters "in public opinion," Jefferson necessarily condemned what, in modern terms, we call official endorsement of religion. He accordingly construed the Establishment Clause to forbid not simply state coercion, but also state endorsement, of religious belief and observance.[5] And if he opposed impersonal presidential addresses for inflicting "proscription in public opinion," all

5. Petitioners claim that the quoted passage shows that Jefferson regarded Thanksgiving proclamations as "coercive": "Thus, while one may disagree with Jefferson's view that a recommendatory Thanksgiving proclamation would nonetheless be coercive . . . one cannot disagree that Jefferson believed coercion to be a necessary element of a First Amendment violation." But this is wordplay. The "proscription" to which Jefferson referred was, of course, by the public and not the government, whose only action was a noncoercive recommendation. And one can call any act of endorsement a form of coercion, but only if one is willing to dilute the meaning of "coercion" until there is no meaning left. Jefferson's position straightforwardly contradicts the claim that a showing of "coercion," under any normal definition, is prerequisite to a successful Establishment Clause claim. At the same

the more would he have condemned less diffuse expressions of official endorsement.

During his first three years in office, James Madison also refused to call for days of thanksgiving and prayer, though later, amid the political turmoil of the War of 1812, he did so on four separate occasions. Upon retirement, in an essay condemning as an unconstitutional "establishment" the use of public money to support congressional and military chaplains, he concluded that "religious proclamations by the Executive recommending thanksgivings & fasts are shoots from the same root with the legislative acts reviewed. Altho' recommendations only, they imply a religious agency, making no part of the trust delegated to political rulers." Explaining that "the members of a Govt. . . . can in no sense, be regarded as possessing an advisory trust from their Constituents in their religious capacities," he further observed that the state necessarily freights all of its religious messages with political ones: "the idea of policy [is] associated with religion, whatever be the mode or the occasion, when a function of the latter is assumed by those in power."

Madison's failure to keep pace with his principles in the face of congressional pressure cannot erase the principles. He admitted to backsliding, and explained that he had made the content of his wartime proclamations inconsequential enough to mitigate much of their impropriety. While his writings suggest mild variations in his interpretation of the Establishment Clause, Madison was no different in that respect from the rest of his political generation. That he expressed so much doubt about the constitutionality of religious proclamations, however, suggests a brand of separationism stronger even than that embodied in our traditional jurisprudence. So too does his characterization of public subsidies for legislative and military chaplains as unconstitutional "establishments," for the federal courts. . . .

To be sure, the leaders of the young Republic engaged in some of the practices that separationists like Jefferson and Madison criticized. The First Congress did hire institutional chaplains, and Presidents Washington and Adams unapologetically marked days of "public thanksgiving and prayer." Yet in the face of the separationist dissent, those practices prove, at best, that the Framers simply did not share a common understanding of the Establishment Clause, and, at worst, that they, like other politicians, could raise constitutional ideals one day and turn their backs on them the next. "Indeed, by 1787 the provisions of the state bills of rights had become what Madison called 'mere paper parchments'— expressions of the most laudable sentiments, observed as much in the

---

time, Jefferson's practice, like Madison's, sometimes diverged from principle, for he did include religious references in his inaugural speeches. Homer nodded. . . .

breach as in practice." Kurland, The Origins of the Religion Clauses of the Constitution, 27 Wm. & Mary L. Rev. 839, 852 (1986). Sometimes the National Constitution fared no better. Ten years after proposing the First Amendment, Congress passed the Alien and Sedition Acts, measures patently unconstitutional by modern standards. If the early Congress's political actions were determinative, and not merely relevant, evidence of constitutional meaning, we would have to gut our current First Amendment doctrine to make room for political censorship. . . .

III

While the Establishment Clause's concept of neutrality is not self-revealing, our recent cases have invested it with specific content: the state may not favor or endorse either religion generally over nonreligion or one religion over others. This principle against favoritism and endorsement has become the foundation of Establishment Clause jurisprudence, ensuring that religious belief is irrelevant to every citizen's standing in the political community, and protecting religion from the demeaning effects of any governmental embrace. Now, as in the early Republic, "religion & Govt. will both exist in greater purity, the less they are mixed together." Letter from J. Madison to E. Livingston (10 July 1822). Our aspiration to religious liberty, embodied in the First Amendment, permits no other standard.

A

That government must remain neutral in matters of religion does not foreclose it from ever taking religion into account. The State may "accommodate" the free exercise of religion by relieving people from generally applicable rules that interfere with their religious callings. . . .

In everyday life, we routinely accommodate religious beliefs that we do not share. A Christian inviting an Orthodox Jew to lunch might take pains to choose a kosher restaurant; an atheist in a hurry might yield the right of way to an Amish man steering a horse-drawn carriage. In so acting, we express respect for, but not endorsement of, the fundamental values of others. We act without expressing a position on the theological merit of those values or of religious belief in general, and no one perceives us to have taken such a position.

The government may act likewise. Most religions encourage devotional practices that are at once crucial to the lives of believers and idiosyncratic in the eyes of nonadherents. By definition, secular rules of general application are drawn from the nonadherent's vantage and, consequently, fail to take such practices into account. Yet when enforcement of such rules cuts across religious sensibilities, as it often does, it puts those affected to the choice of taking sides between God and government. In such circumstances, accommodating religion reveals nothing beyond a recognition that general rules can unnecessarily offend the religious conscience when they offend the conscience of secular society not at all. Thus, in freeing the Native American Church from federal laws forbidding peyote use, see Drug Enforcement Administration Miscellaneous Exemptions, 21 C.F.R. §1307.31 (1991), the government conveys no endorsement of peyote rituals, the Church, or religion as such; it simply respects the centrality of peyote to the lives of certain Americans. See Note, The Free Exercise Boundaries of Permissible Accommodation Under the Establishment Clause, 99 Yale L.J. 1127, 1135-1136 (1990).

B

Whatever else may define the scope of accommodation permissible under the Establishment Clause, one requirement is clear: accommodation must lift a discernible burden on the free exercise of religion. Concern for the position of religious individuals in the modern regulatory state cannot justify official solicitude for a religious practice unburdened by general rules; such gratuitous largesse would effectively favor religion over disbelief. By these lights one easily sees that, in sponsoring the graduation prayers at issue here, the State has crossed the line from permissible accommodation to unconstitutional establishment.

Religious students cannot complain that omitting prayers from their graduation ceremony would, in any realistic sense, "burden" their spiritual callings. To be sure, many of them invest this rite of passage with spiritual significance, but they may express their religious feelings about it before and after the ceremony. They may even organize a privately sponsored baccalaureate if they desire the company of likeminded students. Because they accordingly have no need for the machinery of the State to affirm their beliefs, the government's sponsorship of prayer at the graduation ceremony is most reasonably understood as an official endorsement of religion and, in this instance, of Theistic religion. One may fairly say, as one commentator has suggested, that the government brought prayer into the ceremony "precisely because some people want a symbolic affirmation that government approves and endorses their religion, and because many of the people who want this affirmation place little or no value on the costs to religious minorities." Laycock, Summary and Synthesis: The Crisis in Religious Liberty, 60 Geo. Wash. L. Rev. 841, 844 (1992).[8]

8. If the State had chosen its graduation day speakers according to wholly secular criteria, and if one of those speakers (not a state actor) had individually chosen to deliver a religious message, it would have been harder to attribute an endorsement of religion to the

Petitioners would deflect this conclusion by arguing that graduation prayers are no different from presidential religious proclamations and similar official "acknowledgments" of religion in public life. But religious invocations in Thanksgiving Day addresses and the like, rarely noticed, ignored without effort, conveyed over an impersonal medium, and directed at no one in particular, inhabit a pallid zone worlds apart from official prayers delivered to a captive audience of public school students and their families. Madison himself respected the difference between the trivial and the serious in constitutional practice. Realizing that his contemporaries were unlikely to take the Establishment Clause seriously enough to forgo a legislative chaplainship, he suggested that "rather than let this step beyond the landmarks of power have the effect of a legitimate precedent, it will be better to apply to it the legal aphorism de minimis non curat lex. . . ." Madison's "Detached Memoranda" 559. But that logic permits no winking at the practice in question here. When public school officials, armed with the State's authority, convey an endorsement of religion to their students, they strike near the core of the Establishment Clause. However "ceremonial" their messages may be, they are flatly unconstitutional.

JUSTICE SCALIA, with whom THE CHIEF JUSTICE, JUSTICE WHITE, and JUSTICE THOMAS join, dissenting. . . .

[In] holding that the Establishment Clause prohibits invocations and benedictions at public-school graduation ceremonies, the Court — with nary a mention that it is doing so — lays waste a tradition that is as old as public-school graduation ceremonies themselves, and that is a component of an even more longstanding American tradition of nonsectarian prayer to God at public celebrations generally. . . .

I . . .

From our Nation's origin, prayer has been a prominent part of governmental ceremonies and proclamations. The Declaration of Independence, the document marking our birth as a separate people, "appealed to the Supreme Judge of the world for the rectitude of our intentions" and avowed "a firm reliance on the protection of divine Providence." In his first inaugural address, after swearing his oath of office on a Bible, George Washington deliberately made a prayer a part of his first official act as President:

State. Cf. Witters v. Washington Dept. of Services for the Blind, 474 U.S. 481 (1986). But that is not our case. . . .

> it would be peculiarly improper to omit in this first official act my fervent supplications to that Almighty Being who rules over the universe, who presides in the councils of nations, and whose providential aids can supply every human defect, that His benediction may consecrate to the liberties and happiness of the people of the United States a Government instituted by themselves for these essential purposes.

Such supplications have been a characteristic feature of inaugural addresses ever since. Thomas Jefferson, for example, prayed in his first inaugural address: "may that Infinite Power which rules the destinies of the universe lead our councils to what is best, and give them a favorable issue for your peace and prosperity." . . .

Our national celebration of Thanksgiving likewise dates back to President Washington. . . .

> [The] day after the First Amendment was proposed, Congress urged President Washington to proclaim "a day of public thanksgiving and prayer, to be observed by acknowledging with grateful hearts the many and signal favours of Almighty God." President Washington proclaimed November 26, 1789, a day of thanksgiving to "offe[r] our prayers and supplications to the Great Lord and Ruler of Nations, and beseech him to pardon our national and other transgressions. . . ."

This tradition of Thanksgiving Proclamations — with their religious theme of prayerful gratitude to God — has been adhered to by almost every President.

The other two branches of the Federal Government also have a long-established practice of prayer at public events. As we detailed in Marsh, Congressional sessions have opened with a chaplain's prayer ever since the First Congress. And this Court's own sessions have opened with the invocation "God save the United States and this Honorable Court" since the days of Chief Justice Marshall.

In addition to this general tradition of prayer at public ceremonies, there exists a more specific tradition of invocations and benedictions at public-school graduation exercises. By one account, the first public-high-school graduation ceremony took place in Connecticut in July 1868 [when] "15 seniors from the Norwich Free Academy marched in their best Sunday suits and dresses into a church hall and waited through majestic music and long prayers." . . .

II

The Court presumably would separate graduation invocations and benedictions from other instances of public "preservation and transmission of religious beliefs" on the ground that they involve "psychological coercion." [A] few citations of "research in psychology" that have no particular bearing upon the precise issue here, cannot disguise the fact that the Court has gone beyond the realm where judges know what they are doing. The Court's argument that state officials have "coerced" students to take part in the invocation and benediction at graduation ceremonies is, not to put too fine a point on it, incoherent.

A

The Court declares that students' "attendance and participation in the [invocation and benediction] are in a fair and real sense obligatory." But what exactly is this "fair and real sense"? According to the Court, students at graduation who want "to avoid the fact or appearance of participation," in the invocation and benediction are psychologically obligated by "public pressure, as well as peer pressure, . . . to stand as a group or, at least, maintain respectful silence" during those prayers. This assertion — the very linchpin of the Court's opinion — is almost as intriguing for what it does not say as for what it says. It does not say, for example, that students are psychologically coerced to bow their heads, place their hands in a Drer-like prayer position, pay attention to the prayers, utter "Amen," or in fact pray. (Perhaps further intensive psychological research remains to be done on these matters.) It claims only that students are psychologically coerced "to stand . . . or, at least, maintain respectful silence." Both halves of this disjunctive (both of which must amount to the fact or appearance of participation in prayer if the Court's analysis is to survive on its own terms) merit particular attention.

To begin with the latter: The Court's notion that a student who simply sits in "respectful silence" during the invocation and benediction (when all others are standing) has somehow joined — or would somehow be perceived as having joined — in the prayers is nothing short of ludicrous. We indeed live in a vulgar age. But surely "our social conventions" have not coarsened to the point that anyone who does not stand on his chair and shout obscenities can reasonably be deemed to have assented to everything said in his presence. Since the Court does not dispute that students exposed to prayer at graduation ceremonies retain (despite "subtle coercive pressures") the free will to sit, there is absolutely no basis for the Court's decision. It is fanciful enough to say that "a reasonable dissenter," standing head erect in a class of bowed heads, "could believe that the group exercise signified her own participation or approval of it." It is beyond the absurd to say that she could entertain such a belief while pointedly declining to rise.

But let us assume the very worst, that the nonparticipating graduate is "subtly coerced" . . . to stand! Even that half of the disjunctive does not remotely establish a "participation" (or an "appearance of participation") in a religious exercise. The Court acknowledges that "in our culture standing . . . can signify adherence to a view or simple respect for the views of others." (Much more often the latter than the former, I think, except perhaps in the proverbial town meeting, where one votes by standing.) But if it is a permissible inference that one who is standing is doing so simply out of respect for the prayers of others that are in progress, then how can it possibly be said that a "reasonable dissenter . . . could believe that the group exercise signified her own participation or approval"? Quite obviously, it cannot. I may add, moreover, that maintaining respect for the religious observances of others is a fundamental civic virtue that government (including the public schools) can and should cultivate — so that even if it were the case that the displaying of such respect might be mistaken for taking part in the prayer, I would deny that the dissenter's interest in avoiding even the false appearance of participation constitutionally trumps the government's interest in fostering respect for religion generally.

The opinion manifests that the Court itself has not given careful consideration to its test of psychological coercion. For if it had, how could it observe, with no hint of concern or disapproval, that students stood for the Pledge of Allegiance, which immediately preceded Rabbi Gutterman's invocation? The government can, of course, no more coerce political orthodoxy than religious orthodoxy. West Virginia Board of Education v. Barnette, 319 U.S. 624, 642 (1943). Moreover, since the Pledge of Allegiance has been revised since *Barnette* to include the phrase "under God," recital of the Pledge would appear to raise the same Establishment Clause issue as the invocation and benediction. If students were psychologically coerced to remain standing during the invocation, they must also have been psychologically coerced, moments before, to stand for (and thereby, in the Court's view, take part in or appear to take part in) the Pledge. Must the Pledge therefore be barred from the public schools (both from graduation ceremonies and from the classroom)? In *Barnette* we held that a public-school student could not be compelled to recite the Pledge; we did not even hint that she could not be compelled to observe respectful silence — indeed, even to stand in respectful silence — when those who wished to recite it did so. Logically, that ought to be the next project for the Court's bulldozer. . . .

III

The deeper flaw in the Court's opinion does not lie in its wrong answer to the question whether there was state-induced "peer-pressure" coercion; it lies, rather, in the Court's making violation of the Establishment Clause hinge on such a precious question. The coercion that was a hallmark of historical establishments of religion was coercion of religious orthodoxy and of financial support by force of law and threat of penalty. Typically, attendance at the state church was required; only clergy of the official church could lawfully perform sacraments; and dissenters, if tolerated, faced an array of civil disabilities. Thus, for example, in the colony of Virginia, where the Church of England had been established, ministers were required by law to conform to the doctrine and rites of the Church of England; and all persons were required to attend church and observe the Sabbath, were tithed for the public support of Anglican ministers, and were taxed for the costs of building and repairing churches.

The Establishment Clause was adopted to prohibit such an establishment of religion at the federal level (and to protect state establishments of religion from federal interference). I will further acknowledge for the sake of argument that, as some scholars have argued, by 1790 the term "establishment" had acquired an additional meaning — "financial support of religion generally, by public taxation" — that reflected the development of "general or multiple" establishments, not limited to a single church. But that would still be an establishment coerced by force of law. And I will further concede that our constitutional tradition, from the Declaration of Independence and the first inaugural address of Washington, quoted earlier, down to the present day, has, with a few aberrations, ruled out of order government-sponsored endorsement of religion — even when no legal coercion is present, and indeed even when no ersatz, "peer-pressure" psycho-coercion is present — where the endorsement is sectarian, in the sense of specifying details upon which men and women who believe in a benevolent, omnipotent Creator and Ruler of the world, are known to differ (for example, the divinity of Christ). But there is simply no support for the proposition that the officially sponsored nondenominational invocation and benediction read by Rabbi Gutterman — with no one legally coerced to recite them — violated the Constitution of the United States. To the contrary, they are so characteristically American they could have come from the pen of George Washington or Abraham Lincoln himself. . . .

[There] is nothing in the record to indicate that failure of attending students to take part in the invocation or benediction was subject to any penalty or discipline. Contrast this with, for example, the facts of *Barnette*: Schoolchildren were required by law to recite the Pledge of Allegiance; failure to do so resulted in expulsion, threatened the expelled child with the prospect of being sent to a reformatory for criminally inclined juveniles, and subjected his parents to prosecution (and incarceration) for causing delinquency. To characterize the "subtle coercive pressures," allegedly present here as the "practical" equivalent of the legal sanctions in *Barnette* is . . . well, let me just say it is not a "delicate and fact-sensitive" analysis.

The Court relies on our "school prayer" cases. But whatever the merit of those cases, they do not support, much less compel, the Court's psycho-journey. In the first place, *Engel* and *Schempp* do not constitute an exception to the rule, distilled from historical practice, that public ceremonies may include prayer; rather, they simply do not fall within the scope of the rule (for the obvious reason that school instruction is not a public ceremony). Second, we have made clear our understanding that school prayer occurs within a framework in which legal coercion to attend school (i. e., coercion under threat of penalty) provides the ultimate backdrop. In *Schempp*, for example, we emphasized that the prayers were "prescribed as part of the curricular activities of students who are required by law to attend school." *Engel*'s suggestion that the school-prayer program at issue there — which permitted students "to remain silent or be excused from the room" — involved "indirect coercive pressure" should be understood against this backdrop of legal coercion. The question whether the opt-out procedure in Engel sufficed to dispel the coercion resulting from the mandatory attendance requirement is quite different from the question whether forbidden coercion exists in an environment utterly devoid of legal compulsion. And finally, our school-prayer cases turn in part on the fact that the classroom is inherently an instructional setting, and daily prayer there — where parents are not present to counter "the students' emulation of teachers as role models and the children's susceptibility to peer pressure," Edwards v. Aguillard, 482 U.S. 578, 584 (1987) — might be thought to raise special concerns regarding state interference with the liberty of parents to direct the religious upbringing of their children. . . .

IV . . .

[Given] the odd basis for the Court's decision, invocations and benedictions will be able to be given at public-school graduations next June, as they have for the past century and a half, so long as school authorities make clear that anyone who abstains from screaming in protest does not necessarily participate in the prayers. All that is seemingly needed is an announcement, or perhaps a written insertion at the beginning of the graduation Program, to the effect that, while all are asked to rise for the invocation and benediction, none is compelled to join in them, nor will be assumed, by rising, to have done so. That obvious fact recited, the graduates and their parents may proceed to thank God, as Americans have always done, for the blessings He has generously bestowed on them and on their country. . . .

The reader has been told much in this case about the personal interest of Mr. Weisman and his daughter, and very little about the personal interests on the other side. They are not inconsequential. Church and state would not be such a difficult subject if religion were, as the Court apparently thinks it to be, some purely personal avocation that can be indulged entirely in secret, like pornography, in the privacy of one's room. For most believers it is not that, and has never been. Religious men and women of almost all denominations have felt it necessary to acknowledge and beseech the blessing of God as a people, and not just as individuals, because they believe in the "protection of divine Providence," as the Declaration of Independence put it, not just for individuals but for societies; because they believe God to be, as Washington's first Thanksgiving Proclamation put it, the "Great Lord and Ruler of Nations." One can believe in the effectiveness of such public worship, or one can deprecate and deride it. But the longstanding American tradition of prayer at official ceremonies displays with unmistakable clarity that the Establishment Clause does not forbid the government to accommodate it. . . .

I must add one final observation: The founders of our Republic knew the fearsome potential of sectarian religious belief to generate civil dissension and civil strife. And they also knew that nothing, absolutely nothing, is so inclined to foster among religious believers of various faiths a toleration — no, an affection — for one another than voluntarily joining in prayer together, to the God whom they all worship and seek. Needless to say, no one should be compelled to do that, but it is a shame to deprive our public culture of the opportunity, and indeed the encouragement, for people to do it voluntarily. The Baptist or Catholic who heard and joined in the simple and inspiring prayers of Rabbi Gutterman on this official and patriotic occasion was inoculated from religious bigotry and prejudice in a manner that can not be replicated. To deprive our society of that important unifying mechanism, in order to spare the nonbeliever what seems to me the minimal inconvenience of standing or even sitting in respectful nonparticipation, is as senseless in policy as it is unsupported in law.

For the foregoing reasons, I dissent.

Note: Lee v. Weisman

1. *History and/or tradition.* Consider whether the disagreement between Justices Souter and Scalia can be described as a difference over whether

courts should consider the history reflected in the conclusions drawn by the Constitution's drafters (and their generation) after deliberate reflection on fundamental questions of principles, or whether they should consider the history reflected in the practices of the framers' and later generations. If so, on what basis can one choose between these two versions of history/tradition?

2. *Coercion or endorsement.* Does Justice Scalia's treatment of coercion overlook the possibility that some student, in the face of the graduation prayer, will engage in a prayer that he or she would not otherwise have engaged in? Is that accurately described as coercion? (Consider whether someone *can* be coerced into praying, that is, whether the activity that a coerced person engages in could accurately be called a prayer.) If not, is it more accurate to describe the problem in *Lee* as one of government endorsement of religion, which on the margin induces someone to engage in prayer, rather than one of government coercion?

Page 1460. Before section 3 of the note, add the following:

For a recent analysis of Roger Williams's views, see Hall, Roger Williams and the Foundations of Religious Liberty, 71 B.U. L. Rev. 455 (1991).

B. THE ESTABLISHMENT CLAUSE

1. *Impermissible Purposes: The School Prayer Cases*

Page 1492. At the end of note 7, insert the following:

For the interesting suggestion that the "citizenship declaration" in the first sentence of the fourteenth amendment "prohibits the federal and state governments from subverting a citizen's status in the political community because of his or her creed or lack of religious commitment," see Leedes, Rediscovering the Link Between the Establishment Clause and the Fourteenth Amendment: The Citizenship Declaration, 26 Indiana L. Rev. 469 (1993). According to Leedes, "the immunity associated with citizen status does *not* need to come into play when nonpreferential, noncoercive state aid to religion advances legitimate secular objectives and does not stigmatize members of religious outgroups. It needs to come into play if, and only if, noncoercive state aid to religion marginalizes citizens who do not share the creed of the aided religion." Is it possible to construct an argument that nonpreferential, noncoercive aid necessarily stigmatizes religious outgroups (for example, by conveying the suggestion that those whose religious beliefs do not impel them to accept such aid are less worthy than others)? Leede's argument restricts the coverage of the Establishment Clause to citizens (or, more pejoratively, allows governments to use religion as one of the ways they marginalize non-citizens; is that troubling?

Page 1495. At the end of note 2, add the following:

In a concurring opinion in Lamb's Chapel v. Center Moriches Union Free School District, — S. Ct. — (1993), Justice Scalia analogized the *Lemon* test to "a ghoul in a late-night horror movie that repeatedly sits up in its grave and shuffles abroad, after being repeatedly killed and buried. [It] is there to scare us (and our audience) when we wish it to do so, but we can command it to return to the tomb at will. When we wish to strike down a practice it forbids, we invoke it; when we wish to uphold a practice it forbids, we ignore it entirely. Sometimes, we take a middle course, calling its three prongs 'no more than helpful signposts.' Such a docile and useful monster is worth keeping around, at least in a somnolent state; one never knows when one might need him." He would repudiate the test entirely. The majority was "somewhat diverted by [this] evening at the cinema," but said that there were better ways to overrule established precedent.

Page 1504. Before note 2, add the following:

Zobrest v. Catalina Foothills School Dist., 113 S. Ct. — (1993), held that the Establishment Clause would not be violated if a school district paid the salary of a sign-language interpreter for a deaf student attending a Roman Catholic high school. Chief Justice Rehnquist's opinion for the Court relied on *Mueller* and *Witters*, which held that "government programs that neutrally provide benefits to a broad class of citizens defined without reference to religion are not readily subject to an Establishment Clause challenge just because sectarian institutions may also receive an attenuated financial benefit." The sign-language interpreter was provided as "part of a general government program that distributes benefits neutrally to any child qualifying as 'handicapped' [without] regard to the 'sectarian-nonsectarian, or public-nonpublic nature' of the school the child attends." Because the statute, "creates no financial incentive for parents to choose a sectarian school, an interpreter's presence there cannot be attributed to state decision-making. [Indeed,] this is an even easier case than *Mueller* and *Witters* in the sense that [no] funds traceable to the government every find their way into sectarian schools' coffers. The only indirect economic benefit a sectarian school might receive [is] the handicapped child's tuition — and that is, of course, assuming that the school makes a profit on each student; that, without an [interpreter,] the child would have gone to school elsewhere; and that the school, then, would have been unable to fill that child's spot." The Court distinguished Meek v. Pittinger and *Ball* because there the "direct grants of government aid [relieved] sectarian schools of costs they otherwise would have borne in educating their students," and because "the task of a sign-language interpreter seems to us quite different from that of a teacher or guidance counselor."

Justice Blackmun, joined by Justice Souter, dissented on the merits; Justices Stevens and O'Connor dissented on procedural grounds. According to Justice Blackmun, the Court's decision "authorized a public employee to participate directly in religious indoctrination. [Even] a general welfare program may have specific applications that are constitutionally forbidden under the Establishment Clause." Unlike *Witters* and *Mueller,* "where governmental involvement ended with the disbursement of funds or lessening of tax[, this] case [involves] ongoing, daily, and intimate governmental participation in the teaching a propagation of religious doctrine."

Does *Zobrest* strengthen or weaken the case for the constitutionality of programs creating "vouchers" that students can use to pay tuition at nonpublic schools? After *Zobrest,* would it be constitutional for a state to pay a portion of the salary of mathematics teachers in nonpublic schools as part of a "general program" of paying the salaries of all mathematics teachers?

C. THE FREE EXERCISE CLAUSE: REQUIRED ACCOMMODATIONS

Page 1510. At the beginning of the Note, add the following:

The Court's discussions of required accommodations of religion have tended to ignore examination of the intentions of the drafters of the first amendment, except by referring in general terms to their interest in religious liberty. McConnell, The Origins and Historical Understanding of Free Exercise of Religion, 103 Harv. L. Rev. 1409, 1512 (1990), concludes on the basis of an examination of pre-1787 practice, the debates over the Constitution and the bill of rights, and contemporaneous political theory that "exemptions were not common enough to compel the inference that the term 'free exercise of religion' necessarily included an enforceable right to exemption. [Without] overstating the force of the evidence, however, it is possible to say that the modern doctrine of free exercise exemptions is more consistent with the original understanding than is a position that leads only to the facial neutrality of legislation." Construct the form of the argument allowing the inference from legislative practices of exemption to a constitutional requirement of exemption.

Page 1530. Before section 3 of the Note, add the following:

d. Church of the Lukumi Babalu Aye v. City of Hialeah, 113 S. Ct. — (1993), invalidated a city's ban on "ritual slaughter," as applied to animal sacrifices conducted by the Church as part of its practice of the Santeria religion. The Court found that the background of the ban, and its specific language and exemptions, demonstrated that it was not neutral under *Smith*, but that "suppression of the central element of the Santeria worship service was the object of the ordinances." The background "demonstrates animosity to Santeria adherents and their religious practices; the ordinances by their own terms target this religious exercise; the texts of the ordinances were gerrymandered with care to proscribe religious killings of animals but to exclude almost all secular killings; and the ordinances suppress much more religious conduct than is necessary to achieve the legitimate ends asserted in their defense." (Note that the Court used the scope of the suppression to measure its "object," rather than to assess whether the suppression was justified.) The ordinances did not satisfy the "rigorous scrutiny" required of regulations that are not neutral or of general application, because they were "not drawn in narrow terms to accomplish" the objectives of protecting animals from inhumane slaughter or avoiding unhealthy methods of disposing of animal carcasses.

Justice Souter indicated his belief that *Smith* was probably erroneously decided. Justice Blackmun, joined by Justice O'Connor, concurred in the judgment, saying that "when a law discriminates against religion as such, [it] automatically will fail strict scrutiny [because] by definition, [it] is not precisely tailored to a compelling governmental interest."

Page 1531. Before the Note, add the following:

4. *The commentators' reaction.* Legal commentary has not been receptive to *Smith.* See, e.g., McConnell, Free Exercise Revisionism and the *Smith* Decision, 57 U. Chi. L. Rev. 1109 (1990). Marshall, In Defense of *Smith* and Free Exercise Revisionism, 58 U. Chi. L. Rev. 308, 310, 319 (1991), concedes that, while the opinion in *Smith* "is neither persuasive nor well-crafted," the result can be defended because "exemption analysis threatens free exercise values because it requires courts to consider the legitimacy of the religious claim of the party seeking the exemption," and because "granting exemptions only to religious claimants promotes [a] constitutional preference for religious over non-religious belief systems." (How should Marshall respond to the claim that the first amendment itself expresses such a preference? See id. at 325-327.)

David Williams & Susan Williams, Volitionalism and Religious Liberty, 76 Cornell L. Rev. 769, 772, 777, 908 (1991), argue that *Smith* resulted from "the Court's profound discomfort with nonvolitionalist beliefs," which they define as beliefs that "acknowledge the possibility that some religious consequences for individuals may be caused by activities or events over which they had no free choice or control," as in *Lyng* and Bowen v. Roy. On their analysis, free exercise claims lie along a spectrum ranging from "exemption" claims to "ordering" claims, "the remedy for which consists primarily of reordering some aspect of the government's program not limited in application to the individual claimant." They suggest that, under a pre-*Smith* analysis, "ordering" claims, which typify those made by people with nonvolitionalist beliefs, "are, as a practical matter, likely to impose greater burdens on the government than will exemption claims." Does this raise troubling questions about denominational preference? Greene, The Political Balance of the Religion Clauses, 102 Yale L. J. 1611 (1993), argues that the Establishment Clause bars "enacting legislation for the express purpose of advancing the values believed to be commanded by religion," and that "precisely because religion should be excluded from politics in this way, [the] Free Exercise Clause requires the recognition of religious faith as a ground for exemption from legal obligation. [These] exemptions are merely the appropriate remedy for the damage that precluding religious values from grounding law causes religious people." The Establishment Clause ban arises because, when legislation is enacted for the express purpose of advancing religious values, "a nonbeliever is effectively denied participation in the political process because the nonbeliever cannot discuss the matter on the terms that the religious believers have set." According to Greene, because one type of argument is thereby excluded from political negotiations, those who would make it are entitled to a compensatory offset.

5. *A legislative response.* Members of Congress, relying in part on Katzenbach v. Morgan, have introduced legislation to instruct the courts to return to the test of Sherbert v. Verner. Some opposition has arisen on the ground that such a statute might be construed to create an enforceable right to an abortion. Construct and analyze that argument.

D. PERMISSIBLE ACCOMMODATION

Page 1541. At the end of section 1 of the Note, add the following:

See also McConnell, Accommodation of Religion: An Update and a Response to the Critics, 60 Geo. Wash. L. Rev. 685 (1992).

Page 1541. After the first paragraph of note 2a, add the following:

The Court invalidated a school district's restriction on the use of its facilities after hours by religious groups in Lamb's Chapel v. Center Moriches Union Free School District, — S. Ct. — (1993), finding the restriction viewpoint-based. The district argued that "to permit its property to be used for religious purposes would be an establishment of religion forbidden by the First Amendment." The Court responded that "the posited fears of an Establishment Clause violation are unfounded. [There] would have been no realistic danger that the community would think that the District was endorsing religion or any particular creed, and any benefit to religion or to the Church would have been no more than incidental. As in *Widmar,* permitting District property to be used to exhibit the film involved in this case would not have been an establishment of religion under the three-part test articulated in Lemon v. Kurtzman."

Chapter Nine

Economic Liberties, "Redistribution," and the Constitution: The Contracts and Taking Clauses

A. THE CONTRACTS CLAUSE

Page 1564. Before section 4 of the Note, add the following:

In General Motors Corp. v. Romein, 112 S. Ct. 1105 (1992), the Court upheld a substantial change in a workers' compensation program. In 1980, Michigan had raised the level of maximum benefits; in 1981, it allowed employers to decrease the level of the relevant benefits to disabled employees who could receive compensation from other employer-funded sources. The Michigan Supreme Court ruled that under the 1981 law, employers could reduce benefits to all workers, including those injured before the statute's effective date. In 1987, the legislature repudiated this ruling and said that employers must make refunds to the previously disabled workers. According to the Supreme Court, there was no problem under the contracts clause because the allegedly impaired contracts contained "no contractual agreement regarding the specific workers' compensation terms allegedly at issue." The Court rejected the claim that their statutory right to rely on past payment periods as "closed" was incorporated by law into employment contracts. "[W]e have not held that all state regulations are implied terms of every contract entered into while they are effective. . . ."

The Court added:

> The 1987 statute did not change the legal enforceability of the employment contracts here. . . . Moreover, petitioners' suggestion that we should read every workplace regulation into the private arrangements of employers and employees would expand the definition of contract so far that the constitutional provision would lose its anchoring purpose, i.e., "enabl[ing] individuals to order their personal and business affairs according to their particular needs and interests." Instead, the Clause would protect against all changes in legislation. . . .

B. THE EMINENT DOMAIN CLAUSE

Page 1568. Before Pennsylvania Coal Co. v. Mahon, add the following:

Rubenfeld, Usings, 102 Yale L. J. 1077 (1993) argues that the takings clause is directed only against governmental "usings" of private property.

Page 1591. Before section 3 of the Note, add the following:

The Court continued to emphasize the issue of physical invasion in Yee v. Escondido, 112 S. Ct. 1522 (1992). At issue was a local rent control ordinance, applied to mobile home owners and in particular to owners of mobile home "parks." The ordinance set rents at a 1986 level, prohibited unapproved rent increases, and specified the factors that must be considered for any increases. Mobile home park owners contended that under this system, they could no longer set rents or decide who their tenants will be, and that as a result, the mobile home owner becomes an effective perpetual tenant of the park, indefinitely enabled to occupy the home's "pad." Thus an interest in land — the right to occupy it at sub-market rent — has been transferred from the park owner to the mobile home owner. According to the park owners, there was in this sense a physical invasion of their property.

The Court disagreed. It said that "government effects a physical taking only where it requires the landowner to submit to the physical occupation of the land." Here, however, "[p]etitioners voluntarily rented their land to mobile home owners. . . . [N]either the City nor the State compels petitioners, once they have rented their property to tenants, to continue doing so." In the Court's view, "no government has required any physical invasions of petitioners' property. Petitioners' tenants were invited by petitioners, not forced upon them by the government." Thus the laws at issue "merely regulate petitioners' use of their land by regulating the relationship between landlord and tenant."

The fact that there was a transfer of wealth from park owners to incumbent mobile home owners was not decisive, since many forms of land use regulation "can also be said to transfer wealth from the one who is regulated to another." But the Court noted that a "different case would be presented" if the statute compelled "a landowner over objection to rent his property or to refrain in perpetuity from terminating a tenancy."

In the first year course in property, it is often emphasized that property is a bundle of rights — not a "thing," and not merely a brute fact called physical possession. Has the Constitution disregarded this insight? If the Constitution incorporated the understandings of the first year property course, would rent control laws generally be in jeopardy?

LUCAS v. SOUTH CAROLINA COASTAL COUNCIL
112 S. Ct. 2886 (1992)

JUSTICE SCALIA delivered the opinion of the Court.

In 1986, petitioner David H. Lucas paid $975,000 for two residential lots on the Isle of Palms in Charleston County, South Carolina, on which he intended to build single-family homes. In 1988, however, the South Carolina Legislature enacted the Beachfront Management Act, which had the direct effect of barring petitioner from erecting any permanent habitable structures on his two parcels. A state trial court found that this prohibition rendered Lucas's parcels "valueless." This case requires us to decide whether the Act's dramatic effect on the economic value of Lucas's lots accomplished a taking of private property under the Fifth and Fourteenth Amendments requiring the payment of "just compensation."

I

A

South Carolina's expressed interest in intensively managing development activities in the so-called "coastal zone" dates from 1977 when, in the aftermath of Congress's passage of the federal Coastal Zone Management Act of 1972, the legislature enacted a Coastal Zone Management Act of its own. . . .

In the late 1970's, Lucas and others began extensive residential development of the Isle of Palms, a barrier island situated eastward of the City of Charleston. Toward the close of the development cycle for one residential subdivision known as "Beachwood East," Lucas in 1986 purchased the two lots at issue in this litigation for his own account. [At] the time Lucas acquired these parcels, he was not legally obliged to obtain a permit from the Council in advance of any development activity. His intention with respect to the lots was to do what the owners of the immediately adjacent parcels had already done: erect single-family residences. He commissioned architectural drawings for this purpose.

The Beachfront Management Act brought Lucas's plans to an abrupt end. Under that 1988 legislation, the Council was directed to establish a "baseline" connecting the landward-most "points of erosion . . . during the past forty years" in the region of the Isle of Palms that includes

Lucas's lots. In action not challenged here, the Council fixed this baseline landward of Lucas's parcels. That was significant, for under the Act construction of occupiable improvements was flatly prohibited seaward of a line drawn 20 feet landward of, and parallel to, the baseline. The Act provided no exceptions.

Lucas promptly filed suit in the South Carolina Court of Common Pleas, contending that the Beachfront Management Act's construction bar effected a taking of his property without just compensation. Lucas did not take issue with the validity of the Act as a lawful exercise of South Carolina's police power, but contended that the Act's complete extinguishment of his property's value entitled him to compensation regardless of whether the legislature had acted in furtherance of legitimate police power objectives. Following a bench trial, the court agreed. Among its factual determinations was the finding that "at the time Lucas purchased the two lots, both were zoned for single-family residential construction and . . . there were no restrictions imposed upon such use of the property by either the State of South Carolina, the County of Charleston, or the Town of the Isle of Palms." The trial court further found that the Beachfront Management Act decreed a permanent ban on construction insofar as Lucas's lots were concerned, and that this prohibition "deprived Lucas of any reasonable economic use of the lots, . . . eliminated the unrestricted right of use, and rendered them valueless." The court thus concluded that Lucas's properties had been "taken" by operation of the Act, and it ordered respondent to pay "just compensation" in the amount of $1,232,387.50. . . .

Prior to Justice Holmes' exposition in Pennsylvania Coal Co. v. Mahon, 260 U.S. 393 (1922), it was generally thought that the Takings Clause reached only a "direct appropriation" of property, Legal Tender Cases, 12 Wall. 457, 551 (1871), or the functional equivalent of a "practical ouster of [the owner's] possession." Transportation Co. v. Chicago, 99 U.S. 635, 642 (1879). Justice Holmes recognized in *Mahon*, however, that if the protection against physical appropriations of private property was to be meaningfully enforced, the government's power to redefine the range of interests included in the ownership of property was necessarily constrained by constitutional limits. If, instead, the uses of private property were subject to unbridled, uncompensated qualification under the police power, "the natural tendency of human nature [would be] to extend the qualification more and more until at last private property disappeared." These considerations gave birth in that case to the oft-cited maxim that, "while property may be regulated to a certain extent, if regulation goes too far it will be recognized as a taking."

Nevertheless, our decision in *Mahon* offered little insight into when, and under what circumstances, a given regulation would be seen as going "too far" for purposes of the Fifth Amendment. In 70-odd years of succeeding "regulatory takings" jurisprudence, we have generally eschewed any " 'set formula' " for determining how far is too far, preferring to "engage in . . . essentially ad hoc, factual inquiries," Penn Central Transportation Co. v. New York City, 438 U.S. 104, 124 (1978) (quoting Goldblatt v. Hempstead, 369 U.S. 590, 594 (1962)). See Epstein, Takings: Descent and Resurrection, 1987 Sup. Ct. Rev. 1, 4. We have, however, described at least two discrete categories of regulatory action as compensable without case-specific inquiry into the public interest advanced in support of the restraint. The first encompasses regulations that compel the property owner to suffer a physical "invasion" of his property. In general (at least with regard to permanent invasions), no matter how minute the intrusion, and no matter how weighty the public purpose behind it, we have required compensation. . . .

The second situation in which we have found categorical treatment appropriate is where regulation denies all economically beneficial or productive use of land. . . .[7]

We have never set forth the justification for this rule. Perhaps it is simply, as Justice Brennan suggested, that total deprivation of beneficial use is, from the landowner's point of view, the equivalent of a physical appropriation. See San Diego Gas & Electric Co. v. San Diego, 450 U.S., at 652 (Brennan, J., dissenting). "For what is the land but the profits thereof?" 1 E. Coke, Institutes ch. 1, §1 (1st Am. ed. 1812). Surely, at least, in the extraordinary circumstance when no productive or economically beneficial use of land is permitted, it is less realistic to indulge our usual assumption that the legislature is simply "adjusting the benefits and burdens of economic life," *Penn Central Transportation Co.*, in a manner

7. Regrettably, the rhetorical force of our "deprivation of all economically feasible use" rule is greater than its precision, since the rule does not make clear the "property interest" against which the loss of value is to be measured. When, for example, a regulation requires a developer to leave 90% of a rural tract in its natural state, it is unclear whether we would analyze the situation as one in which the owner has been deprived of all economically beneficial use of the burdened portion of the tract, or as one in which the owner has suffered a mere diminution in value of the tract as a whole. [Unsurprisingly,] this uncertainty regarding the composition of the denominator in our "deprivation" fraction has produced inconsistent pronouncements by the Court. The answer to this difficult question may lie in how the owner's reasonable expectations have been shaped by the State's law of property — i.e., whether and to what degree the State's law has accorded legal recognition and protection to the particular interest in land with respect to which the takings claimant alleges a diminution in (or elimination of) value. In any event, we avoid this difficulty in the present case, since the "interest in land" that Lucas has pleaded (a fee simple interest) is an estate with a rich tradition of protection at common law, and since the South Carolina Court of Common Pleas found that the Beachfront Management Act left each of Lucas's beachfront lots without economic value. [Relocated footnote — EDS.]

that secures an "average reciprocity of advantage" to everyone concerned. *Mahon.* And the functional basis for permitting the government, by regulation, to affect property values without compensation — that "Government hardly could go on if to some extent values incident to property could not be diminished without paying for every such change in the general law" — does not apply to the relatively rare situations where the government has deprived a landowner of all economically beneficial uses.

On the other side of the balance, affirmatively supporting a compensation requirement, is the fact that regulations that leave the owner of land without economically beneficial or productive options for its use — typically, as here, by requiring land to be left substantially in its natural state — carry with them a heightened risk that private property is being pressed into some form of public service under the guise of mitigating serious public harm. As Justice Brennan explained: "From the government's point of view, the benefits flowing to the public from preservation of open space through regulation may be equally great as from creating a wildlife refuge through formal condemnation or increasing electricity production through a dam project that floods private property." *San Diego Gas & Elec. Co.*, (Brennan, J., dissenting). . . .

We think, in short, that there are good reasons for our frequently expressed belief that when the owner of real property has been called upon to sacrifice all economically beneficial uses in the name of the common good, that is, to leave his property economically idle, he has suffered a taking.[8]

The trial court found Lucas's two beachfront lots to have been rendered valueless by respondent's enforcement of the coastal-zone construction ban. . . .

It is correct that many of our prior opinions have suggested that "harmful or noxious uses" of property may be proscribed by government regulation without the requirement of compensation. For a number of reasons, however, we think the South Carolina Supreme Court was too quick to conclude that that principle decides the present case. . . .

8. Justice Stevens criticizes the "deprivation of all economically beneficial use" rule as "wholly arbitrary," in that "[the] landowner whose property is diminished in value 95% recovers nothing," while the landowner who suffers a complete elimination of value "recovers the land's full value." This analysis errs in its assumption that the landowner whose deprivation is one step short of complete is not entitled to compensation. Such an owner might not be able to claim the benefit of our categorical formulation, but, as we have acknowledged time and again, "the economic impact of the regulation on the claimant and . . . the extent to which the regulation has interfered with distinct investment-backed expectations" are keenly relevant to takings analysis generally. Penn Central Transportation Co. v. New York City, 438 U.S. 104, 124 (1978). . . .

When it is understood that "prevention of harmful use" was merely our early formulation of the police power justification necessary to sustain (without compensation) any regulatory diminution in value; and that the distinction between regulation that "prevents harmful use" and that which "confers benefits" is difficult, if not impossible, to discern on an objective, value-free basis; it becomes self-evident that noxious-use logic cannot serve as a touchstone to distinguish regulatory "takings" — which require compensation — from regulatory deprivations that do not require compensation. A fortiori the legislature's recitation of a noxious-use justification cannot be the basis for departing from our categorical rule that total regulatory takings must be compensated. If it were, departure would virtually always be allowed. The South Carolina Supreme Court's approach would essentially nullify *Mahon*'s affirmation of limits to the noncompensable exercise of the police power. . . .

Where the State seeks to sustain regulation that deprives land of all economically beneficial use, we think it may resist compensation only if the logically antecedent inquiry into the nature of the owner's estate shows that the proscribed use interests were not part of his title to begin with. This accords, we think, with our "takings" jurisprudence, which has traditionally been guided by the understandings of our citizens regarding the content of, and the State's power over, the "bundle of rights" that they acquire when they obtain title to property. [We] think the notion pressed by the Council that title is somehow held subject to the "implied limitation" that the State may subsequently eliminate all economically valuable use is inconsistent with the historical compact recorded in the Takings Clause that has become part of our constitutional culture.

Where "permanent physical occupation" of land is concerned, we have refused to allow the government to decree it anew (without compensation), no matter how weighty the asserted "public interests" involved, though we assuredly would permit the government to assert a permanent easement that was a pre-existing limitation upon the landowner's title. We believe similar treatment must be accorded confiscatory regulations, i.e., regulations that prohibit all economically beneficial use of land: Any limitation so severe cannot be newly legislated or decreed (without compensation), but must inhere in the title itself, in the restrictions that background principles of the State's law of property and nuisance already place upon land ownership. A law or decree with such an effect must, in other words, do no more than duplicate the result that could have been achieved in the courts — by adjacent landowners (or other uniquely affected persons) under the State's law of private nuisance, or by the State under its complementary power to abate nuisances that affect the public generally, or otherwise.

On this analysis, the owner of a lake bed, for example, would not be entitled to compensation when he is denied the requisite permit to engage in a landfilling operation that would have the effect of flooding others' land. Nor the corporate owner of a nuclear generating plant, when it is directed to remove all improvements from its land upon discovery that the plant sits astride an earthquake fault. Such regulatory action may well have the effect of eliminating the land's only economically productive use, but it does not proscribe a productive use that was previously permissible under relevant property and nuisance principles. The use of these properties for what are now expressly prohibited purposes was always unlawful, and (subject to other constitutional limitations) it was open to the State at any point to make the implication of those background principles of nuisance and property law explicit. . . .

The "total taking" inquiry we require today will ordinarily entail (as the application of state nuisance law ordinarily entails) analysis of, among other things, the degree of harm to public lands and resources, or adjacent private property, posed by the claimant's proposed activities, the social value of the claimant's activities and their suitability to the locality in question, and the relative ease with which the alleged harm can be avoided through measures taken by the claimant and the government (or adjacent private landowners) alike. The fact that a particular use has long been engaged in by similarly situated owners ordinarily imports a lack of any common-law prohibition (though changed circumstances or new knowledge may make what was previously permissible no longer so. So also does the fact that other landowners, similarly situated, are permitted to continue the use denied to the claimant.

It seems unlikely that common-law principles would have prevented the erection of any habitable or productive improvements on petitioner's land; they rarely support prohibition of the "essential use" of land, Curtin v. Benson, 222 U.S. 78, 86 (1911). The question, however, is one of state law to be dealt with on remand. We emphasize that to win its case South Carolina must do more than proffer the legislature's declaration that the uses Lucas desires are inconsistent with the public interest, or the conclusory assertion that they violate a common-law maxim such as sic utere tuo ut alienum non laedas. As we have said, a "State, by ipse dixit, may not transform private property into public property without compensation. . . ." Webb's Fabulous Pharmacies, Inc. v. Beckwith, 449 U.S. 155, 164 (1980). Instead, as it would be required to do if it sought to restrain Lucas in a common-law action for public nuisance, South Carolina must identify background principles of nuisance and property law that prohibit the uses he now intends in the circumstances in which the property is presently found. Only on this showing can the State fairly claim that, in proscribing all such beneficial uses, the Beachfront Management Act is taking nothing. . . .

The judgment is reversed and the cause remanded for proceedings not inconsistent with this opinion.

So ordered.

Statement of JUSTICE SOUTER.

I would dismiss the writ of certiorari in this case as having been granted improvidently. After briefing and argument it is abundantly clear that an unreviewable assumption on which this case comes to us is both questionable as a conclusion of Fifth Amendment law and sufficient to frustrate the Court's ability to render certain the legal premises on which its holding rests. . . .

JUSTICE KENNEDY, concurring in the judgment. . . .

In my view, reasonable expectations must be understood in light of the whole of our legal tradition. The common law of nuisance is too narrow a confine for the exercise of regulatory power in a complex and interdependent society. Goldblatt v. Hempstead, 369 U.S. 590, 593 (1962). The State should not be prevented from enacting new regulatory initiatives in response to changing conditions, and courts must consider all reasonable expectations whatever their source. The Takings Clause does not require a static body of state property law; it protects private expectations to ensure private investment. I agree with the Court that nuisance prevention accords with the most common expectations of property owners who face regulation, but I do not believe this can be the sole source of state authority to impose severe restrictions. Coastal property may present such unique concerns for a fragile land system that the State can go further in regulating its development and use than the common law of nuisance might otherwise permit.

The Supreme Court of South Carolina erred, in my view, by reciting the general purposes for which the state regulations were enacted without a determination that they were in accord with the owner's reasonable expectations and therefore sufficient to support a severe restriction on specific parcels of property. The promotion of tourism, for instance, ought not to suffice to deprive specific property of all value without a corresponding duty to compensate. Furthermore, the means as well as the ends of regulation must accord with the owner's reasonable expectations. Here, the State did not act until after the property had been zoned for individual lot development and most other parcels had been improved, throwing the whole burden of the regulation on the remaining lots. This too must be measured in the balance.

With these observations, I concur in the judgment of the Court.

JUSTICE BLACKMUN, dissenting. . . .

I first question the Court's rationale in creating a category that obviates a "case-specific inquiry into the public interest advanced," if all economic value has been lost. If one fact about the Court's taking jurisprudence can be stated without contradiction, it is that "the particular circumstances of each case" determine whether a specific restriction will be rendered invalid by the government's failure to pay compensation. . . .

This Court repeatedly has recognized the ability of government, in certain circumstances, to regulate property without compensation no matter how adverse the financial effect on the owner may be. . . .

These cases rest on the principle that the State has full power to prohibit an owner's use of property if it is harmful to the public. "Since no individual has a right to use his property so as to create a nuisance or otherwise harm others, the State has not taken' anything when it asserts its power to enjoin the nuisance-like activity." *Keystone Bituminous Coal*. . . .

Ultimately even the Court cannot embrace the full implications of its per se rule: it eventually agrees that there cannot be a categorical rule for a taking based on economic value that wholly disregards the public need asserted. Instead, the Court decides that it will permit a State to regulate all economic value only if the State prohibits uses that would not be permitted under "background principles of nuisance and property law."

Until today, the Court explicitly had rejected the contention that the government's power to act without paying compensation turns on whether the prohibited activity is a common-law nuisance. . . .

[Common-law] public and private nuisance law is simply a determination whether a particular use causes harm. There is nothing magical in the reasoning of judges long dead. They determined a harm in the same way as state judges and legislatures do today. If judges in the 18th and 19th centuries can distinguish a harm from a benefit, why not judges in the 20th century, and if judges can, why not legislators? There simply is no reason to believe that new interpretations of the hoary common law nuisance doctrine will be particularly "objective" or "value-free." . . .

The Court makes sweeping and, in my view, misguided and unsupported changes in our taking doctrine. While it limits these changes to the most narrow subset of government regulation — those that eliminate all economic value from land — these changes go far beyond what is necessary to secure petitioner Lucas' private benefit. One hopes they do not go beyond the narrow confines the Court assigns them to today.

I dissent.

JUSTICE STEVENS, dissenting. . . .

In addition to lacking support in past decisions, the Court's new rule is wholly arbitrary. A landowner whose property is diminished in value 95% recovers nothing, while an owner whose property is diminished 100% recovers the land's full value. . . .

Moreover, because of the elastic nature of property rights, the Court's new rule will also prove unsound in practice. In response to the rule, courts may define "property" broadly and only rarely find regulations to effect total takings. . . .

The Court's holding today effectively freezes the State's common law, denying the legislature much of its traditional power to revise the law governing the rights and uses of property. Until today, I had thought that we had long abandoned this approach to constitutional law. More than a century ago we recognized that "the great office of statutes is to remedy defects in the common law as they are developed, and to adapt it to the changes of time and circumstances." Munn v. Illinois, 94 U.S. 113, 134 (1877). As Justice Marshall observed about a position similar to that adopted by the Court today: "If accepted, that claim would represent a return to the era of Lochner v. New York, 198 U.S. 45 (1905), when common-law rights were also found immune from revision by State or Federal Government. Such an approach would freeze the common law as it has been constructed by the courts, perhaps at its 19th-century state of development. It would allow no room for change in response to changes in circumstance. The Due Process Clause does not require such a result." PruneYard Shopping Center v. Robins, 447 U.S. 74, 93 (1980) (concurring opinion).

Arresting the development of the common law is not only a departure from our prior decisions; it is also profoundly unwise. The human condition is one of constant learning and evolution — both moral and practical. Legislatures implement that new learning; in doing so they must often revise the definition of property and the rights of property owners. Thus, when the Nation came to understand that slavery was morally wrong and mandated the emancipation of all slaves, it, in effect, redefined "property." On a lesser scale, our ongoing self-education produces similar changes in the rights of property owners: New appreciation of the significance of endangered species, the importance of wetlands, and the vulnerability of coastal lands, shapes our evolving understandings of property rights.

Of course, some legislative redefinitions of property will effect a taking and must be compensated — but it certainly cannot be the case that every movement away from common law does so. There is no reason, and less sense, in such an absolute rule. We live in a world in which changes in the economy and the environment occur with increasing frequency and importance. If it was wise a century ago to allow Government " 'the largest legislative discretion' " to deal with " 'the special exigencies of the moment,' " it is imperative to do so today. The rule that should govern a decision in a case of this kind should focus on the future, not the past. . . .

The Court's categorical approach rule will, I fear, greatly hamper the efforts of local officials and planners who must deal with increasingly complex problems in land-use and environmental regulation. . . .

[Even] assuming that petitioner's property was rendered valueless, the risk inherent in investments of the sort made by petitioner, the generality of the Act, and the compelling purpose motivating the South Carolina Legislature persuade me that the Act did not effect a taking of petitioner's property.

Accordingly, I respectfully dissent.

Note: **Lucas** *and Regulatory Takings*

1. Lucas*'s importance. Lucas* appears to be one of the most important recent cases in the law of takings. But how could anyone object to the idea that compensation is due when government has rendered property completely valueless?

2. *Takings and the common law.* Does the *Lucas* test depend on the common law background, or on the legal background in general? Suppose that the state had said by statute, before Lucas purchased the property, that certain lands must not be developed in order to promote tourism and protect flora and fauna. Would the result be different?

3. *Defining the property taken.* How can we tell if property has been rendered valueless? In footnote 7, the Court suggests that the answer depends on how one defines the property; hence it might be sufficient if 90% of the property is rendered valueless. But if this is right, does it follow that *Lucas* is not really limited to cases of complete valuelessness?

Chapter Ten

The Constitution and the Problem of Private Power

A. STATE ACTION, FEDERALISM, AND INDIVIDUAL AUTONOMY

2. *State Action and Individual Autonomy*

Page 1600. Before the last sentence on the page, add the following:

Consider the following suggestion in Shane, The *Rust* that Corrodes: State Action, Free Speech, and Responsibility, 52 Louisiana L. Rev. 1585, 1587 (1992):

> In deciding what is public and what is private in state action [cases], courts should assess the impacts of either determination on society's discharge of its responsibilities to individuals, the fulfillment of each person's responsibilities to other individuals and to the community as a whole, and the autonomy individuals must enjoy if they are to have any capacity for responsible behavior.

B. PURE INACTION AND THE THEORY OF GOVERNMENT NEUTRALITY

Page 1610. Before section 2 of the Note, add the following:

For an argument that child abuse is analogous to slavery and that the Thirteenth Amendment therefore imposes an affirmative obligation on the state to prevent it, see Amar & Widawsky, Child Abuse as Slavery: A Thirteenth Amendment Response to *Deshaney*, 105 Harv. L. Rev. 1359 (1992). See also West, Toward an Abolitionist Interpretation of the Fourteenth Amendment, 94 W. Va. L. Rev. 111, 129, 142 (1991):

> [The] plainest possible meaning of the Fourteenth Amendment mandate that no state shall deny to any citizen "equal *protection* of the law" is that no state

may deny to any citizen the protection of its criminal and civil law against private violence and private violation. [The] equal protection clause on this reading is at root a guarantee not of equal justice nor of substantive equality, but of sole sovereignty: the state, and only the state, shall be sovereign over each and every citizen. . . .

The major premise of the [*DeShaney*] that there is no constitutional right to a police force is squarely wrong. The right to a police force, or more specifically, the right to the state's protection against the subjugating effects of private violence, are the paradigm Fourteenth Amendment rights. [It] follows that little Joshua DeShaney [did] indeed suffer a constitutional violation. This violation was not *because* the state had sufficiently intervened into the family's life so as to satisfy the state action requirement as (indirectly) argued by the dissent, but, rather, because it did not intervene *enough*. Through its inaction, not its action, the state failed to provide equal protection of the law.

C. CONSTITUTIONALLY IMPERMISSIBLE DEPARTURES FROM NEUTRALITY: STATE SUBSIDIZATION, APPROVAL, AND ENCOURAGEMENT

1. *State Subsidization of Private Conduct*

Page 1637. At the end of the Note, add the following:

4. Edmonson. In Edmonson v. Leesville Concrete Co., 111 S. Ct. 2077 (1991), the Court, in an opinion by Justice Kennedy, held that a private civil litigant who utilized peremptory challenges to exclude jurors on account of race was a state actor for constitutional purposes. The Court based this conclusion in part on the "overt, significant assistance of state officials" in the discriminatory conduct.

> [A] private party could not exercise its peremptory challenges absent the overt, significant assistance of the court. The government summons jurors, constrains their freedom of movement, and subjects them to public scrutiny and examination. [Without] the direct and indispensable participation of the judge, who beyond all question is a state actor, the peremptory challenge system would serve no purpose. By enforcing a discriminatory peremptory challenge, the court "has not only made itself a party to the [biased act], but has elected to place its power, property and prestige behind the [alleged] discrimination." [*Burton.*]

Justice O'Connor, joined by Chief Justice Rehnquist and Justice Scalia, dissented:

> It is the nature of a peremptory that its exercise is left wholly within the discretion of the litigant. [The] peremptory is, by design, an enclave of private action in a government-managed proceeding. . . .

> That [government activity] may be necessary to a peremptory challenge — in the sense that there could be no such challenge without a venire from which to select — no more makes the challenge state action than the building of roads and provision of public transportation makes state action of riding on a bus. . . .
>
> The government "normally can be held responsible for a private decision only when it has exercised coercive power or has provided such significant encouragement, either overt or covert, that the choice must in law be deemed to be that of the State" [*Blum*]. . . .
>
> A judge does not "significantly encourage" discrimination by the mere act of excusing a juror in response to an unexplained request."

D. CONSTITUTIONALLY REQUIRED DEPARTURES FROM NEUTRALITY: THE PUBLIC FUNCTION DOCTRINE

Page 1656. At the end of subsection 1e of the Note, add the following:

In Edmonson v. Leesville Concrete Co., 111 S. Ct. 2077 (1991), the Court relied in part on the public function doctrine to hold that private litigants in civil cases were state actors for constitutional purposes when they utilized peremptory challenges to eliminate jurors on the basis of race. Writing for six justices, Justice Kennedy argued that

> [t]he peremptory challenge is used in selecting an entity that is a quintessential governmental body, having no attributes of a private actor. . . .
>
> If a government confers on a private body the power to choose the government's employees or officials, the private body will be bound by the constitutional mandate of race-neutrality. [At] least a plurality of the Court recognized this principle in [Terry v. Adams]. There we found state action in a scheme in which a private organization known as the Jaybird Democratic Association conducted whites-only elections to select candidates to run in the Democratic primary [elections]. . . .
>
> The principle that the selection of state officials, other than through election of all qualified voters, may constitute state action applies with even greater force in the context of jury selection through peremptory challenges. Though the motive of a peremptory challenge may be to protect a private interest, the objective of jury selection proceedings is to determine representation on a governmental body.

Justice O'Connor, joined by Chief Justice Rehnquist and Justice Scalia, dissented:

> Peremptory challenges are not a traditional government function; the "tradition" is one of unguided private choice. . . .

> In order to constitute state action under [the governmental function] doctrine, private conduct must not only comprise something that the government traditionally does, but something that *only* the government traditionally does. Even if one could fairly characterize the use of a peremptory strike as the performance of the traditional government function of jury selection, it has never been exclusively the function of the government to select juries; peremptory strikes are older than the Republic.

See also Georgia v. McCollum, 112 S. Ct. 2348 (1992) (holding that a defense attorney in a criminal trial who utilizes peremptory strikes on a racially discriminatory basis is a government actor for constitutional purposes).